FOUNDATION PRESS

TORTS STORIES

Edited By

ROBERT L. RABIN

A. Calder Mackay Professor of Law
Stanford Law School

and

STEPHEN D. SUGARMAN

Agnes Roddy Robb Professor of Law
University of California at Berkeley School of Law

FOUNDATION PRESS
New York, New York
2003

THOMSON

WEST

Foundation Press, a division of West Group, has created this publication to provide you with accurate and authoritative information concerning the subject matter covered. However, this publication was not necessarily prepared by persons licensed to practice law in a particular jurisdiction. Foundation Press is not engaged in rendering legal or other professional advice, and this publication is not a substitute for the advice of an attorney. If you require legal or other expert advice, you should seek the services of a competent attorney or other professional.

TEXT IS PRINTED ON 10% POST CONSUMER RECYCLED PAPER

Torts Stories

Introduction 1
      Robert L. Rabin and Stephen D. Sugarman

Chapter 1: *United States v. Carroll Towing Co.*: The Hand
      Formula's Home Port 11
      Stephen G. Gilles

Chapter 2: *MacPherson v. Buick Motor Co.*: Simplifying the
      Facts While Reshaping the Law 41
      James A. Henderson, Jr.

Chapter 3: *Rowland v. Christian:* Hallmark of an Expansionary
      Era 73
      Robert L. Rabin

Chapter 4: *Tarasoff v. Regents of the University of California*:
      The Therapist's Dilemma 99
      Peter H. Schuck and Daniel J. Givelber

Chapter 5: *The Wagon Mound Cases*: Foreseeability,
      Causation, and Mrs. Palsgraf 129
      Saul Levmore

Chapter 6: *Hymowitz v. Eli Lilly and Co.*: Markets of
      Mothers 151
      Anita Bernstein

Chapter 7: *Murphy v. Steeplechase Amusement Co.*: While
      the Timorous Stay at Home, the Adventurous Ride
      the Flopper 179
      Kenneth W. Simons

Chapter 8: *Rylands v. Fletcher*: Tort Law's Conscience 207
      Kenneth S. Abraham

Chapter 9: *Escola v. Coca Cola Bottling Co.*: Strict Products
      Liability Unbound 229
      Mark Geistfeld

Chapter 10: *Vincent v. Lake Erie Transportation Co.*: Liability
      for Harm Caused by Necessity 259
      Stephen D. Sugarman

Contributors 291

Acknowledgments 293

*

FOUNDATION PRESS

TORTS STORIES

*

Introduction

Robert L. Rabin and Stephen D. Sugarman

I

Torts, as much as any subject area of the law, presents a human face to the reader of leading cases. Nonetheless, the student of torts, relying exclusively on casebook learning, comes away with a highly selective perspective on the torts system. A first-rate casebook, of course, does more than present the doctrinal foundations of torts as revealed by judiciously selected appellate opinions. But, because there is so much tort law to cover in a first year course, edited cases, law journal excerpts, supplemental notes and questions can only take one so far.

Behind each notable case are a host of concerns and considerations that are hidden even from the discerning eye, focused as it is on the court's selective recitation of the facts and its characterization of the issues and arguments presented to it. Often, much more can be learned from digging beneath the surface to find out more about the parties, the events giving rise to the claimed injury, and the corresponding context of socio-economic circumstances in which the case arose. And then the lawyers enter the picture. How did they perceive and present the case—what were their lawyering strategies and how did they shape the way the case ultimately turned out? So, too, what of roles played by the trial judge, and in some instances, an intermediate appellate court?

As these lines of inquiry are meant to suggest, every tort case begins with a particular misadventure of its own, and runs the course of a system in which distinct contributions are made by a variety of participants along the way to final resolution. To view these elements in fine detail is to understand the dynamic character of tort law—indeed, the dynamic character of the common law, more generally—in a fashion that by its very nature cannot be fully conveyed in an appellate judicial opinion.

Even so, the story of a landmark case is more than just a narrative of how the case arose, and wound its way to its bound version in the law reports—often with highly surprising twists and turns. If a case has achieved a certain lasting distinction, there is a sequel to be told. Why has the case shown great staying power, and what does that tell us about the aims and purposes of tort law more generally? And what precisely does it mean for a particular case to stand the test of time: That it is widely followed? That it has <u>recast</u> the framework of tort law in some important way? That its notoriety has triggered a continuing dialogue? That it came to define the concerns of a particular moment in time? Or is it some combination of all these factors?

II

One torts story that has already been told—explaining our decision not to retell it in detail in this volume—is the famous case of *Palsgraf v. Long Island Railroad*,[1] arguably the most famous of all American tort cases. Many torts professors could offer testimony from alumni gatherings at which former students from different eras bring up this case when talking about what they remember best, not only from class, but from the entire first year of law school.

Palsgraf's fame has multiple explanations, and one should not discount the power of the plaintiff's last name. Perhaps the case would be much less remembered if Mrs. Smith had been the name of the plaintiff who was injured when a passenger dropped some wrapped-up fireworks while being pushed onto a departing train by a railway station guard. That the fireworks then exploded and caused a scale located further down the platform from the blast to topple over onto Mrs. Palsgraf made for a dramatic, if exotic, event that is vividly remembered by so many who read the majority and dissenting opinions in the 1928 decision of the New York Court of Appeals. The facts nicely raise the question of who should pay for bizarre injuries of this sort, and most torts casebooks give large prominence to both opinions, which adopt radically different analytical approaches to the problem. Indeed, even today courts around the nation have not reached a consensus as to how unexpected consequences of a negligent act should be handled as a doctrinal matter, and a very substantial scholarly literature exists debating the legal puzzle raised by the case. For these reasons and probably as well because Judge Benjamin Cardozo's opinion for the majority offers a characteristic rendition of his unique stylistic approach, most torts instructors devote a substantial amount of class time to *Palsgraf*.

Although the chapter in this book by Saul Levmore on the *Wagon Mound* cases includes a side discussion of *Palsgraf*, there is no separate chapter on the case because those who are interested can turn, among other places, to Judge John Noonan's *Persons and Masks of the Law*, Judge Richard Posner's *Cardozo: A Study in Reputation*, and Professor Andrew Kaufman's biography *Cardozo*, each of which has a chapter that

---

[1] 162 N.E. 99 (N.Y.1928).

discusses the case in detail.[2] These separate portrayals of the *Palsgraf* story together illustrate several themes that run through the ten stories in this book.

(1) Although the edited appellate opinions found in casebooks typically set out the "facts" of the incident that lead up to the injury in question, a better understanding of what "really happened," as well as uncertainties about what the facts "really were," may be gained by a fuller telling of the story based on an examination of the trial record, the briefs, external accounts of the event, and more.

It turns out that the explosion that harmed Mrs. Palsgraf was sufficiently newsworthy to receive front page coverage in the New York Times on August 25, 1924, the day after the accident. The Times story describes "a terrific roar, followed by several milder explosions, and a short-lived pyrotechnic display." Thirteen victims were named in the story as suffering from injuries such as abrasions, burns, and lacerations. Helen Polsgraf (sic) was listed as one of two suffering from "shock." Nothing has been uncovered as to whether any other victims sued.

The Times reported "the force of the detonation also ripped away some of the platform and overthrew a penny weighing machine more than ten feet away. Its glass was smashed and its mechanism wrecked." Nothing was said about the scale striking Mrs. Palsgraf. Dean William Prosser later surmised that the scale was actually knocked over by the panicked crowd. But at the trial of her case Mrs. Palsgraf stated that "the scale blew and hit me on the side," and an eyewitness testified that the blast, not the crowd, knocked the scale over.

There has also been some controversy about just how far Mrs. Palsgraf was from the passenger with the package of explosives. Cardozo's opinion in the case, which talks of the scale being "at the other end of the platform, many feet away," can be read to suggest that she was considerably further away than she probably was. When Mrs. Palsgraf was asked on cross-examination, "And how near were you to the place where the explosion took place?" she replied, "That I can't exactly tell; I don't know what train took the explosion." It does seem clear, however, that she was more than 10 feet way, as suggested by the story in the Times, so that she was not at risk of being struck by the bundle as it fell. These questions of distance from danger and directness of injury help to frame the liability issue, and lend color to the instrumental selection of facts by a judge to achieve greater persuasive power.

(2) Judges writing appellate opinions purposively report only some of the "facts" leaving others out. This not only can leave the reader with

---

[2] John T. Noonan, Jr., *Persons and Masks of the Law* ch. 4 (1976); Richard A. Posner, *Cardozo: A Study in Reputation* ch. 3 (1990); Andrew L. Kaufman, *Cardozo* ch. 16 (1998).

an incomplete picture of the story, but it can also situate the case doctrinally rather differently from where it might be seen to fit were more facts revealed.

This theme is illustrated in *Palsgraf* when we turn to a consideration of the actual harm suffered by Mrs. Palsgraf. (From Cardozo's opinion, one gets the impression that Mrs. Palsgraf was alleging conventional physical consequences from being struck by the falling scale. But, as already noted, the Times story described her as suffering from "shock," and the complaint filed by her lawyer makes this same claim) A more textured understanding of what this meant may be gained from the testimony of the doctor who treated Mrs. Palsgraf the day after the accident. He stated that he found her "extremely nervous and very shaky, and shook up" with "some small bruises on her shoulder and side." He then testified that two or three days later she began "stuttering," and that over the next two months he saw her about twenty times in his office and ten times at her home. Throughout that period, he stated, "she couldn't answer the words," that her condition had remained the same, and that he thought the problem was likely to be permanent. He also testified that there was no doubt that the accident caused this condition.

The trial transcript does not indicate that Mrs. Palsgraf was having trouble responding to questions put to her by either her lawyer or opposing counsel on cross-examination, although perhaps the written record covers up the reality of her speech. For example, she testified that after the Sunday explosion, "I didn't tremble, until about Wednesday morning. . . . my speech was affected." And in reply to the question, "Has your speech been stuttering and stammering ever since that day, as it is now?" she replied, "Ever since the day of the accident." And then to the question, "Has it been any better or worse?" she replied, "Worse."

An expert physician, Dr. Hammond, later testified for the plaintiff that when he examined Mrs. Palsgraf two days before the trial "she stammered quite a good deal and it was with difficulty that she could talk at all. If she persisted she would get the words out." He said that she was "trembling" and "when I placed her on her feet—feet together and eyes closed—she fell over." He diagnosed her condition as "traumatic hysteria" and then, quite astoundingly, he stated, "while her mind is disturbed by litigation she will not recover, but after litigation ceases, she should make a fairly good recovery in about three years."

Dr. Hammond appears to have been overly optimistic. Fifty years after the case was decided, a reporter for the Harvard Law Record interviewed one of Mrs. Palsgraf's two daughters who had been with her on the platform that day. According to the journalist, the daughter "stated that her mother became mute for much of her life and had health problems until she died in October, 1945."

As Judge Posner emphasizes, Cardozo's opinion tells us nothing about the shock and the serious speech difficulties it allegedly caused. But, then, as Posner noted, if the decision could have been categorized by later judges as relevant only to "shock" cases, it was unlikely to have the lasting influence that Cardozo clearly intended for it as a threshold scope of duty requirement of a foreseeable plaintiff.

(3) Most appellate opinions are presented in torts casebooks with little or no attention to the victim's station in life before the accident, her claimed losses from the accident, or to the damages that she was awarded; instead, "plaintiffs" are typically regarded as abstractions, devoid of human features and circumstances. Judge Noonan is particularly critical of this bloodless approach, and strives to put a human face on Helen Palsgraf, and correspondingly, to emphasize the monolithic character of the defendant Long Island Railroad in his *Palsgraf* portrayal.

Mrs. Palsgraf testified that before the accident she served as a janitor in the building where she lived, for which she apparently got $10 a month off her rent, and that she did housework for others two or three days a week earning about $8 a week. In total, these efforts may have brought her somewhat over $500 a year. But after the accident Mrs. Palsgraf gave up her outside housework, and nearly two years after the accident she gave up her janitorial work, as well. Although by the time of the trial all of her children—then ages 21, 18 and 15—were working, she also said that she had not yet paid her treating doctor's bill of $70.

Noonan makes much of the fact that Mrs. Palsgraf was poor and that not only was the defendant railroad quite wealthy, but also the judges who then sat on the Court of Appeals themselves were from the upper middle class. Surely it is not the primary role of tort law to transfer money from the rich to the poor. Noonan's point nonetheless seems to be that, in crafting the contours of tort liability of railroads to their customers, Cardozo and the majority were inappropriately indifferent to the consequences for the actual parties of casting the net of responsibility a bit wider or a bit narrower, which, in the end, is what is at stake in the case.

Although Mrs. Palsgraf's complaint originally asked for $50,000, the jury awarded her only $6,000. Just how that number was reached is not at all clear, and there is no transcript available of the lawyers' arguments to the jury. We do know that Mrs. Palsgraf was 40 years old at the time of the accident, and if she were viewed as having permanently had to give up her work as a result of the accident, then $500 a year for, say, 25 years would amount to $12,500. Possibly, her lawyer figured that she was roughly entitled to that amount plus three times that sum for pain and suffering arising from the stuttering, stammering and associated trembling.

Perhaps the jury believed Dr. Hammond, however, and assumed that three years after the trial (which would be six years after the injury), Mrs. Palsgraf would be able fully to return to her prior life. On that basis, perhaps it roughly settled on $500 a year for lost income for each of those years, plus an equal sum for pain and suffering.

Of course, because the majority of the Court of Appeals reversed her victory, Mrs. Palsgraf never saw any of that money. Noonan is dismayed that the Court of Appeals not only reversed her verdict, but also adhered to the default rule and awarded costs of $350 to the railroad against Mrs. Palsgraf, a sum equal to more than two-thirds of her prior annual income. But it appears that her lawyer never asked that costs not be awarded against the losing party, and Posner is probably correct when he speculates that the railroad never made any attempt to recover those costs.

(4) Many famous torts cases that establish doctrinal breakthroughs are rather paradoxically notable for their uninspired lawyering, in which opposing counsel had little influence over what was eventually decided.

Palsgraf illustrates this theme as well. Noonan is surely correct that the lawyers on both sides litigated *Palsgraf* in a mundane manner. The plaintiff's lawyer, Matthew Wood, never made very clear in the way he presented evidence precisely what the railroad's employees, had they been careful, would have done differently. Since Cardozo himself suggests in passing that "it may very well be doubted" whether there was a wrongful act, Wood appears to have flirted with dismissal on grounds of no negligence—which would have entirely eliminated the need to discuss the issue of unexpected consequences. Furthermore, as suggested above, Wood might have been unwise to have called Dr. Hammond as an expert witness. On the other side, cross-examination by William McNamara, the defense counsel, was generally half-hearted with no evident purpose in mind. In fact, the defense rested after the close of the plaintiff's case without calling a single witness.

It appears that the lawyers viewed the case essentially as one in which the issue was whether the defendant's employees were careless or not. When it came time to instruct the jury, Burt Jay Humphrey, the trial judge, outright rejected one theory that Wood had urged in the complaint but for which he offered no evidence. Humphrey explicitly told the jury that the defendant could not be blamed for failing to examine all the packages that people brought onto the platform. Rather, in order to find the defendant liable, Humphrey told the jurors that they would have to find that the guards were careless in the way they handled the passenger who, it turned out, was carrying fireworks.

McNamara, for the defense, asked the judge to tell the jury that the defendant could not be found negligent unless it knew or should have known that the bundle contained fireworks, but the judge refused this request. Hence, Judge Humphrey seemed to believe that the guards could be found careless simply for pushing the passenger at all, or perhaps for the way they pushed him in dislodging a package that must have had some value to the passenger regardless of its contents.

At that point, McNamara asked the judge to charge the jury that if the guards were helping the man with the package onto the train and in doing so knocked the package from his hands, their acts could not be the proximate cause of the plaintiff's injuries. But the judge refused this request as well. McNamara failed to make clear why he sought this instruction, but from the transcript it seems possible that his idea was that the passenger's decision to carry fireworks was a "superceding cause." In any event, Judge Humphrey apparently believed that if the guards were careless towards the passenger, then, as a matter of law, they were liable to Mrs. Palsgraf. The interesting point is the failure to achieve any real dialogue among the lawyers and the trial judge on the issue that turned out to be most salient to the outcome of the case (and to its landmark status): liability for unexpected consequences.

The Appellate Division clearly understood that the case at least presented an issue of proximate cause, and the judges there split 2–1 on the question. Judge Lazansky argued in dissent "the negligence of defendant was not a proximate cause of the injuries to plaintiff. ... The explosion was not reasonably probable as a result of defendant's act of negligence." Judge Andrews, dissenting in the Court of Appeals, also clearly saw the case as raising a proximate cause question, except for him the close proximity in time, space and physical connection between the explosion and Mrs. Palsgraf's harm meant that the plaintiff should win on the proximate cause issue.

Hence, neither the lawyers, nor the trial judge, nor the judges in the Appellate Division seemed to have any awareness of the issue that Cardozo viewed as critical in deciding the case—that is, whether Mrs. Palsgraf had to show that the defendants were negligent "towards her."

(5) A richer understanding of a case may enhance one's critical evaluation of what has become a famous decision.

As there is already a huge legal literature on the doctrinal aspects of *Palsgraf*, only two points will be made here about Cardozo's opinion. First, as mentioned above, there was rather little basis for the jury finding the defendant negligent at all, and based on his opinions in other cases, one might have expected Cardozo to hold for the defense as a

[Handwritten margin note at top: "Most likely, b/c of this, Cardozo et al simply didn't believe the RR shd pay. But how to reach that gut reaction in words and doctrine because their difficulty."]

matter of law on this ground. After all, if the guards could have no idea what was in the package, what exactly should they have done differently? This seems to have been what the defense counsel was arguing in his effort to obtain more precise jury instructions. Should the guards really not have helped the passenger onto the train, thereby risking his falling and perhaps being seriously hurt? The Appellate Division, in upholding Mrs. Palsgraf's favorable verdict in the case, clearly states that the jury might well have found the guards at fault for not discouraging the passenger and warning him not to try boarding the moving train.

These days, of course, plaintiff lawyers might well offer evidence that the train door entries should have been designed differently, or that there should have been barriers preventing the man with the fireworks from trying to board the train as it began to move out, or that warning signs should have been in place. But none of this was suggested in the actual case, and given the evidence that was presented, it seems odd to blame the guards for providing assistance to someone apparently determined to join his friend who had already succeeded in boarding.

[Handwritten margin note: "negligence / fraud / sending the issue to cause"]

Possibly, the guards simply were careless in knocking the package out from under the passenger's arm while assisting him, and that seems to be the way the case is understood by many today. But there was no testimony suggesting that it would have been feasible for them to help the passenger aboard in a way that did not risk causing the package to fall.

Second, Cardozo compounds the confusion on this matter when he offers up a hypothetical in which a guard stumbles on what he perceives to be a bundle of newspapers, but which turns out to have a concealed can of dynamite inside. In such a case, as well, it is difficult to see how the guard could be found negligent at all, thereby allowing one to put off for another day having to decide whether one who is negligent in one respect should be held liable to an unforeseeable victim of that negligence.

III

In sum, this brief foray into the *Palsgraf* story illustrates several themes that occur in the full torts stories offered in this book. Consider again, the proposition that the "real" facts of a case are different from what they may seem in reading the appellate opinion, suggested by *Palsgraf*. This proposition is developed in James A. Henderson, Jr.'s chapter on *MacPherson v. Buick Motor Co.* and Kenneth W. Simons' chapter on *Murphy v. Steeplechase Amusement Co.* (both, incidentally, also involving landmark opinions written by Judge Cardozo). The proposition that judges are able to marshal facts selectively in order to turn a decision into one that is not directly responsive to the question the parties thought they were fighting over, is demonstrated in the chapter on *Rowland v. Christian*, by Robert L. Rabin, and the chapter on *Escola v. Coca Cola Bottling Co.*, by Mark Geistfeld. A richer human side of famous cases is revealed in the story of *Tarasoff v. Regents of the University of California*, by Peter H. Schuck and Daniel J. Givelber, and the rendition of *Hymowitz v. Eli Lilly and Co.*, by Anita Bernstein. Although *Palsgraf* was instantly regarded as an important decision, as were the *Wagon Mound* cases related by Saul Levmore, and many of the others just mentioned, fame came only later to what today are leading cases, as the stories of *United States v. Carroll Towing Co.*, told by Stephen G. Gilles, and *Vincent v. Lake Erie Transportation Co.*, related by Stephen D. Sugarman, reveal.

As might be expected, other important themes developed in the narratives in this book are not features of the *Palsgraf* story. For example, an especially prominent aspect of the *Tarasoff* story is the behavioral responses to a famous decision. And, the influence of contemporaneous socio-economic circumstances is a central element in the story of *Rylands v. Fletcher*, as related by Kenneth S. Abraham. More generally, the stories related in this book each tell their own tale. Collectively, we have tried to demonstrate the variety of themes found in the leading cases, rather than to diminish the stories by presupposing a set of common propositions.

Like *Palsgraf*, all the cases featured in the ten stories in this book are recognized as leading decisions. Although not necessarily as famous as *Palsgraf*, they all appear in the leading torts casebooks, usually as substantial opinions or occasionally in long notes connected to a related case. Like *Palsgraf*, they all have attracted considerable scholarly attention. And yet, we believe, each is enriched by the narrative account that follows.

The stories have been arranged roughly in the order that they are taken up in many torts courses. From a doctrinal perspective, *Carroll Towing*, the initial story, focuses on the issue of breach of duty; *MacPherson*, *Rowland* and *Tarasoff*, which follow, address the issue of scope of duty; *Wagon Mound*, like *Palsgraf*, involves the issue of proximate cause; *Hymowitz* deals with the question of cause in fact; *Murphy* centers on the defense of assumption of risk; *Rylands* raises the question of strict liability for abnormally dangerous activities; and *Escola* introduces the issue of strict liability for product-related injuries. *Vincent* provides one story from what is conventionally viewed as the field of intentional torts.

If our principal aim has been to assemble a set of narratives that either selectively, or as a whole, will enrich a basic torts course, we have in mind, as well, that some instructors will find these stories sufficiently interesting to serve as the text for a torts seminar. Whatever the case, we hope that the reader will find these stories as interesting as we did in preparing them.

1

Stephen G. Gilles

United States v. Carroll Towing Co.: The Hand Formula's Home Port

Fifty-six years after its publication in 1947, Judge Learned Hand's opinion in *United States v. Carroll Towing Co.*[1] has been cited in scores of judicial decisions and hundreds of law review articles, and "designated as emblematic and significant by unanimous vote of the authors of currently-published casebooks."[2] Yet unlike many leading torts cases, in which important legal principles are announced in a memorable factual setting, *Carroll Towing* purports to apply settled tort doctrine, and the facts it recites are mundane, complicated, and forgettable.

Why then is *Carroll Towing* a leading case? Because it contains a "famous formulation of the negligence standard"[3] by a famous judge.[4] Hand wrote that the duty to take reasonable care is "a function of three variables: (1) The probability [of an accident]; (2) the gravity of the resulting injury . . .; (3) the burden of adequate precautions. Possibly it serves to bring this notion into relief to state it in algebraic terms: if the probability be called P; the injury, L [for loss]; and the burden, B; liability depends upon whether B is less than L multiplied by P: i.e., whether B is less than PL."[5] This formulation—sometimes called the *Carroll Towing* Formula, but nowadays more often known simply as the

---

[1] 159 F.2d 169 (2d Cir.1947).

[2] Patrick J. Kelley, *The* Carroll Towing Company *Case and the Teaching of Tort Law*, 45 St. Louis U. L.J. 731, 733 (2001).

[3] Richard A. Posner, *A Theory of Negligence*, 1 J. Legal Stud. 29, 32 (1972).

[4] *See generally* Gerald Gunther, *Learned Hand: The Man and the Judge* (1994).

[5] 159 F.2d at 173.

Hand Formula—has become *the* paradigmatic example of how a judge can use economic analysis to illuminate the meaning of an important legal concept.

Judge (then Professor) Richard Posner deserves much of the credit for the celebrity status *Carroll Towing* and the Hand Formula now enjoy. In a seminal 1972 article,[6] Posner made Hand's opinion in *Carroll Towing* the centerpiece of his economic theory of negligence law. Posner argued that the Hand Formula interpreted negligence in economic, cost-benefit terms, and that in so doing the Formula merely made explicit what judges had long done implicitly.[7]

Posner's claims ignited a debate that continues to this day. Many torts scholars argue that the Hand Formula is really an attempt to *replace* the traditional reasonably prudent person standard with an impersonal, economic negligence standard.[8] That attempt, some believe, has been largely unsuccessful—as witness standard jury instructions, which generally define negligence as failure to act like a reasonably prudent person, while making no mention of the Hand Formula.[9] In addition, Hand Formula negligence has been criticized as incoherent in principle and unworkable in practice.[10]

This chapter begins with a close look at the *Carroll Towing* case and Hand's use of his Formula to help decide it. The chapter then examines how the Hand Formula approach works in practice, the rationales for using it, the most important objections to it, and how it compares with the leading alternative approaches. The chapter concludes with some comments on the status of the Hand Formula in tort law today.

The Facts of the Carroll Towing Case

The facts of *Carroll Towing* are surprisingly complicated. Who would have guessed that a routine barge accident would prompt litiga-

---

[6] Posner, *supra* note 3, at 29. Even prior to Posner's article, some casebooks treated *Carroll Towing* as a leading case. *See, e.g.*, Charles O. Gregory & Harry Kalven, Jr., *Cases and Materials on Torts* 72 (1959)

[7] Posner, *supra* note 3, at 32.

[8] *See, e.g.*, Michael D. Green, *Negligence = Economic Efficiency: Doubts >*, 75 Tex. L. Rev. 1605 (1997); Richard W. Wright, *The Standards of Care in Negligence Law*, in *Philosophical Foundations of Tort Law* 249 (David G. Owen ed., 1995); Patrick J. Kelley, *Who Decides? Community Safety Conventions at the Heart of Tort Liability*, 38 Clev. St. L. Rev. 315 (1990).

[9] *See, e.g.*, Patrick J. Kelley & Laurel A. Wendt, *What Judges Tell Juries About Negligence: A Review of Pattern Jury Instructions*, 77 Chi.-Kent L. Rev. 587 (2002); Stephen G. Gilles, *The Invisible Hand Formula*, 80 Va. L. Rev. 1015, 1016–20 (1994).

[10] *See, e.g.*, Ronald Dworkin, *Is Wealth A Value?*, 9 J. Legal Stud. 191 (1980); Gregory C. Keating, *Reasonableness and Rationality in Negligence Theory*, 48 Stan. L. Rev. 311 (1996).

tion among four different corporate defendants plus the federal government? To keep things manageable, we will begin with a barebones sketch of the facts, and then flesh out the relationships among the parties.

The claims at issue in *Carroll Towing* all stemmed from the accidental sinking of the barge "Anna C" in New York harbor in January 1944. Today, the Hudson River piers that line lower Manhattan are empty and decaying. Five months before the Allies' massive D–Day invasion of Europe, they were swarming with war-related traffic. As one of the opening statements at trial explained:

> "[D]uring the height of the war shipping on these docks and harbor created a crowded and congested condition beyond limits, with boat loads of material waiting to be shipped, and ships waiting to be convoyed across the ocean. The Government was sending in its barge loads; obviously they could not all be loaded into the ship at once, and the slips became congested, and they had to find places where they could be put temporarily while waiting to be loaded into the ships."[11]

The events that culminated in the sinking of the Anna C began shortly after she was taken to just such a temporary berth. The United States had hired the Pennsylvania Railroad to carry 200 tons of government-owned flour by rail from Buffalo to New York and then load it onto a barge for delivery to a trans-Atlantic ship. The Railroad, which had leased the barge Anna C from her owner, Conners Marine Co., duly loaded her with the government's flour—3,996 hundred-pound bags, to be precise—and had her taken to Pier 58, where the ship was taking on cargo. But there was no room at Pier 58, so on January 2d the Anna C was towed by tug to a temporary berth at the end of Pier 52.[12] Her bargee moored her to Pier 52 with two stout lines, and she lay waiting her turn, apparently in complete safety.

On the night before the accident, events took a turn for the worse. An unknown tug crew moored a tier of five barges to the Anna C, extending out into the river and adding their weight to the lines connecting the Anna C to Pier 52.[13] This maneuver, which had become

---

[11] Transcript of Record (Tr.) at 82 (statement of Robert S. Erskine, counsel for the Grace Line).

[12] The Anna C's bargee testified that the tug Carroll towed the Anna C to Pier 52. *Id.* at 97. The Carroll's captain denied having done so. *Id.* at 181.

[13] Mysteriously, the tug responsible for creating the underlying danger was not named as a party. It is hard to believe the identity of that tug could not have been discovered.

commonplace due to the wartime congestion in New York harbor, enabled more barges to be moored at each pier.[14] But it placed a strain on the Anna C's lines. To reduce that strain, the interlopers also ran a "cross line" between the fourth barge in the Anna C's tier and the fourth (and outermost) barge in a parallel tier that was moored at the next pier to the north (the "Public Pier").[15]

Around noon on the day of the accident, the tug "Carroll" arrived on the scene. The Carroll, owned by Carroll Towing, was working as a "shifting tug" for the Grace Line, the shipping company that operated Pier 58. The Grace Line regularly rented the services of tugs such as the Carroll to tow barges from berth to berth in the harbor. When the Grace Line wanted a tug to shift a particular barge, the Grace Line pier boss would send a Grace Line "harbor master" (despite the fancy title, in reality an ordinary longshoreman) to give directions to the tug captain and go with the tug "to help the deckhand with the lines and see that they get the boat placed right."[16] Consequently, there were three men aboard the Carroll as she approached the Anna C: her captain and deckhand, both employed by Carroll Towing, and the harbor master, employed by the Grace Line.

The Anna C, however, was not the Carroll's target. The Carroll's mission was to tow the "Camden"—one of the tier of barges at the Public Pier—upriver for unloading at Pier 58. But in order to "drill out" the Camden, the Carroll first had to remove the obstructing cross line that had been placed between the Anna C's tier of barges and the tier in which the Camden lay. The captain of the Carroll sent the deckhand and harbor master to do this job. Recognizing that the wind and tide were increasing the strain on the Anna C's lines, the captain told them to make sure that the Anna C's tier of barges was safely moored before throwing off the obstructing line. The deckhand and harbor master went aboard the Anna C and her five companions, readjusted the lines to their satisfaction, removed the obstructing line, and re-boarded the Carroll. While they were doing all this, the Carroll held the Anna C's tier of six barges in place by nosing up against the outermost barge, running her engines against the tide, and pulling on a temporary line she had run to one of the middle barges in the tier.

When these maneuvers were finished, the Carroll backed away to get the Camden. Almost immediately, the lines between the Anna C and

---

Busy as the harbor was, tiers of five barges, complete with bargees and paperwork, surely did not materialize at the Public Pier without a trace.

[14] Tr. at 107.

[15] *Id.* at 93.

[16] *Id.* at 189 (testimony of Grace Line harbor master Al Brun).

Pier 52 gave way, causing the entire tier of six barges to break adrift. The Carroll tried to hold the barges against the wind and tide. But the inner end of the tier, including the Anna C, sagged down toward the next pier to the south (Pier 51). The Anna C collided with—"bumped into" might be a more accurate way of describing it—a tanker lying on the north side of Pier 51. Unbeknownst to anyone, the tanker's propeller broke a hole in the Anna C near her bottom, and she began to take on water.

Meanwhile, the Carroll had summoned a nearby Grace Line tug to help her get the barges safely back to Pier 52. Both tugs had powerful pumps on board, and could have kept the Anna C afloat had they known she was leaking. Either because he was absent or because he was inattentive, however, the Anna C's bargee failed to alert the tugs that the Anna C was leaking; and the tug crews did not inspect the Anna C themselves because they were preoccupied with rescuing the whole flotilla. Shortly after the tugs managed to push the barges into the slip between Piers 51 and 52, the Anna C capsized, dumped her cargo, and sank.

The Litigation and Trial

This initial description of the accident suggests several plausible negligence claims: Conners, owner of the Anna C, had claims against Carroll Towing and the Grace Line based on the alleged negligence of their employees in handling the Anna C's lines. Carroll Towing and the Grace Line could claim that Conners was contributorily negligent because its bargee had failed to alert the tugs that the Anna C was leaking. And the United States had colorable claims that Conners, Carroll Towing, and the Grace Line were vicariously liable for the negligent destruction of its flour by their employees.

Ironically, although all of these tort claims eventually became part of the *Carroll Towing* case, the litigation began with the filing by Conners of a *contract* claim alleging that the Railroad was in breach for failing to return the Anna C undamaged at the end of the rental period. Next, in anticipation of impending tort claims, Carroll Towing filed a special "limitation" petition pursuant to a federal admiralty statute that limits a shipowner's liability for most losses to the value of the vessel and its freight.[17] The statute required all four claimants against the tug

---

[17] Carroll Towing claimed that the tug's value did not exceed $15,000. Petition of Carroll Towing Co. (In re Carroll), Tr. 39. The value of the lost flour was $10,588. Penn. R.R. Brief at 2. The Railroad paid approximately $2,000 to salvage the Anna C, Claim of the Pennsylvania Railroad Co. (In re Carroll), Tr. 48, and the estimated cost of repairing the Anna C was $5,172. Conners Exh. 2, Tr. 215.

Carroll–Conners, the Grace Line, the Railroad, and the United States[18]—
to file their negligence claims in a single limitation action. The negligence claims and Conners' contract claim were consolidated into a single
admiralty trial before Judge Moskowitz in the Eastern District of New
York.[19] As is traditional in admiralty, there was no jury.

The main issue at trial was which, if any, of the parties had been
negligent in connection with the loss of the Anna C and her cargo.
(There was also a vigorous battle over who was in charge of adjusting
the Anna C's lines—the Grace Line harbor master, the Carroll's captain
and deckhand, or both). The three principal witnesses at trial were the
tug captain, the harbormaster, and the bargee.[20] The only dramatic
moments came during the bargee's testimony.[21]

The bargee told an unlikely story: on the morning of the accident he
arrived for work at 8AM and observed the tier of five barges newly
moored to the Anna C. Although he realized that these barges placed an
unsafe strain on the Anna C's lines, he did not add more lines.[22] He was
still on board the Anna C when the longshoremen from the Carroll
began adjusting lines sometime after 1 p.m. Although he recognized that
the removal of the line connecting the two tiers of barges would further
increase the strain on the Anna C's lines, he again did nothing.[23]
Strangest of all, the bargee testified that after the Anna C struck the
tanker, he looked inside the hold and could see no water. (It was, he said,
a "kind of dark foggy day").[24] A little later, he noticed that the Anna C
was listing, whereupon he ran onto the pier and telephoned both
Conners and the Railroad.[25] But by then it was too late.

---

[18] The United States did not play an active part in the trial. By the time of trial, the
Railroad had agreed to pay the United States for its flour, and the United States had
agreed that the Railroad would consequently be subrogated to the government's claims
against the other parties. Tr. at 129.

[19] For discussion of the admiralty background, see Matthew P. Harrington, *The
Admiralty Origins of Law and Economics*, 7 Geo. Mason L. Rev. 105, 111–115 (1998).

[20] The deckhand, who was no longer employed by Carroll Towing at the time of trial,
was present in the courtroom but not called as a witness. *See* Tr. at 187.

[21] Unlike the other witnesses, who were called by their respective employers, the
bargee was called by the Railroad, *id.* at 90, and then cross-examined by the attorneys for
Conners, the Grace Line, and Carroll Towing. In light of the subsequent attack on the
bargee's credibility, one wonders whether Conners' counsel declined to call the bargee in
the belief that some of his testimony would be false.

[22] *Id.* at 108, 126.

[23] *Id.* at 118.

[24] *Id.* at 115.

[25] *Id.* at 95.

On cross-examination, counsel for Grace Line mounted a Perry Mason-style attack on the bargee's testimony: "Q. Now, I am going to suggest to you, Captain, you weren't on this boat at the time of the accident; isn't that so? A. No, I do not think so. The Court: What? The Witness: No, I was there."[26] A startled Judge Moskowitz immediately announced "a short recess."[27] There ensued a determined effort to get the bargee to change his story. Yet despite being warned that the testimony of the deckhand and harbormaster would contradict him,[28] and even after point-blank questioning by the judge himself, the bargee insisted that he was aboard the Anna C when she broke adrift.[29]

Later in the trial, the bargee's story was duly contradicted by the harbormaster, who claimed that he and the deckhand found no one aboard when they boarded the Anna C to readjust her lines.[30] The deckhand's affidavit, which was also in evidence, corroborated the harbormaster's testimony.[31]

The Trial Court's Decision

Unsurprisingly, the trial judge credited the harbormaster and deckhand. As he delicately put it, "[a]t the time the lines were shifted by the harbor master and the deckhand on the Anna C, it is believed that the captain of the barge Anna C was absent."[32]

Paradoxically, this was good news for Conners. The bargee's self-serving insistence that he had been on board made him look blatantly negligent. Not only had he observed the strain on the Anna C's lines, and done nothing about it; after the collision, he had unaccountably failed to observe what must have been a very serious leak. But if the bargee had been elsewhere at the time, these lapses vanished, and the question was simply whether his absence amounted to negligence.

On that issue, the trial judge ruled in favor of the bargee and Conners. He first held that the Grace Line harbormaster and the Carroll deckhand had been jointly negligent "in throwing off the line between the two tiers of boats, and in failing to properly secure the boats at the

---

[26] *Id.* at 114.

[27] *Id.* at 114.

[28] *Id.* at 114.

[29] *Id.* at 115.

[30] *Id.* at 196–97.

[31] *Id.* at 220.

[32] Conners Marine Co. v. Pennsylvania Railroad Co., et al., 66 F.Supp. 396, 398 (E.D.N.Y.1946).

end of Pier 52 under the conditions of wind and tide before doing so."[33] He then rejected the suggestion that Conners was also at fault[34] for failing to have a bargee on board:

> The absence of the captain of the Anna C did not in any wise contribute to the accident. He was not required to anticipate negligence of the harbor master, the master and deckhand of the tug Carroll. Under the circumstances here disclosed, the absence of the captain is not in itself negligence.[35]

The judge found precedent for this reasoning in cases deeming absent bargees non-negligent in the absence of apparent dangers such as impending storms.

The Briefs on Appeal

Substantial briefs on appeal were filed by the Grace Line and Carroll Towing as appellants and by Conners as appellee.[36] Interestingly, *none* of the briefs relied on the language in prior Second Circuit opinions (most written by Learned Hand) describing the negligence standard in cost-benefit balancing terms.[37] The Grace Line's brief, however, stressed that

---

[33] 66 F.Supp. at 400.

[34] In 1947, the prevailing rule in American negligence law was that contributory negligence completely barred a plaintiff's claim. In admiralty, however, the rule at that time was one of "divided damages," meaning that each negligent party would bear an equal share of all losses. *See* United States v. Reliable Transfer Co., 421 U.S. 397 (1975) (abolishing this approach in favor of comparative fault).

[35] 66 F.Supp. at 398.

[36] The Pennsylvania Railroad filed a three-page brief that preserved the Railroad's claims against Conners in the event the Second Circuit held the Anna C at fault, but offered no argument on the merits.

[37] *See* Conway v. O'Brien, 111 F.2d 611, 612 (2d Cir.1940) (L. Hand, J.) ("The degree of care demanded of a person by an occasion is the resultant of three factors: the likelihood that his conduct will injure others, taken with the seriousness of the injury if it happens, and balanced against the interest which he must sacrifice to avoid the risk."); Gunnarson v. Robert Jacob, Inc., 94 F.2d 170, 172 (2d Cir.1938) (L. Hand, J.) ("[L]iability depends upon an equation in which the gravity of the harm, if it comes, multiplied into the chance of its occurrence, must be weighed against the expense, inconvenience, and loss of providing against it."); Tompkins v. Erie R. Co., 90 F.2d 603, 605 (2d Cir.1937) (Swan, J.) ("As always in judging of negligence, it is a question of the gravity of the danger, coupled with its likelihood, as compared with the opportunity of avoiding it."); The Charles H. Sells, 89 F.2d 631, 633 (2d Cir.1937) (L. Hand, J.) ("As in all such situations the legal standard is the function of three variables: the actuarial possibility that the event will occur; the gravity of the damage, if it does; the expense and effort necessary to fend against it."); The B.B. No. 21, 54 F.2d 532, 533 (2d Cir.1931) (Swan, J.) ("As always in judging fault, it is a question of the gravity of the danger, coupled with its likelihood, as compared with the opportunity of avoiding it."). Lest readers conclude that Judge Swan originated

the Anna C was lying in a busy spot in which other barges would probably be moored outside her; that the accident occurred during working hours; that "[i]t was all the more important for [the bargee] to be aboard to care for the Anna C because she was loaded with a valuable cargo of flour"; and that the bargee's absence was unexcused and "wrongful."[38] The Grace Line's brief also distinguished between collision and sinking damages, as Hand would later do in his opinion.[39]

The brief for Conners stressed the precedents holding that a bargee's absence from his vessel is not negligence in itself.[40] Conners recognized this did not dispose of the argument that there was a heightened probability of an accident here because other boats were being moored in and removed from berths outside of the Anna C.[41] In response, Conners contended that the district court had correctly ruled that the bargee was not required to anticipate negligence by the harbormaster and deckhand.[42] Beyond that, Conners suggested that since the harbormaster and deckhand knew there was no one aboard the Anna C, they were negligent for failing to inspect her after she collided with the tanker.[43]

The Pre–Conference Memoranda

During Hand's tenure, the judges of the Second Circuit employed the unusual practice of writing pre-conference memoranda.[44] After oral argument, each of the three judges assigned to the appellate panel would circulate to his colleagues a brief memo outlining his views. The panel would then meet face-to-face before making its final decision. Learned Hand saved the pre-conference memos in the thousands of cases he heard during his long service as a Circuit Judge.[45] The memos in *Carroll*

---

the Hand Formula, I hasten to add that Swan's formulation was lifted almost verbatim from Hand's pre-conference memo in *The B.B. No. 21*, which asserted that "[a]s always, it is a question of the gravity of the danger coupled with its likelihood, as compared with the opportunity of escape."

[38] Grace Line Brief at 13, 10.

[39] Grace Line Brief at 11.

[40] Conners Brief at 7.

[41] Conners Brief at 7.

[42] Conners Brief at 8.

[43] Conners Brief at 15.

[44] *See* Gunther, *supra* note 4, at 286–88.

[45] Hand donated his papers to his alma mater, Harvard Law School. The pre-conference memoranda in *Carroll Towing* are in Box 209, Folder 7 of the Hand Papers.

Towing offer a fascinating additional window into the thinking of the panel, which, in addition to Learned Hand, consisted of Judges Harrie Chase and Jerome Frank.

The pre-conference memoranda show that the judges unanimously agreed with the trial judge's ruling that the Grace Line and Carroll Towing were jointly liable for the negligence of the harbormaster and deckhand. The panel was divided, however, on the issue of the bargee's negligence. Learned Hand, who wrote the most thorough memo and was the first to circulate his views, voted to hold the bargee (and hence Conners) liable for the sinking of the Anna C and the loss of her cargo. Hand argued forcefully—but in common-sense language, and with no mention of the Hand Formula—that the bargee's absence constituted negligence:

> I am not content to exculpate the barge herself for such damage as she suffered after the actual collision, or—what is much more important—for the loss of the cargo. We are to take it as a fact— though Moscowitz, J. did not expressly find it—that the bargee was not aboard at the time when the flotilla broke loose at 1 p.m.; and no excuse is offered for his absence. It would have been hard for the Anna C. to excuse him as he said that he was on hand; his absence, which I do not doubt, nevertheless stands unexcused. Although it is true that we have several times held it excusable for a bargee, who has safely tied up his barge, to sleep ashore, so far as I know we have never so held during the day, except when he has to leave to get some food, or the like. Why should he be free to stay away, at least in such a busy time as that was? His barge might have been moved elsewhere at any time; everything was on the move in the Harbor in those days, and he might be called upon to do his duties. If he was hired for anything, it was to be on hand generally; he could not expect to be summoned only when there was immediate occasion for some active service.
>
> If he was at fault for being absent, it seems to me that the situation was such as to charge him for failing to take action to save the cargo and the barge after she struck the tanker. True, the injury was to the bottom; but it is the first duty of a bargee in such cases to go below and see whether the barge is making water; and there is not the slightest reason to suspect that, if he had been on board and had done his duty, he would not have found that she had sprung a leak. If he had, concededly there were tugs about with heavy-duty siphon pumps which he could have hailed to his assistance. Had he done so, the barge would not have lost her cargo and sunk. I can see no answer to this argument; and, although I recognize that apparently

we have never before held a bargee for absence, it has been merely a chance, I submit, that we have not.[46]

Although Hand's memo made a strong case for holding the bargee liable, his arguments initially failed to persuade the other judges. Five days later, Judge Chase circulated a memo in which he voted to affirm. Chase rejected the suggestion that the bargee was negligent, reasoning that "[t]he findings . . . cannot fairly be held clearly erroneous."[47] Judge Frank then circulated a very brief memo announcing that he was undecided: "Assuming that there was a duty to Grace and/or the tug to have a barge on the barge, I think the barge-owner should be held jointly liable for the fact that nothing was done after the barge struck the tanker. But I have some difficulty in seeing that the barge-owner owed either of these parties a duty to supply a bargee."[48] Tentatively, Frank voted to affirm the trial judge's ruling exonerating the bargee and Conners.

Going into conference, then, it appeared that Chase's view would probably prevail. Yet the upshot was a unanimous opinion in line with Hand's pre-conference memorandum. It seems evident that Judge Frank came around to Hand's view of the case. But it also seems clear that Hand must have written his opinion with an eye to keeping Frank on board and persuading Chase to forgo a dissent. This was not a case in which he had an enthusiastic, unanimous panel behind him.

Hand's Opinion for the Second Circuit

After affirming the trial judge's conclusion that the negligence of the harbormaster and deckhand in adjusting the Anna C's lines should be imputed to both Carroll Towing and the Grace Line, Hand turned to whether the bargee's absence constituted negligence. In stating the facts, Hand had already resolved one key factual question left open by the trial judge's finding that the bargee was absent when the accident occurred: *how long* had he been absent? Recall that the bargee had testified that he showed up for work on time at 8 a.m., noticed the strain on the Anna C's lines, and did nothing. Had Hand credited that testimony, he could have argued that the bargee had negligently gone AWOL later in the morning, knowing full well that the Anna C's lines were under severe strain.[49] This would have brought the case squarely within the precedents holding that it was negligent for a bargee to abandon his barge in

---

[46] Memorandum from "L.H." to Judges Chase and Frank, at 1–2 (Dec. 6, 1946).

[47] Memorandum from "H.B.C." to Judges Hand and Frank (Dec. 11, 1946).

[48] Memorandum from "JNF" to Judges Chase and Hand (Dec. 12, 1946).

[49] The Grace Line had made exactly this argument in its brief. Grace Line Brief at 13.

the face of apparent danger. But it would have required a new factual finding in sharp tension with the trial judge's finding that the bargee had left the Anna C safely moored.[50] That would not have sat well with Chase, whose memo had insisted that there was nothing clearly erroneous in the trial court's factfinding.

Perhaps for that reason, Hand posited that the bargee *had never reported for work on January 4*[th] *at all.* So framed, the question was whether a bargee's absence during normal working hours is negligence. To answer that question in the affirmative, Hand had to reckon with three of the trial judge's rulings: that the bargee's absence had not contributed to the accident; that the case law suggested that it was not negligence for a bargee to leave his barge absent some foreseeable danger; and that there was no such danger here, because the bargee had left the Anna C safely moored, and was entitled to assume that anyone who adjusted her lines would use reasonable care.

Rather than rejecting the trial judge's finding that the bargee's presence would not have avoided the breaking away of the Anna C, Hand hastened to agree with it.[51] But the trial judge's finding made no mention of the additional losses caused by the subsequent sinking of the Anna C. Hand was therefore free to argue, as he had in his pre-conference memo, that the bargee's presence *would* have avoided these "sinking damages." If he had been on board, the bargee would have discovered that the Anna C was leaking and alerted the tugs in time to save her.[52]

Next was the matter of precedent. The trial judge had read the decisions dealing with absent bargees to mean that a bargee's absence was not negligence "in itself."[53] The cases he cited suggested that something more is necessary, such as leaving a barge when a storm was threatening.[54] The trial judge seemingly inferred that bargees must stay aboard only if there is some apparent danger (not merely a possibility) that the barge will go adrift.

Though he put it more tactfully, Hand's response amounted to saying that the trial judge had misread the cases and misunderstood the

---

[50] 66 F.Supp. at 397 ("[p]rior to the time that the harbor master and the deckhand of the tug adjusted the lines, the Anna C was safely made fast and lying properly").

[51] Hand reasoned that even if the bargee had been present, the harbormaster and deckhand would not have deferred to his judgment about how to arrange the lines. United States v. Carroll Towing Co., 159 F.2d 169, 172 (2d Cir.1947).

[52] *Id.*

[53] 66 F.Supp. at 398.

[54] None of the three published Second Circuit decisions the trial judge cited involved a bargee's absence during normal working hours.

prevailing meaning of negligence.[55] A review of the case law[56] demonstrated that "there is no general rule to determine when the absence of a bargee or other attendant will make the owner of the barge liable for injuries to other vessels if she breaks away from her moorings."[57] In fact, Hand asserted, "there can be no such rule," because the issue turns on balancing the costs and benefits of a bargee's presence in the particular circumstances of each case:

> Since there are occasions when every vessel will break from her moorings, and since, if she does, she becomes a menace to those about her; the owner's duty, as in other similar situations, to provide against resulting injuries is a function of three variables: (1) The probability that she will break away; (2) the gravity of the resulting injury, if she does; (3) the burden of adequate precautions. Possibly it serves to bring this notion into relief to state it in algebraic terms: if the probability be called P; the injury, L; and the burden, B; liability depends upon whether B is less than L multiplied by P: i.e., whether B is less than PL.[58]

Having announced that Hand Formula balancing is the true test for negligence, Hand proceeded to apply his Formula to the facts as found by the trial judge. He began by pointing out that the likelihood that a barge will break away (P) and the damage she will do (L) increase "if she is in a crowded harbor where moored barges are constantly being shifted about."[59] The presence of a bargee aboard would reduce or eliminate this danger.[60] Turning to B—the burden of precautions—Hand suggested

---

[55] By arguing that the trial judge misunderstood the applicable law, Hand managed to accommodate Judge Chase's view that the trial court's factual findings should not be disturbed. Arguably, Hand read too much into the trial judge's opinion, which did not expressly rely on any "general" rule, and may merely have been a somewhat clumsily-phrased ruling that the bargee could not reasonably foresee that the Anna C would go adrift.

[56] Hand summarized thirteen decisions touching on the general question "whether a barge owner is slack in the care of his barge if the bargee is absent." 159 F.2d at 172. In seven of these cases, a bargee's absence was held negligent; in three, not negligent; and in the remaining three the bargee was held not liable on other grounds (e.g., that the bargee's presence would have made no difference).

[57] 159 F.2d at 173.

[58] 159 F.2d at 173. Hand's emphasis on the risk a runaway barge poses to other vessels, and on the barge owner's resulting "duty," may have been a response to Judge Frank's pre-conference doubts about whether Conners owed a duty to Carroll Towing and the Grace Line.

[59] 159 F.2d at 173.

[60] A bargee's absence increases several risks: the risk of injury to the barge; the risk of injury to her cargo; and the risk that the barge will occasion injury to other vessels and their cargos. In economic terms, it is clear that L in the Hand Formula should include *each*

that it would be unduly burdensome to require bargees to be aboard continuously merely because they are moored in a crowded harbor.[61] Here, however, the question was whether it is "a sufficient answer to a bargee's absence without excuse, during working hours, that he has properly made fast his barge to a pier, when he leaves her."[62] Notice Hand's technique: he has now identified a much *less* burdensome precaution—staying aboard during working hours unless one has a good excuse—that will avoid most of the increased dangers associated with a crowded harbor (and that would have avoided the sinking of the Anna C). This combination of heightened PL and a much lower B makes negligence look likely.

Yet in the same breath, Hand zeroed in on the biggest weakness in the case against the bargee: safely mooring one's barge to a pier before leaving her is a precaution that greatly *reduces* P (and hence PL). Hand's response was that even if PL was quite small, the facts suggested that B must have been trivial. The bargee's "fabricated story was affirmative evidence that he had no excuse for his absence."[63]

At this juncture, Hand could perhaps have ended his analysis by declaring that PL was positive, while B was vanishingly small. The trial judge, however, had ruled that the bargee was "not required to anticipate negligence" on the part of the deckhand and harbormaster in adjusting the Anna C's lines. That ruling was arguably equivalent to a finding that PL was trivially small, at least from the bargee's standpoint. To put it in common sense terms, why should a bargee *need* an excuse for his absence if the barge is safely moored and if those who might interfere with her will presumably exercise reasonable care?

---

of these increased risks, because all of them are costs that could be avoided if the bargee were present. Even today, however, it is unclear whether negligence law is consistent with this conclusion. Indeed, it has recently been argued that most courts erroneously consider only the risk to the plaintiff in determining contributory negligence, and only the risk to others in determining a defendant's negligence. Robert Cooter & Ariel Porat, *Does Risk to Oneself Increase the Care Owed to Others?*, 29 J. Legal Stud. 19 (2000). Hand did not explicitly address this question in Carroll Towing. He framed his Hand Formula discussion in terms of the barge-owner's liability *for injuries to others*, on the grounds that if the barge-owner would be liable as a negligent defendant "obviously" he would be contributorily negligent "if the injury is to his own barge." 159 F.2d at 173. This necessarily implies that a plaintiff can be contributorily negligent either because of risks to self or because of risks to others—and one would think that means they should be added together for purposes of finding PL. Surprisingly, however, when Hand applied his Formula, he focused solely on the risk that a barge will "break from her moorings" and "become a menace to those about her." *Id.*

[61] 159 F.2d at 173.

[62] *Id.*

[63] *Id.* at 173–174.

On this issue, Hand directly challenged the trial judge's reasoning: "At the locus in quo—especially during the short January days and in the full tide of war activity—barges were being constantly 'drilled' in and out. Certainly it was not beyond reasonable expectation that, with the inevitable haste and bustle, the work might not be done with adequate care."[64] Thus, although the Anna C may have been safely moored, there was a residual risk that she might go adrift as a result of negligently performed maneuvers in the busy harbor. So P was not negligible (and L was substantial)—therefore the bargee *did* need an excuse after all, at least "during the working hours of daylight."[65]

Having heralded his Formula as proof that there is no "general rule" governing when a bargee's absence is negligence, it comes as no surprise that Hand framed his holding narrowly: "In such circumstances we hold—and it is all that we do hold—that it was a fair requirement that the Conners Company should have a bargee aboard (unless he had some excuse for his absence), during the working hours of daylight."[66] In a future case, a barge-owner could argue that its bargee's absence was distinguishable on any number of grounds: the harbor was less busy, the bargee had business ashore, and so on. Cautious lawyers might find in Hand's opinion a signal that bargees should be aboard during normal working hours absent a good excuse. But that signal is a suggestion, not a rule of law. Especially in the context of the barge industry—one of whose principal competitive advantages is its comparatively low labor costs as against self-propelled vessels[67]—Hand's diffidence seems sensible.

Why Hand Formula Balancing?

Learned Hand was not the first to propose a cost-benefit conception of negligence (though he was the first to express it in algebraic form).[68]

---

[64] *Id.* at 174.

[65] *Id.* Hand clearly has the better of this argument: longshoremen are not infallible, and presumably their error rate increases when they are overworked. Hand's decision to treat B as tantamount to zero, however, is open to question. Even if the bargee's reason for being absent was one that his employer would normally excuse, he might still have claimed he was present for fear he would be scapegoated because disaster struck while he was absent.

[66] *Id.*

[67] *See* Harrington, *supra* note 19, at 123–24.

[68] As another aspect of the Carroll Towing litigation demonstrates, Hand was quite proficient in the use of algebra. After the Second Circuit issued its decision, Carroll Towing petitioned for rehearing on the ground, *inter alia*, that under the portions of Hand's opinion dealing with damages, it might have to pay more than its share of the cargo and

Henry Terry had done so in a 1915 Harvard Law Review article, and the Restatement of Torts adopted a risk-utility test for negligence in the early 1930s.[69] While there was some authority for this position, it was far from settled law. Terry, the drafters of the Restatement, and Learned Hand all *chose* to recognize cost-benefit negligence as authoritative. The question is, why?

Carroll Towing supplies no answer. It seems likely, however, that Hand and others in the "founding generation" would have agreed with the rationale most often offered nowadays: that cost-benefit negligence tends to advance overall social well-being by inducing actors to take the right level of precautions. In economic theory, society is best off if actors take precautions against accidents when—and only when—the benefits of those precautions exceed their costs. Defining negligence in cost-benefit terms is designed to deter actors from creating risks of personal injury that fail this cost-benefit test, while permitting them to create cost-justified risks without fear of negligence liability.

At the same time, the Hand Formula can be seen as reflecting a particular view of what constitutes reasonable and fair behavior: each of us should refrain from creating "unreasonable" risks to others (risks that can be avoided for less than their expected accident costs) but remains free to create "reasonable" risks (risks it would be excessively burdensome to guard against). According to the Restatement of Torts, this conception of reasonable behavior reflects the idea that everyone should "give an impartial consideration to the harm likely to be done the interests of the other as compared with the advantages likely to accrue to his own interests, free from the natural tendency of the actor, as a party concerned, to prefer his own interests to that of others."[70] Thus,

---

salvage losses. The Second Circuit issued a brief per curiam opinion in which it clarified Hand's original opinion by explaining the circumstances in which Carroll Towing would be allowed a "set-off" against the recovery of the Grace Line and the Conners Company in the limitation proceeding. *United States v. Carroll Towing Co.*, 160 F.2d 482 (2d Cir.1947). Prior to issuance of this per curiam opinion, which he almost certainly wrote, Learned Hand circulated two memos to his colleagues explaining the formidable complexities of this part of the case in non-algebraic terms. The Hand Papers, however, also include an undated, three-page handwritten memo that appears to be authored by Hand, and which uses algebra to analyze the problem. Here is a sample: The memo begins by setting "x = value of tug Joseph Carroll," "y = claim of U.S. (value of flour)," "z = claim of Penn (salvage costs)," "A = collision damages," and "B = sinking damages (i.e. damages to Anna C)." It then reasons that "Carroll's suggestion that recoupment or setoff be allowed is practical in the following situation: Where $x > y + z + \frac{1}{2}A + \frac{1}{6}B$ *and* $\frac{1}{3}(x + y) < 1/6 B$."

[69] Henry T. Terry, *Negligence*, 29 Harv. L. Rev. 40 (1915); Restatement of Torts § 291 (1934).

[70] *Id.* § 283 cmt. a.

Hand Formula negligence can be (and frequently is) justified both on social welfare and fairness grounds.[71]

A Hand Formula Primer

How exactly does the Hand Formula work? A first encounter with *Carroll Towing* leaves many readers baffled on this score. The explanation that will be offered here omits many complexities for the sake of conveying the basic idea—namely, that the Hand Formula is a tool for comparing the costs and benefits of particular "untaken precautions" (that is, precautions an actor failed to take, and that the opposing party insists should have been taken).[72] The costs of taking a precaution are all the disadvantages (pecuniary and non-pecuniary) of adopting it; these are represented by B (for burden) in the Hand Formula. The benefits of taking a precaution are the accident risks it avoids—in other words, the amount by which taking the precaution reduces expected accident losses. These benefits are represented by PL in the Hand Formula: the probability of an accident if the precaution is not taken, multiplied by the expected loss if an accident occurs.

Consider as an example the precaution of having a bargee aboard during normal working hours. (Imagine, if you like, that Conners had not agreed to supply a bargee, and the Railroad had not provided one). The cost of taking this precaution is the cost of hiring a bargee—say, $8/day in 1944.[73] The benefits of taking it equal the difference between expected accident losses with and without a bargee. Suppose that expected accident losses without a bargee are, on average, one $6,000 accident every 200 days, or $30/day. If adding a bargee during normal working hours would completely eliminate these accidents, PL would equal $30/day. But that is unrealistic, because some barge accidents happen at night or are not preventable by a bargee. In order to determine PL, therefore, we need to estimate the probability and magnitude of accidents that would occur even with a bargee. Let's assume that hiring a bargee reduces the expected frequency of an accident to one every 300 days, and the average accident loss to $3,000. Then expected accident losses with a bargee are $10/day ($3,000/300 days), versus $30/day ($6,000/200 days) without one. PL is the difference: $20/day in expected accident costs that will be avoided by hiring a bargee. Applying the Hand

---

[71] *See, e.g.*, Gary Schwartz, *Mixed Theories of Tort Law: Affirming Both Deterrence and Corrective Justice*, 75 Tex. L. Rev. 1801 (1997).

[72] *See* Mark Grady, *Untaken Precautions*, 18 J. Legal Stud. 139 (1989).

[73] The Grace Line harbor master testified that he earned normal longshoreman's wages of $1.25/hour in 1944. Transcript at 197. Bargees presumably earned significantly less.

Formula, B ($8/day) is less than PL ($20/day), and hence it is negligent
not to hire a bargee during normal working hours.

Finding the Hand Formula Facts: The Problems of Information and Error Costs

Now that we have seen how the Hand Formula is supposed to work,
we can consider the first major objection to Hand Formula negligence:
that it is a failure by its own social-welfare standards.[74] Cost-benefit
negligence, the argument goes, flunks cost-benefit analysis: the costs of
operating the tort system—judges, jurors, lawyers, witnesses, and all the
rest—exceed the incentive and fairness benefits it creates. The chief
villain of this story is "information costs," namely the costs to the
parties and the court of obtaining reliable information about B, P, and L
in any given case.[75] High information costs are a problem in the first
instance because they inflate the administrative costs of the negligence
system. Less obviously, they also reduce its benefits: if reliable information is difficult or impossible to obtain, then Hand Formula judgments
will frequently be wrong: actors who take cost-justified precautions will
often be held liable, and actors who fail to take cost-justified precautions
will often escape liability. In turn, these errors will undermine the
negligence system's ability to induce people to take cost-justified precautions.

Although *Carroll* Towing passes over the problem of information
costs in silence, Learned Hand acknowledged elsewhere that it was a
serious difficulty. For example, in *Moisan v. Loftus* he wrote:

> But of [the Hand Formula] factors, care is the only one ever
> susceptible of quantitative estimate, and often that is not. The
> injuries are always a variable within limits, which do not admit of
> even approximate ascertainment; and, although probability might
> theoretically be estimated, if any statistics were available, they never
> are; and, besides, probability varies with the severity of the injuries.
> It follows that all such attempts are illusory; and, if serviceable at
> all, are so only to center attention upon which one of the factors
> may be determinative in any given situation.[76]

Think back to our blithe assumptions a few paragraphs ago that the
presence of a bargee reduced the probability of an accident from 1 per

---

[74] *See* Richard A. Epstein, *Torts* 95–99 (1999).

[75] The second villain is usually said to be the weakness of tort law as an incentive-
creating regime. Consider, for example, the obvious inability of negligence law to deter
actors who are judgment-proof.

[76] 178 F.2d 148, 149 (2d Cir.1949).

200 days to 1 per 300 days, and the average cost of an accident from $6000 to $3000. Statistics like these do not fall like manna from heaven. To construct them, fallible human actors must collect and interpret large amounts of data—hoping all the while that conditions are not changing so fast that their results are no longer valid. Even under the most favorable of circumstances, statistics will furnish a rough estimate, not a precise answer.

That said, Hand's pessimism about radically incomplete information may reflect the fact that Hand Formula negligence was comparatively new and untried when he wrote. If a similar barge accident happened today, the missing "statistics" about P and L might be known to (or ascertainable by) maritime insurance companies, state port authorities, or experts in barge accidents. As the Hand Formula becomes more influential, lawyers are increasingly likely to unearth and present detailed evidence bearing on the Hand Formula factors.

Moreover, despite his pessimism about making exact Hand Formula judgments, Hand thought his Formula could still be helpful in making rough-and-ready ones. *Carroll Towing* is an example: the "determinative" factor turns out to be B, which Hand concluded was negligible. Armed with that datum, Hand did not *need* exact information about PL. It was enough that PL, although small, was not trivial. Here is a second example: defendants often argue that the precaution suggested by plaintiffs would have created other, greater risks of injury.[77] In cases of this kind, the essential issue is whether the precaution would in fact produce a net safety benefit. If not, there is no need to determine exactly how much the precaution would cost.

Courts use a variety of other techniques to reduce the information costs of the Hand Formula approach. Litigants in negligence cases are not expected to present information about the entire range of possible precautions a defendant could have taken, so that the factfinder can decide whether the defendant's actual behavior was "optimal." Instead, as we have already seen, plaintiffs are expected to identify one or more specific "untaken precautions" and offer proof that—as compared with the defendant's actual conduct—their safety benefits outweigh their costs. This practice greatly simplifies the Hand Formula inquiry.

Again, *Carroll Towing* is illustrative. If Conners had not hired a bargee to be aboard the Anna C during normal working hours, the litigation would have focused on whether Conners was negligent for omitting that customary precaution. Because Conners *had* hired a bargee, Hand could assume that the benefits of having a bargee aboard during normal working hours normally exceeded the cost of hiring a

---

[77] *See* Cooley v. Pub. Serv. Co., 10 A.2d 673 (N.H.1940).

bargee.[78] But the fact that Conners had provided a bargee forced the
other litigants to argue that Conners was *vicariously* liable because the
bargee had negligently been absent. The question then became whether
the costs *to the bargee* of performing his duties on January 4th were for
some reason so high as to excuse his absence. Answering that question
required a manageable amount of information: why had the bargee
chosen not to report for work? The bargee, of course, elected not to
reveal his motive by insisting that he was present throughout—but then
Hand could fairly assume that he had taken the day off for no good
reason.

These various strategies for reducing information costs and increasing accurate adjudication are sensible refinements of the Hand Formula
approach. Whether they are sufficiently effective to enable a system of
cost-benefit negligence to survive cost-benefit scrutiny is a large empirical question we cannot pursue here. This much at least is clear: although
any negligence standard will have high information costs as compared
with a regime of strict liability, American courts are firmly committed to
negligence as the general standard of liability in tort. The real issue,
therefore, is whether information costs are a bigger problem for Hand
Formula negligence than for competing approaches to negligence. We
will return to that question shortly.

Evaluating the Hand Formula Factors: The Problem of Incommensurability

The second major objection to the Hand Formula is more fundamental. The claim is that the Hand Formula cannot be implemented in a
coherent, principled way—even if complete, accurate information about
each variable is available—because the variables are *incommensurable*
(that is, not comparable in terms of a common metric). At first blush,
this objection seems strange. One might think that once B, P, and L are
known, they can simply be plugged in to the Hand Formula equation to
determine whether the actor is negligent. In reality, however, the Hand
Formula cannot be applied unless PL and B can be expressed in terms
that permit the factfinder to make a quantitative comparison between
them.

Suppose, for example, that by putting a blade guard on its handheld
power saws a manufacturer can eliminate a 1 in 10,000 chance that

---

[78] Economic analysis confirms Hand's judgment. The custom attested that it was in the
joint interests of barge-owners and charterers to pay a bargee to perform a wide variety of
mundane barge-related duties during normal working hours. Plainly, then, only a small
fraction of the bargee's paycheck was attributable to his responsibility to call for help in
the unlikely event that the barge sprung a leak. As a rough approximation, therefore, the
bargee's presence during working hours should be taken as a given, and the focus should
be on the costs to the bargee of staying aboard.

users will lose a finger in an accident. This gives us B (a blade guard) and PL (a .0001 chance of losing a finger). But in order to determine which is greater—the cost of a blade guard or the benefit of avoiding a .0001 chance of losing a finger—we need to be able to describe them in terms of a common metric. And that undeniably poses a problem, because fingers and blade guards *as such* obviously cannot be quantitatively compared.[79]

One plausible strategy is to try to *price* (or "monetize") the relevant costs and benefits. In some cases, this strategy works quite well. If the untaken precaution is "hiring a bargee during normal working hours," and if the expected accident costs involve only property damage, B and PL can readily be expressed and compared in dollar terms. But this strategy quickly runs into problems if the expected accident costs include personal injuries or deaths. In our power saw example, the unit price of a blade guard can be calculated, but pricing the risk of losing a finger presents stubborn difficulties. Some of the associated losses, such as medical expenses and lost earnings, can at least be estimated in monetary terms. But there are no market prices for others, such as pain and suffering and the impaired functioning of the injured hand; they are literally "priceless," (though certainly not infinitely costly).

For some years Posner—the foremost champion of Hand Formula negligence—argued that courts could solve these problems by estimating what people would be willing to pay to avoid risks of personal injury. He has subsequently acknowledged, however, that the "[c]onceptual as well as practical difficulties in monetizing personal injuries" mean that "[f]or many years to come juries may be forced to make rough judgments of reasonableness, intuiting rather than measuring the factors in the Hand Formula."[80]

Some people think this concession is fatal.[81] As they see it, without a common metric the whole enterprise of cost-benefit balancing comes to a crashing halt. Posnerian judges and juries may *think* they are making reasoned judgments when they "intuit" values for B and PL. But the skeptics view these intuitions as nothing more than arbitrary expressions of the decisionmaker's own values and preferences.

---

[79] The problem of "incommensurability" is not peculiar to the Hand Formula. It is a standard objection to cost-benefit analysis in *any* context, and has generated a scholarly literature too extensive even to summarize here. *See, e.g., Incommensurability, Incomparability, and Practical Reason* (Ruth Chang ed., 1997).

[80] *McCarty v. Pheasant Run, Inc.*, 826 F.2d 1554, 1556 (7th Cir.1987).

[81] Others think it is premature. *See* Louis Kaplow & Steven Shavell, *Fairness Versus Welfare* 15–38 (2002) (arguing that costs and benefits *can* be commensurated and analyzed in terms of the well-being of individuals).

Learned Hand was skeptical, but not *that* skeptical. Although he did not mention it in *Carroll Towing*, in other opinions Hand emphasized that the application of the Hand Formula requires the decisionmaker to make value judgments about PL and B.[82] Moreover, throughout his long career, Hand consistently adhered to the position that values are incommensurable[83]: there is no true metric that will enable us to compare, say, the value a bargee attaches to taking a spontaneous holiday from work with the value of the increased risks of harm his absence imposes on the barge, her cargo, and other vessels. Indeed, the proposition that there is no common metric for weighing the conflicting values and interests of different individuals and groups was, for Hand, an important argument in favor of legislative primacy and judicial restraint.[84] Precisely because there were no legal or scientific principles for resolving conflicting interests, he reasoned, these contests should generally be decided by the people's elected representatives.

Hand was well aware, however, that it would be utterly impractical for legislatures to resolve the sorts of fact-specific value conflicts that arise in negligence (and other common law) cases. In particular, judges and juries are charged with resolving the conflicting interests of parties in negligence cases—as well as in a variety of other legal contexts in which the law mandates a standard of "reasonableness." Hand's position was that in applying these reasonableness tests decisionmakers should first identify the relevant interests, and then balance those interests in line with prevailing social values.[85]

Hand did not pretend that social values were a definitive solution to the problem of incommensurability. Sometimes the community's values would be too vague or heterogeneous to yield a clear answer. But there would also be cases in which the judge could be confident that widely-held values would assign greater weight to one interest than another. A bargee who takes an unscheduled holiday from his safely moored barge merely because he "feels like it" is negligent because the community places less value on such whims than on the small residual risk of a serious accident in his absence. And whether the answer is clear or not, when society delegates the determination of negligence to the judge he

---

[82] *See, e.g.*, Conway v. O'Brien, 111 F.2d 611, 612 (2d Cir.1940) (applying the negligence standard "always involves some preference, or choice between incommensurables").

[83] *See, e.g.*, United States v. Levine, 83 F.2d 156, 157 (2d Cir.1936) ("As so often happens, the problem is to find a passable compromise between opposing interests, whose relative importance, like that of all social or personal values, is incommensurable.").

[84] *See* Learned Hand, *The Bill of Rights* 37–42 (1958).

[85] He suggested that this task is often committed to juries rather than judges because "their decision is thought most likely to accord with commonly accepted standards, real or fancied." *Conway v. O'Brien*, 111 F.2d at 612.

must find the facts and estimate the values as best he can. Thus, for Hand, the pervasiveness of value-incommensurability was not a sufficient reason for courts to refrain from making practical cost-benefit comparisons. On the contrary, it was a reason for making those cost-benefit judgments only after careful attention to the Hand Formula variables *and* to prevailing social values.

The Hand Formula and Its Rivals: The Foreseeable Danger and Community Expectations Approaches

Now that we've seen how Learned Hand applied the Hand Formula, and how he dealt with the most pressing problems with his approach, it is time to take a brief look at the competition. Two alternatives to Hand Formula balancing have been especially influential in Anglo–American negligence law: I will refer to them as the "foreseeable-danger" approach and the "community expectations" approach. Like the Hand Formula, they are attempts to give content to the traditional—but vague—definition of negligence as the failure to do what a reasonably prudent person would have done in like circumstances.

As we have seen, the Hand Formula uses cost-benefit balancing to supply that content: reasonably prudent persons, it implies, take cost-justified precautions—not all *possible* precautions—against foreseeable risks to others occasioned by their conduct. To many people, however, it seems only fair that when an actor creates a foreseeable danger to others, the actor should be responsible if injury results—whether eliminating the risk would have been ridiculously easy or extremely difficult. That view of fairness animates the foreseeable-danger approach, which holds that reasonably prudent persons are expected to do everything possible to avoid creating foreseeable dangers to others. This " 'non-balancing' interpretation of negligence"[86] was endorsed by Holmes in his influential book *The Common Law*,[87] and many early twentieth-century courts (including the New York courts) apparently favored it.[88] Above the threshold level of foreseeable danger—which is not quantifiable, but simply determined by the factfinder in light of the probability and gravity of the risk—actors are liable regardless of "the difficulty of remedial measures."[89] Below the threshold of foreseeable danger, actors are not liable even if remedial measures would have been easy.

---

[86] Thomas C. Grey, *Accidental Torts*, 54 Vand. L. Rev 1225, 1279 n.168 (2001).

[87] Holmes argued that an actor is negligent if "he might and ought to have foreseen the danger, or, in other words, [if] a man of ordinary intelligence would have been to blame for acting as he did." O.W. Holmes, Jr., *The Common Law* 110 (1881).

[88] *See* William E. Nelson, *From Fairness to Efficiency: The Transformation of Tort Law in New York, 1920–1980*, 47 Buff. L. Rev. 117, 142–143 (1999).

[89] *Bolton v. Stone* , [1951] A.C. 850, 867 (Lord Reid).

The community-expectations approach also rejects Hand Formula balancing, in the belief that social understandings and norms are a better guide to what is in society's best interests (and what we can fairly expect from each other) than cost-benefit analysis.[90] Its central tenet is that a reasonably prudent person conforms to the prevailing expectations in the community about consideration for the safety of others. On this view, the law should not try to guide the jury's inquiry by setting up an independent legal benchmark for what constitutes reasonable care. Instead, the jury should decide in accord with community expectations concerning safe behavior under the circumstances.[91] Jurors may find those norms in the evidence at trial, in their own knowledge and experiences, or both. No doubt those norms will sometimes point to the same result as a Hand Formula analysis (or a foreseeable-danger analysis). But under the community-expectations approach, that is coincidental. Actors should follow the community's safety norms because they are, so to speak, the rules of the game.

We can use the setting of *Carroll Towing* to illustrate the practical differences among these three approaches. Under the Hand Formula approach, the bargee was negligent because, although PL was small, B was completely negligible. Under the foreseeable-danger approach (which the trial judge seems to have favored) the bargee probably wins, because the risk (PL) falls below the threshold of dangerousness given that he left the barge safely moored. As this illustrates, the seemingly stricter foreseeable-danger approach is actually less strict than Hand Formula balancing in low-risk cases.[92] But if we tinker with the facts—say, if the bargee left the barge during a storm because he was sick and needed to get medical attention—the outcomes flip: the bargee would certainly be negligent under the foreseeable-danger test (because PL is high), but might not be negligent under the Hand Formula (because B is also high).

---

[90] *See* Patrick J. Kelley, *Who Decides? Community Safety Conventions at the Heart of Tort Liability*, 38 Clev. St. L. Rev. 315 (1990).

[91] For simplicity, the account I present here lumps together the view that the jury should decide by reference to a *pre-existing* community norm and the view that jurors should *construct* or *imagine* what a reasonably prudent person would do. In practice, both views deny that jurors are expected to balance costs and benefits, and look instead to jurors' socially-influenced expectations about safety. I acknowledge that these views may differ in other respects, and those differences may be important for negligence theory.

[92] It is possible to modify the foreseeable-danger approach so that defendants are liable without balancing if the threshold for danger is crossed, but are subject to liability under a balancing test for risks that are small but not negligible. *See* Overseas Tankship (U.K.) Ltd. v. The Miller Steamship Co. (The Wagon Mound No.2), [1967] 1 A.C. 617, 643–44 (Lord Reid). This modification moves the foreseeable-danger approach closer to Hand Formula negligence; how much closer depends on where the line between small risks and foreseeable dangers is drawn.

Because several competing safety norms were arguably in play, it is unclear how *Carroll Towing* would have come out under the community-expectations test. First, the trial judge apparently believed that bargees customarily relied on tug crews to rearrange lines properly when shifting barges. Choosing that norm would entail finding that the bargee was not negligent. Learned Hand's pre-conference memo, by contrast, suggested that the reason for having a bargee on board during working hours was to ensure that he would be available to help if something went wrong. Following that norm would mean that the bargee's absence was negligent. And here is a third possibility (unfortunately not explored at trial): there may have been a common understanding among bargees and their employers about what constituted an acceptable excuse for going ashore during working hours. If so, that waterfront-community norm could have been used to judge the bargee's conduct.

Does this mean that the community-expectations approach is hopelessly indeterminate, or that it collapses into the Hand Formula approach? Not at all. The decisionmaker (in *Carroll Towing*, a judge; more often, a jury) is supposed to decide which of these alleged norms best represents the actual expectations of the relevant community concerning the behavioral issue in question. That judgment is not supposed to depend on—or even to consider—which alleged norm is best in Hand Formula terms. And while it would be surprising if community norms were wildly at odds with a Hand Formula analysis, it would be even more surprising if they always reached the same results.[93]

The Hand Formula and Its Rivals: A Normative Comparison

Which of these competing conceptions of negligence you prefer is likely to depend on which account of reasonable consideration for the safety of others you find persuasive. Should people do everything possible to avoid substantial risks to others? Should they take their bearings from social expectations and norms of acceptably safe behavior? Or

---

[93] Some community norms may coincide with the Hand Formula in most situations, but fail to provide for exceptions that a Hand Formula analysis would recognize. Consider this example from *Carroll Towing*: during cross-examination of the tug's captain, the attorney for the Grace Line tried to establish that the deckhand and harbormaster should have *shifted* the obstructing cross-line to a different barge, rather than just removing it. The common sense behind this suggested untaken precaution was that doing so would have allowed the Carroll to gain access to the Camden, while continuing to relieve the strain on the Anna C's lines by means of a cross-line between the two tiers of barges. The Carroll's captain indignantly retorted, "That ain't our duty to do that stuff, to go from pier to pier and attend to somebody else's ropes." Tr. at 153. The captain's homespun account of who-is-expected-to-do-what may make good economic sense in general. On the facts of *Carroll Towing*, however, this community-expectations norm seems at odds with Hand Formula analysis because of the high *ex ante* risk that the barges would break away if the cross-line were simply removed.

should they decide how careful to be based on a disinterested evaluation of the costs and benefits of additional precautions, expressed in terms of social values?

Resolving this normative dispute is an undertaking far too ambitious to be pursued here. But whichever your preference, it is important to understand that each of these approaches is endorsed by many reasonable people—and yet that each of them also has serious practical shortcomings. We've already seen that high information costs and incommensurability pose problems for the Hand Formula approach. Similar problems dog foresight-based negligence and community-expectations negligence too.

By refusing to balance the costs and benefits of precautions, the foreseeable-danger approach reduces information costs (because precaution costs (B) need not be determined). Information costs remain high, however, because determining whether there is foreseeable danger requires knowing P and L, which are often the hardest variables to get accurate information about. Similarly, while refusing to compare B and PL avoids one kind of incommensurability, a related measurement problem promptly arises: what level of PL counts as foreseeable danger, and why? In order to answer that question coherently—something that, so far as I know, no court has ever even attempted to do—it would be necessary to compare levels of PL in different cases. (If a 1/1,000 chance of losing a foot constitutes foreseeable danger, but a 1/10,000 chance does not, what about a 1/1,000 chance of losing a finger?) Moreover, from a social welfare standpoint the foresight-based approach builds in two types of errors: some defendants are held liable although it would have been excessively burdensome for them to avoid injuring the plaintiff, while other defendants escape liability although they could easily have avoided the accident.

The information costs of the community-expectations approach look low at first glance: juries can just rely on what "everyone knows" about prevailing norms in the community. Often, however, there may be no community expectations directly on point. Beyond that, the open-endedness of the community expectations approach invites each party to invest heavily in persuading the jury to adopt its preferred substantive test for liability, thereby creating information costs of a different sort. As for incommensurability, the community expectations test avoids the problem by relying on society to have done the hard work already. But society's expectations may not be coherent—indeed, they may be contradictory: which is it, "better safe than sorry" or "waste not, want not"? The community expectations approach thus seems vulnerable to the objection that it merely conceals the problem of incommensurability behind the veil of jury verdicts that typically do not explain the jury's thumbs-up or thumbs-down.

The Hand Formula and Its Rivals: A Descriptive Comparison

We've seen that there is no knockdown winner in the normative contest between the Hand Formula and its rivals, the foreseeable-danger and community-expectations tests. But which approach have the courts adopted, and which arguments have persuaded them? To an astonishing degree, the answer to these questions cannot be found in the explicit language of judicial opinions. Few courts have even acknowledged that there are important choices to be made in defining the reasonably prudent person standard and in communicating that definition to juries, let alone offered reasons for the choices implicit in their practices.

That said, it is clear that Hand Formula negligence is increasingly important in American negligence law. The vast majority of appellate courts have endorsed some version of a cost-benefit balancing test for negligence, and virtually none have rejected balancing. By the same token, the foreseeable-danger approach, which repudiates balancing, is far less influential now than it was when *Carroll Towing* was written.

The community-expectations approach, however, is very much alive and well. When judges and juries apply the reasonably prudent person standard without using the Hand Formula, they presumably draw on their background beliefs about what is considered safe and prudent behavior in their communities. Strikingly, in the half-century since *Carroll Towing*, a wide gap has opened up between doctrine and practice: although appellate courts endorse balancing (and sometimes engage in it), trial judges typically give juries an undefined reasonably prudent person instruction, in which nothing is said about the Hand Formula or any other version of balancing. Under these circumstances, it seems clear that much of the content of the negligence standard is being supplied by jurors' understanding of societal expectations about appropriately safe behavior. Jurors may sometimes engage in common-sense versions of balancing on their own motion (or because they are persuaded to do so by counsel for one of the parties). But there is good reason to think that many jurors strongly resist (indeed, sometimes are angered by) the proposition that safety issues should be decided by balancing costs and benefits.[94]

One can argue that this divergence between Hand Formula doctrine and community-expectation instructions shows that the courts have perceptively dealt with a third problem with the Hand Formula: institutional fitness. On this view, even if cost-benefit analysis is a valuable tool for regulatory agencies and judges reviewing jury verdicts, it is not a

---

[94] *See* Gary T. Schwartz, *The Myth of the Ford Pinto Case*, 43 Rutgers L. Rev. 1013, 1038 (1991).

technique juries are comfortable with or competent to apply. Giving Hand Formula instructions may confuse and antagonize jurors who will reach more sensible results more often if they are simply told to consult their intuitions about how reasonable people are expected to behave in our society.

This argument would carry more weight if courts articulated and defended it, which they generally have not. Beyond that, the Hand Formula approach, as actually implemented in litigation, is hardly "rocket science." Ordinary people make many everyday choices—including choices about safety—by informally balancing the costs and benefits of their options. The Hand Formula variables and the relationships among them are thus already familiar to most jurors (though not by name). Hand Formula instructions may therefore be more workable than courts seem to believe.[95]

Even if Hand Formula jury instructions are not in the offing, the Hand Formula remains an increasingly important feature of negligence law. Learned Hand proposed his Formula in the evident hope that it would help judges—many of whom were already "balancing" in deciding negligence cases—to balance more carefully and consistently. That aspiration has met with some success. Many judges now use the Hand Formula to "sharpen thinking about negligence" and bring "structure to what would otherwise be rather loose speculation as to how a reasonable person would or would not act in particular circumstances."[96] Just as importantly, so do many lawyers. Whether they represent plaintiffs or defendants, today's litigators routinely employ the Hand Formula to help frame their litigation strategies, negotiating positions, and sometimes even jury arguments. What is more, today's law students are the second generation of young lawyers for whom the Hand Formula represents a powerful and familiar way to understand the meaning of negligence. As they rise in the ranks of the legal profession, it seems likely that the Hand Formula's influence will continue to grow.

The Impact of *Carroll Towing* and Its Author on Hand Formula Negligence

This brings us to one final question: How much of the Hand Formula's influence is attributable to Learned Hand, and to *Carroll*

---

[95] Products liability law suggests, by analogy, a possible compromise along the following lines: when specific and well-defined community expectations exist, juries should be told to decide on that basis; when they do not, juries should be instructed to apply the Hand Formula in light of prevailing social values. *Cf.* Soule v. General Motors Corp., 882 P.2d 298 (Cal.1994) (a product is defective if its design violates widely shared consumer expectations, or, in the absence of such expectations, if it fails a cost-benefit analysis).

[96] Richard A. Posner, *Law and Legal Theory in England and America* 40–41 (1996).

Towing in particular? As we've seen, Henry Terry and subsequently the Restatement of Torts endorsed versions of cost-benefit negligence long before Hand wrote *Carroll Towing*. But Hand was deeply involved in the Restatement project, and history may eventually show that he influenced the Restatement as much or more than it influenced him. However that may be, the fact that a jurist of Hand's stature endorsed cost-benefit negligence in no uncertain terms (and did so repeatedly before and after *Carroll Towing*)[97] lent further credibility to the Restatement's claim that its position faithfully described the prevailing judicial understanding of negligence. At a minimum, Hand played an important part in bringing cost-benefit thinking into the mainstream of common law doctrine.

As for *Carroll Towing*, it is the most famous of Hand's several Hand Formula opinions for a mixture of good and not-so-good reasons. *Carroll Towing* stands out as Hand's fullest and subtlest application of the Hand Formula. Yet if in 1972 Posner had used a different Hand opinion to showcase the Hand Formula, this chapter might have told the story of that case instead. Moreover, in terms of Hand's own jurisprudence Posner's choice was an odd one. *Carroll Towing* omits the cautions about information costs and incommensurability with which Hand qualified most of his other Hand Formula opinions. Those qualifications are central to the skeptical, self-restrained spirit in which Hand thought judges should use the Hand Formula. Hand may have been mistaken, of course, but surely his views deserve careful consideration. It would be a sad irony if *Carroll Towing*'s celebrity caused Learned Hand's diffident appraisal of his Formula to be overlooked or brushed aside.

---

[97] *See supra* note 37 and cases cited therein.

*

2

James A. Henderson, Jr.

MacPherson v. Buick Motor Company: Simplifying the Facts While Reshaping the Law

The Facts Leading Up To Trial

What Happened on the Day of the Accident: No Good Deed Goes Unpunished

It was a clear Tuesday afternoon in late July 1911, and Donald MacPherson was on a mission of mercy. The Carr brothers, John and Charles, had called him earlier that day to ask if he would take them in his automobile to the hospital in Saratoga Springs. John Carr, age 27, had a painful infection in his hand that required immediate medical attention, very likely surgery. MacPherson had agreed to help his friends. After he and his wife, Johanna, finished their dinner (lunch, in the modern vernacular), he had climbed into his 1911 Buick runabout around 2:30 p.m. and headed for the Carrs' house. The car was not new, or even nearly new; the MacPhersons had owned it for over a year and had put it to hard use. Once under way, Donald took the back road from Galway Village, the hamlet in Upstate New York where he and Johanna lived, driving east toward the Village of Ballston, eight miles distant.

Halfway to Ballston, MacPherson turned off the road a mile or so to pick up the Carr boys. John, with his swollen hand, got in the left front passenger seat (the steering wheel was on the right side in those days) and Charles, John's older brother, climbed in the oversized rumble seat in back. They got back on the road and drove east to Ballston, where they stopped at the West Building garage to get gas. A few minutes later, just after 4:00 p.m., they continued traveling east to the state road where they turned left to head north toward Ballston Spa and, beyond that, Saratoga Springs. By then Donald MacPherson was in a hurry. It would take them at least half an hour to drive the remaining twelve miles to Saratoga Springs, more time to reach the hospital, and several hours on top of that for John Carr to have his hand treated. By the time MacPherson got the Carr boys back to their house and got himself home to Johanna, it would be very nearly dark.

Once on the paved state road headed north toward Saratoga Springs, MacPherson shifted the Buick into high gear and pushed the speed up to over 30 miles an hour. At that speed, he overtook and passed several other vehicles traveling at more normal speed (15 to 20 m.p.h.) in the same direction. He had confidence in himself and his automobile, which he referred to as "the machine." He had owned and operated several other automobiles prior to this one, and was an experienced driver. This particular Buick was a 1911 Model 10 "runabout," so called because it was lightweight (1800 pounds; most cars in 1911 weighed more) and had a relatively powerful four-cylinder engine (22 ½ horsepower; many cars in 1911 had less). In the popular press the Model 10 was known as the "Baby Buick" and was said to be "cute." It could reach 50 m.p.h. in high gear; had no top or windshield; traveled on 30–inch, wooden-spoked wheels with air-filled rubber tires; and sported a list price of $1,000.[1] MacPherson's Buick was off-white ("French gray," if you please) with the wheels and trim painted a slightly darker shade of the same color.

MacPherson had bought the car new over a year earlier in May 1910, from the Close Bros. dealership in Schenectady, New York, for $825 ($750 cash and a $75 trade-in allowance). He and one of his grown sons had driven it from May to early December 1910 in connection with his grave marker and headstone business in Galway. (He had opted for a double-sized rumble seat to carry stones and markers.) From December 1910 until the following May they had stored the car in the barn, out of the elements, and then had used it again from May through July of 1911. The MacPhersons had driven the car all over that part of upstate New York (north of Albany, the capital) on all kinds of surfaces, including rough country roads. Thus, as Donald MacPherson drove at a brisk pace toward Saratoga Springs that Tuesday afternoon, he had confidence in the safety of his doing so. He had driven his Baby Buick for a year on rough roads with a lot of weight aboard, and the car had never given him any reason to doubt that all parts of it, including the wheels, were soundly built. He was driving on a good, dry road, paved with crushed stone, under good weather conditions. And his friend needed help. Why

---

[1] In today's dollars, this would be $19,600, about the base price of a Ford Taurus.

shouldn't he push the Buick into the upper ranges of its well-advertised capacity for speed?

Unfortunately, the answer came as MacPherson and his passengers approached the southerly outskirts of Saratoga Springs. At that point, without forewarning, the Buick encountered a stretch of loose gravel, approximately four inches deep, that had been spread on the road earlier by a maintenance crew. When the Buick entered the gravel, MacPherson lost control and the automobile slid off the road to the right. As it left the roadway, it struck a telephone pole with the front right bumper, spun around 180 degrees from its own momentum, and fell, pointed the way it had come, into a three-foot ditch. When the automobile landed in the ditch, the left rear wheel broke under the sudden force of the impact, rolling the car over to its left and causing it to land on top of Donald MacPherson with the motor still running. The Carr brothers were thrown free and escaped serious injury. MacPherson broke his right wrist, cracked several ribs, and suffered head lacerations. Passers-by stopped at the accident scene, and a small crowd of motorists and gawkers gathered. In spite of his injuries, while still at the accident scene MacPherson picked up two wooden spoke fragments that he found in the grass by the side of the road, one in the ditch and one near the top of the banking. He put those pieces in his pocket and took them home with him that evening. Other bystanders found and retrieved broken wheel spokes from the crash site, most of which were preserved and presented into evidence at the second trial. All of these spokes were found near the badly damaged automobile; none was found in the road south of the telephone pole.

One of the motorists who had stopped at the scene, whom MacPherson had passed on the road several minutes earlier, gave MacPherson and the Carr brothers a ride to the same hospital toward which they had been headed not long before. While being treated at the hospital for his injuries, MacPherson told several different people that he did not know how the accident happened and that he was sorry for having been in such a hurry to help his friend. He repeated essentially the same things to the person who took him home from the hospital later that day. At no time did MacPherson mention anything about a wheel breaking or collapsing prior to the Buick landing in the ditch.

What Happened Prior to the Accident: Buick's Efforts to Avoid Defects

The wooden-spoked wheels on MacPherson's Buick were manufactured by the Imperial Wheel Company, a major manufacturer of automobile wheels. Each wheel had twelve spokes made of hickory wood, as did most wagon and automobile wheels at that time. Automobile wheels had been adapted from wagon wheels, and therefore had a sufficient safety margin so that even several spokes of inferior wood would not have compromised the overall strength of the wheel. Only a very small percentage of spokes were made of bad wood to begin with. Every one of the individual spokes was inspected visually at the Imperial Wheel factory before the wheels were assembled and primed. The chances of a wheel ending up with enough bad spokes to cause it to fail in normal use were so small as to be nonexistent. Imperial painted the wheels with primer at their factory in order to prevent the spokes from drying and shrinking, and thus possibly weakening the wheels, after assembly.

The assembled wheels arrived at the Buick factory ready to be painted the appropriate color and installed on the automobiles. Buick did not inspect the wheels again except for aesthetic defects because it reckoned that inspection for structural defects at that point would have been costly and practically useless. Hydraulic pressure applied at the hubs, later mentioned at trial as a possibility by one of plaintiff's witnesses, would not have been effective and could have weakened otherwise sound wheels. Buick road tested all of its finished vehicles under rigorous conditions, including sharp turns at high speed that put considerable pressure on the wheels. Of the many tens of thousands of automobiles that the Buick Company had shipped and the 80,000 wheels that Imperial had supplied to Buick, not one instance of spontaneous wheel failure during normal post-sale use had ever been reported.

What Happened After the Accident: Shaping a Scenario

Donald MacPherson returned to the accident scene after several weeks of recuperation. Having suffered injuries that threatened both his eyesight and his self-employment as a stone cutter, he understandably sought to determine, after the fact, if the cause of the accident might, after all, have been something wrong with his automobile. Examining the place where his car had crashed, he observed a scrape mark in the stone roadway south of the telephone pole, such as might have been made by the left rear axle of his car if it had dragged on the road surface. He also noted a mark on the telephone pole approximately where the car must have struck it. From his subsequent testimony at trial he seems to have concluded that the wheel must have collapsed—why else would he, an experienced driver, have driven off the road? He appears also to have concluded that he must have slowed the vehicle considerably before it hit the telephone pole—he would certainly not have been driving at a reckless rate of speed. Upon reflection, after he had examined the scene of the accident and contemplated its implications, the collapsing wheel scenario must have come to him like a message from on high. He apparently remembered for the first time—he had not mentioned it to anyone on the afternoon of the accident nor in the days following—that he had heard an unusual sound just before he lost control of the automobile, and had felt the left rear of the car go down. (What he heard may have been the car wheels grinding into four inches of dry gravel and what he felt may have been the rear end of the car swinging to the left through that gravel as he lost control.) He had found wheel fragments near the wrecked car, had he not? And what about the scrape mark on the road?

When MacPherson sought legal counsel, the lawyer to whom he turned, a prominent politician in the area, undoubtedly supported, appropriately enough, his conclusion that a broken wheel had caused the accident, rather than the other way around. And then the lawyer must have instructed him on the most effective way to express his belief that the wheel had failed him. When experts were located who were willing to criticize the quality of the wood in the spokes and to suggest that an inspection by Buick might have revealed the defect, the scenario to be pursued at trial was complete. On the view that the plaintiff had come to accept, a negligently overlooked manufacturing defect in the left rear wheel of MacPherson's Baby Buick had nearly taken his life and had left him seriously disabled. It was only fair that Buick should pay for its callous neglect of his welfare.

The Facts as They Came Out at Trial

The trial in this case was not the first time MacPherson had brought his claim against Buick to court. Earlier, he had suffered dismissal of the same complaint on privity grounds and had won a reversal and remand in the Appellate Division.[2] In an era when a tort plaintiff's contributory negligence was a complete bar to recovery,[3] it is understandable that MacPherson's story at trial was that he had been driving eight miles per hour, not the 30–plus miles per hour that several disinterested eyewitnesses estimated he had been traveling just before the accident. Once again, he probably believed his testimony to be accurate in this regard. What difference did his speed make, anyway? It was a defective wheel that had brought him to grief, in any event. Moreover, the plaintiff testified that he had, in an effort to regain control, reduced his speed even further, from twelve to eight miles an hour, by the time he struck the telephone pole.

The problem with MacPherson's story was that it was premised on a physical impossibility. Uncontradicted expert testimony from defendant's experts showed that, at such a low speed in high gear, the Buick would have stalled in its tracks—the engine could not possibly have continued to operate in four inches of gravel—and the car would have come to a

---

[2] MacPherson v. Buick Motor Co., 138 N.Y.S. 224 (N.Y.App.Div.1912).

[3] *See Restatement (Second) of Torts* § 467 (1965).

stop almost immediately. Especially if the left rear wheel had suddenly collapsed and the axle had been dragging on the road, as plaintiff testified, it was not physically possible for the car to reach the telephone pole on the side of the road, much less to have sufficient momentum to pivot 180 degrees around the pole and end up facing in the opposite direction with the motor still running. At 30–plus miles per hour on four good wheels such events were quite possible; but they could not have occurred with a broken wheel at the eight miles an hour MacPherson claimed he had been driving.

To be sure, MacPherson testified under oath that he had heard the sound of the wheel breaking just before the collision: "This sound that I heard when I looked back was the breaking of the wheel, the breaking of wood. It wasn't a blow out. It was the breaking of the spokes."[4] And he testified that he had felt and seen the left rear of the car go down, as though something had collapsed beneath it. Moreover, Charles Carr, the passenger in the rumble-seat, testified that, moments before the accident, he "felt the hind end go down, and a sound like wood breaking."[5] Even if one assumes sincerity on their part in so testifying, as one must assume given the jury's verdict in favor of the plaintiff, their testimony that the wheel spontaneously collapsed is contradicted by the physical facts implicit in their testimony regarding how the subsequent collision with the telephone pole happened.

In response to Buick's insistence that the automobile could not have pivoted around the pole at such a low speed with a collapsed left rear wheel, the plaintiff speculated that the right rear wheel continued to turn and must have pushed the car around the pole at low speed. But defendant's experts demonstrated that such a sequence was not physically possible, especially with a collapsed left rear wheel. For one thing, the right rear wheel was not positioned to provide the necessary leverage to turn the car around the pole. For another, the differential in the rear axle housing would have caused the right rear wheel to stop delivering power when the left rear wheel collapsed. The plaintiff never introduced an expert witness to explain how, in theory, the accident could possibly have happened the way the plaintiff testified that it had. Defendant Buick Motor Company argued before both the trial judge and the jury that the plaintiff's version of the accident was inherently impossible, that the only way that the car could have ended up where it did, in high gear with the engine still running, was if it had been going much faster, on four good wheels, when it hit the telephone pole. But Buick's arguments, even though resting on incontrovertible physical laws, fell on decidedly deaf ears.

---

[4] Record on Appeal in the New York Court of Appeals, p. 104.

[5] *Id*. at 129.

Part of the judge's and the jury's hardness of hearing most likely reflected understandable local bias against the out-of-town, big-shot defendant and its army of arrogant engineers from Detroit. Even the lawyers who ran the trial for Buick were from Michigan.[6] In contrast, the plaintiff and every one of his witnesses were local people from that region of upstate New York. The plaintiff's lawyer was a successful local politician, State Senator Edgar T. Brackett, who represented Saratoga County and was popular in the area.[7] (Everyone, including the judge, referred to him as "Senator Brackett" throughout the trial.) And the presiding judge of the County Court (who himself ran for election every ten years and must have been politically connected) and the jurors (all male) were upstate New Yorkers, as well. Indeed, the MacPherson trial was held in the Saratoga County Courthouse in Ballston Spa, one of the towns through which Donald MacPherson and the Carr brothers had driven on their fateful trip northward to Saratoga Springs. The accident itself, reported the next day in the local newspaper, had happened only a few miles from the courthouse, just a short distance up the state road that MacPherson and his Buick had traveled a year and a half earlier. No wonder, then, that the trial judge and the local jury were ready to take Donald MacPherson's word, given under solemn oath, over the dubious implications of Newton's laws of physics.

Given that the plaintiff had sworn under oath that the left rear wheel suddenly collapsed while the car was being driven at only eight miles an hour, the issue of Buick's negligence in failing to inspect the wheel became a major focus of the trial. On this issue, the plaintiff's witnesses offered largely anecdotal testimony. Yes, they said, a good "spokes man" could probably spot a bad spoke just by looking at it, at least if it had not already been painted. And yes, some of the broken wood fragments from the Baby Buick's left rear wheel looked "brash" (brittle) and had not "broomed up" (split longitudinally into splinters) when they broke, indicating inferior hickory had been used. One of the plaintiff's witnesses recalled that at least one wheel manufacturer in his experience had applied hydraulic pressure horizontally to the hubs of wooden-spoked wheels to test their fitness. The same witness admitted on cross-examination that such a pressure test had never, to his knowledge, revealed a wheel to be defective and might, itself, damage sound wheels in the process.

---

[6] Defendant was represented by local counsel from Saratoga Springs, of course, but the lawyers who ran the show were from Michigan.

[7] Brackett was instrumental in helping to save the mineral springs for which the region was widely regarded. A granite monument to his efforts stands to this day in Saratoga Springs.

In the end, the defendant's failure to subject the wheels to close inspection while in its possession, relying instead on the testing conducted by Imperial and its own road testing of the finished automobiles before shipping, convinced the judge and jury that Buick had been derelict in its handling of the wheel that allegedly collapsed under Donald MacPherson, and that this dereliction led directly to the accident. Buick should have inspected every spoke in every wheel, and, if they had done so, they would have caught the bad spokes in MacPherson's wheel and thereby prevented the accident. Seemingly ignored in this reasoning process was the circumstance that this particular Buick had been subjected before the accident to more than twelve months of driving, carrying heavy loads over rough country roads, without any problems. If the wheel had, in fact, originally been made of sufficiently defective wood such as to cause it to crumble into fragments, one would have expected it to fail long before the accident that injured Donald MacPherson. But the jury found for the plaintiff and against the defendant on the negligence issue

In addition to these issues of fact that were extensively litigated at trial, Buick argued from the outset that it owed no duty of care to MacPherson because there was no privity of contract between them. Because MacPherson had had an earlier complaint dismissed for lack of privity and had won reversal in the Appellate Division, the law of the case at trial was that lack of privity presented no obstacle to plaintiff's recovery. The privity issue would have to await eventual appeal to New York's highest court.

The Facts as They Came Out on Appeal

In the Appellate Division

Based on the trial record, Buick arguably had grounds to appeal not only on circumvention of the privity rule but also on the inadequacy of credible evidence to support the jury's findings of original defect and negligent failure to inspect. And yet, for reasons that can only be guessed at, Buick chose to appeal only on the grounds that it owed no duty of care to those, like MacPherson, with whom it was not in privity of contract and that, in any event, it had not breached any such duty. Although Buick Motor Company had contested the facts of the accident vigorously at trial and had insisted that MacPherson's story was inherently incredible, in its briefs before the Appellate Division, Buick focused exclusively on the issues of its alleged negligence and the lack of contractual privity between defendant and plaintiff. Having lost at trial, Buick conceded the issue of original defect causing the accident and placed its hopes entirely on the legal issues involving the alleged breach of its duty of care that Buick owed or, as they argued, did not owe, to

MacPherson. Although Buick's appellate brief alludes to the disagree-ments at trial regarding how the accident happened, including a refer-ence to the automobile hitting the telephone pole and landing eight or nine feet beyond it, in its summary of facts Buick describes the accident as having happened when the left rear wheel "broke down while [the car was] traveling on a State Road, at about fifteen miles an hour or less, and [plaintiff] was injured."[8] The plaintiff's appellate brief contains a more extensive description of what happened, including the part of plaintiff's story that Buick had argued at trial could not physically have happened—that a low-speed impact with the telephone pole turned the car completely around. But Buick's brief does not argue that such an event was physically impossible.

It is interesting to speculate regarding Buick's decision to play down the facts about the accident in its appellate brief. What apparently concerned Buick most was not maximizing the opportunity to win reversal on the inadequacy of plaintiff's proof of the facts but rather the prospect of losing on the law governing the legal duties that it owed generally to the motoring public who bought and used its automobiles. This tactical decision may have been driven in part by the fact that the Appellate Division had already decided against Buick on the privity issue in MacPherson's earlier appeal from dismissal of its complaint. Were Buick to win the case on its facts and gain another remand, a second trial in the same venue would almost certainly reach the same outcome, probably on a better-looking record for the plaintiff. And if they won a directed verdict on the facts in the Appellate Division, the earlier decision by that court, setting lack of privity aside as a legal defense, would stand as damaging precedent until the next case came along. So taking the privity issue to the Court of Appeals may have been the better of bad choices. In any event, having lost at trial, Buick conceded defeat on the facts regarding how the accident happened and focused on winning on the law by persuading the appellate courts—really, the Court of Appeals—that it had not been negligent and that New York should retain the privity rule.

Turning from Buick's arguments on appeal to the actual decision by the Appellate Division, a unanimous panel affirmed the verdict and judgment for plaintiff.[9] Regarding the privity rule, the court's willingness to disregard it was a foregone conclusion in light of the same court's decision just two years earlier remanding MacPherson's claim for trial. Regarding how the accident happened, the opinion contains the following description:

---

[8] *See* Buick's Brief in Appellate Division, p. 4.

[9] *See* MacPherson v. Buick Motor Co., 145 N.Y.S. 462 (N.Y.App.Div.1914).

The plaintiff claimed that he and two others were riding in the automobile, upon a good road, at a speed of about eight miles per hour, when the spokes in the left rear wheel broke and the wheel collapsed, the automobile went into the ditch and the plaintiff was thrown out and injured. The defendant claimed that the plaintiff was going at the rate of about thirty miles per hour when he struck several inches of loose gravel upon the road, and that the gravel and the high rate of speed caused the automobile to go into the ditch and the spokes were broken when the wheel collided with a telegraph (sic) pole. The verdict of the jury has established the fact that the wheel collapsed under the circumstances claimed by the plaintiff, and that his injury is due entirely to the weak and defective wheel.[10]

Regarding Buick's negligence in failing to inspect the wheel that allegedly collapsed, the court concluded:

If the defendant had purchased its wheels unpainted, a wood expert would have been of great assistance in determining the quality of the wood used. If it purchased the wheel painted some of the paint could have been removed, the wheel could have been weighed, and an expert could have formed some judgment as to the quality of the wood used. There is some evidence of other tests and it must be there is some way of determining the quality of the wood in such a wheel; if not, it must be negligence to purchase a wheel in such a forward state of construction that it is impossible to determine what it is made of. . . . All workers in wood examine and throw aside defective material, using only that which, upon examination, proves satisfactory.[11]

Each of these treatments of the facts by the Appellate Division is remarkable in its own way. Having chosen to go into the factual dispute between the parties regarding how the accident happened, the Appellate Division could have been expected to refer to the important element on which both sides agreed—to wit, the collision with the telephone pole and the pivoting of the car completely around it. The opinion suggests that the plaintiff had denied hitting the pole. Moreover, contrary to the Appellate Division's opinion, the defendant never suggested, let alone tried to prove, that the left-rear wheel shattered when the wheel struck the telephone pole. The court's recitation of the facts of how the accident happened is, therefore, somewhat garbled. And the court's statement of what Buick should have done to inspect each and every wheel is no less interesting. For the court to suggest that workers in the Buick factory could "examine and throw aside defective material," presumably wheel-by-wheel and spoke-by-spoke, implies that Buick was causally negligent

---

[10] *Id.* at 462.

[11] *Id.* at 464.

by the very fact that it had delegated the wheel making function to a reliable wheel manufacturer who had, itself, undertaken the spoke-by-spoke inspection that the court describes.

In the Court of Appeals

The description of the facts in Cardozo's famous opinion is sufficiently succinct to allow it to be quoted in full:

> The defendant is a manufacturer of automobiles. It sold an automobile to a retail dealer. The retail dealer resold it to the plaintiff. While the plaintiff was in the car, it suddenly collapsed. He was thrown out and injured. One of the wheels was made of defective wood, and its spokes crumbled into fragments.... The wheel was not made by the defendant. It was bought from another manufacturer. There is evidence, however, that its defects could have been discovered by reasonable inspection, and that inspection was omitted.... [The defendant] was not at liberty to put the finished product on the market without subjecting the component parts to ordinary and simple tests.[12]

Cardozo's recitation of the facts is starkly simple and gives no hint of the inherently controversial nature of the conclusions reached at trial. Anyone reading his description would reasonably assume that the car was new (it wasn't) and that the collapse of the wheel occurred during normal, routine driving (it didn't). Cardozo does not mention the collision with the telephone pole that had loomed so large in the plaintiff's scenario at trial and to which both the Appellate Division and both parties' appellate briefs alluded. Regarding Buick's negligence in allowing a defective product to leave its factory, Cardozo overstates the simplicity and clarity of plaintiff's proof of how Buick might have inspected every spoke in every wheel. In contrast to the case presented at trial, in Cardozo's majority opinion in the Court of Appeals the case appears, on its facts, to be as clean and simple as one could imagine such a case to be. As Cardozo and a majority of his colleagues present the matter in the court's decision, the only obstacle left standing between the plaintiff and the justice that he so clearly deserved was the inexplicably arbitrary privity rule, which Cardozo thereupon dispatched with the logic and reason for which his opinion in *MacPherson* is rightly famous.

Why Simplifying the Facts in *MacPherson* was Important to Dispensing with Contractual Privity

An Overview: The Privity Rule as a Screen Against Unmanageable Claims

The important point about the facts in *MacPherson* is not that the

---

[12] MacPherson v. Buick Motor Co., 111 N.E. 1050, 1051 (N.Y.1916).

case was decided wrongly at trial, although it may have been.[13] Certainly if the case were tried today, it might well be decided for the defendant as a matter of law, notwithstanding that privity has not been a problem for physically injured tort plaintiffs for more than half a century.[14] Rather, the point is that the facts in *MacPherson* had to appear clear and compelling in Cardozo's opinion in order for the death of privity to appear necessary and appropriate. Pressures to dispense with privity had been building in the late nineteenth century. However, as shall be explained subsequently, the rule had served the institutionally important function of keeping relatively unmanageable defect claims out of court. Thus, the privity rule in New York, together with its exceptions for inherently dangerous products such as poisons, explosives, and the like, helped to assure that, for the most part, only relatively manageable claims of negligently-caused defects reached trial. Dispensing with the privity rule threatened to confront New York courts with a steady stream of defect claims that would be difficult to resolve at trial.

From this institutional perspective, the facts in *MacPherson* presented something of a dilemma. The same aspects that made the case attractive politically—automobiles epitomized the emerging culture of mass-produced, nationally-distributed consumer products—made it unattractive institutionally: defect claims in that context were going to present unmanageable issues. Not only were the claims of original, time-of-sale defects difficult to verify in many instances, but reviewing the adequacy of manufacturers' systems of quality control was quite difficult. On any fair assessment of its facts, *MacPherson* was the sort of questionable case that the privity rule had been keeping out of New York trial courts. The claim of original defect at the time of manufacture was questionable and the claim of Buick's negligence, even more so. Given that the privity rule had become unacceptable politically, nothing would be gained by waiting for a more manageable case, because unmanageability was inherent in the nature of such claims. Moreover, from the perspective of Cardozo and his colleagues on the Court of Appeals, the Appellate Division's reversal and remand of the *MacPherson* case four years earlier, combined with Buick's decision to limits its appeal to the issues of privity and negligence, left them no real choice in the matter. The time for review of the privity rule was upon them and there was no

---

[13] Plaintiff's proof of original defect was sufficiently weak to have failed as a matter of law. Had the wheel at the time of original sale been unsound enough to collapse spontaneously under the weight of the Carr brothers going eight miles an hour on a smooth, paved road, it would have collapsed long before that under the greater weight of gravestones being carried at greater speeds for more than a year over rough, country roads.

[14] Not only was the proof of original defect very weak (*see supra* note 13), but modern courts would require plaintiff's experts to advance a theoretically plausible explanation for how the accident could have happened the way MacPherson claimed it had.

ducking the issue. It follows that, in order to render the rejection of privity in *MacPherson* plausible and sensible, it was important that the case appear more factually compelling than it actually was. Thus, Cardozo's simplification of the facts was more than merely stylistic; it served an important purpose. The legitimacy of appellate courts recasting the facts in this manner will be considered after this part of the story of *MacPherson* and the demise of the privity rule has been told.

Why Courts Must Screen Factually Unmanageable Tort Claims

All rules of tort law call for liability to follow from delineated sets of facts, employing an **If-Then** format: "*If* A kicks B without sufficient reason, *then* A is liable in damages to B."[15] For liability rules to produce rational, consistent outcomes, the liability rules must refer to facts that (1) are verifiable at trial and (2) present issues that can be resolved within an adversarial system of adjudication.[16] Examples of potentially unverifiable facts in tort disputes include subjective states of mind and unwitnessed, single-party accidents in which the only direct evidence is likely to consist of the plaintiff's self-serving testimony. Examples of relatively unadjudicable issues include those that call for reasonableness assessments of complex, technically sophisticated patterns of conduct, such as whether, everything considered, reliance on the internal combustion engine is good for America. Claims that rest on unverifiable factual premises and that present issues that exceed the limits of adjudication are here referred to as "unmanageable."

It is important to appreciate how a typical product defect claim under a negligence regime threatens courts with unmanageability. As reflected in the *MacPherson* litigation, the two factual elements in a negligence-based product defect claim are (1) defect at time of original sale, causing the accident; and (2) negligence by the manufacturer in producing the defect. A classic example presenting difficulties with both elements is a claim based on a exploding bottle of carbonated soda. The element of original defect in such a case rests on events prior to the explosion that are usually witnessed only by the plaintiff. "Yes, your honor, neither I nor anyone else ever abused the bottle of soda, and I was opening the bottle carefully when it exploded in my face." After the accident, the shattered bottle typically cannot be examined effectively for original defect because of the destructive effects of the explosion. In many cases what caused it to explode is, in truth, anybody's guess. The point is not that events relating to product defects are never observed by disinterested witnesses, or that products can never effectively be exam-

---

[15] *See generally* James A. Henderson, Jr., et al., *The Torts Process* 17–20 (5th ed. 1999).

[16] *See generally* James A. Henderson, Jr., *Process Constraints in Tort*, 67 Cornell L. Rev. 901, 907–11 (1982).

ined, after the accident, for signs of original defect. Rather, it is that the original defect issues in a significant percentage of routine product defect cases are, as in many exploding bottle cases, factually problematic in that they are not objectively verifiable. Only when the products are relatively new, and fail in circumstances that effectively eliminate causes other than original defect, are such claims circumstantially verifiable.

And the issue of the manufacturer's negligence is typically even more problematic than the issue of original product defect. Although exploding bottle cases involve what today are classified as manufacturing defect claims to which strict liability applies,[17] plaintiffs in MacPherson's time had to prove that the manufacturer's negligence caused the defect. And that part of the claim involved judicial review of the design of the manufacturer's system of quality control.[18] Many factual considerations are properly relevant to such a judicial inquiry, including the technical feasibility of alternative ways of reducing defects; the costs of each such alternative, including the monetary costs of testing and the possible negative effects of such testing on the integrity of the products tested; the likelihood that original product defects that escape detection will cause accidents; the costs of those accidents; and so forth. Claims that a manufacturer negligently produced a defective product are difficult to resolve without specific legal standards, which are typically not available. It is hardly surprising that the courts in the *MacPherson* case adopted the conceptually erroneous but institutionally helpful view that allowing even a single defect to reach market, or failing to employ redundant and essentially useless methods of inspection, constituted sufficient proof of a manufacturer's negligence.[19]

Courts Traditionally Have Framed Liability Rules to Screen Factually Unmanageable Claims

Reflecting upon the form and structure of the common law of torts, one is struck by the extent to which that body of legal doctrine seems self-consciously designed to avoid feeding courts a steady diet of factually unmanageable cases. This is hardly surprising, in light of the preceding discussion; but it is often overlooked by students who are focusing intently on the substantive goals of tort. Clearly, the conceptual structures of intentional torts satisfy the requirement that most tort claims

---

[17] *See Restatement (Third) of Torts: Products Liability* §§ 1, 2(a) (1998).

[18] Today, even under strict liability, courts review the reasonableness of product designs in determining whether they are defective. *See generally* James A. Henderson, Jr. & Aaron D. Twerski, *Products Liability: Problems and Process* 473–643 (4th ed. 2000).

[19] Even a careful manufacturer will produce a few defective units out of hundreds of thousands of products. To draw an inference of negligence from a single defect is to impose the functional equivalent of strict liability. *See* Escola v. Coca Cola Bottling Co. of Fresno, 150 P.2d 436 (1944) (Traynor, J., concurring).

be manageable in court. The formal definitions of assault, battery, and false imprisonment replace generalized reasonableness assessments with discrete factual elements that the plaintiff must prove to establish a prima facie case.[20] And where the subjective element of intent threatens courts with unverifiability, the objective concept of constructive intent, based on the relative certainty with which an outcome will follow the actor's conduct, steps in to clean things up.[21] Beyond the prima facie case are issues of legal privilege, with respect to which the defendant bears the burdens of production and persuasion. Here again, the common law rules governing privileges present discrete and manageable factual issues, with apparent consent helping, as did constructive intent, to render that element objectively verifiable.[22] To be sure, the privilege of self-defense relies explicitly on the reasonableness of the actor's belief that force is necessary, and such assessments are potentially problematic.[23] However, because self-defense always arises in the context of individual human conduct, the traditional "reasonable person" construct allows judges and jurors to apply channeled intuition and common sense in reaching rational outcomes.[24]

It follows that the formal, layered structures of most intentional torts, over which outcome-oriented first year law students often chafe and balk, serve to deliver to the courts claims that are relatively manageable. The one exception might arguably be the tort of "intentional infliction of mental upset;" but courts have successfully kept such claims from becoming unmanageable by relying on quantitative modifiers like "extreme and outrageous conduct" causing "severe emotional upset."[25] These modifiers work to screen open-ended, potentially unmanageable emotional upset claims from reaching trial.

Common law negligence claims, as the discussion of the exploding bottle hypothetical indicates, are more problematic than are claims based

---

[20] The elements of harmful battery, for example, are (1) an act; (2) with the intent to cause harmful or offensive contact with another's person or apprehension of such contact; (3) resulting in harmful contact. *See Restatement (Second) of Torts* § 13 (1965).

[21] *See Restatement (Second) of Torts* § 8A (1965) (An actor intends to cause the consequences of his act when he desires to cause those consequences, "or he believes that the consequences are substantially certain to result from it.").

[22] *See* O'Brien v. Cunard S.S. Co., 28 N.E. 266 (Mass.1891).

[23] *See* Courvoisier v. Raymond, 47 P. 284 (Colo.1896).

[24] *See generally* James A. Henderson, Jr., *Judicial Review of Manufacturers' Conscious Design Choices: The Limits of Adjudication*, 73 Colum. L. Rev. 1531, 1541 n.32 (1973).

[25] *See Restatement (Second) of Torts* § 46 (1965) ("outrageous conduct causing severe emotional distress").

on intentional torts, primarily because the negligence concept is inherently more unstructured and open-ended.[26] And yet, even here, a number of common law concepts and doctrines introduce sufficient formality in many contexts to reduce the difficulties to manageable proportions. A good example of such a formal rule structure concerns the duties of care owed by possessors of land to those who enter the premises and suffer injury. Traditionally, courts believed that such duties should reflect the values embedded in the rights of possessors to prevent others from entering land without permission. Rather than leave those values to be factored into liability decisions by triers of fact responding to vague, open-ended instructions, common law courts worked out a relatively elaborate system of reciprocal rights and duties based on the formal status of the entrant in any given instance. Trespassers, who enter without permission, are owed little in the way of care on the part of the possessor. Invitees are owed considerably more, and there are a number of gradations in between. Whether or not one agrees with the values reflected in this traditional rule structure, the point here is that, given common law courts' commitments to those values, the formal structures render disputes between possessors and entrants manageable on a case-by-case basis.[27]

This same injection of rule formality into the potentially unmanageable concept of "reasonableness under all the circumstances" takes other forms in other contexts. Thus, courts recognize flat-out immunities from negligence-based liability in certain areas, such as disputes among close family members[28] and claims against governmental agencies,[29] where the evaluative issues would otherwise threaten to exceed judicial capabilities. And courts treat violations of safety statutes and regulations in ways that render the vague reasonableness standard of negligence more specific and the issues for decision more manageable.[30] For the significant residue of negligence claims to which none of these more formal rules

---

[26] *See generally* James A. Henderson, Jr., *Expanding the Negligence Concept: Retreat From the Rule of Law*, 51 Ind. L.J. 467, 467–77 (1976).

[27] *See id.* at 510–14.

[28] *See id.* at 502–05.

[29] *See id.* at 505–10. Actions against the federal government are regulated by the Federal Tort Claims Act, 60 Stat. 812 (1946). Reflecting the management concerns described in the text, the federal government consents to be sued in tort in those areas that do not require courts to review the reasonableness of broad discretionary exercises of executive and legislative authority.

[30] *See, e.g.,* Martin v. Herzog, 126 N.E. 814 (N.Y.1920) (famous Cardozo opinion holding that unexcused violation of a "lights on vehicles after dark" statute constituted "negligence per se").

applies, the general coping mechanism upon which courts rely is the flesh-and-blood "reasonable person" construct that hopefully allows both judges and juries to bring intuition and common sense to bear in cases involving individual human actors engaged in everyday human activities.[31]

The main problem with product defect claims, of course, is that they do not involve individual human defendants engaged in everyday activities. In that context, the reasonable person construct does not serve to channel intuition and common sense, leaving triers of fact at sea. Since the turn of the last century, American courts have increasingly been called upon to render reasonableness assessments in cases where the defendants are corporate actors engaged in highly technical activities capable of doing harm on a massive scale. In these contexts, in the absence of one or another of the more formal common law coping mechanisms, the "reasonable person" rubric is out of its element entirely and courts are threatened with floundering in oceans of technical, interdependent data. When the institutional actors against whom technologically complex negligence claims are brought are employed by the state, governmental immunities may be available.[32] But when the defendant is in the private sector, things can get out of hand in a hurry.

Not surprisingly, the common law of torts adjusted early and innovatively to meet these challenges in at least one significant area of technically complex activity—the professional delivery of medical and other health care services. For courts to attempt independently to review the reasonableness of the designs of various courses of medical treatment would have threatened to drown them in unmanageability. To avoid these problems, courts traditionally deferred to the medical profession to set the specific standards by which the actions of individual physicians and other health care providers are judged. When a doctor performs an appendectomy, the court does not independently assess the reasonableness of the design of that procedure; instead, the focus of inquiry is whether the individual doctor conformed to the specific design established by the relevant medical community.[33] In this way, by generally deferring to the objectively verifiable standards set by medical custom,

---

[31] See supra note 24 and accompanying text.

[32] See supra note 29 and accompanying text.

[33] See generally James A. Henderson, Jr. & John A. Siliciano, *Universal Health Care and the Continued Reliance on Custom in Determining Medical Malpractice,* 79 Cornell L. Rev. 1382 (1994). This traditional rule may be eroding to some extent. See Phillip G. Peters, Jr., *The Quiet Demise of Deference to Custom: Malpractice Law at the Millennium,* 57 Wash. & Lee L. Rev. 163 (2000). But even in those contexts, custom plays a significant role that helps keep the claims institutionally manageable.

courts have avoided the unmanageability of trying to determine the reasonableness of technically complex medical procedures.

Why These Common Law Screening Techniques Were Not Available in Connection with Negligence–Based Product Defect Claims at the Turn of the Last Century

As in *MacPherson*, the main issues in a product defect case in the late nineteenth century were time-of-sale (original) defect and seller's negligence. As has been explained, negligence-based defect claims tend to be unmanageable, threatening to exceed the institutional capabilities of courts. And the sorts of coping mechanisms that the common law developed in other areas of tort were not readily available for judicial use in connection with defect claims at that time. The inherent unverifiability of the "I was opening the bottle of soda carefully when it exploded in my face" type of claim might have been dealt with by analogy to the doctrine of res ipsa loquitur.[34] If the soda bottle were relatively new, and could be shown to have been handled carefully since its purchase, an inference of original defect would have been appropriate.[35] But the res ipsa concept had been traditionally used in assessing defendant's negligence, not in determining factual causation, and the development of the res ipsa concept as a bridge to strict products liability was then still many decades in the future.[36]

Things were equally problematic in connection with proving that the manufacturer had been negligent. Judicial deference to industry custom, as courts routinely deferred to medical custom in malpractice actions, was unacceptable.[37] In contrast to judicial deference to the medical profession, courts were not willing to trust commercial industries to set the standards of care by which the conduct of their constituent members toward the public was to be judged. It follows that, at the turn of the nineteenth century, no legal techniques other than the privity rule were readily available with which to deal with the difficulties presented by product defect claims. Almost by default, the contractual privity requirement became the primary means by which courts protected themselves from factual unmanageability in connection with routine product defect claims.

---

[34] This is, of course, the basic fact pattern in Escola v. Coca Cola Bottling Co. of Fresno, 150 P.2d 436 (Cal.1944), in which the Supreme Court of California stretched res ipsa to impose a form of strict liability. See the chapter on *Escola* in this book by Professor Mark Geistfeld, *Escola v. Coca Cola Bottling Co.: Strict Liability Unbound.*

[35] This is the rule recognized in *Restatement (Third) of Torts: Products Liability* § 3 (1998).

[36] The *Escola* decision, which is credited with providing this bridge, was decided in 1944.

[37] *See, e.g.,* The T.J. Hooper, 60 F.2d 737 (2d Cir.), cert. denied 287 U.S. 662 (1932).

How the New York Version of the Privity Rule Screened Factually Unmanageable Claims While Allowing Manageable Claims to Proceed to Trial

Most of what has been written about the *MacPherson* decision and the contractual privity rule it displaced has focused on the substantive economic implications of the holding and the masterful way in which Cardozo dealt with applicable precedents to make the death of privity seem easy and natural.[38] While these analyses are undoubtedly useful, this analysis adds a third perspective, largely overlooked until now. An important function of the New York privity rule prior to *MacPherson* was to screen factually unmanageable product defect claims, sending only relatively manageable claims to trial. Viewed from this process perspective, the beneficiaries of the privity rule and its exceptions were not simply product manufacturers who might have been threatened if the floodgates had been opened—very few of the privity decisions prior to *MacPherson* had involved mass-produced products.[39] The privity rule also benefited the trial courts of New York, who were thereby spared from having to adjudicate claims that relied heavily on self-serving testimony about unverifiable events and called for judicial review of emerging technologies in the absence of adequately specific legal standards. The point here is not that the floodgates concerns were less important than the institutional concerns. To the contrary, from the very beginning, courts justified the privity rule on the ground that it held back a tidal wave of claims that would otherwise overwhelm defendants. Rather, the point is that the privity rule also served important institutional purposes, largely overlooked until now.

The privity rule caught on early in New York[40] and showed surprising staying power. In its application later on to mass-produced products, the rule all but insulated manufacturers from liability. While suits by purchasers against retailers were not barred, proving retailer negligence was very difficult. Thus, while retailers may have had rights of indemnity against manufacturers, most often there was no retailer liability for manufacturers to indemnify. Thus, in its pure form, before New York courts recognized a fairly broad range of exceptions, the privity rule arguably represented overkill. It solved the potential unmanageability

---

[38] *See, e.g.,* Martin P. Golding, *Legal Reasoning* 112–143 (1984); Edward H. Levi, *An Introduction to Legal Reasoning* 8–25 (1962); Walter Probert, *Applied Jurisprudence: A Case Study of Interpretive Reasoning in* MacPherson v. Buick *and Its Precedents*, 21 U. C. Davis L. Rev. 789 (1988).

[39] *See* Gary T. Schwartz, *Commentary: Cardozo as Tort Lawmaker*, 49 De Paul L. Rev. 305, 310 (1999).

[40] The first decision in the Court of Appeals to recognize the privity rule also created a limited exception based on "inherently dangerous products." *See* Thomas v. Winchester, 6 N.Y. 397 (N.Y. 1852).

problems of many product defect claims by keeping all such claims out of court. To some observers, this must have seemed like a doctor killing his patient outright in order to prevent a skin rash from spreading. Not surprisingly, in the middle to late nineteenth century, exceptions to the general no-duty rule increasingly began to allow deserving plaintiffs into court, but, as a general rule, only when doing so did not threaten courts with unmanageability.

How the New York courts accomplished this objective sheds light on why the Court of Appeals handled *MacPherson* the way it did. The leading case to recognize an exception to the privity rule was *Thomas v. Winchester*, relied upon by Cardozo in *MacPherson*, involving mislabeled poison.[41] In allowing the injured plaintiff to reach trial, the New York Court of Appeals in *Thomas* held that claims based on products that, like poison, were "inherently dangerous" were not barred by lack of contractual privity because their intrinsic danger supported the conclusion that the defendant's duty of care extended to third-party victims. While substantively this reasoning made sense, from the process perspective developed in this analysis its logic was impeccable. By connecting plaintiff's right to recover to the inherent destructiveness of the poison, as a practical matter the court limited the plaintiff to claims of mislabeling. (Adulteration was not a problem because poison is already highly dangerous.) And claims based on defendant's mislabeling the poison were typically amenable to objective proof after the event.[42] Moreover, attaching the wrong label to a bottle of poison was not only obviously unreasonable, it constituted a violation of the producer's own standard of care. Given the predictably disastrous (and fairly certain to follow) consequences of the defendant's neglect, justifying a heightened level of care in labeling the poison, the negligence case was what today would be referred to as a "no-brainer."[43]

One further example, to which Cardozo's opinion in *MacPherson* also makes specific reference, will help to make this point. Another exception to the privity rule, *Devlin v. Smith,* involved a scaffold that had been nailed together rather than, as was then the custom among scaffold makers, being tied together with ropes.[44] The nails worked loose,

---

[41] *See id.*

[42] One could almost say that the design of the poisonous product was inadvertently defective; design defects, unlike manufacturing defects, do not present problems of verifiability. In any event, the mislabeling was usually provable by direct, rather than by circumstantial, evidence.

[43] Given that mislabeling would, with almost certainty, turn the product into an engine of destruction, and that the defendant without doubt knew this full well, a zero-defect rate was clearly called for.

[44] *See* Devlin v. Smith, 89 N.Y. 470 (N.Y.1882).

the scaffold came apart, and the plaintiffs' decedents plunged to their deaths. The New York Court of Appeals applied the same "inherently dangerous" rubric as in *Thomas* and allowed the negligence claim to proceed, although the defendant had not sold the scaffold directly to the decedents, but to their employer. Once again, allowing the claim in *Devlin* did not threaten the trial court with unverifiable assertions of unwitnessed events—the facts relating to the accident and the inferior construction of the scaffold were, by their inherent nature, objectively verifiable after the accident. Nor did sending the case to trial require a reasonableness judgment in the absence of adequate legal standards—dangerous departures from specific industry custom have long constituted adequate proof of negligence, even if conformance to industry custom does not necessarily constitute due care.[45]

It is also important to observe that most of the cases in which the New York Court of Appeals refused to apply the "inherently dangerous" exception involved factually unmanageable claims that would have been difficult to resolve at trial. Most of the cases referred to in Cardozo's opinion as pro-defendant precedents conform to this pattern. Thus, in *Losee v. Clute*, the defendant sold a steam boiler to a paper company for use in its business operations.[46] The paper company took delivery of the boiler, inspected it and maintained it until it exploded three months later, injuring bystanders and damaging properties near the paper company's factory. The trial court dismissed the complaint of one of the nearby property owners on the authority of the privity rule, notwithstanding allegations of the defendant seller's causal negligence. The Court of Appeals affirmed, observing that, after acceptance by and testing of the boiler by the purchaser, "the said defendants had nothing whatever to do with the boiler, and had no care or management of it at the time of explosion, but that the [paper] company had the sole and exclusive ownership, management and conduct of it."[47]

The quoted passage reflects the court's concern over the potential difficulties involved in determining whether a defect in the boiler caused the accident and, if so, whether the defect arose before or after sale by the defendant manufacturer.[48] Of course, through modern eyes one may

---

[45] The rule that applies both to conformance with, and departure from, industry custom is that evidence of custom is admissible on the issue of defendant's negligence, but does not control. As a practical matter, however, evidence that the defendant departed from a specific, industry-wide custom that was aimed at safety and, if conformed to, would have saved the plaintiff, is quite damning and assures the plaintiff of reaching the jury. *See, e.g.,* Pittsburgh, S. & N. R.R. v. Lamphere, 137 F. 20 (3d Cir.1905).

[46] *See* Losee v. Clute, 51 N.Y. 494 (N.Y.1873).

[47] *Id.* at 494.

[48] The privity rule also barred claims where proof of time-of-sale defect was strong but the court's judgment about who should be responsible for the defect was ambivalent. *See,*

say that it is a case in which the conduct of the purchaser, including inspection of the boiler, intervened to break any proximate cause connection between the supplier's original negligence and the plaintiff's ultimate loss. But that simply helps to prove the point here being made. Sophisticated proximate causation analysis was yet in-the-making when *Losee* was decided.[49] Privity was a readily available, bright-line means of ridding the court of a potentially unmanageable claim.

Why, By the Early Twentieth Century, the New York Privity Rule's Days Were Numbered

What emerges from a review of the New York privity rule as it functioned in the decades preceding *MacPherson* is a perfectly understandable picture of courts protecting themselves from having to resolve factually unmanageable claims involving a variety of original product defects that allegedly caused harm. On the whole, manageable claims against remote sellers went to trial, but factually problematic claims did not. From this perspective, the privity rule with its exceptions was aimed not only at protecting the economic well-being of burgeoning industry but also at helping to protect the institutional integrity of New York trial courts. The privity rule served both objectives, but the latter has been thus far overlooked. To be sure, the privity rule accomplished the latter objective by something of a subterfuge. Had the New York Court of Appeals offered judicial self-protection explicitly as the reason for allowing some defect claims to reach trial while refusing many others, they would have opened themselves to embarrassment in the absence of a formal liability standard upon which to base traditional sufficiency-of-proof rationales on a case-by-case basis.[50] So the duty-based concept of contractual privity was brought into service as a gatekeeper, for as long as it could be patched together as a viable screening device.

With the help of hindsight, the New York privity rule had begun to show serious signs of instability at the turn of the last century. Several factors contributed to these developments. First, the idea that legal duties were personally relational was becoming increasingly shopworn; foreseeability of harm seemed a better measure of duty's reach than did one-on-one contractual relationships.[51] Second, the "inherently danger-

---

e.g., Loop v. Litchfield, 42 N.Y. 351 (N.Y.1870) (defect was known to purchaser and product was used for five years before defect caused explosion that killed plaintiff's decedent).

[49] Cardozo's famous opinion in *Palsgraf v. Long Island R.R.*, 162 N.E. 99 (N.Y.1928) was then more than 50 years distant.

[50] After *MacPherson*, courts did develop a consistent approach to the circumstantial proof of defect, borrowing from the res ipsa loquitur concept in connection with the negligence issue. *See infra* note 59 and accompanying text.

[51] This trend is reflected in Cardozo's other famous tort decision in *Palsgraf v. Long Island Railway*, 162 N.E. 99, 100 (1928) ("the risk reasonably to be perceived defines the

ous" exception had shown increasing signs of conceptual instability; if the scaffold in *Devlin* was inherently dangerous, why was not a large boiler like the one in *Losee*, operating under great pressure? From the process perspective developed here, the different treatment made sense; but the conceptual vehicle of "inherent danger" was being asked to carry a load that it could not comfortably bear. And third, significant substantive pressures were building relentlessly to replace privity with an approach that was more generous toward injured plaintiffs. After all, the era of mass-produced, nationally-distributed products had arrived, and manufacturers were addressing their advertising directly to consumers on a global scale. Increasingly, privity seemed an arbitrary, unfair, anti-consumer holdover from the past. Thus, to any knowledgeable observer, it must have been apparent at the turn of the last century that the days of the privity rule were numbered. When the Appellate Division in the first *MacPherson* appeal in 1912 reversed the trial court's privity-based dismissal of the complaint and remanded the case to the Saratoga County Court for trial,[52] the demise of privity must have seemed not only probable, but imminent.

Why Simplifying the Facts in MacPherson Helped to Facilitate the Death of Privity

The reasons why the simplification of the facts in *MacPherson* was important to the persuasiveness of its holding should now be clear. Several aspects of the case made it an attractive instrumentality—one hesitates to say "vehicle"—for implementing the legal change that was about to take place. The American automobile industry at the turn of the last century epitomized the coming age of mass-produced and nationally-distributed consumer products. Moreover, manufacturing defects could be expected to cause injuries and deaths in increasing numbers. But a major problem with inviting these cases into court was that manufacturing defect claims involving automobiles were likely to be factually unmanageable, at least in many instances. When something went wrong with an automobile and a violently destructive accident resulted, it would be difficult in many cases to determine whether a defect had caused the accident, and even more difficult to determine whether the defect had arisen during manufacture or later, as a result of hard driving on bad roads. (Through modern eyes, of course, automobiles arguably should be able to take a fair amount of abuse without breaking down. But that way of thinking implicates possible inadequacies in automobile designs, a subject still far in the future in *MacPherson*'s time.) And even if an original defect were found to be the culprit, reviewing the reason-

---

duty to be obeyed"). Of course, *Palsgraf* can be read, especially in contrast to Andrews' dissent, as strongly relational, albeit in a sense other than one-on-one contractual.

[52] *See* MacPherson v. Buick Motor Co., 138 N.Y.S. 224 (N.Y.App.Div.1912).

ableness of automobile manufacturers' quality control systems under a negligence standard would, in the absence of more specific legal standards, strain the limits of adjudication.

It follows that Donald MacPherson's defect claim presented something of a mixed blessing for the New York appellate courts. On the one hand, it was attractive on its merits. It epitomized the type of claim for which, given the reality that car dealers were mere conduits through which consumers purchased automobiles from national manufacturers, the privity rule was manifestly inappropriate.[53] On the other hand, MacPherson's claim on its particular facts was institutionally unattractive. In all likelihood the accident had been caused not by a manufacturing defect but by fast driving on a gravel-covered road. And the Buick Company's conduct, fairly assessed, appeared to have been reasonable. Buick's duty clearly was not to inspect every single spoke to make sure that it was perfect; all it was required to do was to exercise reasonable care to prevent an unreasonably high rate of defects. And in any event it would be difficult for a court honestly and rationally to second-guess Buick's conduct. If these problems had in any way been unique to *MacPherson*, it might have made sense for Cardozo and his colleagues to dispose of the case on its particular facts and wait for a more appealing one with which to effect this important change in the law. But the decision by the Appellate Division in 1912, remanding the case for trial notwithstanding lack of privity, had called the Court of Appeal's hand. And *MacPherson* was not all that unique on its facts. It epitomized the type of claim to be expected once privity was no longer available as a screening mechanism. So *MacPherson* was as good a case as any to get on with changing the law.

Besides the significance of its legal holding that the privity rule no longer applied in negligence actions based on defective products, the most interesting aspect of the *MacPherson* case is the way in which a factually problematic claim came to appear quite normal and compelling. Highly questionable events became plausible, and then undeniable. Negligence that was arguably nonexistent became debatable, and then self-evident. Part of this remarkable recasting of the facts came at the hands of the judge and jury at trial, who responded favorably to the plaintiff in the face of inherently unbelievable dubious testimony. Part of it stemmed from Buick's tactical decision not to pursue the factual aspects of the case on appeal, when arguably there were grounds for doing so. And part of it flowed from the penchant for simplification on the part of the appellate judges. Accepting Cardozo's statement of the facts in *MacPherson* on its face, no clearer claim for negligence-based tort

---

[53] *See* Schwartz, *supra* note 39, at 310 ("[I]n this mass production context, the manufacturer's argument in favor of tort-liability-based-only-on-privity was highly unattractive, perhaps even a reduction to absurdity.").

recovery could be imagined. As Cardozo described what had happened to the plaintiff, the requirement that Donald MacPherson must have dealt directly with the Buick Motor Company revealed itself as an unfair and arbitrary vestige of a bygone era. Presenting no apparent factual or institutional difficulties, MacPherson's claim clearly should be compensable, and one of the most influential judges on one of the most prestigious American state courts proceeded to reach exactly that conclusion.

The Aftermath of *MacPherson*

The Effects of MacPherson on the Privity Rule

Some commentaries about the aftermath of *MacPherson* create the impression that it eliminated the privity requirement cleanly and relatively quickly, opening the way wide for plaintiffs to reach juries with negligence-based product defect claims against remote manufacturers.[54] Once again, the common wisdom about this famous case is not quite accurate. The privity requirement in negligence actions did, indeed, succumb eventually to the force of Cardozo's reasoning. By transforming a relatively bright-line no-duty rule into one of "duty under all the circumstances," Cardozo doomed the privity rule as an effective gatekeeper. But it took quite a bit longer, especially in New York, than one might have assumed.[55]

From the perspective developed in this analysis, it is hardly surprising that privity died a relatively slow death. The important institutional interests served by the privity rule continued to require attention after *MacPherson* was decided. And Cardozo's opinion supplied the necessary conceptual apparatus to assure that those interests would continue, for a time, at least, to be served:

> We hold, then, that the principle of *Thomas v. Winchester* is not limited to poisons, explosives, and things of like nature, to things which in their normal operation are implements of destruction. If the nature of a thing is such that it is reasonably certain to place life and limb in peril when negligently made, it is then a thing of danger. Its nature gives warning of the consequences to be expected. If to the element of danger there is added knowledge that the thing

---

[54] *See, e.g.,* William L. Prosser, *The Assault Upon the Citadel (Strict Liability to the Consumer),* 69 Yale L.J. 1099, 1099–103 (1960). ("During the succeeding years [*MacPherson*] swept the country. . . ."). In fairness, Prosser went on to observe that New York courts continued to "talk the language of 'inherent danger.' " *Id.* at 1102.

[55] *See generally* Robert M. Davis, *A Re–Examination of the Doctrine of* MacPherson v. Buick *and Its Application and Extension in the State of New York,* 24 Fordham L. Rev. 204 (1955).

will be used by persons other than the purchaser, and used without new tests, then, irrespective of contract, the manufacturer of this thing of danger is under a duty to make it carefully. That is as far as we are required to go for the decision of this case. There must be knowledge of a danger, not merely possible, but probable.[56]

Why did Cardozo hedge his holding with these caveats? Perhaps he realized that it would take time for New York courts to adjust to life after privity. Or perhaps he wanted to make the law side of the transition look as smooth as he had made the fact side look easy.

In any event, a number of courts, both within New York and without, interpreted the foregoing language to mean that courts had a continuing responsibility to screen negligence-based defect claims from reaching trial.[57] In effect, they read *MacPherson* to expand upon, but not altogether to eliminate, the "inherently dangerous product" approach begun in *Thomas v. Winchester*. Cardozo's masterful treatment of judicial precedents in *MacPherson* led many courts to interpret his opinion as gradually extending, rather than abruptly overturning, *Thomas v. Winchester*; and thus they continued to apply Cardozo's language, quoted above, in ways that protected them from unmanageable claims. That it took so long for the vestiges of privity to die bears witness to the powerful institutional interests that the privity rule had served.

Significant Fall–Out Effects of the MacPherson Decision on American Products Liability Law

The most significant fall-out effect of *MacPherson* was the ascendancy of strict liability over negligence as the legal basis of manufacturers' liability for product defects. Notwithstanding that the remnants of privity played out longer than some might have expected, no one doubts that Cardozo's opinion in *MacPherson* marked the beginning of the end of the privity rule in American products liability jurisprudence. To the extent that courts, for the first time, began to face the prospect of reviewing the reasonableness and adequacy of manufacturers' quality control systems under the general negligence principle, with no prospect of borrowing specific standards from industry custom, pressures escalated to replace negligence with strict liability. From the institutional perspective of protecting the integrity of the judicial process, strict liability was just as attractive as had been the strict immunity afforded by the privity rule. What was clearly unattractive institutionally was trying to occupy the middle ground of reviewing defendants' systems of quality control under the general negligence standard. Just as the privity rule had aligned the institutional interests of the courts with the

---

[56] *See* MacPherson v. Buick Motor Co., *supra* note 12 at 1053.

[57] *See* Davis, *supra* note 55; *see also* Prosser, *supra* note 54, at 1102 & n.24.

economic interests of commercial suppliers, now the demise of privity aligned the institutional interests of the judiciary with the economic interests of the plaintiff's bar in an ongoing struggle to adopt strict liability in tort. Given this new alignment, the fall of privity in negligence actions led inexorably to the rise of privity-free strict liability.[58] Because this transition was facilitated, in part, by concepts of implied warranty borrowed from contract, surmounting the barrier of contractual privity prolonged the struggle toward strict tort liability. But *MacPherson* clearly got everything into motion.

The other important effect of the *MacPherson* decision was the extension of res ipsa loquitur principles to the task of determining whether a time-of-sale defect had caused the plaintiff's injuries. Prior to *MacPherson*, the chief stumbling block to such an innovative extension had been the fact that res ipsa traditionally applied only to the issue of defendant's negligence, not to the related, but separate, issues of causation and product defect.[59] Of course, so long as the privity rule succeeded in keeping the lion's share of factually unmanageable defect claims at bay, there had been no great need for courts to develop innovative techniques for dealing with the defect issue. With the demise of privity, the need for such conceptual innovation increased significantly. The end result, accomplished within a matter of decades, is a fairly robust, sensible approach that relies on the relative newness of the product unit (in contrast to its inherent dangerousness) and the objective circumstances of the product's failure to perform its manifestly intended function.[60]

Notwithstanding these developments in the decades following *MacPherson*, proof-of-defect problems continue to challenge American courts to this very day. Even under the current regime of strict liability for manufacturing defects, the plaintiff must prove that the product was defective at the time of sale;[61] and that issue can raise difficult problems of proof with which courts continue to struggle mightily.[62] In fact, the plaintiff's evidence in *MacPherson*, which courts of that era held to be

---

[58] *See* Prosser, *supra* note 54.

[59] *See, e.g.,* Myrlak v. Port Auth. of New York & New Jersey, 723 A.2d 45 (N.J.1999) ("We hold that the traditional negligence doctrine of res ipsa loquitur generally is not available [to prove defect] in a strict products liability case.").

[60] *See Restatement (Third) of Torts: Products Liability* § 3 cmt. a (1998) ("As products liability law developed, cases arose in which an inference of product defect could be drawn from the incident in which a product caused plaintiff's harm.").

[61] *See id.* § 1.

[62] *See, e.g., Myrlak v. Port Authority of New York and New Jersey, supra* note 59.

sufficient to support a judgment, would arguably not be deemed sufficient today under current rules governing proof of original defect.[63]

Was Cardozo's Part in Simplifying the Facts in *MacPherson* Legitimate?

As this analysis reveals, a substantial disparity exists regarding the facts in *MacPherson*. On the one hand are the facts relating to Buick's conduct and the events on the day of the accident as they must have actually happened and as they were brought out at trial. On the other are the facts as Cardozo recounted them in his famous opinion on appeal. As observed throughout this analysis, part of this disparity can be attributed to the process of an appellate court accepting the facts as they were found by a trial jury. And Buick chose not to question on appeal the legitimacy of those implicit findings or the sufficiency of the evidence supporting them, at least in connection with the accident itself. Nevertheless, the factual disputes at trial regarding how the accident happened were a significant part of the record with which the Court of Appeals was presumably familiar. By choosing to ignore the factual controversies that came out at trial and to which the parties alluded in their appellate briefs, Cardozo simplified the basic narrative to the point that it would have been unrecognizable to anyone who had either witnessed the accident or been involved in the manufacture of MacPherson's Baby Buick.

One can understand why Cardozo would want to present the strongest factual case for circumventing the privity rule. But did he go too far in this regard? The opinion in the Appellate Division, it will be recalled, did refer to the dispute at trial concerning the speed at which MacPherson had been driving and alluded to the fact that Buick, at least, claimed that the car struck a telephone pole. In contrast, Cardozo's opinion in the Court of Appeals contains none of that. Indeed, Cardozo clearly implies that the Buick was new when the accident happened and that, therefore, a manufacturing defect must have caused the wheel suddenly to collapse. It remains, then, to consider the legitimacy of this recasting of the facts in the context of an appellate court making a significant change in the law. To put the question in perspective, it is useful to consider the two important functions performed by an appellate decision:

---

[63] The plaintiff's version of how the accident happened would likely be ruled unacceptable as a matter of law as manifestly against the undisputed physical facts of the case. *See* Thornberry v. Smith, 346 S.W.2d 727 (Ky.1961). The circumstantial evidence of original defect would very probably be ruled inadequate, given the twelve months of heavy usage over rough roads between the sale and the accident. *See supra* notes 13–14 and accompanying text.

deciding the actual case before the court on appeal, and making law for the future. Every appellate decision performs both of these functions, although clearly some decisions accomplish more by way of the second than do others. Of the two functions, the first is the more basic and logically precedes the second; without the first function being performed, in most cases the second cannot take place.[64]

Regarding the first function, given the Buick Company's decision not to appeal on the weakness of plaintiff's proof of what caused the accident, Cardozo's recasting of the facts did not contribute to the case being decided wrongly on appeal. Interestingly, in at least one other equally famous torts case, *Palsgraf v. Long Island Railway Co.*,[65] the loser on appeal (in that case, the plaintiff) challenged Cardozo's treatment of the trial record in his celebrated appellate opinion on the ground that it caused the case to be decided wrongly in the Court of Appeals. In that case, the Court of Appeals reversed a plaintiff's verdict and judgment against the defendant railroad company. According to Cardozo, injury to the plaintiff was, as a matter of law, unforeseeable by the defendant because the plaintiff had been standing some distance from where a railroad employee had committed a seemingly innocuous negligent act. The plaintiff petitioned for rehearing on the ground that it was undisputed that she had been standing much closer to the negligent employee than Cardozo's majority opinion suggested. In a one-sentence per curiam decision, believed by many to have been written by Cardozo, the Court of Appeals denied a rehearing, asserting that, in any event, any such disparity would not have affected the outcome.[66] As in *Palsgraf*, Cardozo's recasting of how the accident happened in *MacPherson* did not affect the outcome, because Buick did not pursue that avenue on appeal. And Cardozo's simplification of the nature of Buick's negligence did not affect the outcome because, on that issue, the plaintiff arguably had raised a triable issue for the jury to decide.[67]

Even if Cardozo's recasting of the facts in *MacPherson* did not affect the outcome on appeal, was it legitimate for him to simplify the factual record in order to render more attractive his exercise of the court's law-

---

[64] One notable exception is the growing practice of federal courts in diversity actions to certify questions of law to state courts to be answered without a decision of the underlying case or controversy by the state court.

[65] 162 N.E. 99 (N.Y.1928); *see also supra* note 39.

[66] *See* Palsgraf v. Long Island R.R., 164 N.E. 564 (N.Y.1928).

[67] Given the open-endedness of the negligence issue and the fact that the plaintiff had introduced experts who testified that some sort of inspection was possible, the issue may have been for the trier of fact.

making authority? Clearly a court's holding on appeal is a function of what the court says the relevant facts are, not what the record reveals those facts to be.[68] But how free ought an appellate court be to manipulate the facts to affect the reception that the holding is likely to receive in the broader legal community? Cardozo spoke to this question in a well-known essay on appellate judging:

> There is an accuracy that defeats itself by the overemphasis of details. I often say that one must permit oneself, and that quite advisedly and deliberately, a certain margin of misstatement. Of course, one must take heed that the margin is not exceeded, just as the physician must be cautious in administering the poisonous ingredient which magnified will kill, but in tiny quantities will cure. On the other hand, the sentence may be so overloaded with all its possible qualifications that it will tumble down of its own weight. "To philosophize," says Holmes in one of his opinions—I am quoting him from uncertain and perhaps inaccurate recollection—"to philosophize is to generalize, but to generalize is to omit." The picture cannot be painted if the significant and the insignificant are given equal prominence. One must know how to select.[69]

Did Cardozo "exceed the margin" in his opinion for the majority in *MacPherson*?

Clearly Cardozo believed that MacPherson's claims of original defect and manufacturer's negligence could be assumed, almost hypothetically, in order to reach the important issue of law in the case—the continued vitality of the privity rule as a gatekeeper in New York products liability law. Just as he hedged the new law with caveats to make it more palatable, so also he managed the facts by recasting and simplifying them. For this latter liberty, however, he may be forgiven. To be sure, if appellate judges, even illustrious judges like Benjamin Cardozo, are free to conjure what amount to hypothetical fact patterns on which to base their decisions, they take considerable power unto themselves. But the holding of the Court of Appeals in *MacPherson* concerned a formal gatekeeper rule that was, in its own terms, largely insensitive to the relative strength of plaintiff's proof of defect and defendant's fault. For Cardozo to reduce the facts to hypothetical form had no direct bearing on the legal conclusion he reached, even if it made that holding more appealing than it would have been had he based it on a more accurate,

---

[68] *See generally* Arthur L. Goodhart, *Determining the Ratio Decidendi of a Case*, 40 Yale L.J. 161 (1930).

[69] *See* Benjamin N. Cardozo, *"Law and Literature," in Selected Writings of Benjamin Nathan Cardozo* 341 (Margaret E. Hall ed., 1947).

"warts and all" recitation of the trial record. And, after all, he got the substance right. Moreover, by circumscribing his new rule with important caveats, he gave New York courts the necessary time to work out new ways of keeping product-defect claims manageable. In the modern era, with its emphasis on claims of defective product design and marketing, that struggle continues to this day.

*

3

Robert L. Rabin

Rowland v. Christian: Hallmark of an Expansionary Era

Halcyon Days

An observer of the mid-twentieth century tort scene, scanning the recent past, might have detected occasional tremors hinting that something big was about to happen in California, land of seismic disturbances. Among other indicators, *Escola v. Coca Cola Bottling Co. of Fresno*,[1] featured Justice Traynor's concurring opinion calling for a paradigm shift from negligence to strict liability in defective product cases. From the very same term of the California Supreme Court, there was *Ybarra v. Spangard*,[2] providing a strikingly expansive application of *res ipsa loquitur* to a medical malpractice case. And four years later, *Summers v. Tice*[3] offered an unorthodox shift in the burden of proof on causation in a joint tortfeasor case. But these blips on the tort screen could easily be dismissed as random events. Nothing really had appeared on the landscape to suggest the momentous shift that would occur nationwide, with the California Supreme Court in the vanguard, over the two decades beginning in 1960.

In a series of landmark cases, the California court set its sights on reshaping the basic framework of liability for accidental harm to an extent unprecedented in the annals of American tort law. A brief roll call

---

[1] 150 P.2d 436 (Cal.1944). *Escola* is examined in detail in this volume. *See* Mark Geistfeld, *Escola v. Coca Cola Bottling Co.: Strict Products Liability Unbound*.

[2] 154 P.2d 687 (Cal.1944).

[3] 199 P.2d 1 (Cal.1948).

gives a sense of the sweeping developments. In *Greenman v. Yuba Power Products, Inc.*[4] and a series of succeeding cases,[5] the Court resurrected Justice Traynor's *Escola* concurrence and established the foundations for strict liability in tort for product injuries. In *Tunkl v. Regents of University of California*,[6] the Court sharply limited the circumstances in which exculpatory clauses could be relied on to impose waivers of liability for negligent conduct. In *Muskopf v. Corning Hosp. Dist.*[7] and *Gibson v. Gibson*,[8] the Court overturned longstanding governmental and intrafamily immunities from negligence liability. In *Li v. Yellow Cab Co.*,[9] the Court overturned the doctrine of contributory negligence, which had served as an absolute bar to recovery from the inception of the negligence era. In *Dillon v. Legg*[10] and *Molien v. Kaiser Foundation Hospitals*,[11] the Court lowered the barriers to recovery for negligently inflicted emotional distress. And in *Tarasoff v. Regents of University of California*,[12] the Court established a duty to exercise reasonable care when threats of violence to third persons are made in the course of a therapist-patient relationship.

In 1968, near the midpoint of this singular era, the Court decided *Rowland v. Christian*,[13] abolishing the categories of invitee, licensee, and trespasser, which had limited the duties owed by land occupiers for accidental harm based on the status of the land entrant—limitations that had stood as an integral part of the common law of tort in California from the earliest days of statehood.[14] *Rowland* can appropri-

---

[4] 377 P.2d 897 (Cal.1963).

[5] In particular, see *Vandermark v. Ford Motor Co.*, 391 P.2d 168 (Cal.1964) (holding that the newly-enunciated standard of liability extended to other defendants in the sales chain, such as retailers, as well) and *Elmore v. American Motors Corp.*, 451 P.2d 84 (Cal.1969) (extending the strict liability in tort duty to bystanders injured by the defective product).

[6] 383 P.2d 441 (Cal.1963).

[7] 359 P.2d 457 (Cal.1961).

[8] 479 P.2d 648 (Cal.1971).

[9] 532 P.2d 1226 (Cal.1975).

[10] 441 P.2d 912 (Cal.1968).

[11] 616 P.2d 813 (Cal.1980).

[12] 551 P.2d 334 (Cal.1976). *Tarasoff* is examined in detail in this volume. *See* Peter H. Schuck & Daniel J. Givelber, *Tarasoff v. Regents of the University of California: The Therapist's Dilemma*.

[13] 443 P.2d 561 (Cal.1968).

[14] The leading treatise on California law, in an edition prior to *Rowland*, cites an 1890 case on the limited duty owed to trespassers and a 1904 case on the limited duty owed to licensees. *See* B.E. Witkin, 2 *Summary of California Law* 1444, 1449 (6th ed. 1960).

ately be viewed as a prime entry in this registry of pathbreaking opinions issued in a remarkable era.[15]

Moreover, upon close observation *Rowland* reveals itself as a prototypical instance of proactive judicial decisionmaking, providing insights beyond the special moment in time and distinctive spirit of reform that characterized the California Supreme Court from 1960 to 1980. In fact, *Rowland* can be told as many stories and not just one. The case affords a pathway to exploration of fundamental issues that have given tort law a particularly dynamic character from its earliest origins to the present time: the tension between rules and standards, the distinction between misfeasance and nonfeasance, the role of liability insurance in reformulating the goals of the system, among others. And at the outset, against the backdrop of the California Supreme Court's landmark holding, the case reveals the dynamics of adversary presentation by parties whose immediate concerns may be far-removed from those of an appellate court with an agenda of its own. The examination of *Rowland* that follows is meant to be illuminating on these many dimensions.

The Opinion: A Landmark Waiting to Happen

Procedural Paradoxes

Nothing is as simple as it seems in *Rowland v. Christian*, beginning with the posture of the case as it came before the Court. After indicating that the plaintiff James Rowland was appealing from summary judgment in favor of defendant Nancy Christian, Justice Ray Peters' opinion begins in noncommittal fashion with a recitation of the facts from the written pleadings. Rowland alleged that Christian failed to warn him of a

---

[15] An era of retrenchment began not long thereafter, although most of these landmark cases (not *Molien*) survived relatively unscathed. *See* Stephen D. Sugarman, *Judges as Tort Law Un–Makers: Recent California Experience with "New" Torts*, 49 DePaul L. Rev. 455 (1999) (discussing the California case law, 1984–98, and finding, for the most part, a far more conservative pattern of decisions). Sugarman attributes this shift principally to the politically conservative appointments made by two Republican governors who served during this period. For a similar assessment of tort law retrenchment beginning at roughly the same time on the national scene, see Gary T. Schwartz, *The Beginning and the Possible End of the Rise of American Tort Law*, 26 Ga. L. Rev. 601 (1992).

Not all of this retrenchment came in the judicial forum. Another Supreme Court pronouncement of the era that appeared likely to have major ramifications was *Coulter v. Superior Court*, 577 P.2d 669 (1978), in which the Court imposed a duty on social hosts to avoid unreasonable provision of liquor to a guest who subsequently caused personal injury to a victim of his driving while drunk. The state legislature reacted not only by overturning *Coulter*, but also an earlier case that had created civil liability against commercial sellers. *See* Cal. Bus. & Prof. Code § 25602 (Deering 2003); Cal. Civ. Code § 1714(c) (Deering 2003). The state legislature also revisited *Rowland*, but narrowed the holding only slightly (in the case of injured felonious trespassers). *See infra* note 66.

cracked bathroom faucet handle in her rented apartment of which she
had knowledge, and as a consequence, when he turned off the water
after washing his hands, he suffered severed tendons and nerves from
the defective condition of the sink. Christian, in turn, responded that
Rowland was a social guest, and although admitting that she had
knowledge of the defect—indeed, that she had complained about it to the
building manager—averred that he was contributorily negligent and
failed to use his "eyesight." She did not deny that the porcelain handle
had broken in his hand as he turned off the faucet and caused the
injuries that were the grounds for the suit. If there is anything amiss
here, at first blush, it is a certain vagueness about the circumstances of
the injury: Was this crack in the faucet apparent, or was it hidden?

Not to be deterred, the Court immediately remarks that summary
judgment is a "drastic" procedure, a tip-off as to what is coming. And
then Justice Peters engages in a bit of legerdemain. Both parties had
submitted affidavits along with their respective motion and countermo-
tion. But somewhat mysteriously, Rowland failed to allege that the
defect was concealed, and Christian, apart from a bare assertion in her
answer that plaintiff failed to use his eyesight, mentioned nothing about
the crack being noticeable. Justice Peters addresses this factual vacuum
in arresting fashion, remarking that "Without in any way contradicting
[defendant's] affidavit or [plaintiff's] own admissions, plaintiff at trial
could establish ... that defendant should have expected that he would
not discover the danger."[16]

True enough. But if concealment was a necessary element of the
plaintiff's claim—and as we shall see, plaintiff was arguing no more than
that as a social guest he was owed an obligation of warning about
concealed defects—then it is a puzzle why plaintiff survives summary
judgment without alleging at least a colorable claim that the defect was
hidden, however defendant might have characterized the facts in her
motion for dismissal. In short, the Court subtly shifts the burden of
pleading a triable issue of fact to defendant to allege nonconcealment,
rather than requiring plaintiff to have pleaded facts indicating concealment.

This fast dealing is only necessary, of course, if the defendant's
obligation to warn turned on the plaintiff's fitting into the traditional
social guest/licensee pigeonhole, which required a hidden defect before
any obligation to warn would be recognized. No such gyrations would
have been required to survive summary judgment if the defendant owed
a general obligation of due care to a guest on the premises, irrespective
of his status as trespasser, licensee, or invitee. And, getting ahead of our
story, this is precisely the proposition for which *Rowland v. Christian*

---

[16] *Rowland* at 563.

stands, in magisterially abolishing the status-based categories. Oddly, then, the Court works hard to provide procedural window-dressing for a substantive display that never sees the light of day. It is as though the Court is unaware of where it is going in the succeeding discussion and holding in the case.

And the oddity is compounded at the end of the opinion. After providing a host of reasons for why the status-based, limited duty categories have outlived their usefulness, Justice Peters returns to the case at hand, which now, he says, "presents no substantial difficulties."[17] But surprisingly, he then recasts the facts, seemingly unselfconsciously. We must assume, Peters asserts, that defendant Christian not only knew that the faucet was defective and dangerous, but "that the defect was *not obvious*." It follows, he says, that "[w]here the occupier of land is aware of *a concealed condition* involving . . . an unreasonable risk of harm" and fails to warn or repair, her conduct constitutes negligence.[18]

Note the transformation here. The defect which both parties steered clear of describing as latent or patent—the closest approximation is Christian's statement that if Rowland had used his "eyesight" he would have been aware of the cracked faucet—has suddenly become, in the Court's apparent enthusiasm for sealing the case, a concealed defect. But the effect, in so closing the circle, is to make entirely gratuitous the change in the law that marks *Rowland* off as a landmark case. If indeed the defect was concealed, summary judgment was improperly granted under the then prevailing view of obligations owed to a social guest under the categories.[19]

As we shall see, California arguably did not subscribe to this prevailing view, but instead required something like a recklessly maintained trap to trigger an obligation to warn a social guest.[20] But even so, once the Court characterizes the facts as presenting a concealed condition, the summary judgment could readily have been overturned by simply adopting the plaintiff's argument for adhering to the generally accepted view that *any* hidden defect, not just spring gun-type condi-

---

[17] *Id.* at 568.

[18] *Id.* (emphasis added).

[19] This prevailing view, discussed at greater length in the text, *infra*, was that the possessor of land was under an obligation to disclose to social guests "any concealed dangerous conditions of the premises of which he had knowledge." William L. Prosser, *Handbook of The Law of Torts* 390 (3d ed. 1964) (citing Restatement of Torts § 342).

[20] As the *Rowland* court put it, "the general rule is that a trespasser and licensee or social guest are obliged to take the premises as they find them insofar as any alleged defective condition thereon may exist, and that the possessor of the land owes them only the duty of refraining from wanton or willful injury." *Rowland* at 565.

tions, required warning to a social guest. Having come this far, however, the Court was not to be denied. The categories had to go.

In fact, although never mentioned in the *Rowland* opinion or the court of appeals decision under review, less than two years earlier, the Court had possibly tipped its hand. In *Ross v. DeMond*,[21] an openly reluctant court of appeals had sustained a judgment notwithstanding the verdict for defendant in a case involving a plaintiff who tripped and fell, badly injuring herself, on a darkened front step that had settled over a period of time, leaving a considerable rise to the porch of her friend's home. The defect was not hidden, although perhaps obscured by the shadow cast by the porch light; indeed plaintiff had been to the defendant's home on other occasions. Under the circumstances, the court felt bound by the plaintiff's limited status as a social guest/licensee. But in the course of its opinion, the *Ross* court noted disdainfully the "Procrustean bed" of the categories by which it felt bound.[22]

The California Supreme Court, by a 6–1 vote, then granted an appeal in *Ross*. But the case settled, prior to a hearing. So arguably the handwriting was on the wall. One year later, when Rowland's lawyer sought an appeal in a context that was far less than ideal, as we will see in greater detail below, the Court appears to have felt the time was ripe for change, whatever the particulars of the immediate case.

The Rationale: Constructing the Foundation for a New Edifice

But why should the categories have appeared so anomalous to the Court? Although respected commentators had questioned their continuing vitality,[23] the framework of land occupier obligations, anchored in the tripartite division of land entrants into invitees, licensees, and trespassers, was universally accepted by American state courts and buttressed by continuing acceptance in the prestigious Restatement Second of Torts.[24]

---

[21] 48 Cal.Rptr. 743 (Cal.App.1966).

[22] *Ross* at 752. Among other citations, the court discusses two highly critical earlier opinions by Justice Ray Peters, who would write the opinion in *Rowland* abolishing the categories, *Fernandez v. Consolidated Fisheries*, 219 P.2d 73 (Cal.App.1950) (written years earlier when Peters was still on the court of appeals, in which he was able to distinguish the case at hand as involving active negligence—an exception to the limited duty category) and *Chance v. Lawry's, Inc.*, 374 P.2d 185 (Cal.1962)(in which the Court, per Justice Peters, refused to allow an independent contractor to avail himself of the land occupier's limited duty obligations).

[23] *See, e.g.*, Fowler Harper & Fleming James, *The Law of Torts* ch. XXVII (1956).

[24] As Prosser cogently articulated the framework:

Those who enter upon land are divided into three categories: trespassers, licensees, and invitees, and there are subdivided duties as to each. They make out, as a general pattern, a rough sliding scale, by which, as the legal status of the visitor improves, the possessor of the land owes him more of an obligation of protection.

Moreover, the categories had not proven resistant to change. A more elaborate framework of rules had developed with the passage of time: commercial establishments were held to an obligation of due care to anyone who was lawfully on the premises; discovered and tolerated trespassers were upgraded to licensee status; special rules, incorporating obligations of due care, were recognized in the case of child trespassers.[25] What might consequently have been regarded as rule flexibility, however, was instead characterized as evidence of confusion and over-complexity by the *Rowland* court.

The Court constructed its foundation for a new edifice on a set of propositions that for the most part, like the elusive concealed defect, appear nowhere in the arguments made by the parties.[26] The opening thrust of Justice Peters' opinion, in fact, cuts a far wider swath than the obligations of land occupiers. Those heretofore limited obligations, the Court suggests, are something of an anomaly in view of the sweeping language of Section 1714 of the California Civil Code, enacted almost a century earlier in 1872, which provides that "[e]veryone is responsible . . . for an injury occasioned to another by his want of ordinary care in the management of his property or person, except so far as the latter has . . . brought the injury upon himself."[27] This provision, the Court remarks, is often taken "as the foundation of our negligence law." Strikingly, it had not occurred to the plaintiff's attorney to mention this statutory provision in his brief. But then he could hardly have been criticized on this score, since Section 1714 had resided alongside the limited duties owed to land entrants—and indeed, as a sort of hortatory proclamation, beside every no-duty or limited duty rule subscribed to by the common law of the state—from time immemorial (or more precisely,

---

Prosser, *supra* note 19, at 365.

The Restatement section spelling out the particular duty owed to licensees is § 342, entitled *Dangerous Conditions Known to Possessor*, and provides:

A possessor of land is subject to liability for physical harm caused to licensees by a condition of the land if, but only if, a) the possessor knows or has reason to know of the condition and should realize that it involves an unreasonable risk of harm to such licensees, and should expect that they will not discover or realize the danger, and b) he fails to exercise reasonable care to make the condition safe, or to warn the licensees of the condition and the risk involved, and c) the licensees do not know or have reason to know of the condition and the risk involved.

Restatement (Second) of Torts § 342 (1965).

[25] *See* Prosser, *supra* note 19, at 364–408.

[26] The *Rowland* case file, which I have obtained and examined, contains every written document submitted by the parties from date of filing to eventual settlement after remand. These submissions are discussed in the text that follows.

[27] Cal. Civ. Code § 1714 (Mathew Bender 1968).

since 1872).[28]

But Section 1714 is simply the lynch-pin for the Court to enunciate a set of duty factors—factors meant to be determinative of whether departure is warranted from the "fundamental principle" of ordinary care—that are perhaps the hallmark of the opinion. Indeed this "balance of considerations," which came to be known as the *Rowland* duty factors, has served as a guidepost for the development of California tort law to the present date:

> The foreseeability of harm to the plaintiff, the degree of certainty that the plaintiff suffered injury, the closeness of the connection between the defendant's conduct and the injury suffered, the moral blame attached to the defendant's conduct, the policy of preventing future harm, the extent of the burden to the defendant and consequences to the community of imposing a duty to exercise care with resulting liability for breach, *and the availability, cost, and prevalence of insurance for the risk involved.*[29]

The italicizing of the insurance factor is mine—and is done to a purpose. For the *Rowland* duty factors do not in fact originate in *Rowland.* They are taken verbatim from a case decided by the Court a decade earlier, *Biakanja v. Irving,*[30] and had been cited in a number of succeeding cases[31]—with one highly conspicuous exception: None of the earlier formulations had mentioned insurance as a factor in determining whether a general duty of due care, rather than a no-duty or limited duty rule, should be applicable.

Clearly, the Court was up to something here. But it was not by way of suggestion of the parties. Just as with Section 1714 of the Civil Code, neither plaintiff nor defendant made mention of insurance as a factor that might play a role in influencing the outcome of the case. As it happens, defendant Christian, although an apartment-dweller of modest means, did carry renter's insurance—a rarity in her circumstances back then. And her lawyer was in reality an attorney for the insurance carrier, who was the real party in interest. But all of this goes unsaid in the pleadings, supporting affidavits, decision below, and the Court's

---

[28] Among the landmark cases of the *Rowland* era, referred to *supra*, in text accompanying notes 4–12, only *Li, supra* note 9, relies in any substantial way on § 1714, and it was decided seven years after *Rowland.* Interestingly, *Li* acknowledges that the Civil Code was meant to encapsulate the existing common law at the time it was enacted. But at the same time, the Court argues that the legislature in 1872 meant to have the Code's provisions liberally construed—and by liberal interpretation the Court finds in the language of § 1714 a basis for moving from contributory to comparative fault. *See Li* at 865–67.

[29] *Rowland* at 564.

[30] 320 P.2d 16 (Cal.1958).

[31] Those cases are cited in *Rowland* at 564, along with the *Biakanja* cite.

opinion. All we have as a clue to the significance of liability insurance in the recasting of the law of land occupier's obligations is this additional duty factor, introduced by the Supreme Court as a policy consideration for the first time, without a word of comment.

The *Rowland* court next puts forward arguments sounding in judicial administrability and fairness. Thus, as the Court sees it, the accretion of sub-categories of land entrants, mentioned earlier, constituted an effort to accommodate an antiquated "heritage of feudalism"—highly protective of land occupiers—to modernity by stretching the definitions of "active operations" and "traps" to broaden the scope of the ordinary care requirement.[32] For the Court, these efforts, however well-intentioned, simply bred confusion and over-complexity. They demonstrated the need to scrap the categories entirely in the name of effective judicial administration, rather than retain them. By contrast, the *Rowland* attorneys had singlemindedly pitched their battle on the conceptual terrain of conflicting definitions of what constituted a "trap"—the furthest thing from their minds was to suggest that the categories had lost their vitality.

And from all appearances in the written pleadings, motions and briefs, broad precepts of "fairness" were well outside the purview of the parties as well, preoccupied as they were with doctrinal refinements. Yet, it is here that the Court most unequivocally states the grounds for its impatience with continued resort to the categories:

> A man's life or limb does not become less worthy of protection by the law nor a loss less worthy of compensation under the law because he has come upon the land of another without permission or with permission but without a business purpose. Reasonable people do not ordinarily vary their conduct depending upon such matters, and to focus upon the status of the injured party as a trespasser, licensee, or invitee in order to determine the question whether the landowner has a duty of care, is contrary to our modern social mores and humanitarian values.[33]

At a later point, I will return to the Court's assertion that the categories are "contrary to our modern social mores and humanitarian values." Now, however, it is time to put aside the *Rowland* opinion itself, and peer behind the scenes—beyond the glimpses I have offered of a proactive court unconcerned about the parties' conceptions of the litigation—to view in greater detail how a modest case, in every respect, grew into a landmark decision.[34]

---

[32] *Rowland* at 565–66.

[33] *Id.* at 568.

[34] I should add that Justice Burke filed a brief dissenting opinion in *Rowland*, joined by Justice McComb, maintaining that the traditional approach "provides the degree of

A Modest Case Transformed

James Rowland had a plane to catch and didn't want to leave his car at the airport if he could avoid it, while he was away from San Francisco in Portland. He went looking for his friend, Bob Kohler, thinking that he might leave his car in front of Kohler's apartment and get a ride from him to the airport. No luck, Kohler was out. But it occurred to him that Kohler might just be nearby at the apartment of Nancy Christian, a mutual friend, whom Kohler had been dating. He had been there once before at a party given by Christian. So he phoned her, only to find out that Kohler was not there. But when he mentioned his reason for calling, Christian offered to give him a ride to the airport.

When he arrived Christian was busy painting the apartment, which she had just moved into a month earlier. They had a drink and then Rowland asked to use the bathroom facilities before they left for the airport. The rest is history—tort history. A cracked bathroom faucet that cut him badly enough to sever tendons and nerves, requiring hospitalization, came between Rowland and his Western Airlines flight to Portland. It was November 30, 1963—just over five years before the California Supreme Court would decide *Rowland v. Christian*.

In his complaint, Rowland avers in standard legalese that "said bathroom fixtures were dangerous to all persons using them, which said fact was well known to the defendants."[35] Dangerous, perhaps, but as indicated earlier, no mention is made of whether the danger was concealed. Elusively, earlier in the complaint Rowland asserts that "the cold water faucet on the bathroom sink was cracked and should be replaced"—and, as we have seen, he alleged that Christian had knowledge of the crack in the cold water faucet (which she did not dispute). But neither in the complaint, nor in his supporting affidavit, is there even the barest description of the bathroom facilities.

Christian, in turn, does no better in bringing the matter towards joinder. As indicated earlier, her answer claims in conclusory fashion that Rowland was "guilty of contributory negligence" and that he failed to use "his natural faculties, including that of eyesight." Nowhere,

stability and predictability so highly prized in the law," and that "[s]weeping modifications of tort liability law fall more suitably within the domain of the Legislature." *Rowland* at 569.

[35] Note the plural, *defendants*. The other defendants were the building owners. Rowland had greater immediate success against them. The trial judge who entertained the landlords' summary judgment motion—a different trial judge, even though the cases were consolidated—ruled in Rowland's favor. But this parallel proceeding never went any further. It was put on hold until the appeals were exhausted in the case against Christian, and then settled along with the claim against her (as discussed later).

however, in her answer or affidavit in support of her motion for summary judgment, does she describe the appearance of the faucet. Neither party makes the factual assertion that could have been so critical to the appropriate resolution of the motion for dismissal on the pleadings.

Years later, when I interviewed her, Nancy Christian was more revealing about the real-life setting alluded to so obscurely in the written pleadings. The apartment, which she had moved into slightly more than a month earlier, was "a pigsty"—a total mess, as she recollected. Indeed, she eventually moved out in desperation when an army of cockroaches descended during re-decoration of the upstairs apartment precipitated by the tenant above her vacating the premises.

As to the faucet, the crack wasn't really concealed as she recalls it, but it was caked in dirt and grime. She surmised that Rowland might not have noticed the defective condition. These observations are many years later, of course. Nonetheless, Christian's recollections clearly suggest indifferent lawyering, at best, on the part of Rowland's attorney, whose only realistic hope for avoiding summary judgment, under the circumstances, had been to raise a colorable factual claim that the defect was concealed.

But what motivated Rowland's attorney to sue Christian, a young woman of modest means, in the first place? The answer is at once both unsurprising and surprising. Unsurprising, in that Christian was only a nominal defendant; she turns out to have had renter's insurance. At the same time, it is rather surprising that she had such insurance at all. It was quite uncommon for big-city apartment renters of modest means to carry liability insurance in the early 1960s. In fact, she carried the insurance not out of regard for personal liability concerns, but because she had some valuable sterling silverware that was a family heirloom. Such are the fortuities that led this case to be brought—and launched it on its uncertain path to the California Supreme Court.

As befits her nominal presence in the case, Christian had virtually no relationship with her attorney. John Healy was a small-time insurance defense lawyer who was handling the case for her insurance carrier. Christian's sole contact with him was in the preparation of her affidavit and deposition testimony. In a surprising twist, however, she was in fact a good friend of Rowland's attorney, Jack Berman—a good enough friend in fact that two months into the case, when Berman moved to a new office, he gave Christian his carpeting to help along her continuing efforts to make her apartment more livable! Indeed, it is only a short step, although not certain from this point in time, to conjecture that Rowland retained Berman, who was primarily a criminal defense lawyer not a personal injury practitioner, as his attorney on the suggestion of

Christian, who had known Berman socially for some time before the case arose.[36]

Jack Berman and John Healy were "street lawyers," as an attorney who knew both of them well back in the 1960s described them to me. He was not speaking pejoratively. Berman was a well-known figure in the criminal courts, and indeed something of a colorful San Francisco character, according to news accounts and the reminiscences of surviving friends.[37] But he was not primarily a plaintiffs' lawyer and by all accounts he was not an appellate lawyer who took cases to the state Supreme Court. Healy seems to have been more in his element, at least before the trial court, in defending what appeared to be a routine premises liability case. But he, too, was not an appellate practitioner. In short, these were not test case lawyers—and this is transparent in the written record, discussed below, which Justice Peters and his colleagues had before them when they decided to hear an appeal in the case.

But that written record can only be understood in the context of a closer look at the obligations owing to a social guest when James Rowland had his fateful encounter with the cracked faucet. Like every other state, California at the time subscribed to the tripartite invitee-licensee-trespasser framework. Significantly, however, California appeared to do so in the most begrudging fashion. To be sure, as far as entrants on *business* premises were concerned, the California Supreme Court, in *Oettinger v. Stewart*,[38] had followed the step taken by most states in broadly recognizing an obligation of due care, without reference to the particularities of whether the proprietor stood to recognize an economic benefit from the entrant's presence. If Rowland's injury had occurred in the bathroom at his neighborhood café, he would have been owed a full obligation of due care, even if he stopped in solely to use the facilities.

---

[36] Nancy Christian does not recall whether she suggested Berman to Rowland, but thinks that it was certainly a possibility.

[37] In an obituary that appeared in the San Francisco Chronicle, S.F. Chron., April 12, 2002, at A23, Berman is described by a number of old friends, all politically-connected San Franciscans, as an avid gambler with a passion for the Las Vegas gaming tables; a longtime enthusiast of jazz, the prize fights, and hanging out at a well-known bar across from City Hall. He also went south in the 1960s as a civil rights activist and served many years, in colorful style, as a local trial court judge beginning in 1982. His second wife describes him as "a total character." He was earlier married for a few years, prior to her political career, to Senator Dianne Feinstein.

[38] 148 P.2d 19 (Cal.1944). In dictum, the *Oettinger* court also states that California recognized an obligation of due care to licensees when the land occupant was engaged in "active operations," a recognized exception in the Restatement to the otherwise limited duties owed to licensees. *Oettinger* involved a landlord who accidentally tripped and fell onto an apartment seeker, seriously injuring her, as she was seeing her down some stairs after telling her that there were no vacancies in the building.

Social guests in a private residential setting, however, were another matter. Here, confusion reigned among the lower appellate courts and the California Supreme Court had done virtually nothing to clarify matters. A number of appellate court cases suggested that the social guest took the premises as he or she found them; in other words, that the land occupier had no obligation to take safety precautions beyond whatever seemed personally adequate for the immediate family.[39] Translated into a rule of conduct applicable to licensees, this was frequently taken to mean that the land occupier in California owed no duty beyond avoiding willful and wanton injury to a visitor.[40]

By contrast, the vast majority of states required a warning to a social guest whenever the host had knowledge of a danger that he had reason to expect would not be discovered, a rule enunciated in the Restatement Second of Torts, § 342.[41] In short, the Restatement required warning of known concealed dangers, without reference to a standard of concealed risk created by the land occupier's conduct that bordered on reckless misconduct.

The confused state of the law in California, and indeed the uneven doctrinal developments in other states as well, frequently boiled down to definitional haggling over what constituted a "trap." In earlier times, and in contemporaneous California decisions, the illustration often relied on was a spring gun—surely suggesting a far more limited obligation from premises occupiers than if they had to concern themselves about a range of "traps" including obscured banana peels in the front yard and slippery spots on the dining room floor. But for William Prosser in the edition of his authoritative treatise on torts contemporaneous with *Rowland*, "trap" had taken on a new, and more expansive, meaning:

> [Trap] originally was used in the sense of presenting an appearance of safety where it did not exist; but the significance which gradually became attached to it was not one of intent to injure, or even of any active misconduct, but was merely that the possessor of the land was

---

[39] This was the reading of the California case law in *Ross v. Demond*, the appellate court case in which the Supreme Court had granted a hearing just two years before *Rowland* (only to have the case settle). *Ross* cites a number of earlier cases in support of this narrow characterization of the licensee category. *See Ross*, 48 Cal. Rptr. at 747–49.

[40] *See Rowland* at 565. Another way of viewing this limited duty obligation is from the perspective of the traditional common law distinction between misfeasance and nonfeasance. Willful and wanton misconduct eliminates the nonfeasance protection ordinarily afforded land occupiers by spilling over into *active* misconduct. In fact, this indirect route to extending the ordinary care obligation to social guests had been taken in some cases by broadly defining "active operations" on the part of private hosts. *See Oettinger, supra* note 38. I discuss the common law distinction between misfeasance and nonfeasance in greater detail in the next section.

[41] *See* Restatement (Second) of Torts § 342 (1965).

under an obligation to disclose to the licensee any concealed dangerous conditions of the premises of which he had knowledge.[42]

Prosser's reference at this point is to the above-mentioned Restatement
Second of Torts, § 342—Prosser, it might be noted, was the Reporter on
the Restatement Second—for what he characterizes as "the overwhelming weight of authority."[43]

This, then, was the battlefield on which Berman and Healy clashed.
Berman, unsurprisingly, was disabled immediately—the trial court
granted summary judgment to defendant on the pleadings—through his
failure to allege what would have been the baseline requirement even in
a majority rule jurisdiction: a concealed defect. Undaunted, he appealed
on behalf of Rowland, steadfastly sticking to his guns in his statement of
the case, opening brief, in the California court of appeals: "Defendant
knew that the handle was cracked and realized that this constituted a
dangerous condition." Once again, there is no averment on Rowland's
behalf that the crack was concealed. But then, almost as an after-
thought, in the argument section of the brief, which runs less than 2½
pages in its entirety, Berman for the first time suggests that "the only
question with which this court is faced is whether the crack qualified as
a concealed danger or deceptive condition." If so, Berman continues,
there is nothing to stop the court from adopting "the trap exception to
the rule of non-liability"—an exception that he inexplicably fails to
define in the handful of succeeding paragraphs in the argument.

And so, the terms of engagement were set: Healy, in his reply brief,
argued that California had never adopted Restatement Second, § 342,
and that the "so-called" trap exception, "[o]utside of deliberate, willful
'entrapment,' such as the maintenance of spring guns and other hideous
devices . . . is largely a myth." Berman, in turn, in a reply brief hardly
over a page in length, rejoins that there is nothing to stop the court from
adopting § 342 in the case at hand. And there the matter ends—not a
word urging the court to venture beyond clarification of the meaning of
hidden defect to reconsider the legitimacy of the categories.[44]

---

[42] Prosser, *supra* note 19, at 390.

[43] *Id.* Consistent with the *Ross* court, Prosser cites a California appellate court
decision, *Fisher v. General Petroleum Corp.*, 267 P.2d 841 (Cal.App.1954), in a following
footnote, for the proposition that there are still occasional "exceptions" (throwbacks, one
might say) to the Restatement approach. But tacitly attesting to the California confusion,
he also cites, in a preceding footnote, a California appellate court case, *Newman v. Fox West
Coast Theatres*, 194 P.2d 706 (Cal.App.1948) in *support* of the Restatement position.

[44] By contrast, plaintiff-appellant's opening brief in the court of appeals in *Ross*, after
claiming that plaintiff made out a conventional case for recovery either as an invitee or
licensee, then argued for abolishing the categories. *See* Brief for Appellant at 15–17, Ross v.
Demond.

The court of appeals set its sights on the arguments in the briefs, and quickly rehearsed three possibilities for addressing the trap exception: that it was no part of California law at all; that it had the narrow meaning suggested by defendant's counsel; or, that it had the broad meaning suggested by plaintiff.[45] And then, not surprisingly, the court held that it need not decide the question at all—although its sentiments quite clearly ran to a narrow obligation, if any, on the part of social hosts—since "[no] source in the record contains any allegation, factual or conclusory, which describes the faucet, its appearance, its location, the lighting, the bathroom, or . . . any other fact which would support the conclusion that plaintiff was injured by a concealed danger."[46]

If, in hindsight, the dominant theme, as the case wound its way to the Supreme Court, was tunnel vision, the petition for a hearing before the high court served as the capstone. A word of context is necessary. At the time *Rowland* was decided there was no independent briefing before the Supreme Court; the Court reviewed cases *de novo* on the basis of briefs filed in the court of appeals—and the petition for a hearing (which could run thirty pages or more).[47] Should the request for a hearing be granted, then, it is critical to note that the petition and reply constituted the final moment for the contesting parties to frame the issue, as they conceived it. True to form, Berman argued exclusively for adoption of § 342, and Healy, taking his cue from the court of appeals decision, replied narrowly that there was no baseline averment of a concealed defect that would warrant reconsideration of the summary judgment in defendant's favor. Neither submission reaches four pages in length, and not a word is devoted to the possibility that the categories might be abandoned.[48]

Healy's reply brief in *Rowland* is only marginally more expansive and illuminating on prior existing case law than Berman's. More than half of the nineteen pages are devoted to copious quotes, mostly of peripheral relevance, from two earlier precedents interpreting obligations to licensees narrowly.

[45] Rowland v. Christian, 63 Cal.Rptr. 98, 102–04 (Cal.App.1967)

[46] *Id.* at 104.

[47] *See* Cal. R. Ct. 28 (Deering 1968). In 1985, a thirty-page limit was imposed on petitions for review. There is no indication of a fixed page limit prior to that time. The Advisory Committee comment explained that the page limit was being imposed because an additional brief on the merits was now expected. *See* Cal. R. Ct. 28 (Deering 1985).

At the time *Rowland* was decided, the Supreme Court could, and sometimes did, request supplemental briefing after granting a hearing. Notably, it chose not to do so in *Rowland*.

[48] Nor were there any amicus parties in the case who might have framed the issues in broader terms. Whether there would have been amicus submissions if the Court had provided some reason to think that it had larger intentions in mind—for example, by a Court request for supplemental briefing—is of course another matter entirely.

Might the possibility of abandoning the categories have been introduced at oral argument? Perhaps, but I can only offer speculation, since oral arguments before the Court were neither transcribed nor recorded at the time. My interviews with court clerks from the *Rowland* era suggest that, in most cases, when oral arguments were heard a draft of the final opinion had already been prepared and circulated by the Justice to whom opinion-writing had been assigned; in short, that oral arguments were viewed as a formality for the most part. Very likely then, if the prospect of abandoning the categories arose at all during oral arguments, it was on the initiative of the Justices rather than the parties.[49] Whatever the case, the battle in the trenches in *Rowland v. Christian* confirms in singular fashion that this was a court prepared to refine and reformulate tort law according to its own lights, a proactive court extraordinaire.

The Aftermath: Perspectives on the Case

After the Supreme Court remanded the case for trial under the newly-enunciated standard of ordinary care owed to all land entrants, Berman referred the case to a San Francisco firm of plaintiffs' litigation specialists, Walkup, Downing, Wallach & Stearns, who quickly settled the matter. In keeping with the modest particulars of the case, surviving attorneys in that firm recall a settlement figure of under $10,000.[50]

Like Berman's, Healy's petition—in response to the request for a Supreme Court hearing—runs four cursory pages. It seems fair to say that the attorneys were operating on a level playing field.

[49] As a side note, Jack Berman may have reached the conclusion at this point that he needed some outside assistance. For the first time in any of the submissions and arguments related to the case, co-counsel for Rowland appears in the Pacific Reporter headnotes (but not those of the official California Supreme Court reports or the California Appellate reports), "Jack K. Berman *and Cyril Viadro*, San Francisco, for plaintiff and appellant." *Rowland* at 562 (emphasis added). Multiple interview sources have confirmed both that Cyril Viadro was a respected local appellate advocate of the period, and that Berman was highly unlikely to have himself argued a case before the Supreme Court. In any event, Berman stands identified as the lawyer who won *Rowland v. Christian* and reformed the law of premises liability, and it was his case from the beginning to settlement negotiations. Surviving associates tell me that Berman took singular pride in this accomplishment, and in fact the biographical entry in Kenneth James Arnold, *California Courts and Judges*, Profiles 63 (7th ed. 1995)—Berman as mentioned, subsequently was appointed to the California superior court, from which he was retired at the time of this entry—published almost thirty years later ends with the following: "Significant cases in which Judge Berman served as attorney of record include *Rowland v. Christian*, [citation] which abolished the distinctions between invitee, licensee, and trespasser with respect to the duty owed by the possessor of premises."

[50] The two attorneys of record from the Walkup firm whom I interviewed drew no distinction between the insurer representing Christian and the landlord defendants in

Apparently, Rowland's injuries had healed without any lasting difficulties. In fact, the major problem in getting the case settled, as one former Walkup attorney recalls, is that Rowland had moved out of the state, and once located, was annoyed about having to make a brief return appearance in a matter that was now far behind him. Nancy Christian herself entirely lost interest in the case once her insurance carrier's lawyer, Healy, had finished deposing her, and never even bothered to inquire as to its outcome. Nor did she ever see Rowland again. None of this diminishes the significance of the case, of course. Some landmarks of the law have lasting impact on the lives of the immediate parties; others, like *Rowland v. Christian*, take on a life of their own, and the parties get on with their personal affairs with hardly a glance backwards.

Makings of a Landmark: Impact on the Law

Doctrinal reformulation can be of great salience for either of two distinct reasons: It may have decisive consequences for future parties in like circumstances, or it may have wide influence through adoption by courts in other jurisdictions. *Rowland* passes muster on both counts.

Future cases, like circumstances

Consider initially how the parties fared in *Rowland* itself, until the Supreme Court stepped in and scrapped the categories. Even under the more liberal Restatement Second version of concealed defect, if the crack in the faucet was apparent—if in the final analysis, the reason Rowland failed to plead concealment was that the crack simply was not concealed, and he used the faucet thinking that it would not be a problem to avoid injuring himself—then there is no case for a jury. The licensee requirement of a hidden condition would bar recovery. More generally, whatever one makes of the *Rowland* facts, there are clearly many scenarios in which injury results from a nonconcealed condition: forgetfulness on the part of a social guest (recall the forgotten gap between top stair and porch landing in *Ross v. Demond*,[51]), inattentiveness, or outright disregard for risk. Obviously, in some of these situations, even under a *Rowland* approach, a defendant could argue contributory fault to the jury. But that is just the point. The cases go to the *jury* under *Rowland* on the question of what constitutes ordinary care—whether a fix-up or warning obligation—and what conduct might count as a defense. By

---

recollecting this total sum. I also located and interviewed one of the attorneys for the landlords, who indicated that, as in the case of Christian, his firm was almost certainly representing an insurer rather than the individual defendants. At this point in time, there is no way to determine how much each of the insurance carriers contributed to the settlement. In any event, *Rowland* clearly is not memorable for the amount of money that exchanged hands.

[51] *See Ross*, 48 Cal.Rptr. 743.

contrast, under the categories, the cases will far more frequently fail to satisfy the threshold requirement of concealment needed to get beyond summary dismissal.[52]

Similarly, on the related licensee requirement conceded in *Rowland*—that defendant was *aware* of the danger and failed to warn—many occasions arise where the host is no more cognizant of the dangerous condition than the guest. Consider the facts of a relatively recent case in Missouri, adhering to the traditional categories, *Carter v. Kinney.*[53] Plaintiff, a social guest and member of a Bible study group, arrived early for a meeting at defendant's house and slipped on ice and snow that had accumulated since defendant last shoveled the driveway the preceding evening. The Missouri Supreme Court affirmed summary judgment dismissing the case on the ground that the condition was unknown to defendant and that therefore as a matter of law he owed no obligation to warn a licensee. Once again, liability would not be a certainty in a *Rowland* jurisdiction. Defendant could argue that plaintiff was contributorily negligent, or simply that due care did not require rising before 7:00 a.m. to clear ice from the driveway for arriving guests. But these matters would be decided by a jury with relatively unfettered discretion, rather than dismissed out of hand on the basis of the categories because of lack of knowledge that a dangerous condition existed.

So the categories do have bite; they are consequential. And note that I have not even mentioned the status of a trespasser, similarly abolished as an independent limited duty category by *Rowland*, which replaces the minimal obligation of refraining from willful misconduct to trespassers with a due care standard (more on trespassers, shortly).[54] In sum, abandoning the categories leads to a shift in allocation of decisionmaking authority from judge to jury in circumstances where knowledge and/or concealment of a dangerous condition of the premises cannot be clearly established.

---

[52] Even under the categories, of course, there is considerable play for jury decisionmaking. Ironically, as my recounting suggests, *Rowland* itself can be taken to be just such a case; if plaintiff had simply pled more clearly that the appearance of the faucet gave no indication of its dangerous condition, possibly there would have been a jury question on liability—at the very least there would have been enough to get beyond summary judgment.

[53] 896 S.W.2d 926 (Mo.1995)

[54] Near the end of the opinion, the Court does add this qualifier, "although the plaintiff's status as a trespasser, licensee, or invitee may in the light of the facts giving rise to such status have some bearing on the question of liability, the status is not determinative." *Rowland* at 568. What the Court seems to have in mind by "some bearing" is that trespassers may stray into odd corners of the premises where it is not foreseeable that dangerous conditions would pose risks to anyone, and in such a case there would be no liability. This is, of course, perfectly consistent with the Court's across-the-board recognition of a standard of due care.

Future cases, other places

Consider next the influence of *Rowland* outside its state of origin. In 1964, when Prosser published the third edition of his authoritative text, abolition of the categories was still but a gleam in the eye of Justice Peters.[55] *Rowland*'s claim was just beginning its slow journey through the California courts, and no other common law jurisdiction had seen fit to follow the advice of commentators like Fowler Harper and Fleming James that the categories be relegated to the scrap heap of tort history.[56] Seven years later, however, when Prosser next revised his text, he saw fit to take special note of the recently-decided *Rowland* and venture a cautious look at what the future held. Only Hawaii, had fallen into line behind California at that point. Nonetheless, as Prosser saw it, "[t]hese decisions are still too recent to permit any guess whether they will be followed elsewhere, although it certainly is not unlikely; ..."[57]

Prosser didn't live to see his guarded prediction borne out. But in 1984, when John Wade and others came out with the fifth edition of the Prosser text, eight states had followed *Rowland* and abolished the categories across the board and another five had erased the duty distinction between invitees and licensees, although retaining only a limited duty to trespassers.[58] The text goes on to caution that after 1979 adoptions in any form "came to a screeching halt"—and reflects approvingly on the possibility, to be discussed below, that this might indicate a more basic dissatisfaction with the 1960s phenomenon of replacing tailored tort rules with a broad due care standard.[59] Whatever the accuracy of the latter general observation, my recent count of *Rowland* jurisdictions indicates that the opinion has shown sustained persuasive influence: As of late 2002, I find ten states that have entirely abandoned

---

[55] Recall Justice Peters' earlier indications of a predisposition to abolish the categories, *supra* note 22.

[56] *See* Harper & James, *supra* note 23. Note, however, that England, the land of common law origin of the categories, had abolished them by legislation in 1957, *see* Occupiers' Liability Act, 1957, 5 & 6 Eliz. 2, c. 31 (Eng.), and the U.S. Supreme Court refused to recognize the categories in admiralty cases in *Kermarec v. Compagnie Generale Transatlantique*, 358 U.S. 625 (1959). Justice Peters refers to both of these precedents in the course of his opinion. *See Rowland* at 566, 568.

[57] William Prosser, *Handbook on the Law of Torts* 399 (4th ed. 1971).

[58] W. Page Keeton et al., *Prosser and Keeton on the Law of Torts* 433 (5th ed. 1984).

[59] *Id.* at 433–34. In striking contrast to Prosser's relative receptiveness to overriding the categories, the new editors, reflecting on the perceived loss of momentum to adopt *Rowland*, sourly noted that "[a]t least it appears that the courts are gaining a renewed appreciation for the considerations behind the traditional duty limitations toward trespassing adults, and that they are acquiring more generally a healthy skepticism toward invitations to jettison years of developed jurisprudence in favor of a beguiling legal panacea."

the categories and thirteen more that have retained only the trespasser category for limited duty treatment.[60] Thus, nearly half the states have recast their law of land occupier liability since *Rowland*, attesting to its influence and staying power.

Makings of a Landmark: Illuminating Broader Concerns

But should one view the glass as half empty or half full? That twenty-seven states retain the categories thirty years after *Rowland* surely suggests that more was at stake in the case than discarding an approach that was plainly, in the words of the court, "contrary to our modern social mores and humanitarian values."[61]

In reality, *Rowland*, without saying so, provokes reassessment of a central guiding principle of tort liability for accidental harm: the distinction between nonfeasance and misfeasance.[62] In its starkest application, that principle has undergirded protection of individual autonomy by refusing to translate the moral approval afforded the Good Samaritan into a legal obligation of affirmative action. As an ethical matter, we may disapprove of the hypothetical bystander's refusal to undertake no-risk rescue of the infant on the railroad tracks from the onrushing train, but tort law does not traditionally recognize a legal obligation on the part of a stranger to protect another from injury.

This precept—no duty of affirmative action—is a *leitmotif* in the law of tort, subject to many exceptions that have developed over time, particularly through the carving out of special relationships.[63] The traditional rules of land occupier liability to various categories of land entrants are a variation on this theme.[64] In modern times, the character-

---

[60] States that have abolished the categories completely according to at least one published appellate opinion are Alaska, California, Washington, D.C., Hawaii, Louisiana, Montana, Nevada, New Hampshire, New York, and Rhode Island. States that have abolished the categories for invitees and licensees, but retained a limited duty to trespassers, include Illinois, Iowa, Maine, Massachusetts, Minnesota, Nebraska, New Mexico, North Carolina, North Dakota, Tennessee, West Virginia, Wisconsin, and Wyoming. In some of the above-mentioned states, as well as the remaining states that have retained the categories, there are on occasion conflicting opinions from different circuits within the state regarding the status of the categories.

[61] *Rowland* at 104. It is possible, of course, that some of the states retaining the categories may not have had occasion to reconsider their adherence to the categories, although after the duration of thirty years I would think that would be a small number, at most.

[62] For discussion in the context of the duty to rescue, see Richard A. Epstein, *A Theory of Strict Liability*, 2 J. of Legal Stud. 151, 197–204 (1973). For a contemporary application, see *Harper v. Herman*, 499 N.W.2d 472 (Minn.1993).

[63] *See* Restatement (Second) of Torts § 314A (1965).

[64] Consider, on this score, that the traditional invitee category reflects the notion of special relationship; in particular the prospect of economic benefit from the land entrant's

ization of these obligations as a vestige of medieval protection of the landed gentry is nothing but a red herring. Rather, the question is whether norms of civility require anything more than offering a home environment that is as free from risk as the host sees fit to make it for family members. Fix-up costs as a property ages often involve substantial investments in time and money that lead homeowners to make do, putting off maintenance and elimination of risk for another day, in the privacy of one's residence. And, it would be unusual to say the least, for this common tendency to live in a certain state of disrepair—as a lifestyle choice, if not for purely economic reasons—to be remediated by posting warning signs around the premises. Whether these homely realities are contrary to "modern social mores and humanitarian values" may well be questioned.

If there has been some discernible reluctance for courts to treat social guests as tantamount to business visitors, obligations of due care to trespassers have evoked even less enthusiasm. As mentioned, less than half the states that have followed *Rowland* in upgrading the status of social guests have been willing to follow suit with regard to trespassers. Once again, the *Rowland* opinion elides a fundamental precept of duty analysis in its hostility to continued recognition of status considerations. But the issue is distinct from the treatment of social guests. Traditionally, tort law has taken a dim view of the claimant who seeks to profit from his own wrongdoing.

The trespasser is a prototypical bad actor of this sort. Consider a California case, after *Rowland*, which offers a concrete illustration. In the early 1980s, a California school district, in the face of the legal uncertainties posed by *Rowland*, decided to settle a case brought by a trespasser who fell through a skylight while crawling on the roof of a school building at night in an effort to illegally remove floodlights.[65] The outcry raised by the case contributed to state legislative action establishing a narrowly limited duty obligation to criminal trespassers in California.[66] Humanitarian values may well counsel against the use of spring guns to spear trespassers. But it is a far cry from setting a spring gun to,

---

presence. Moreover the later development of the "active operations" exception can be seen as directly responsive to the nonfeasance-misfeasance distinction: If the land possessor is engaged in active operations there no longer is a concern that affirmative obligations to act are being imposed by recognizing a duty to act carefully.

[65] The incident, in which the injured trespasser was left a quadriplegic, was settled by the school district for $260,000 plus monthly payments for life of $1,200. See discussion of the case in *Calvillo-Silva v. Home Grocery*, 968 P.2d 65, 71 (Cal.1998).

[66] Cal. Civ. Code § 847 (Deering 2003). *Calvillo-Silva* also discusses a second pivotal case from the legislative history of § 847, in which a motorcycle thief joyriding in a farmer's field was badly injured after hitting a pothole and recovered nearly $500,000. *See Calvillo–Silva* at 71.

for example, allowing hazardous litter to accumulate—broken glass, perhaps—on private beachfront property clearly marked as "no trespassing," let alone the painting over of a school skylight. It seems to strain credulity to regard these latter oversights as a lack of humanitarian values. Yet, they are probably the stuff of most trespasser injuries in which suit would be brought. It seems at best a debatable proposition whether the law should depart from its traditional low regard for those who consciously stray where they don't belong and then sue in injury situations of this sort.

Having come this far, it is time to recognize again the persuasive power of *Rowland*—after all, nearly half the states have fallen into line with its basic holding. What accounts for it? Although there is no magic formula for balancing the *Rowland* factors, I would speculate that here, as in many other areas of accident law, liability insurance—that duty factor quietly introduced explicitly as a general policy consideration into California tort law for the first time in *Rowland*—has borne great weight.[67] For homeowner's insurance is nearly universally carried, the incidence of premises injuries is highly predictable from an actuarial perspective, and the costs of premises accidents are relatively contained (accidental deaths or catastrophic injuries are rare occurrences in the premises liability setting).[68] From a compensation perspective, then, the appeal of respecting homeowner autonomy or punishing trespassers (especially non-felonious trespassers) has been muted in many quarters. Certainly, this was so in the 1960s heyday of tort activism in the California Supreme Court, and undoubtedly a vestige of that spirit survives elsewhere today, as well.

From a more sweeping vantage point, *Rowland* tapped into an intellectual current that was attaining widespread judicial acceptance; indeed, that can be viewed as a dominant theme in the historical evolution of tort law from the nineteenth to the twentieth century. Status-based barriers to liability for negligent conduct, expressed as immunities or limited duty obligations, fell victim to an emerging paradigm that might be characterized as obligations based on scope of

---

[67] *Compare* Gibson v. Gibson, 479 P.2d 648, 653 (Cal.1971) (in which the Court observed, "[W]e feel that we cannot overlook the widespread prevalence of liability insurance and its practical effect on intra-family suits. Although it is obvious that insurance does not create liability where none otherwise exists, it is unrealistic to ignore this factor in making an informed policy decision on whether to abolish parental negligence immunity. We can no longer consider child-parent actions on the outmoded assumption that parents may be required to pay damages to their children.").

[68] Interestingly, just as Nancy Christian carried renter's insurance for first-party reasons—that is, to insure her dinnerware—rather than out of third-party liability concerns, homeowners' insurance is carried primarily to satisfy mortgagors and protect against unexpected loss or damage to real and personal property, rather than due to tort liability concerns.

endangerment.[69] Probably the most notable instance of this shift in perspective is the rejection of the privity requirement in product injury cases in *MacPherson v. Buick Motor Co.*[70] Similarly, the wholesale adoption of workers' compensation laws marked a rejection of the contract-based defenses that had limited recovery for employment-related injuries. The California Supreme Court, in the period identified earlier as the halcyon years, 1960–80, contributed significantly to this movement in cases like *Muskopf* (rejecting blanket immunity from municipal liability), *Gibson* (similarly rejecting intrafamily tort immunity) and *Tunkl* (limiting contractual disclaimers of negligence liability).[71] *Rowland*, eliminating the status-based limitations in premises liability cases, stands at the forefront of this effort.

Afterword

Suppose the case had not settled after remand: Would James Rowland, in the end, have prevailed? Not necessarily. Whether in the haste of the moment before departure for the airport—Nancy Christian perhaps changing out of her paint-splattered clothes, Rowland offhandedly deciding to use the bathroom—her failure to mention the need for caution in using the faucet constituted a lack of ordinary care might well have been decided either way. After all, she had presumably been using the facilities without accident to herself or guests for a month while waiting for the landlord to make repairs. So too, Rowland's contributory negligence (or even assumed risk), in not using his "eyesight"—still a complete bar to recovery at that point—might have emerged more clearly at trial.[72]

In fact, it doesn't seem much of a stretch to speculate that if the *Rowland* scenario were to recur on ten separate occasions, five or more juries might come out one way and the remainder the other. On this score, *Rowland* puts one in mind of the classic pair of cases, *Baltimore & Ohio Railroad Co. v. Goodman*[73] and *Pokora v. Wabash Railway Co.*,[74] in

---

[69] For discussion of the status-based limitations on negligence liability, see Robert L. Rabin, *The Historical Development of the Fault Principle: A Reinterpretation*, 15 Ga. L.Rev. 925 (1981).

[70] 111 N.E. 1050 (N.Y.1916). *MacPherson* is examined in detail in this volume, see James A. Henderson, Jr., *MacPherson v. Buick Motor Company: Simplifying the Facts While Reshaping the Law*.

[71] See text *supra* at notes 6–8.

[72] In this regard, in pretrial admissions of fact Rowland stipulated that he had been to Christian's apartment once before at a party—and used the bathroom facilities.

[73] 275 U.S. 66 (1927).

[74] 292 U.S. 98 (1934).

which the respective opinions of Justices Oliver Wendell Holmes and
Benjamin Cardozo so vividly spelled out the tension between rules and
standards in tort cases—and the concomitant issue of allocation of
decisionmaking authority between judge and jury.

In my experience, most first-year students in torts resonate to
Justice Cardozo's observation that grade-crossing accidents, at least back
then, arose under such varied circumstances that fixed rules governing
appropriate precautionary steps to be taken by drivers approaching
railroad crossings—such as Justice Holmes' edict in *Goodman* to stop,
look and get out of the vehicle if necessary—made no sense; the flexibility of a standard of ordinary care, applied case by case, was more likely to
assure just outcomes.

But Cardozo offered a further qualifier of direct relevance to our
present concerns. After offering a number of hypothetical circumstances
in which a fixed rule requiring getting out of one's vehicle might be
contrary to ordinary care, he observed:

> Illustrations such as these bear witness to the need for caution in
> framing standards of behavior that amount to rules of law. The need
> is the more urgent when there is no background of experience out of
> which the standards emerged. They are then, not the natural
> flowerings of behavior in its customary forms, but rules artificially
> developed, and imposed from without.[75]

Whether the categories reflect just such "natural flowerings of behavior
in its customary forms" is, of course, the issue posed by an assessment of
Rowland.[76]

---

[75] *Id.* at 106.

[76] There is a nice parallel to another of the landmark cases from the *Rowland* era,
Gibson, abolishing intrafamily negligence immunity. Plaintiff's father negligently instructed him to go out on the highway and correct the position of the wheels on a jeep that the
father was towing. Plaintiff was hit by another car, passing on the road. The Court rejected
limitations on abolition of the immunity adopted in other states that would have retained
the immunity in two situations. In other words, these latter states had adopted a rule-
based approach to govern these situations; specifically: "1) where the alleged negligent act
involves an exercise of parental authority over the child; and 2) where the alleged negligent
act involves an exercise of ordinary parental discretion with respect to the provision of
food, clothing, housing, medical and dental services, and other care." *Gibson* at 652
(quoting Goller v. White, 122 N.W.2d 193, 198 (Wis.1963)). (Somewhat similarly, New York
has recognized an exception to negligence liability, meant to respect the diversity of views
on child-raising among various religious and ethnic communities, in cases of "negligent
supervision." *See* Holodook v. Spencer, 324 N.E.2d 338 (N.Y.1974).) The *Gibson* court
rejected any such limitations on liability for negligent conduct:

> [W]e reject the implication of *Goller* that within certain aspects of the parent-child
> relationship, the parent has carte blanche to act negligently toward his child .... In
> short, although a parent has the prerogative and the duty to exercise authority over
> his minor child, this prerogative must be exercised within reasonable limits. The

In the final analysis, perhaps it is fitting that the states should be split roughly evenly over the acceptance of *Rowland*. The tension between rules and standards cannot be resolved in conclusive fashion. It is not overstating the matter to say that it is a theme of classic proportions, reflected in enduring literary works.[77] Add to the mix the conflicting pressures to achieve broad risk-spreading and compensatory goals, on the one hand, and to respect individual autonomy in a residential setting, on the other, and the landmark significance of *Rowland v. Christian* comes into focus.

---

standard to be applied is the traditional one of reasonableness, but viewed in the light of the parental role. Thus, we think the proper test of a parent's conduct is this: what would an ordinary reasonable and prudent *parent* have done in similar circumstances? *Gibson* at 652–53.

[77] *See, e.g.*, Herman Melville, *Billy Budd*.

*

4

Peter H. Schuck and Daniel J. Givelber

Tarasoff v. Regents of the University of California: The Therapist's Dilemma

On October 27, 1969, Prosenjit Poddar, a graduate student at Berkeley, killed Tatiana (Tanya) Tarasoff. The killing was predictable and perhaps preventable. Poddar had developed an interest in Tarasoff, apparently unreciprocated, and her expression of disinterest was followed by severe psychiatric symptoms in Poddar. These led him to seek psychotherapeutic counseling on an outpatient basis at Cowell Memorial Hospital in Berkeley. He had seven sessions with a psychologist, Dr. Lawrence Moore, during which he threatened to kill Tarasoff. These threats and the underlying mental condition persuaded Moore that Poddar should be involuntarily committed for the safety of others. Moore asked the campus police at Berkeley to initiate the commitment. Apparently, the police interviewed Poddar, decided that he did not pose the threat perceived by Moore, and released him with a warning to stay away from Tarasoff. Neither Moore nor anyone from the clinic made any effort to communicate any of this to Tarasoff or her family; indeed, the head of the Cowell Clinic may have forbidden Moore from doing so. And Poddar, too, was left alone; after his release, it appears, he never returned to therapy.

The Tarasoff family learned about these events in a dramatic way—from the testimony at Poddar's criminal trial (about which more later)—and sued all involved for damages. The trial court dismissed the complaint in its entirety, and the Court of Appeals affirmed the dismissal. The California Supreme Court, however, reversed. Initially, it ruled that both the therapists and the police might be liable for failing to warn Tarasoff of her danger (*Tarasoff I*),[1] but finally decided that the police

---

[1] Tarasoff v. Regents of Univ. of Cal., 529 P.2d 553 (Cal.1974).

were immune and that the therapists alone faced possible civil liability (*Tarasoff II*).[2] Ultimately, the Court held that the plaintiffs would state a cause of action if they alleged that the therapists "in fact determined that Poddar presented a serious danger of violence to Tarasoff, or pursuant to the standards of their profession should have so determined, but nevertheless failed to exercise reasonable care to protect her from that danger."[3] Justice Mosk disagreed strongly on this precise point: "should have" was so nebulous, he thought, as to be a dangerous and perhaps impossible standard to impose.[4] Although the Court was careful to formulate the duty in terms of the need to exercise "reasonable care," the mental health profession immediately understood it as the more specific duty to warn foreseeable victims that the Court had prescribed in *Tarasoff I*.[5] Our guess—we have seen no data on point—is that the profession still thinks that *Tarasoff* imposes a duty to warn,[6] and as a practical matter, if not a legal one, this understanding may well be correct. In the wake of the *Tarasoff* decision, the California legislature enacted a statute immunizing therapists from liability for failure to warn except in the case of certain serious threats "against a reasonably identifiable victim or victims."[7]

---

[2] Tarasoff v. Regents of Univ. of Cal., 551 P.2d 334 (Cal.1976). This final decision (hereinafter *Tarasoff II*) starts from the beginning, as though *Tarasoff I* had never been decided—*Tarasoff I* is never even mentioned. According to an attorney then clerking at the Supreme Court, the justices—feeling that their first decision was wide of the mark—made a conscious choice to generalize away from the duty to warn, recognizing that this would not always be the best solution.

[3] *Tarasoff II*, 551 P.2d at 353.

[4] *Id.* at 451–52 (Mosk, J., concurring and dissenting). Justice Mosk concurred in the *Tarasoff* result because the practitioners *did* predict violence; but he wanted "to eliminate all reference to conformity to standards of the profession in predicting violence" when fashioning the duty to third persons in general, because to impose such a standard is to "take us from the world of reality into the wonderland of clairvoyance." *Id.* at 452. Mosk's view has not been ignored by subsequent courts. *See, e.g.*, Boynton v. Burglass, 590 So.2d 446, 448 (Fla.Dist.Ct.App.1991) ("When the duty to be imposed is dependent upon the standards of the psychiatric profession, we are asked to embark upon a journey 'that will take us from the world of reality into the wonderland of clairvoyance.' ").

[5] Daniel J. Givelber et al., Tarasoff, *Myth and Reality: An Empirical Study of Private Law in Action*, 1984 Wis. L. Rev. 443, 467–478. Note that *Tarasoff I* expressed the duty as one "to warn the endangered Tatiana *or those who reasonably could have been expected to notify her* of her peril." *Tarasoff I*, 529 P.2d at 555 (emphasis added). Indeed, the original complaint was not that the doctors did not warn Tatiana, but that they had not warned her parents. *Id.* at 556 n.3.

[6] At a minimum, the *Tarasoff* obligation is being presented to some therapists in training as though it specifically requires warnings. *See, e.g.*, Dean Hepworth et al., *Direct Social Work Practice: Theory & Skills*, 79–80 (5th ed. 1997).

[7] Cal. Civ. Code § 43.92 (West Supp. 2002) (enacted in 1985). Other states have done so as well; *see* Harris, *infra* note 118, at 48.

To appreciate how the Court came to impose this "*Tarasoff* duty," one must understand the factual and procedural settings in which the case reached the Supreme Court. These settings are opaque both in the decision itself and in the torts casebooks that feature the case. We were able to glean them only by examining the briefs in Poddar's criminal case and by contacting lawyers in the case.[8] These facts were highly unusual, even exotic, for a tort dispute. Indeed, we speculate that had the case arisen in a more typical manner, it might have been decided differently; that is, no *Tarasoff* duty would have been imposed. Part I raises this possibility by providing a much richer account of the facts surrounding this dispute than the Court supplied.

In Part II, we extend this contextual account by considering the larger legal and professional milieus in which *Tarasoff* was decided. The then-contemporaneous trend toward expansion of tort liability and the decision's impact on the norms and practices of the mental health profession, we suggest, helped make *Tarasoff* notorious, controversial, and conducive to doctrinal development. Part III analyzes this doctrinal fertility by tracing the *Tarasoff* duty's subsequent career and its legal significance today, using post-*Tarasoff* decisions to show how courts in many jurisdictions have both extended and contracted the *Tarasoff* duty. We conclude by briefly distilling from this history some insights about how judges use the tools of their craft both to guide the development of doctrine and to control the jury, insights that we think are especially serviceable to law teachers and students.

Tarasoff's Exotic Facts

Both Tarasoff and Poddar were born and raised abroad. Tarasoff was born in China to Russian parents and grew up in São Paolo, Brazil before moving with her family to Berkeley, California in 1963, six year before her death. Poddar grew up in a small Bengali village in northern India as a member of the Harijan or "untouchable" caste. Evidently a young man of talent and determination, Poddar managed to surmount severe obstacles of class, caste, and parochialism[9] to graduate from the Indian Institute of Technology in 1961. He came to the U.S. in 1967 to study naval architecture at the University of California.

These achievements could not have been easy for Poddar. First, there was the transition from his humble and despised origins to the

---

[8] Particular thanks to Franklin Brockway Gowdy of Brobeck, Phleger & Harrison in San Francisco, who was Poddar's appellate counsel and who generously provided us with copies of numerous sources—including the briefs of both sides in the criminal case—upon which we have relied heavily.

[9] *See* Appellant's Opening Brief at 2, People v. Poddar, 103 Cal.Rptr. 84 (Cal.Ct.App. 1972) (1/Crim. No. 9547); Respondent's Brief at 3, *Poddar* (1/Crim. No. 9547).

Indian Institute where, according to testimony, his rural table manners, Bengali accent, and Harijan caste isolated him somewhat. In particular, he had little or no contact with women at the Institute, where no dating or other social interchange between the sexes was permitted.[10] The transition from traditional India to the Berkeley campus, whose free-wheeling, liberationist culture in the late 1960s was world-famous, must have been even more wrenching. We shall have more to say about this second transition and its bearing on the *Tarasoff* case.

Tarasoff took at least one class at the university and also spent time at its International House, while attending college in neighboring Oakland. Poddar lived at International House, and they met at a folk dancing party there. According to Poddar, the trouble began when the more liberal, outgoing Tarasoff kissed Poddar at International House on New Year's Eve 1968. Believing that she had some romantic interest in him, Poddar pursued her but she apparently was unresponsive. In January, according to Poddar, he learned that she was having sexual relations with other men. Testimony by his friend from India, Farrokh Mistree, and by others established that his personal habits and research activity began to deteriorate: he was often absent from work and remained in his room for hours on end, listening to tapes that he had made of all of his conversations with Tarasoff as he attempted to understand what he saw as her inconsistent behavior toward him. This continued for several months during which he threatened Mistree, whom he accused of siding with Tanya and of mocking Poddar. In May 1969, Poddar told Mistree that he intended to kill Tanya. When Mistree threatened to report this to the police, Poddar threatened to kill Mistree as well. Poddar discussed with coworkers blowing up Tarasoff's block, then just her house, and finally just her room.

Tarasoff returned to Rio de Janeiro for the summer of 1969, apparently fitting in easily with the culture of her childhood.[11] During her absence, Poddar sought psychotherapeutic counseling at the Cowell Memorial Hospital at Berkeley. On June 5, he saw a psychiatrist on an emergency basis, received medication, and was referred for outpatient treatment with Dr. Moore, a psychologist with whom he then met for seven sessions. Treatment ended on August 20, 1969, when Poddar made the threat against an individual whom therapists could identify as Tarasoff. Moore may have confronted Poddar concerning his threats, and after consulting the psychiatrist who had originally seen Poddar on an

---

[10] *See* People v. Poddar, 103 Cal.Rptr. 84, 88–89 (Cal.Ct.App.1972); Respondent's Brief at 6, *Poddar* (1/Crim. No. 9547); Appellant's Opening Brief at 3, *Poddar* (1/Crim. No. 9547); Appellant's Closing Brief at 6, *Poddar* (1/Crim. No. 9547).

[11] Or so she later told Poddar. *See* Respondent's Brief at 3, 8–9, *Poddar* (1/Crim. No. 9547).

emergency basis, Moore called the campus police and urged them to take steps to commit Poddar to a mental hospital for observation.[12] Moore diagnosed Poddar as suffering from a "paranoid schizophrenic reaction, acute and severe," opining that Poddar "is, at this point, a danger to the welfare of other people and himself." The campus police detained Poddar and searched his rooms, actions from which Poddar evidently inferred that Dr. Moore had communicated Poddar's threat. Poddar seemed rational, however, so they did not implement the commitment request.[13]

Tarasoff returned from Brazil on September 13, 1969, and at this point Poddar's condition worsened. During her absence, he missed classes, meals, and workdays, while spending more time in bed, but he found her return unendurable. Tarasoff recounted her romantic escapades in Brazil and Poddar learned that she was having relations with other men.[14] He looked into purchasing a gun, but also offered one of her former sexual companions $100 to act as an intermediary to procure her sexual favors for him.[15] He said that he would take the gun to the proposed meeting with Tarasoff and 'save' her by pointing out the error of her ways. He began to stalk her, contriving to meet her at bus stops, her college, and the University.[16]

A bizarre twist in this tragedy is that Alex Tarasoff, Tanya's brother, had been living with Poddar for about three months before the killing; they shared an apartment up until the murder took place in October. Indeed, as we shall see, Alex may even have contributed unwittingly and indirectly to her subsequent death. Alex had once answered the phone at the Tarasoff home when Poddar was calling for Tanya; although Alex warned Poddar to "lay off," Poddar—undaunted—asked to meet him. Alex agreed and met Tanya and Poddar at the gas station where Alex worked. At this meeting, Poddar sought to win Alex over to his side. Alex, who apparently understood the cultural gulf between Poddar and Tanya, tried to explain to Poddar why, in the American context, Tanya's behavior was unexceptionable.[17]

The two men had some technical interests in common and became close friends and then roommates—first in International House during

---

[12] *Tarasoff I*, 529 P.2d at 556.

[13] The letter to the police is reprinted in Vanessa Merton, *Confidentiality and the "Dangerous" Patient: Implications of* Tarasoff *for Psychiatrists and Lawyers*, 31 Emory L.J. 263, 289–290 n.57 (1982).

[14] *See* Respondent's Brief at 7, 8–9, *Poddar* (1/Crim. No. 9547); Appellant's Opening Brief at 4, 6, *Poddar* (1/Crim No. 9547).

[15] Appellant's Opening Brief at 6, *Poddar* (1/Crim. No. 9547).

[16] Respondent's Brief at 8–9, *Poddar* (1/Crim. No. 9547).

[17] *Id.* at 3–4.

Tanya's summer 1969 visit to Brazil, and then, beginning in September, in an apartment near Alex's job. Poddar once asked Alex, who tried to discourage Poddar's obsession with Tanya, if Alex's pellet gun could be used to kill a person. When Alex replied that he did not know, Poddar asked where he could purchase a regular gun. Alex said that he did not think an alien was permitted to do so. Although Alex later testified that he did not believe that Poddar meant to kill his sister, Poddar's friendship with Alex enabled Poddar to learn when he would find Tanya alone at her family's home on October 27, 1969, the day of her death. Although some of the details of the killing are unclear, it seems that Poddar argued with her, shot her with a pellet gun, chased her outside to the sidewalk, and stabbed her 17 times with a kitchen knife, the cause of death.

Tanya's death led to a criminal prosecution, one that (like the subsequent tort case) went all the way up to the Supreme Court of California. The criminal proceeding—in which Poddar was convicted of second degree murder—is a key to understanding the tort case for several reasons. First, the criminal trial and appeals unearthed many of the facts that we have just recounted. But of even greater interest is the likelihood that the Supreme Court's familiarity with the facts of the criminal case, particularly Poddar's mental state and the conduct of the therapists and police, affected the tone of the opinion in the tort case as well as the substantive decision. Although the tort case reached the Court only on the pleadings, the justices already knew the facts, which had been revealed in the criminal trial. *Tarasoff I*, upholding the Tarasoff family's tort complaint, was issued only ten months after the Court found the evidence of Poddar's mental illness so compelling that it refused to sustain even a manslaughter conviction unless a jury had an opportunity to consider this evidence under proper instructions. Some of the evidence came from the defendant therapists and campus police who had evaluated Poddar *before* he killed Tarasoff; their testimony in the criminal trial supported the claim that Poddar should not be held legally responsible for Tarasoff's death because of his condition.

In considering the defendants' motion to dismiss in the tort case, therefore, *the Court had no need to speculate about what a reasonable therapist might conclude because it already knew that the treating therapist had in fact concluded that Poddar posed a threat, and that the police and the chain of command at the Cowell clinic knew this.*[18] The Court also knew that once the campus police rejected Dr. Moore's request to commit Poddar, no one lifted a finger to help Tarasoff. It is not much of a stretch, we think, to assume that the justices, who accepted the tort case in September 1973 while Poddar's criminal appeal was still pending

---

[18] In *Tarasoff II*, Justice Mosk concurred with the result only, on the ground that the therapists had in fact predicted Poddar's future violence. *Tarasoff II*, 551 P.2d at 451.

before them,[19] wanted to assign blame for the tragedy that, they had already concluded, the tort defendants helped to cause.

The justices could not fully accomplish this in the criminal case. They reversed Poddar's conviction for second-degree murder and remanded for a new trial. Because of his troubled state of mind, the California Court of Appeal had already reduced his second-degree murder conviction to manslaughter, but the California Supreme Court ruled that even manslaughter might be too harsh under the circumstances. At trial, Poddar had advanced a defense of insanity, offering the testimony of those who had evaluated and treated him at Cowell. The prosecution had depicted him as a "love sick puppy" who did not handle rejection well.[20] The defense, however, hoped to educate the jury about the very different world-view that Poddar had brought with him from India, and to show that his behavior reflected a "diminished capacity" due largely to culture shock, a condition that the defense claimed negated the necessary criminal intent.[21]

To accomplish this, the defense wanted to call as an expert witness a cultural anthropologist who was a professor of international studies.[22] It would ask her to give the jury a crash course in Indian culture. She could explain about Bengali folkways, the caste system and especially the Harijan caste, Indian family life, arranged marriages, and the norms of male-female interactions.[23] She was uniquely qualified, according to the defense, to testify about the adjustment difficulties of Indian students who attended American universities.[24] Since she had interviewed Poddar, she could help the jurors put themselves in his shoes.[25] She would testify "that he was simply unfit to cope with the . . . stress and strain that he found in this country."[26]

---

[19] The Court issued its decision in the criminal case, *People v. Poddar*, 518 P.2d 342 (Cal.1974), on February 7, 1974, and in the tort case (*Tarasoff I*) on December 23.

[20] Appellant's Opening Brief at 11, *Poddar* (1/Crim. No. 9547).

[21] His brief to the Court of Appeal stated: "American jurors don't have an understanding of the nature of male-female relationships in India. They don't know the outlook of a rural Indian boy who is confronting a sophisticated urban culture. They can't appreciate the emotional stress that was engendered by the activities of the victim in this case. Nor can they understand the effects of the kind of rejection that occurred here upon one who was born into the lowest strata of a rigid and invidious caste system." *Id.* at 12.

[22] *Id.* at 9.

[23] Respondent's Brief at 15–16, *Poddar* (1/Crim. No. 9547).

[24] People v. Poddar, 103 Cal.Rptr. 84, 88 (Cal.Ct.App.1972); *see also* Appellant's Opening Brief at 9, *Poddar* (1/Crim. No. 9547).

[25] Appellant's Opening Brief at 10, *Poddar* (1/Crim. No. 9547).

[26] Appellant's Closing Brief at 7, *Poddar* (1/Crim. No. 9547).

The trial court doubted that an anthropologist's testimony could sustain a finding of diminished capacity, but it proposed to allow limited testimony about cross-cultural tension, which defense counsel could then use to question psychiatrists and psychologists about Poddar in particular.[27] The defense rejected the offer, as it did not want to filter the anthropologist's limited testimony through the mental health witnesses.[28] The defense also knew that those witnesses had attributed Poddar's problem to paranoid-schizophrenia, not to cross-cultural stress.[29] The trial court therefore barred the testimony, and the Court of Appeals agreed.[30]

The Supreme Court did not even address this issue. It ordered a retrial—not because the anthropologist's testimony had been excluded but because the trial court had failed to instruct the jury about how diminished capacity might affect the specific intent necessary for a second-degree murder verdict.[31] Poddar, however, was never retried. Instead, the state allowed him to return to India where (according to one commentator, citing no evidence) he married a lawyer and lived an ostensibly normal life.[32]

It seems possible, then, that the California Supreme Court, unable to condemn the therapists' passivity in the criminal case, did so indirectly in the tort case by creating the *Tarasoff* duty and allowing the jury to apply that duty to the university clinicians. The Court in effect lifted some of the burden of criminal responsibility from Poddar's shoulders while imposing a burden of civil responsibility on the clinicians.

Tarasoff's Legal and Professional Contexts

Tort Liability Expansion

These judicial moves were very much creatures of their time. The *Tarasoff* duty, announced in 1976, was part and parcel of a larger liability-expanding effort by the Court and by many other state courts

---

[27] *Poddar*, 103 Cal. Rptr. at 88.

[28] *Id.*

[29] Respondent's Brief at 14, *Poddar* (1/Crim. No. 9547). The government notes that the defense had a day to try to frame hypotheticals for the psychiatrists based upon the anthropologist's proposed testimony, but then "acknowledged" that the information she would provide would not be relevant to the psychiatrists' testimony. *Id.* This helps explain why the anthropologist was important in the first place: she provided an independent opportunity for the jury to view Poddar sympathetically.

[30] *Poddar*, 103 Cal. Rptr. at 88.

[31] *Poddar*, 518 P.2d at 344.

[32] Merton, *supra* note 13, at 290.

that often followed its lead. This effort took a variety of forms. In a 1981 article, the late torts scholar Gary Schwartz detailed how the courts were imposing new legal duties to protect third parties from risks created by others.[33] As Schwartz later noted, the *Tarasoff* court sought to legitimate its expansion of liability by linking its action to the "expanding . . . list of special relationships which will justify" the imposition of affirmative duties of protection.[34]

In an earlier article, one of us identified some other ways in which the courts were expanding tort liability at the time of the *Tarasoff* decision.[35] First, judges at this time were busily enlarging the discretion of civil juries. For example, judges formulated legal duties in ever more general terms, increasing the jury's freedom to interpret and apply those duties as the jury saw fit. Indeed, the Court in *Tarasoff* demonstrated this tendency when it abandoned its specific "duty to warn" standard in *Tarasoff I* in favor of a more flexible "duty of reasonable care" standard in *Tarasoff II*.

Second, judges were extending tort liability to relationships that previously had been largely or exclusively governed by contract law, relationships in which the parties' promises—rather than a jury's determination of reasonableness—defined their duties to one another. Although doctor-patient relationships have long been governed by tort law as well as by contract law, the relationship in *Tarasoff* was built on an especially compelling promissory element: the traditional—and in this case perhaps explicit—assurance of confidentiality by the defendant therapist. Accordingly, the Court's decision to override this solemn promise in favor of a tort duty to protect third parties exemplifies this subordination of contract to tort in a rather dramatic fashion.

In addition to cutting back on contract defenses, judges were also narrowing traditional tort defenses such as assumed risk, prior warning, contributory negligence, misuse, proximate cause, and charitable and other immunities.[36] This trend, which was evident in virtually all areas of tort law, made the *Tarasoff* duty even more expansive than it might initially appear because it strengthened plaintiffs' *prima facie* cases and deprived defendants of the ability to exculpate themselves before trial by showing—in *Tarasoff*, for example—an unheeded warning to the police,

---

[33] Gary T. Schwartz, *The Vitality of Negligence and the Ethics of Strict Liability*, 15 Ga. L. Rev. 963 (1981).

[34] Gary T. Schwartz, *The Beginning and the Possible End of the Rise of Modern American Tort Law*, 26 Ga. L. Rev. 601, 684 (1992), citing *Tarasoff II*, 551 P.2d at 343 n.5.

[35] Peter H. Schuck, *The New Judicial Ideology of Tort Law*, in *New Directions in Liability Law* 4 (Walter Olson ed., 1988).

[36] For some examples, see Schwartz, *supra* note 33, at 964–70.

an extended time period between the threat and the tortious act, or intervening events or supervening relationships (for example, Alex's friendship with Poddar) that might cut off the defendant's causal responsibility.[37]

More generally, tort judges were moving from a conception of tort law concerned with corrective justice in the individual case to a more functional ideal in which judges viewed themselves as risk regulators, cost-benefit analysts, and social problem-solvers rather than as adjudicators of isolated, morally self-contained disputes. This new functionalism not only changed how parties litigated tort cases and how judges and juries rationalized their decisions. It also systematically enlarged the scope of tort liability. Indeed, courts (and most tort scholars) took each of the legal system's policy goals—even administrative efficiency, the Achilles' heel of tort law—as another reason to expand tort responsibility, if not quite moving all the way to strict liability.

Tarasoff's functionalist reasoning, rhetoric, and result exemplified the general trend. This was widely perceived, as evidenced by the swiftness with which the authors of leading torts casebooks added *Tarasoff* to the canon, a prominence that they have accorded it ever since.[38] We examined five leading casebooks that not only include *Tarasoff* as a main case but also present lengthy excerpts from the Court's decision and discuss its implications in the notes following the case.[39] It is surprising, then, that these casebooks present *Tarasoff* out of its factual context. None of them includes even the rather skeletal facts recited in the Court's opinions, much less the exotica that we readily

---

[37] *Tarasoff* provides a compelling example of this phenomenon. The plaintiff had alleged that Moore's supervisor directed him to take no further action with respect to Poddar. Moore urged the court that the complaint ought to be dismissed against him since the plaintiff's complaint acknowledged that he was not free to take any further action. The court noted that because the *plaintiff's* complaint did not give enough specifics about when the order to take no action was given and whether it bound Moore, the court would not grant Moore relief on the pleadings. *Tarasoff II*, 551 P.2d at 442 n.16.

[38] Given *Tarasoff*'s canonicity—and the fact, noted below, that its name is probably as well-known by non-lawyers as any in the canon, see discussion *infra* pp. 114–15,—it is puzzling that the case is not even mentioned in the latest draft of the *Restatement (Third) of Torts, Restatement (Third) of Torts: Liability for Physical Harm (Basic Principles)* (Tentative Draft No. 2, 2002), although it was cited in the *Discussion Draft*, Apr. 5, 1999, at 247. The new Reporter, Professor Michael Green, does not know the reason for this discrepancy.

[39] Dan B. Dobbs & Paul T. Hayden, *Torts and Compensation* (4th ed. 2001); Richard A. Epstein, *Cases and Materials on Torts* (6th ed. 1995); Marc A. Franklin & Robert L. Rabin, *Tort Law and Alternatives* (7th ed. 2001); James A. Henderson, Jr. et al., *The Torts Process* (5th ed. 1999); Victor E. Schwartz et al., *Prosser, Wade and Schwartz's Torts Cases and Materials* (10th ed. 2000).

culled from the official records and presented in Part I,[40] exotica that would fire future lawyers' imaginations about just what happened and why, and how the unusual interaction of the criminal and civil proceedings may have affected the *Tarasoff* judges and juries.

The Mental Health Profession Responds

Tarasoff I unleashed a firestorm of protest in the mental health establishment. The leading organization of psychiatrists, joined by other mental health professions,[41] filed an *amicus* brief seeking a rehearing of the decision. This brief predicted that the ruling would produce dire outcomes—for example, more reluctance among mental health professionals to treat potentially violent patients, less willingness among such patients to seek treatment, and diminished effectiveness in whatever treatment was undertaken. (After all, Poddar himself seems to have avoided treatment after Moore warned the police.) To some mental health professionals, *Tarasoff I* seemed like a cruel joke. Less than a year after the California Supreme Court held in *Tarasoff I* that mental health professionals had a duty to warn whenever they *reasonably should have determined* that a patient might be violent, it ruled in another case that such predictions are inherently unreliable.[42] How, critics wondered, could

---

[40] Of the casebooks we reviewed, only Schwartz mentions Poddar's romantic motivation ("he intended to kill Tatiana Tarasoff because she had spurned Poddar's romantic advances"). Schwartz et al., *supra* note 39, at 429–30. It is also the only one that notes the two-month time lag between the Clinic's decision to take no further action against Poddar and the murder, and it is the only one to describe the violent nature of the attack. *Id.* at 430.

[41] The American Psychiatric Association, joined by local or state branches of psychologists, social workers, and hospitals, filed the brief.

[42] People v. Burnick, 535 P.2d 352, 364–66 (Cal.1975). Ruling that proof beyond a reasonable doubt rather than simply proof by the preponderance of the evidence was required in order to commit someone as a mentally disordered sex offender, the Court stated:

> In the light of recent studies it is no longer heresy to question the reliability of psychiatric predictions. Psychiatrists themselves would be the first to admit that however desirable an infallible crystal ball might be, it is not among the tools of their profession. It must be conceded that psychiatrists still experience considerable difficulty in confidently and accurately *diagnosing* mental illness. Yet those difficulties are multiplied manyfold when psychiatrists venture from diagnosis to prognosis and undertake to predict the consequences of such illness: "A diagnosis of mental illness tells us nothing about whether the person so diagnosed is or is not dangerous. Some mental patients are dangerous, some are not. Perhaps the psychiatrist is an expert at deciding whether a person is mentally ill, but is he an expert at predicting which of the persons so diagnosed are dangerous? Sane people, too, are dangerous, and it may legitimately be inquired whether there is anything in the education, training or experience of psychiatrists which renders them particularly adept at predicting dangerous behavior. Predictions of dangerous behavior, no matter who makes them, are incredibly inaccurate, and there is a growing consensus that psychiatrists are not

a court that discounted the validity of predictions of violence then create a duty triggered by a professional's *reasonable* belief that the patient was likely to be violent?

Anomalies such as these encouraged many in the mental health community to view *Tarasoff* as only the latest example of the law's assault upon their professional autonomy and well-being. This assault came on two fronts. First, the 1970s witnessed the first medical malpractice crisis. Insurers' perception that plaintiffs were increasingly suing health care providers and recovering large judgments led insurers in many jurisdictions to raise their premiums, limit coverage, or cease writing policies altogether. This crisis not only increased the cost of practicing medicine, but also generated fears about the continuing availability and quality of medical care. Many policy analysts feared that health professionals would practice "defensive" (i.e., excessively costly and risk-averse) medicine or withdraw from certain fields of practice altogether. Professional meetings and journals began to discuss these legal developments with alarm, and California, among other states, enacted a statute reforming malpractice law.[43]

The second legal assault on the health professions came in the form of the due process revolution. If psychiatrists were at the periphery of

---

uniquely qualified to predict dangerous behavior and are, in fact, less accurate in their predictions than other professionals."

Id. at 365 (citations omitted).

[43] The malpractice crisis led to legislative attention nationwide. In 1975, the California legislature was convened in extraordinary session by Governor Brown, whose proclamation recalling the legislature said that "[t]he inability of doctors to obtain [medical malpractice] insurance at reasonable rates is endangering the health of the people of this State" and asked the legislature to "enact laws which will change the relationship between the people and the medical profession, the legal profession and the insurance industry" in ways to reduce insurance costs. Proclamation of the Governor, 1975 Cal. Stat. 2d Ex. Sess. 3947 (May 16, 1975). The legislature responded by passing the Medical Injury Compensation Reform Act (MICRA), which was signed by the governor on September 23, 1975. 1975 Cal. Stat. 2d Ex. Sess., 3949, codified as amended in scattered sections of Cal. Bus. & Prof. Code, Cal. Civ. Code, Cal. Civ. Proc. Code, and Cal. Ins. Code. For a discussion of MICRA, see Martin Ramey, Comment, *Putting the Cart Before the Horse: The Need to Re-examine Damage Caps in California's Elder Abuse Act,* 39 San Diego L. Rev. 599, 625–47 (2002) (describing MICRA's history, its recent evolution and plans for further reform), and Jonathan J. Lewis, Recent Developments, *Putting MICRA Under the Microscope: The Case for Repealing California Civil Code Section 3333.1(a),* W. St. U. L. Rev. 173 (2001).

The malpractice insurance crisis was not limited to California: also in 1975, for instance, in order to ensure that medical care remained available to the general public, Louisiana enacted its "Medical Malpractice Act," which imposed a $100,000 cap on recovery for any single plaintiff, and mandated a medical review panel before a case could go to court. This law later intersected with *Tarasoff* when it became important to decide whether or not a physician's failure to protect third parties was "malpractice" or not. *See* Hutchinson v. Patel, 637 So.2d 415, 419 (La.1994) (a failure to protect a third party is *not* malpractice, and therefore not protected by the cap on damages).

the malpractice crisis (as opposed to obstetricians, for example), they were at the heart of the legal movement to change the coercive treatment of the mentally ill. Lawyers "discovered" the institutionalized mentally ill during the 1960s, and attacked both the standards leading to commitment and the quality of post-commitment care.[44] For decades psychiatrists had been treated as valued partners in the social response to criminality and aberrant behavior. Now, they found themselves cast as villains, not heroes. In criminal law, the rehabilitative ideal—the belief that punishment for criminal conduct should aim to rehabilitate the criminal through treatment or otherwise—was vigorously challenged during the 1970s as much research cast doubt on the efficacy of rehabilitation and as concern grew about the abuses committed in its name.[45] The law increasingly demanded that the institutionalized mentally ill be either treated or released,[46] yet rendering such treatment grew more difficult. The courts required due process hearings to justify both an initial commitment and continued involuntary detention,[47] and gave detainees the right to resist forcible medication administered under the guise of treatment.[48] Courts and legislatures, with possibly tragic consequences for those like Tanya, required more exacting procedures for emergency involuntary commitment.[49]

The psychiatrists' *amicus* brief apparently[50] did its work; the California Supreme Court agreed to rehear *Tarasoff*. However, the revised

[44] Ralph Reisner et al., *Law and the Mental Health Profession* 639 (3d ed. 1999). The authors note: "In the early 1970s, the pendulum swung again. Influenced by the civil rights movement of the 1960s, by exposés of poor hospital conditions and commitment abuses, and by a growing distrust of psychiatric expertise and the medical model of mental illness upon which it is based, groups of lawyers, mental health professionals and patients successfully exerted pressure for legal reform."
Id.

[45] Andrew Von Hirsh, *Doing Justice* 11–18 (1976). By the mid–1980s, spurred by this movement, the federal sentencing guidelines rejected rehabilitation as a justification for criminal sentencing. 28 U.S.C.A. § 994 (West 1993 & Supp. 2002).

[46] O'Connor v. Donaldson, 422 U.S. 563 (1975).

[47] *See, e.g.*, Fasulo v. Arafeh, 378 A.2d 553 (Conn.1977).

[48] *See, e.g.*, Rogers v. Okin, 634 F.2d 650 (1st Cir.1980).

[49] Lessard v. Schmidt, 349 F.Supp. 1078 (E.D.Wis.1972) (Wisconsin civil commitment procedures invalid for not providing enough substantive and procedural rights to those committed); Lanterman–Petris–Short Act, Cal. Welf. & Inst. Code §§ 5000–5500 (West 1998 & Supp. 2002) (enacted in 1967 "[t]o protect mentally disordered person" and guarantee them and the public appropriate and fair treatment; *see id.* § 5001). One observer noted that contacting the police but not Tanya or her family appeared to be what California law concerning confidentiality required. Merton, *supra* note 13, at 293.

[50] We use "apparently" advisedly. While *Tarasoff* is famous for what it said about tort duties generally and about mental professionals particularly, the major substantive change

opinion, *Tarasoff II*, brought little comfort to the mental health community. While the Court substituted a general duty to exercise reasonable care to protect the third party victim for a specific duty to warn, it rejected fears that this duty placed therapists in an untenable ethical and therapeutic position. The Court did not think that this exception to confidentiality would hamper the treatment of the potentially violent by compromising the therapy or discouraging the patient from either seeking therapy or revealing violent thoughts to the therapist. The Court also dismissed the claim that grounding therapists' liability on something as unreliable as their ability to predict violence was unwise and unjust, replying that therapists need only follow the standards of their profession in predicting violence. The Court seemed confident that such standards existed.

The Court based the therapist's duty to protect those threatened by the patient on his or her relationship with the patient. This idea made more sense as an exercise in formalist legal reasoning than as effective social policy. Assuming (as the Court did) that the therapeutic relationship is vital and can help people deal effectively with violent feelings, it might have been more prudent for the potential victim to be warned by a police officer, bartender, or other person with no on-going, confidential, and therapeutic relationship with the dangerous person. If there are powerful policy arguments against holding the police liable, the Court did not address them. Instead, it simply observed that the mental health defendants had a therapeutic relationship with Poddar, while the police did not. It did not address the possibility that this fact might cut precisely the other way in terms of who should bear liability.

Tarasoff's stark facts probably overwhelmed the nuanced legal and policy arguments that the professionals advanced against creating the new duty. Whether or not professional standards for assessing dangerousness existed, the Cowell clinicians had in fact concluded that Poddar was sufficiently dangerous to warrant commitment. This must have emboldened the Court to think that such standards are possible, particularly when the subsequent events in the case before it actually bore out their predictions. Whatever the deleterious effects of breaching therapeutic confidentiality, moreover, Dr. Moore had already breached it when he asked the campus police to detain Poddar. The California Supreme Court noted that neither the statutory protection for confidentiality in therapy nor codes of medical ethics prohibited the disclosure of confidential

---

wrought by *Tarasoff II* involved the liability of the campus police for failing to warn Tarasoff. *Tarasoff I* had upheld the complaint against the campus police on this score but *Tarasoff II* dismissed it. 551 P.2d at 349 n.18. Although this issue received almost no discussion in the majority opinion in either *Tarasoff* decision, the grant of rehearing may have been motivated in part by the Court's desire to address this issue.

information when such disclosure is necessary to protect another.[51] On the other hand, nothing in the then existing law or in medical ethics *required* that disclosure. Although it may often be desirable for the law to encourage the mental health profession to develop its own ethical and behavioral norms for treating situations like *Tarasoff* and then encourage judicial deference to those norms, the professionals in *Tarasoff* apparently operated under these norms but nevertheless handled Poddar's violent threat in a fatally incomplete manner. The Court balanced the abstract possibility that bad results *might occur* in the future if therapists felt compelled to disclose, against the reality of what *did in fact happen* to Tanya when the decision about disclosure had been left to the discretion of therapists. It opted for a rule designed to prevent the concrete harm it knew about and to discount the theoretical harm that its new rule might produce.

Indeed, the *Tarasoff* facts may have signaled more than a single instance of professional nonfeasance. The psychologist and psychiatrist in *Tarasoff* were genuinely concerned about Poddar's potential violence yet they retreated from the scene entirely once the campus police declined to detain him. The *Tarasoff* complaint alleged that the head of the clinic directed that no action be taken to detain Poddar. We speculate that this demand was motivated by the clinic's concern about Poddar's legal rights and its own potential liability for infringing those rights.[52] If professionals as sophisticated as those who dealt with Poddar were uncertain about how to balance the safety and privacy interests, perhaps the court could help to provide some guidance. The *Tarasoff* decision did succeed in clarifying what had previously been uncertain: the therapists' overarching duty was to the identifiable victim's safety, not to the patient's privacy.

The profession, as noted earlier, initially responded to *Tarasoff* with alarm.[53] A quarter of a century later, we know that the alarmists were wrong. *Tarasoff* has been woven into clinical practice and has become a professional standard of practice among providers. We know of no evidence that it has adversely affected the practice of psychotherapy,[54]

---

[51] *Tarasoff II*, 551 P.2d at 346–47.

[52] The defendants claimed that the recently revised California mental health statute provisions (Lanterman–Petris–Short Act, *supra* note 49, § 5328–5328.9) relating to the release of confidential information about a patient prohibited them from warning Tarasoff. While the court, over Justice Clark's dissent, rejected this position, it is certainly possible that this is what those in charge of the Cowell clinic believed and may have been an explanation for the failure to advise Tarasoff of Poddar's threats. *Tarasoff II*, 551 P.2d at 348–49.

[53] Alan Stone, *The* Tarasoff *Decisions: Suing Psychotherapists to Safeguard Society*, 90 Harv. L. Rev. 358 (1976).

[54] It has affected the practice of psychotherapy somewhat. *See* D.L. Rosenhan et al., *Warning Third Parties: The Ripple Effects of* Tarasoff, 24 Pac. L.J. 1165 (1993); Toni Wise,

led to a diminution in the availability of treatment for the potentially dangerous, caused an increase in the rate of involuntary commitments, or generated an increase in violence among those who do not seek treatment because of concerns about confidentiality.[55]

Few if any tort decisions are as well known outside the legal community as *Tarasoff*. It has remarkably high "name recognition" within the therapeutic community. Surveys of California psychiatrists and psychologists conducted within ten years after the decision revealed that somewhere between 85 and 95% of respondents knew the name of the case.[56] Nor was this simply local knowledge: nearly nine out of ten psychiatrists *outside* California had heard of *Tarasoff*, as had more than half of the psychologists.[57] Enter "Tarasoff & warn" into the search engine Google.com, and more than1500 web sites containing these words appear. Just the name "Tarasoff" yields 5980 hits; by contrast, entering "Palsgraf" yields only 1660.[58] Psychiatric textbooks discuss *Tarasoff* by name, clarifying that most practitioners nationwide have *Tarasoff* duties to protect, not just to warn.[59]

Therapists appear to be more familiar with the case name *Tarasoff* and the idea that one must warn a potential victim than they are with

---

Where the Public Peril Begins: A Survey of Psychotherapists to Determine the Effects of Tarasoff, 31 Stan. L. Rev. 165, 187–189 (1978). Rosenhan et al. summarize the effects they found as follows:

> As a result of *Tarasoff*, therapists (1) are more inclined to discuss dangerousness with their patients, (2) focus more often on their patients' less serious threats, (3) are more inclined to consult with other professionals when involved with potentially dangerous patients, and (4) have changed the manner in which they keep their records.

Rosenhan et al., *supra*, at 1224. Assuming that each effect exists and can be attributed to *Tarasoff*, it is hard to see that these are bad as opposed to salutary or neutral outcomes. At an absolute minimum, these effects bear no resemblance to the Armageddon predicted by the amicus brief.

[55] Givelber et al., *supra* note 5, at 472–83.

[56] *Id.* at 459 (Table I); Rosenhan et al., *supra* note 54, at 1202.

[57] Givelber et al., *supra* note 5, at 459 (Table I). Even in foreign jurisdictions, practitioners have felt the impact of *Tarasoff. See, e.g.,* Thomas Hadjistavropoulos & David C. Malloy, *Making Ethical Choices: A Comprehensive Decision–Making Model for Canadian Psychologists,* 41 Canadian Psychol. 104 (2000) (using *Tarasoff* throughout the article as a "familiar example" in outlining the authors' framework for psychologists in Canada to resolve ethical dilemmas).

[58] Search conducted on February 3, 2003.

[59] Texts used by psychiatry students pay careful attention to *Tarasoff. See, e.g.,* 2 Benjamin J. Sadock & Virginia A. Sadock, *Kaplan and Sadock's Comprehensive Textbook of Psychiatry* 3297–98 (7th ed. 2000) (giving students an overview of *Tarasoff I and II,* though with incorrect dates); Julie A. Rand & Constance J. McKee, *Legal Issues in Psychiatry, in Clinical Psychiatry for Medical Students* 882, 891 (Alan Stoudemire ed., 3d ed. 1998).

the actual holding of the case or, for that matter, with the law that currently regulates their behavior when they confront a patient making a credible threat of harm to another. A national survey conducted in 1980 found that therapists both within and without California were far more likely to believe that *Tarasoff* required warning a potential victim (*Tarasoff I*'s holding) than that it required reasonable care (*Tarasoff II*).[60] Indeed, such is the grip of *Tarasoff I* on the therapeutic imagination that 65% of California therapists responding to a 1987 survey believed that a statute enacted in order to make the *Tarasoff* duty more precise requires them to warn the victim of a credible threat.[61] Only 30% of the respondents understood that the statute actually requires them to warn both the police and the victim.[62] Therapists learned about *Tarasoff* not from lawyers or judges but from professional associations and publications,[63] which emphasized warnings.

Therapists now warn potential victims when their patients utter credible threats, and the percentage of therapists who did so doubled after the *Tarasoff* decisions.[64] Interestingly, the respondents to the various surveys conducted after *Tarasoff* indicated their belief that such behavior was required as a matter of personal and professional ethics,[65] an ethical insight absent from both the profession's *amicus* brief in *Tarasoff* and the discussions of the case in the professional literature.[66] Perhaps personal and professional ethics together would have led most therapists to act to protect potential victims, if not Tanya herself, prior to *Tarasoff*; but nothing in the litigation indicated that this was so.

So far as one can tell, *Tarasoff*'s mandated breach of confidentiality in the face of a credible threat has not proved to have the deleterious effects that many predicted.[67] Instead, many therapists routinely discuss the limits on confidentiality at the outset of treatment while others

[60] Givelber et al., *supra* note 5, at 468 (Table VI–B).

[61] Rosenhan et al., *supra* note 54, at 1205–1206.

[62] *Id.* at 1205–06; Cal. Civ. Code § 43.92 (West Supp. 2002).

[63] Givelber et al., *supra* note 5, at 459 (Table II).

[64] Rosenhan et al., *supra* note 54, at 1217. The pre-*Tarasoff* figure was 16.7%; post-*Tarasoff* it was 39%.

[65] Givelber et al., *supra* note 5, at 474–475 (Tables IX–A, IX–B); Fillmore Buckner & Marvin Firestone, *"Where the Public Peril Begins": 25 Years After* Tarasoff, 21 J. Legal Med. 187, 219 (2000).

[66] A study conducted within a year of *Tarasoff II* found that a "substantial percentage" of California respondents had warned potential victims even before *Tarasoff I* and noted that "the duty to warn, as an ethical or professional, if not a legal matter, therefore may not be so foreign to therapists as the amici had argued." Wise, *supra* note 54, at 183–84.

[67] Buckner and Firestone, *supra* note 65, at 219–20.

discuss these limits when the situation appears to call for it.[68] Clinical advice about how to deal with this issue abounds.[69] Interestingly, the therapeutic community appears to have integrated the *Tarasoff* exception to confidentiality into their practice, while courts continue to struggle with how to integrate the tort duty to protect third parties with the evidentiary privilege to exclude testimony about therapeutic communications. For example, two federal circuit courts recently came to opposite conclusions about whether a therapist is free to testify in court about a threatening statement made by a patient against a third party. According to the Tenth Circuit, once a therapist has issued a warning pursuant to *Tarasoff*, she can be compelled to testify in court about the patient's threat. In contrast, the Sixth Circuit ruled that even when an appropriate *Tarasoff* warning is given, the patient retains the privilege and can prevent the therapist from testifying about the therapeutic communication.[70]

Predicting future violence—the foresight that triggers the *Tarasoff* duty—remains the decision's most contested feature. Therapists continue to emphasize their limited ability to anticipate when someone will act upon a threat, and the evidence on just how accurate those predictions are is mixed. The 1987 survey of California therapists found that two-thirds of the respondents believed that their ability to predict future dangerousness was no better than chance whereas one third thought that they could perform this task somewhere between "somewhat" and "very accurately."[71] As noted, some researchers have suggested that *Tarasoff*'s requirement that therapists do what many insist they are not competent to do leads some of them to overreact to threats, focus too intensely upon possible violence, ignore other therapeutic issues, and avoid treating patients who might possibly be violent.[72]

As a legal matter, of course, *Tarasoff* does not require a therapist to predict accurately. It only demands that he or she act "reasonably" under existing professional standards. Therapists believe that such standards exist. When asked whether respected professional colleagues would *agree* with their prognosis in the most recent case in which they dealt

---

[68] Rosenhan et al., *supra* note 54, at 1211–16.

[69] *See, e.g., The Potentially Violent Patient and the* Tarasoff *Decision in Psychiatric Practice* (James C. Beck ed., 1985).

[70] United States v. Hayes, 227 F.3d 578 (6th Cir.2000); United States v. Glass, 133 F.3d 1356 (10th Cir.1998). For an examination and explanation of the cases, see Note, *Evidence—Sixth Circuit Holds That* Tarasoff *Disclosures Do Not Vitiate Psychotherapist–Patient Privilege—United States v. Hayes*, 114 Harv. L. Rev. 2194 (2001).

[71] Rosenhan et al., *supra* note 54, at 1207–09.

[72] *Id.* at 1206–10. For a somewhat different view of some of these issues, see Givelber et al., *supra* note 5, at 479–83.

with a dangerous patient, the vast majority of therapists responded that between 90 and 100% would agree. Tort law defers to the standards of learned professions without inquiring into the validity of those standards. Tort law, then, provides standards against which a therapist's prediction of future violence can be measured. Are these standards valid? Research indicates that therapists can predict future violence with greater than random accuracy, albeit far from perfectly.[73] Perhaps more significantly, "[v]iolence risk assessment is a critical and expanding part of the practice of mental health law in the United States."[74] The evidence contradicts the claim by some mental health professionals that they have nothing to contribute to violence risk assessment.

In the end, whether *Tarasoff* has had a salutary impact on mental health practice turns upon an assessment of the importance of responding to potentially violent out-patients. Whatever else may be said about the *Tarasoff* decision, it focused attention on this problem and has generated apparently sound clinical approaches to it. Concentrating on potential dangerousness may produce clinically awkward interventions or may blind therapists to other compelling therapeutic issues. The changes wrought by *Tarasoff* have their costs. Still, social policymaking requires the weighing of those costs against the benefits. Whether or not the California Supreme Court was the appropriate policymaking forum, it now appears that Justice Tobriner may have been correct in opining that "the protective privilege ends where the public peril begins."[75]

Post–Tarasoff Doctrinal Development

As anyone trying to shepardize *Tarasoff* quickly learns, it has been a subject of comment in nearly every jurisdiction, including the courts of all but four states. The decision has been cited well over 1,000 times in legal writing, including in about 600 cases.[76] In the more than quarter-century since the decision came down, courts have reshaped the *Tarasoff* duty, sometimes expanding and sometimes limiting it. To understand

---

[73] John Monahan, *Violence Risk Assessment: Scientific Validity and Evidentiary Admissibility*, 57 Wash. & Lee L. Rev. 901 (2000) (comprehensively reviewing and evaluating empirical research concerning clinicians' ability to predict violence in outpatient settings).

[74] *Id.*

[75] *Tarasoff II*, 551 P.2d at 347.

[76] Shepardizing *Tarasoff* online yields 1,305 citing references, including 606 cases; the remaining citations are to other legal sources including A.L.R. annotations, statutes, and law review articles. The other citator, Westlaw's KeyCite, returns 1,610 citations, including Restatements, treatises, and administrative materials. These results were found by running online searches on February 3, 2003; the number of citations will only increase. The four states which have not addressed *Tarasoff* as yet are Arkansas, North Dakota, Rhode Island, and West Virginia.

this evolution, we have examined a small subset of these cases with five specific and related questions in mind. To which types of defendants (other than mental health professionals) have subsequent courts extended the duty? Have courts defined the duty differently than *Tarasoff* did (i.e., in terms of general reasonableness)? How attenuated are the chains of causality that the courts have allowed juries to ascribe to defendants? How have the courts defined the nature, quality, and cost of the risk information available to defendants that may suffice to trigger the *Tarasoff* duty? Which legal doctrines have the courts developed to limit the potential liability of defendants under the duty? We call these the questions of defendant type, definition of duty, proximate cause, risk information, and defenses.

Defendant Type

A common link in cases finding a duty to protect third parties is the existence of a "special relationship" between the defendant and either the person causing the harm or the victim of the harm. This is consistent with the *Second Restatement*, which asserts that such a special relationship is the *only* justification for imposing such a duty.[77] When no such relationship exists, courts typically will not impose a duty—and will dismiss the case at the threshold.[78] In *Tarasoff* and most of its progeny, this special relationship has been one between a psychotherapist and his patient,[79] but it has also been found in a variety of other professional settings. This is hardly surprising given *Tarasoff*'s own facts and the California Supreme Court's focus in *Tarasoff* on the law surrounding the therapeutic relationship. In several cases, the defendant has been a residential facility of one type or another: for the mentally impaired,[80] for

---

[77] *Restatement (Second) of Torts* § 315 (1965).

[78] *See, e.g.*, Sellers v. United States, 870 F.2d 1098 (6th Cir.1989) (no special relationship between a psychiatrist and a voluntary patient giving rise to a duty to confine); Clarke v. Hoek, 219 Cal.Rptr. 845 (Cal.Ct.App.1985) (a physician observing a negligently performed operation had no special relationship with the patient which would impose a duty to intervene).

[79] *See, e.g.*, Rivera v. New York City Health & Hosps. Corp., 191 F.Supp.2d 412 (S.D.N.Y.2002) (psychotherapists treating a homeless man, who knew that he was homeless and without a social safety net to help prevent predictable violence, owed a duty of care to the general public); Evans v. United States, 883 F.Supp. 124 (S.D.Miss.1995) (statute prevented a psychotherapist treating a Vietnam War veteran suffering emotional and psychological problems from disclosing information to the patient's family); Currie v. United States, 644 F.Supp. 1074 (M.D.N.C.1986) (creating a "psychotherapist judgment rule" in a case where a psychotherapist had an ongoing outpatient relationship with a worker harboring violent thoughts towards his colleagues).

[80] *See, e.g.*, Shively v. Ken Crest Ctr. for Exceptional Persons, 2001 WL 209910 (Del.Super.Ct. Jan.26, 2001) (residential facility for the mentally impaired has duty to protect the public from residents' foreseeable harm).

disturbed and ungovernable children,[81] or simply for the homeless.[82]

Some of the cases, however, involve defendants in the health care industry who are not mental health providers. Closest to the classic *Tarasoff* defendant categories was a medical doctor engaged in prescribing medication.[83] Like the suit against the homeless shelter, many *Tarasoff* claims have been asserted against defendants who are in no way part of the health care sector. For example, a sexual predator's family members were sued for failing to warn his new girlfriend or her eight year-old son about his past.[84] Of perhaps greatest interest to many of our readers, a growing number of lawyers have been sued under a *Tarasoff* theory.[85]

Other types of defendants have included a long-term residential care facility sued by nurses' husbands for breaching its duty of care to the husbands by not adequately preventing the spread of diseases brought home by the nurses,[86] an out-of-state diocese sued for failing to warn victims of a priest's sexual tendencies,[87] a landlord sued by third parties for failing to protect them from tenants who assaulted the passerby,[88] the U.S. government, sued by auto accident victims injured by a soldier whose vision was known to the government to be poor,[89] a television talk

---

[81] *See* Nova Univ. v. Wagner, 491 So.2d 1116 (Fla.1986) (center for disturbed children has a duty to protect the public from children's foreseeable harm, after two residents killed a four year old boy and maimed his six year old sister).

[82] *See Rivera*, 191 F.Supp.2d 412 (homeless shelters may have a duty to third parties imposed upon them depending on the circumstances, but declining to impose such duty in this case).

[83] McKenzie v. Hawai'i Permanente Med. Group, Inc., 47 P.3d 1209 (Haw.2002) (doctors have duty to third parties to warn patients about the effects of medication, but not to prescribe only safe medications). *See infra* notes 97–98 and accompanying text for an examination of this decision.

[84] Eric J. v. Betty M., 90 Cal.Rptr.2d 549 (Cal.Ct.App.1999). In this case, the recidivist molester sexually assaulted the young boy on numerous occasions—many of them in the homes of the offender's family. The Court did not, however, impose a duty on the family, which had hoped—and had reason to believe—that he had repented and reformed.

[85] *See infra* notes 100–102 and accompanying text.

[86] Bolieu v. Sisters of Providence in Wash., 953 P.2d 1233 (Alaska 1998) (imposing duty).

[87] Tercero v. Roman Catholic Diocese, 48 P.3d 50 (N.M.2002) (no duty because New Mexico's long-arm statute did not provide for in personam jurisdiction).

[88] Spencer v. Nesto, 764 A.2d 224 (Conn.Super.Ct.2000) (no duty when not foreseeable that tenants would harm third party).

[89] Basaloco–Lapo v. United States, 1991 WL 172381 (9th Cir.1991) (citing *Tarasoff* to show that the government had no duty because its doctor was in no position to control the soldier's behavior).

show, sued by the estate of a man who was murdered by a male friend
after the taping of a TV show in which the deceased disclosed his sexual
interest in the friend,[90] and even classmates of students who were killed
in a school shooting tragedy, sued because they did not warn about the
attacker's previous behavior.[91]

Definition of Duty

Some post-*Tarasoff* decisions expressly rejected any *Tarasoff* duty,
even for psychiatrists,[92] and most of those that do recognize such a duty
define it simply as a general duty of reasonable care in the protection of
third parties at risk.[93] A few decisions, however, have defined the duty in
more specific ways than *Tarasoff* did. In one case, for example, the court
imposed a duty on psychotherapists to commit a patient whom the
therapist reasonably foresees will endanger any potential victim even
(indeed, especially) where that victim is not readily identifiable.[94] In
Brady v. Hopper,[95] the psychiatrist of John Hinkley was sued by others

---

[90] Graves v. Warner Bros., 656 N.W.2d 195 (Mich.Ct.App.2002) (reversing jury judgment and award of nearly $30 million because defendant had no duty to anticipate and prevent the attack, which took place three days after the taping). *See* Margaret Cronin Fisk, *$29 Million 'Jenny Jones' Award Erased*, Nat'l L.J., Oct. 28, 2002, at A4.

[91] James v. Wilson, 95 S.W.3d 875 (Ky.Ct.App.2002) (classmates had no duty to warn others about potential attack by other student). The Court said, "[T]here is no legal duty to report the commission of a crime by another, let alone the possibility of a crime being committed by another." *Id.* at 889.

[92] *See, e.g.*, Gregory v. Kilbride, 565 S.E.2d 685, 692 (N.C.Ct.App.2002) ("North Carolina does not recognize a psychiatrist's *duty to warn* third parties.") (emphasis in original).

[93] *See, e.g.*, Hamman v. County of Maricopa, 775 P.2d 1122, 1128 (Ariz.1989) ("duty to exercise reasonable care to protect the *foreseeable victim* of [a] danger") (emphasis in original); Naidu v. Laird, 539 A.2d 1064, 1072 (Del.1988) ("affirmative duty to persons other than the patient to exercise reasonable care in the treatment and discharge of psychiatric patients"); HaseneI v. United States, 541 F.Supp. 999, 1012 n. 24 (D.Md.1982) ("reasonable action to prevent any harm to [readily identifiable] victims").

[94] Currie v. United States, 644 F.Supp. 1074 (M.D.N.C.1986) In *Currie*, the federal court was purporting to apply North Carolina law—which *Gregory*, 565 S.E.2d 685, found to reject such a duty. In *Currie*, the Court held that while there is a duty to commit when there is any foreseeable potential victim, liability will only be imposed if the psychotherapist's failure to commit was not in "good faith." Creatively borrowing from corporate law's "business judgment rule," it crafted this liability limitation as the "psychotherapist judgment rule." *Currie*, 644 F.Supp. at 1083. The apparent conflict between *Gregory* and *Currie* is partially answered by the fact that *Currie* was a federal court's attempt to apply North Carolina law although that state "ha[d] not directly considered the issue" by the time *Currie* was resolved. *Id.* at 1077. Sixteen years later, in *Gregory*, a state appeals court simply ignored *Currie* in declaring that "North Carolina does not recognize a psychiatrist's *duty to warn* third persons." *Gregory*, 565 S.E.2d at 692 (emphasis in original). Indeed, *no* North Carolina court has *ever* cited to *Currie*.

[95] 570 F.Supp. 1333 (D.Colo.1983).

injured in the assassination attempt on President Reagan. The court held that a duty could not be imposed unless a "specific threat" of violence was directed toward "identifiable victims."[96]

In another very recent decision involving a physician who allegedly prescribed medication without warning the patient that it might cause drowsiness that could affect his driving, the Hawaii Supreme Court imposed a duty on the physician, for the benefit of third parties, to warn the patient about the danger this side-effect might pose to those third parties. The court, however, rejected a second duty asserted by the plaintiffs—namely, that the doctor's duty to third parties should also include the duty to refrain from prescribing negligently. The court recognized that because "a physician already owes a duty to his or her patient under existing tort law to warn the patient of such a potential adverse effect[, the] imposition of a duty for the benefit of third parties is not likely to require significant changes in prescribing behavior."[97] But the court feared that allowing the third party to sue the physician directly would alter the physician's prescribing behavior, potentially discouraging physicians from prescribing what might actually be in their *patients'* best interests.[98] A *Tarasoff* duty for the benefit of—but not directly to—at-risk third parties has also been imposed on physicians in other cases.[99]

Some courts, sometimes without mentioning *Tarasoff* explicitly, have recognized a more specific *Tarasoff I*-type duty to warn possible victims under certain circumstances. Several of these suits were brought against criminal lawyers who knew of their clients' dangerous propensi-

---

[96] *Id.* at 1338.

[97] McKenzie v. Hawai'i Permanente Med. Group, Inc., 47 P.3d 1209, 1219 (Haw.2002).

[98] *Id.* at 1216. In so ruling, the court considered and rejected several cases that had refused, under similar circumstances, to impose a duty upon a doctor for the benefit of non-patient third parties. Some of those decisions had simply rejected the duty rationales. *See, e.g.*, Conboy v. Mogeloff, 567 N.Y.S.2d 960 (N.Y.App.Div.1991) (because he did not have the authority to control his patient, a physician who incorrectly told a mother that she could drive after taking sedatives did not owe a duty to her children, who were passengers when she lost consciousness and had an accident); Werner v. Varner, Stafford & Seaman, P.A., 659 So.2d 1308 (Fla.Dist.Ct.App.1995) (when a physician failed to warn against driving when prescribing anti-epileptic drugs, there was no duty to a victim who was not readily identifiable as required by Florida law).

[99] *See, e.g.*, Reisner v. Regents of Univ. of Cal., 37 Cal.Rptr.2d 518 (Cal.Ct.App.1995) (physician had a duty to patient's boyfriend to warn patient of her HIV-positive status, because she would have warned her boyfriend and prevented his infection); Pate v. Threlkel, 661 So.2d 278 (Fla.1995) (physicians diagnosing genetically transferable diseases may have a duty to patient's children, dischargeable by warning the patient herself); Tenuto v. Lederle Labs., 687 N.E.2d 1300 (N.Y.1997) (doctor owed duty to father to warn that he could contract polio if his newly-immunized baby's excrement came into contact with an open wound).

ties but failed to warn endangered third parties. In one, the court reluctantly accepted in principle a duty to warn where the client firmly intended to inflict serious personal injuries on an unknowing third person, but the court declined to apply this duty to a victim (the client's mother) who already knew about the danger.[100] In another, the court imposed a duty on the lawyer to warn a judge who the lawyer knew was unaware of the risk of personal harm from the lawyer's client.[101] A third case raised the *Tarasoff* duty issue in a more unusual context. A lawyer representing a violent patient who was seeking release from a mental hospital mentioned *Tarasoff* obliquely in open court in an effort to signal to the judge that the lawyer considered his client dangerous, thereby discharging (so the lawyer hoped) his *Tarasoff* duty. When the judge denied the patient's release, the patient appealed and filed a *habeas corpus* petition, arguing that the lawyer's mention of *Tarasoff* in effect disadvantaged his own client, constituting "a constructive denial of counsel" that justified reversal. The appellate court rejected this argument because the lawyer's mention of *Tarasoff* had not in fact affected the trial judge's decision.[102]

Some versions of the *Tarasoff* duty on lawyers are more demanding than the ethical rules that the legal profession imposes on itself. Rule 1.6(b)(1) of the American Bar Association's Model Rules of Professional Conduct permits lawyers to reveal information they reasonably believe necessary "to prevent the client from committing a criminal act that the lawyer believes is likely to result in imminent death or substantial bodily harm." The fact that the Rule permits lawyers to protect third parties from their clients but does not require them to do so *even in the case of imminent death* suggests the persistence in the legal community, more than 25 years after *Tarasoff*, of a claim of immunity from a duty of protection that other professionals, also bound by confidentiality norms, must bear.[103]

[100] Hawkins v. King County Dep't of Rehabilitative Servs., 602 P.2d 361 (Wash.Ct.App. 1979). For liability being limited because the plaintiff already knew about the threat, see also *Matter of Votteler's Estate,* 327 N.W.2d 759, 761–62 (Iowa 1982), in which the plaintiff was run over by a psychiatrist's patient, but no duty was imposed since the plaintiff *did* know of the threat.

[101] State v. Hansen, 862 P.2d 117 (Wash.1993).

[102] People v. Hopkins, 2002 WL 44251 (Cal.Ct.App.2002).

[103] At least one commentator seeks to justify the difference in duty between attorneys and psychotherapists. See Marc L. Sands, *The Attorney's Affirmative Duty to Warn Foreseeable Victims of a Client's Intended Violent Assault,* 21 Tort & Ins. L.J. 355 (1986). See also Alan Kirtley, *The Mediation Privilege's Transition from Theory to Implementation: Designing a Mediation Privilege Standard to Protect Mediation Participants, the Process and the Public Interest,* 1995 J. Disp. Resol. 1, 48.

Proximate Cause

As a matter of traditional proximate cause doctrine, the ten weeks separating the defendant's knowledge of the danger to Tanya and her death is a relatively long period of time. During the interval between the threat and the harm, many other events intervened as a factual matter and perhaps supervened as a legal matter. These intervening events— the involvement of the campus police, the meetings and communications between Poddar and Tanya, Alex's relationship to both of them and his own opportunities to warn Tanya, and the near certainty that Tanya and her family already knew of the danger well before the killing—affected the nature and magnitude of the risk that Poddar posed and the distribution of causal responsibility for Tanya's death. Because the case never went to trial after the *Tarasoff II* remand,[104] neither the court nor the jury had occasion to address the proximate cause issue. Yet courts have been reluctant to allow defendants—including in cases where the intervals are far greater than the ten weeks in *Tarasoff*—to escape liability for lack of proximate cause.

In some cases, the court adjudicates only the question of whether a *Tarasoff* duty exists without going on to discuss proximate cause.[105] In still others, the court, having determined the existence of a *Tarasoff* duty, will allow the jury to resolve the causal issues rather than to decide them as a matter of law.[106] Even so, the chain of events in some post-*Tarasoff* cases is sufficiently attenuated that difficult proximate cause issues are raised. In one case involving a doctor's failure to warn a patient of her HIV-positive status, years elapsed between the doctor's knowledge and the third party's infection.[107] In another recent case, a patient received four units of HIV-contaminated blood during surgery five years before her marriage, which led to the death of her and her child. The defendant hospital was under a *Tarasoff* duty to her husband, who was "within the class of identifiable third persons at risk."[108] In *Naidu v. Laird*,[109] the temporal sequence extended over five and a half

---

[104] According to the Tarasoff family's lawyer, the case was settled "within the range for wrongful death of a college girl." Merton, *supra* note 13, at 295.

[105] *See, e.g.*, Hamman v. County of Maricopa, 775 P.2d 1122 (Ariz.1989) (reversing summary judgment in favor of psychiatrist and imposing duty, leaving proximate cause to the lower court); Bolieu v. Sisters of Providence in Wash., 953 P.2d 1233, 1237 (Alaska 1998) ("Any genuine dispute about whether Our Lady's conduct actually caused injury . . . should be resolved in the context of causation, not duty.").

[106] *See, e.g.*, Myers v. Quesenberry, 193 Cal.Rptr. 733, 737 (Cal.Ct.App.1983) ("proximate causation presents questions of fact for the jury").

[107] Reisner v. Regents of Univ. of Cal., 37 Cal.Rptr.2d 518 (Cal.Ct.App.1995).

[108] Estate of Amos v. Vanderbilt Univ., 62 S.W.3d 133, 138 (Tenn.2001).

[109] 539 A.2d 1064 (Del.1988).

months and encompassed many factors that may have altered the dynamics of both risk and causation.[110] Courts have disagreed about whether to impose a *Tarasoff* duty extending to patients' future children in cases in which the defendant's negligence caused an inter-generational transfer of a disease risk.[111]

Risk Information

In the post-*Tarasoff* cases we examined, the quality of the risk information that the defendant possessed was generally similar to that of the therapists (and police) in the *Tarasoff* case itself. Where the defendants were therapists, their patients had expressed to them an intention to injure the third party victim,[112] and the therapists sometimes had access to input from others with direct knowledge of the risk.[113] Where the defendant was a prescribing physician, he knew the patient's medical history and the risks posed by the prescribed drug.[114] Homeless shelter

---

[110] *Naidu*, 539 A.2d at 1069. In *Naidu*, the defendant's psychiatric patient had been committed to various mental hospitals nineteen times between 1965–77; his relationship with the defendant began in 1969 with his third commitment. In March 1977, the defendant released the patient without reviewing the voluminous medical records, which might have suggested that the patient was not taking his medicine and might be a danger to himself or others. Over the five and a half months between the patient's release and his purposeful collision, while in a psychotic state, with plaintiff's decedent, the patient "led a rather unremarkable life" and had even enrolled in college classes. The court left the proximate cause issue to the jury.

[111] *Compare* Albala v. City of New York, 429 N.E.2d 786 (N.Y.1981) (no duty owed to son with permanent brain damage caused by mother's earlier negligently performed abortion), *with* Renslow v. Mennonite Hosp., 367 N.E.2d 1250 (Ill.1977) (duty owed to child suffering permanent damage because of mother's negligently performed blood transfusion years before pregnancy).

[112] *See, e.g.*, Rivera v. New York City Health & Hosps. Corp., 191 F.Supp.2d 412 (S.D.N.Y.2002); Mlynarczyk v. Smith, 2001 WL 1004183 (Conn.Super.Ct.2001) (psychiatrist who knew that patient had "vengeful thoughts" and exhibited threatening behavior towards colleagues owed duty to third party victims); Emerich v. Philadelphia Ctr. for Human Dev., Inc., 720 A.2d 1032 (Pa.1998) (mental health professional who knew of specific danger from patient against third party satisfied duty to her by warning her not to go to patient's apartment); Currie v. United States, 644 F.Supp. 1074 (M.D.N.C.1986). Conversely, when the facts make clear that the psychiatrist has *no* reason to suspect any violent tendency at all, courts tend to terminate proceedings at the summary judgment stage. *See, e.g.*, Suzuki v. Eli Lilly & Co., 2002 WL 258263 (Cal.Ct.App.2002) (union leader who shot himself and others had never been shown to be a danger to himself or others); Fraser v. United States, 674 A.2d 811, 816 (Conn.1996) (no "imposition of liability [against psychotherapists] for harm to unidentifiable victims or unidentifiable classes of victims of outpatients with no history of dangerous conduct or articulated threats of dangerous behavior").

[113] *See, e.g.*, Gregory v. Kilbride, 565 S.E.2d 685 (N.C.Ct.App.2002) (even the patient's own father had requested commitment).

[114] *See* McKenzie v. Hawai'i Permanente Med. Group, Inc., 47 P.3d 1209 (Haw.2002). In *Powell v. Catholic Med. Ctr.*, 749 A.2d 301 (N.H.2000), a phlebotomist was harmed when

and residential facility defendants had observed the violent propensities of the individuals in question.[115] The lawyer-defendants also possessed reliable information about the risk to third parties.[116] On the other hand, some plaintiffs have asserted, unsuccessfully, a *Tarasoff* duty on the basis of weaker, more ambiguous, or more conflicting risk information than that possessed by Dr. Moore in *Tarasoff*.[117]

Defenses

One kind of defense to assertions of a *Tarasoff* duty—apart from the claim that the common law does not impose one—is based on a state statute that eliminates or bars such a duty. Many states have enacted statutes limiting the release of medical information or providing immunity to some categories of people who fail to use such information to

---

drawing a blood sample from a stroke victim who was suffering confusion and memory problems. The treating physician had noted in daily reports that the patient often lunged forward and became agitated; the New Hampshire Supreme Court upheld a trial court verdict against the doctor for failing to warn the phlebotomist. *Id.* at 303.

[115] *See supra* notes 80–82 and accompanying text.

[116] *See supra* notes 100–102 and accompanying text. In *Hawkins v. King County Dep't of Rehabilitative Servs.*, 602 P.2d 361 (Wash.Ct.App.1979), one of the key arguments was that the attorney had been warned specifically by both a family attorney and a psychiatrist that his client was dangerous. *Id.* at 363.

[117] This does not mean that courts accept claims based on weak risk information: in *Rojas v. Diaz*, 2002 WL 1292996 (Cal.Ct.App.2002), plaintiffs' decedent was a gardener killed by his employer's niece's husband. The employer knew that her niece had been threatened by her husband, and for this reason allowed the niece to stay with her for only a short time; the husband, discovering that she was there, came with a female accomplice and murdered a host of individuals in the home, something host he had never threatened. Neither aunt nor niece was present at the time. The Court emphatically rejected a *Tarasoff* duty: this "is *not* a problem governed by our Supreme Court's famous decision about the future acts of a specific human being in *Tarasoff* . . . because the holding in the *Tarasoff* case was predicated on the fact the human being who committed the crime actually confided an *intention* to commit the crime prior to doing so." *Id.* at *3 (emphasis in original).

Other courts have also resisted premising a *Tarasoff* duty on the possession of weak risk information. In *Timofeyev v. Taber Consultants*, 2003 WL 121169 (Cal.Ct.App.2003), a safety officer sued a geologist for injuries sustained while the plaintiff put himself in the same perilous position that he had been hired to prevent other employees from entering. The Court, however, did not impose a duty, viewing the plaintiff's risk information as greater than that possessed by the geologist. In *Gold v. Greenwich Hosp. Ass'n*, 811 A.2d 1266 (Conn.2002), the plaintiff had assumed a care-taking role over a woman who suffered a violent allergic reaction during dinner. The defendant hospital gave the patient injections and told plaintiff that her charge would likely sleep through the night, but the patient awakened and violently attacked plaintiff. The Court granted the hospital summary judgment because plaintiff had not stated a claim for medical malpractice, but the Court also noted that a long-term care-giver might have superior risk information about a patient's mental state than an emergency room physician who thinks that he is dealing only with an allergy problem.

protect third parties in *Tarasoff*-type situations.[118] In addition to statutory immunity, at least one court has provided that the *Tarasoff* duty is satisfied by a good faith professionally-based decision not to protect the third party.[119] A number of courts have declined—often as a matter of policy—to extend an established *Tarasoff* duty to certain categories of defendants[120] or victims.[121]

Perhaps the most common limitation of the *Tarasoff* duty is for courts to require that the danger the defendant can reasonably foresee be a danger not just to a general class of potential victims but to victims

---

[118] *See* Evans v. United States, 883 F.Supp. 124, 126–27 (S.D.Miss.1995), construing Miss. Code Ann. § 41–21–97 (1990). Immunity from a duty to release information in the context of AIDS has been explicitly granted by Cal. Health & Safety Code § 121015(c) (West 1996) (initially codified as § 199.25(c) in 1987) ("[n]o physician has a duty to notify any person of the fact that patient is reasonably believed to be infected by the probable causative agent of" AIDS), but subsections (a) and (b) *allow* disclosure to certain individuals under strict guidelines (the physician must first discuss it with the patient and seek patient's consent, only inform individuals with particular relationships with the patient that might put them at risk, and must refer the at-risk individuals for appropriate care). For recent discussion of disclosure rules focusing on the tension between public health and privacy, including analysis of *Tarasoff* ramifications, see Lawrence O. Gostin & James G. Hodge, Jr., *Piercing the Veil of Secrecy in HIV/AIDS and Other Sexually Trasmitted Diseases: Theories of Privacy and Disclosure in Partner Notification*, 5 Duke J. Gender L. & Pol'y 9 (1998) and Benjamin F. Neidl, Note, *The Lesser of Two Evils: New York's New HIV/AIDS Partner Notification Law and Why the Right of Privacy Must Yield to Public Health*, 73 St. John's L. Rev. 1191 (1999).

Some involuntary commitment statutes have been interpreted to create a duty to third parties, while others have not. For an overview of state statutes concerning psychotherapist privilege and how psychotherapists can avoid liability in various circumstances, see George C. Harris, *The Dangerous Patient Exception to the Psychotherapist–Patient Privilege: The* Tarasoff *Duty and the* Jaffee *Footnote*, 74 Wash. L. Rev. 33, 41–44 (1999). For states that have adopted *Tarasoff* by statute or decision, see *id.* at 47–48.

[119] Currie v. United States, 644 F.Supp. 1074, 1083 (M.D.N.C.1986).

[120] *See, e.g.*, J.L. v. Kienenberger, 848 P.2d 472 (Mont.1993) (parents of thirteen year-old rapist, who was under the influence of alcohol and marijuana when he attacked victim, did not owe duty to victim in spite of inadequately supervising their son), *abrogated by* Crisafulli v. Bass, 38 P.3d 842 (Mont.2001); Popple v. Rose, 573 N.W.2d 765 (Neb.1998) (parents of babysitter who sexually assaulted child did not know their son had a propensity to sexual abuse and therefore no duty was imposed, but in general, parents have a duty to warn of child's alleged dangerous traits).

[121] *See, e.g.*, Lester *ex rel.* Mavrogenis v. Hall, 970 P.2d 590 (N.M.1998) (no duty owed to third party injured by physician's patient while driving). New Jersey took the opposite approach in *Reed v. Bojarski*, 764 A.2d 433 (N.J.2001), where "the duty to communicate with a patient who is found to be ill is non-delegable," regardless of whether the physical is paid for by employers. *Id.* at 443 For a summary of cases going both ways on whether to impose duty on physicians to third parties in driving cases, see *Lester*, 970 P.2d at 596–98, and Neil J. Squillante, Comment, *Expanding the Potential Tort Liability of Physicians: A Legal Portrait of "Nontraditional Patients" and Proposals for Change*, 40 UCLA L. Rev. 1617 (1993) (showing that most courts do not find duty in this circumstance).

who are identifiable with a significant degree of specificity. Statutory grants of immunity for failure to warn absent identifiability has been one approach.[122] Many courts have adopted similar specific identifiability requirements as a matter of common law.[123] Courts that reject such a limitation almost always substitute another, as in the previously-noted *Currie* case where the court preferred a good faith "psychotherapist judgment rule."[124] These two limitations, however, are not coterminous and indeed address different factors—the victim's specificity versus the defendant's state of mind.

Conclusion

Tarasoff is a unique tort case, studied not only by nearly every law student, but by nearly every medical student in the United States. It possesses an important but rare pedagogical value as one of the very few tort cases whose actual effects on the behavior of the group targeted by the legal rule—here, mental health professionals—has been studied empirically. In general, judges and scholars know little about the behavioral consequences of legal rules. Their ignorance is particularly dismaying because tort law's justificatory rhetoric in both the courts and the academy increasingly invokes functional-instrumental goals rather than corrective justice.

Nor is this ignorance easily remedied. Unintended consequences are endemic to law, but especially to today's more policy-oriented tort law.[125]

---

[122] *See, e.g., supra* note 7 and accompanying text.

[123] *See, e.g.,* Fraser v. United States, 674 A.2d 811 (Conn.1996) ("[O]ur decisions defining negligence do not impose a duty to those who are not identifiable victims [and] in related areas of our common law, we have concluded that there is no duty except to identifiable persons."); Bradley v. Ray, 904 S.W.2d 302 (Mo.Ct.App.1995) ("We recognize a right to sue only for failure to warn of specific risks of future harm to readily identifiable victims."); Emerich v. Philadelphia Ctr. for Human Dev., Inc., 720 A.2d 1032, 1040 (Pa.1998) ("[T]he duty to warn will only arise where the threat is made against a specifically identified or readily identifiable victim. Strong reasons support the determination that the duty to warn must have some limits."); Limon v. Gonzaba, 940 S.W.2d 236, 239 (Tex.Ct.App.1997) ("Where there is no allegation of a threat or danger to a readily identifiable person, we . . . are unwilling to impose a blanket liability upon all hospitals and therapists for the unpredictable conduct of their patients with a mental disorder."). But note that statutes imposing a duty on health care providers when the potential victim is specifically identifiable are not necessarily construed as immunity from a standard negligence action when the victim is *not* specifically identifiable: in *Powell v. Catholic Med. Ctr.*, 749 A.2d 301 (N.H.2000), *see supra* note 114, the statutory duty was to warn identifiable victims, but the court did not find a repeal of ordinary common law duty. *Id.* at 304.

[124] *Currie*, 644 F.Supp. at 1083.

[125] The remainder of this paragraph draws on a more extensive discussion in Schuck, *supra* note 35, at 15–16. *See generally* Peter H. Schuck, *The Limits of Law: Essays on Democratic Governance* 424–34 (2000).

After all, judges are trained as generalist lawyers (usually as litigators), not as policy specialists, and they are unlikely to acquire, or know how to exploit, the kinds of information that a competent policy analysis requires. The litigants represent only a few of the many social interests affected by the disputed legal rule, and the litigated cases are unlikely to be representative of the social reality that a policy should address. Courts lack any reliable way to obtain feedback on their rules' real-world effects. Indeed, unless courts write their opinions with unmistakable specificity—and maybe not even then—they have no control over how their rulings will be understood by those who will be affected by them. Perhaps most inimical to a sound policy-making framework are the deep structures of tort law—its vestigial moralism, its adversarial, party-centered control of litigation, its radical decentralization and non-accountability, its glacial accumulation of precedents, its factual diversity and particularity, its rejection of specific rules in favor of general standards, and its view of problems only in a hindsight that is transfixed, and perhaps distorted, by the sight of palpable human suffering. Even if courts could readily determine the correct social policy for distributing risk, they would be hard put to implement that policy through a tort rule expressed in terms of "reasonable behavior" and applied by *ad hoc* juries, requiring A (more likely A's insurer) to pay B a certain sum of money.

If studying *Tarasoff* gives us a rare opportunity to compare the law's ambitions to its actual effects—and to confirm that tort rules sometimes do accomplish what the courts intended (while having some unintended effects as well, such as making some therapists more wary of potentially violent patients)—it also enables the law student to observe and grapple with the generativity of legal rules, as courts confront the perennial need for line-drawing and containment of legal duty in the face of relentless pressures to extend the logic of the general rule to new, ostensibly analogous fact situations. *Tarasoff* is an especially rich source of insights into this generative process because the legal duty that it imposed—to protect third parties against serious dangers of which one has special knowledge threatened by those for whom one bears some special responsibility—is both morally compelling and readily susceptible to being extended to encompass other relationships, while at the same time demanding limitations by virtue of the nature and source of the information on which that knowledge is based. By studying *Tarasoff*, we learn how tort law goes about resolving this tension—and read an arresting, intensely human tort story to boot.

5

Saul Levmore

The Wagon Mound Cases: Foreseeability, Causation, and Mrs. Palsgraf

Introduction: The Role of Foreseeability

Every damage remedy must have its limit. A tort leaves the world a different place, and no legal system can hope to engineer a perfect reconstruction, fashioning things as they would have been had the tort never occurred. Law needs mechanisms with which to limit damages, even as it compensates victims and deters wrongdoers. Two of the more obvious limiting devices in tort law are the doctrines of emotional harm and pure economic loss; damages that fall in these categories will, in most circumstances, go unrecoverable. If, for example, A hits B and B is then unable to walk to her favorite restaurant owned by C, C is unable to recover for any lost business.

The most significant of these limiting tools is proximate cause; the law will not make a tortfeasor pay for losses it may have brought about, or "caused in fact," if these losses are found not to have been "proximately caused." Plaintiff must normally show that defendant was negligent and that this negligence proximately caused plaintiff's injury. It is not enough to show that "but for" the defendant's act, plaintiff would not have been injured. But this requirement of proximate causation is sometimes confusing and often unhelpful in predicting whether a given defendant will be held responsible for some particular damage. It is unhelpful because the stated rules give the courts much room to decide the cases one way or the other. And one source of confusion is the link between liability and foreseeability; it is sometimes asserted that there is no proximate cause if the wrongdoer could not have foreseen the damage that occurred, but of course there are few things that can be foreseen with great precision and yet almost everything can be anticipated at some level of generality. This Chapter explores the most famous cases dealing with this connection between foreseeability and the requisite sort of causation. The cases are *Polemis*, *Palsgraf*, and two cases known as *Wagon Mound (No. 1)* and *Wagon Mound (No. 2)*.[1] The centerpiece of our story is the Wagon Mound, a vessel that spilled furnace oil in Sydney Harbor off the eastern coast of Australia in 1951. The cases arising out of this incident are, as we will see, paradoxical, and the resolution of that paradox reveals an important lesson about foreseeability and causation.

All readers know that if a tortfeasor, A, kicks, or otherwise negligently or intentionally injures another, B, then A pays B for the latter's damages—including B's "thinskull" or "eggshell" damages, should there be such extreme losses. For instance, in the famous case of *Vosburg v. Putney*[2] (and in a manner quite unlike comparable contracts cases), where Putney kicked Vosburg, who had a precondition of an infected knee, Putney was required to pay for the more serious damage his kick caused even though he was unaware of Vosburg's temporary fragility. Vosburg collected full damages, which is to say far more than the expected or foreseeable damage normally associated with bruising another's knee.

We might say that Putney's liability extends to unforeseeable consequences, but this can be a confusing or circular expression. That someone's knee might have recently been injured is hardly unforeseeable; a great many things are simply unusual, surprising, or normally unexpected. We could imagine a rule requiring the tortfeasor to pay the average damages that could or ought to have been expected to follow from the tort, or a rule under which the tortfeasor pays the actual damages generated by the tort so long as these do not exceed the expected or average damages normally anticipated from a tort of the kind committed. But the prevailing rule is in fact that the tortfeasor takes the victim as he or she finds him, infected knee and thinskull included.

But does the tortfeasor take the circumstances, as well as the persons, as given? We can ask this question about the negligence calculus itself, which is to say about the risks and benefits associated with some action, and the answer is fairly clear—and negative. A defendant is not deemed to be negligent if a reasonable person assessing

---

[1] In re Polemis, 3 K.B. 560 (C.A.1921); Palsgraf v. Long Island R.R. Co., 162 N.E. 99 (N.Y.1928); Overseas Tankship (U.K.) Ltd. v. Mort's Dock & Eng'g Co. (*The Wagon Mound (No. 1)*), [1961] A.C. 388 (P.C.) (appeal taken from Austl.); Overseas Tankship (U.K.) Ltd. v. The Miller Steamship Co. (*The Wagon Mound (No. 2)*), [1967] 1 A.C. 617 (P.C.) (appeal taken from Austl.).

[2] Vosburg v. Putney, 50 N.W. 403 (Wis.1891).

normal risks would not have thought the action or behavior unreasonable. For example, it may be reasonable to open a particular door quickly when one is in a rush to get to work or to assist with an emergency. If it then happens to be the case that someone is standing on the other side of the doorway with a valuable antique, which is broken by the untimely swing of the door, we will not hold the door opener liable. A defendant's behavior is judged according to what a reasonable person should have expected in average circumstances, and so the presence of the plaintiff or the antique on the other side of the door is regarded as unforeseeable. The negligence calculus calls for an ex ante, or before the fact, analysis of whether the defendant's behavior was reasonable. In this calculation it is the expected, or average, damages that matter, and in this hypothetical case the quick opening of the door was reasonable because valuable antiques are so rarely on the other side. To be sure, if strict liability, rather than negligence, is the rule governing the activity in question, then we avoid this reasonableness calculation and need ask only whether the plaintiff's damages were proximately caused by the defendant. But where negligence is at issue, the law asks whether, judged by "foreseeable" consequences, the defendant acted responsibly.

Assuming then that negligence has been found (or that strict liability governs), the next question is whether the injury is too remote, indirect, or non-proximate (to use three oft-stated words or tests) to be included in the set of losses that defendant must make whole. This is essentially the question up for grabs in the several cases discussed here. Let us begin with the earliest of these cases, *Polemis*, decided in 1921.

Polemis and Alternatives to the Foreseeability/Unforeseeability Distinction

In *Polemis*, the defendant's employees negligently dropped a plank down into the hold of a ship, the Polemis, from a higher deck. The cargo included a number of containers of benzine that had begun to leak during the ship's previous voyage. Local stevedores were hired to relocate these leaking containers into another part of the hull so that they could be safely delivered to the next port. To this end, they rigged a series of slings and platforms to move the heavy containers. During this process, one of the planks broke loose and fell into the hull. The impact of the fallen plank was immediately followed by a rush of flames from the lower hold that eventually resulted in the total destruction of the Polemis. Let us stipulate that the dropping of the plank was negligent behavior if only because the gain from incautiously assembling planks into platforms, without either warning all below to clear the way or taking steps to prevent the free fall of a plank, was small compared to the expected costs of hitting someone down in the hold. If the falling plank had hit someone on the head, the case would be simple. The very foreseeable harm that had been contemplated and included in the negligence calculus associated with working on an upper deck with planks would then have occurred. Defendant obviously pays for such foreseeable injuries that themselves cause a mode of operation to be deemed negligent. But in *Polemis*, the plank hit no one on the head but rather apparently generated a spark when it scraped or collided with the hull or other cargo. The spark in turn generated the fire, and the question is whether this rather unanticipated result of a (negligent) plank-dropping is the responsibility of the defendant or whether it is too "remote." The *Polemis* court held that there was indeed liability because foreseeability is relevant to the negligence calculus alone; once there is negligence, the defendant pays for the damage that it causes, foreseeable or not, so long as it is sufficiently "direct."

Note that this approach to foreseeability and causation avoids the need to draw a line between foreseeable and unforeseeable damages but puts more pressure on line drawing with respect to directness or some other categorical distinction that comes into play, because every damage remedy must have some limit. Imagine, for example, that the Polemis fire had spread and destroyed every ship in the harbor and then every building in the port city, causing large-scale dislocation. We can be sure that the defendant would not have been made to pay for all these losses. Similarly, if the raging fire brings out additional firefighters who rush to the fire, and one firefighter accidentally hits a pedestrian on the way to the flames, there will again be no liability on the part of the plank-dropping defendant. Nor would such line drawing be avoided if *Polemis* had held that there was no liability for the plank-induced fire. In this case, we can imagine that there would one day be the question of liability after a flying plank frightened someone enough to drop a fragile object. And if that consequence is also found too remote for liability, then something a bit closer to the plank-on-the-head will be the subject of litigation. A line must be drawn somewhere, even under the *Polemis* approach of including all direct consequences, and the doctrine of proximate cause as well as the language of foreseeability are the tools with which this line is to be drawn. These are the tools for sorting consequences into the set of those payable by the tortfeasor, and the set of those found too distant, or not sufficiently proximate, to be attributed to the tortfeasor.

One conventional way to draw these lines is to look at the kind of injury that might have been foreseen and compare it to what actually occurred. This approach is especially convenient for rationalizing the coexistence of the thinskull rule itself and the practice of not holding a tortfeasor liable for injuries that seem remote, such as the (hypothetical) one caused by the firefighter who rushes to a fire and injures a pedestrian on the way. The pedestrian's injury might be labeled as "unforesee-able," but so could the thinskull damages associated with Vosburg's infected knee. One ready distinction, to justify opposite results in these two cases, is that liability extends to injuries of a greater degree than those normally foreseeable, but not to injuries of a different kind from those which are reasonably foreseeable. The infected knee is gravely injured by a kick, but then this is just a greater degree of harm than that expected from a kick to a normal knee. On the other hand, a dropped plank may hit someone on the head or cause damage in a ship's hull, but a pedestrian's injury at the hands of a firefighter heading to the ship is of a completely different kind than the earlier, foreseeable injury. This degree/kind distinction is occasionally appealing, and perhaps even the basis of a good answer on a bar exam or a respectable point to advance on behalf of a client. Some courts use a variant in the form of a manner/type distinction; negligent tortfeasors are said to be responsible for consequences that are of the same type as the foreseeable harms, even though they come about in an unforeseeable manner. In many cases, however, the degree/kind (or manner/type) distinction is difficult to make without torturing language and defying common sense. *Polemis*, for example might be regarded as incorrectly decided by an observer who relied on the degree/kind distinction, because it is arguable that igniting the cargo below and causing a fire is not a kind (or type) of injury to be expected when a ship's cargo is negligently moved about with heavy equipment.

It is noteworthy that the *Polemis* court sought to avoid the confu-sion of such distinctions (specifically that which associated liability with "natural and probable" consequences rather than unnatural and im-probable ones) by simply requiring the negligent actor to pay for all the results of its negligence. But by relying on the distinction between direct and indirect consequences as a way of bringing the chain of causation to an end, the *Polemis* court simply relocated the confusion. Indirectness, remoteness, unforeseeability, improbability, and unnaturalness are hard-ly self-executing standards for limiting liability. Each creates confusion and the need for line drawing. The *Polemis* court articulated its rule as one distinguishing between culpability and compensation. Foreseeability is relevant only to determine culpability, or negligence, and then liability is meant to follow for all "direct" harms, foreseeable or not. The *Polemis* world is thus one in which lawyers and judges must master a distinction with no firm basis. Such mastery may be impossible.

The Wagon Mound Circumstances

The Wagon Mound cases arose out of a series of events in the harbor near Sydney, Australia. Overseas Tankship (U.K.), Ltd., was a charterer by demise of the Wagon Mound, an oil-carrying ship. A demise charter is similar to a lease, except that the charter succeeds to more of the shipowner's rights and obligations. On the morning of October 29, 1951 the Wagon Mound entered Mort Bay, off the coast of a working-class suburb known as Balmain. It was to deliver a cargo of petrol, or gasoline, to Caltex corporation, and then to bunker, or load up, with furnace oil to transport overseas.

Caltex Corporation maintained a jetty in Mort Bay, an oil operation at the tip of a small peninsula known as Ballast Point. The Wagon Mound moored to the jetty at about 9:35 that morning and unloaded its cargo of gasoline. Evidently there was no direct way to load the furnace oil into the ship from the Caltex jetty, so the Vacuum Oil Company brought around barges to load the fuel oil into the Wagon Mound's tanks from the bay side. Mr. Cullen–Ward, chief bunkering officer of the Vacuum Oil Company, testified that he had boarded the Wagon Mound at approximately 11:00 that morning and had remained on board until the bunkering was complete, which was at about 4:00 the next morning, October 30. His job was to make sure the hoses and other connections between the barge and the Wagon Mound functioned properly. Nonetheless, at some point during this operation the Wagon Mound began to leak oil, not because of any problem with the connection to the Vacuum Oil Company's barges, but because someone left open a different hatch to another part of the Wagon Mound's tank, the farthest forward lower tank door. Unfortunately, furnace oil was going into one end of the tank, and coming out the other, though at a slower rate. Nobody noticed this disaster until Mr. Cullen–Ward left early that next morning and observed oil bubbling out as well as a slick extending across the bay. Cullen–Ward promptly reported the spillage to the officers of the Wagon Mound, and was told not to worry about it for it was not his responsibility. The open valve was beyond the control of Vacuum Oil and, in any event, inasmuch as the oil had already been delivered to the ship, it was the Wagon Mound's fault that it had overflowed. There was some evidence that the officers attempted to slow the leak by diverting the oil into another tank, but their efforts were frustrated by a stuck valve. Captain Craven, a witness to the extent of the oil spill at 10:30 that morning, testified that the spill extended roughly 500 yards from the tip of Ballast Point, an area encompassing more than half of Mort Bay. No other action was taken to disperse or otherwise deal with the substantial quantity of oil that had spilled into the bay. The Wagon Mound simply pushed away at about 11:00 a.m. heading overseas, clearing the Heads of the Sydney Bay area around noon, and perhaps leaving a trail of oil behind. Arrangements had been made with a Mr. Durack, depot manager at Caltex, to act as an agent on the Wagon Mound's behalf regarding the immediate ramifications of the spill.

Mort's Dock and Engineering Company was located in the "corner" of Mort Bay. It was an immediate neighbor of Caltex, though the wharf and the Wagon Mound were about 500 yards apart. The company had a substantial ironworking operation on land adjacent to the bay, in addition to shipbuilding and repair services which took place on the Sheerlegs Wharf. Its position in this corner, combined with the inflowing tidal motion, meant that a substantial amount of the oil washed up and around their wharf. At the time of the spill the dock was repairing the Corrimal, a 1,100 ton collier (coal carrying ship), as well as a smaller ship called the Audrey D. Workers were using electric torches and an oxy-acetylene welding apparatus, a torch that burned at 6,300 degrees Fahrenheit, in order to refit the Corrimal so that it could work the coal run between Newcastle and Sydney. The oil around the wharf was so thick and black that when a boilermaker for the company picked up a bit of concrete and threw it into the oil, "it was just like seeing it go into sloppy cement; it just like bubbled a bit, and I knew that was very thick. That was what made me go up to Mr. Parkin." Mr. Parkin was works manager of Mort's Dock. He immediately ordered the cessation of all welding work on the wharf. Unaware of the source of the spill, but guessing that it had something to do with his large oil company neighbor, Parkin telephoned Caltex's Durack, who came to Mort's Dock at about 10 a.m. He assured Parkin that the oil was quite safe for normal work to continue. Relying entirely on this single suggestion, and without ever inquiring as to Durack's understanding of "normal work," Parkin ordered the resumption of welding operations on the large wharf, which was the size of two football fields. Business at the wharf had only been interrupted for a few hours. The wharf itself was built entirely of timber, supported by wooden piles, with spaces up to two inches wide between planks of the decking, all of which was substantially mucked by this very thick oil.

Two and a half days later, with the thick oil still surrounding and invading the wharf, and with welding and other work continuing there, the oil and then the wharf caught fire.[3] Ironically, Parkin first learned of the fire from Durack, who called him at about 2:00 p.m. on November 1 to ask permission to bring someone over to inspect the property damage being caused by the oil muck. Before Parkin could answer, Durack saw the flames from his office and exclaimed, "Good Lord, your place has gone up in flames." The fire spread very quickly, and the heat that it generated caused the oxy-acetylene cylinders to explode with such force

---

[3] The next morning's newspaper described the oil as having been around for weeks before the fire, thus suggesting an earlier source of oil, and perhaps the Caltex facility. But this is a lone observation and one that is inconsistent with other reported facts. I assume that it was derived from a comment by a worker on the scene who may have exaggerated his frustration with the surrounding oil mess.

that the tank fragments pierced the steel sides of the Corrimal. Yet no one was killed. A front page newspaper report the next morning in the Sydney Morning Herald offered dramatic stories of people who jumped to safety, were rescued at the corner of the dock moments before the flames engulfed the spot where they had been standing, and were forced to flee so suddenly that they did not even manage to turn off their torches. The dock was a complete loss, and the Corrimal and Audrey D suffered extensive damages. The newspaper reports depict the workers as having been quite fearful of, but resigned to, the oil. "We have been expecting a fire here . . . it had to come sooner or later with so much oil about." One worker even overheard another comment, "That oil slick is on fire at last," a few seconds before the whole wharf and ship were an inferno.

As it turns out, the fire marked the beginning of the end for Mort's Dock and Engineering Company. Once the largest private employer in Sydney, with over 1,300 iron workers in 1889, Mort's closed in 1958, seven years after the fire. Business had slowed after the war, and the dock operations were never rebuilt after this fire. It is apparent that there was a decrease in the demand for these services, quite apart from the fire, but it is possible that at the time it would have seemed that the fire alone brought about the end of this substantial business.

A series of suits followed the spill and fire. Claims filed by the owners of the Corrimal and the Audrey D against Caltex and against Vacuum Oil never made it to court, but suits brought against the owner of the Wagon Mound by the owner of Mort's Dock and then by the owners of the Corrimal and the Audrey D found their way up through the Australian legal system, eventually becoming known as the Wagon Mound Cases. The final decisions in both cases were issued by the Privy Council, a court that would today not have jurisdiction over these matters, inasmuch as the High Court of Australia has become the final court of appeal. The Privy Council consisted of five members of the House of Lords sitting as an appellate court—and one from which there was no further appeal. The House of Lords is of course the unelected chamber of the British parliament, and it provides judges to serve as the final court of appeals for most civil cases in the British Commonwealth. At the time of the Wagon Mound Cases, the Council had jurisdiction to hear some appeals from some Commonwealth countries, including New Zealand and Australia. The Privy Council's decisions were treated as persuasive authority, but not directly binding on English Courts. Indeed, the Privy Council's power to overrule other cases—like *Polemis* itself, which was decided by the Court of Appeal whose members were also drawn from the Lords—was debated. As we will see, *Wagon Mound (No. 1)* did in fact overrule *Polemis*, though perhaps only in nominal fashion. But all this gets ahead of our story. The Privy Council, it should be noted, presents its advisory opinion as a single unanimous opinion, so that there is little opportunity to gather hints about the debate that might have taken place behind its closed doors in the event the judges be divided.

We do, however, have a lower court opinion in *Wagon Mound (No. 1)* with which to begin.[4] It is from the Supreme Court of New South Wales. Mort's Dock sued the Wagon Mound to recover for the loss of the wharf. Judge Kinsella, sitting with no jury, conducted hearings for eleven days, concluding on March 18, 1958. One important issue was the foreseeability of fire arising out of this sort of oil spill. The court heard testimony from Professor Hunter, a Professor of Chemical Engineering at the University of Sydney, whose past experience included experiments aimed at determining whether oil in the English Channel could be ignited as a means of defending against an invasion of England. He carried out over 300 experiments for the Wagon Mound litigation and found that furnace oil floating on water was unlikely to ignite when molten materials were dropped onto its surface. On the other hand, with a burning object floating on the surface of the oil, ordinary furnace oil might well ignite. He concluded that the fire at Mort's Dock required some kind of wick, partially floating in the oil and partially above it, which may have caught fire when a spark or piece of molten metal fell onto it through the wide spaces between the planks of the wharf. The wick must have been fanned by a breeze of not more than 20 miles an hour, and the oil must have been more than 1/8 of an inch thick. Two employees of Mort's Dock corroborated the chemical engineer's theory with the observation that they had seen a small flame emanating from a smoldering piece of material atop some bark floating in the water shortly before the dock ignited. We can imagine that welding and other work on the dock did not join with other circumstances to cause a fire until the right debris and breeze came along, more than two days after welding resumed.

The court also learned that furnace oil was not the only thing leaking from the Wagon Mound. Mr. Cullen–Ward testified that he also saw gasoline leaking onto the deck, at about the rate at which water comes out of a garden hose. The fourth mate of the ship insisted that this leak occurred while they were testing connections to a hose before full pressure was applied, and that the leak was negligible. Judge Kinsella found that this leak did not contribute to the fire. The amount of gasoline was not very great, and Professor Hunter testified that 98.2% of this sort of gasoline would have evaporated within five hours, and thus the highly volatile and flammable elements would no longer have been around when the actual fire erupted, some sixty hours later.

---

[4] Mort's Dock & Eng'g Co. v. Overseas Tankship (U.K.) Ltd., (1958) 1 Lloyd's Rep. 575 (N.S.W.).

Much time was spent hearing witnesses opine as to whether they, which is to say reasonable and ordinary people, would expect heavy oil like furnace oil to catch fire upon the water. Most did not but of course that depended on the work being done on the wharf above the oil. In April, Judge Kinsella issued a ruling in favor of Mort's Dock. The opinion sets out the rule of *Polemis* and its meaning for the Australian litigation. The *Polemis* rule is said to be that "the presence or absence of reasonable anticipation of damage determines the legal quality of the act as negligent or innocent. If it be thus determined to be negligent, then the question whether particular damages are recoverable depends only on the answer to the question whether they are direct consequences of the act ... and not due to the operation of independent causes having no connection with the negligent act, except that they could not avoid its results." Judge Kinsella conceded that furnace oil in the open was generally regarded as safe, and that the Wagon Mound's workers and agents were negligent in spilling oil, though not negligent in advising that welding was safe, but he found the Wagon Mound liable because the fire was a direct consequence of the spill. Brushing aside the Wagon Mound's lawyers' emphasis on the time and actions that intervened between the oil spill and the fire, Judge Kinsella concluded that some kind of damage to the dock was foreseeable, if only because oil would muck up the dock and its equipment, and therefore the more extensive damage (from the fire) was also the defendant's responsibility. In short, the unanticipated damage to the wharf was simply more extensive than the damage that was foreseeable, and it was a direct enough consequence of the negligent act to warrant liability under the *Polemis* rule.

The appeal went to a panel of three new judges on the same court.[5] The findings of fact in the earlier litigation were not contested. Still, there were four days of hearings devoted mainly to the definition of directness and to the merits of the rule of *Polemis*—which, as the court noted, had stood for nearly forty years, and thus had absorbed its share of academic and judicial criticism. The lawyers debated a variety of precedents and argued the question of whether *Polemis*, a breach of contract case (because the employer of the plank dropper, the shipowner, and the owner of the cargo were all in contractual relationships), ought to be much of a precedent for these Australian tort cases. The damage rules in tort and contract cases are famously distinct, and hinge on foreseeability, so that there was some doubt or perhaps merely confusion as to whether foreseeability, insofar as causation is concerned, is also something to be treated differently in these two areas of law. But in the end, this appeal failed and the *Polemis* rule stood firm; that the oil spill would somehow damage the dock was to be anticipated, and so the

---

[5] Mort's Dock & Eng'g Co. v. Overseas Tankship (U.K.) Ltd., (1959) 2 Lloyd's Rep. 697 (N.S.W.).

defendant should also bear responsibility for the fire damage to the dock. The court conceded that "if a logical analysis is made of this series of events, there is very strong support for the view that there were intervening circumstances of a kind which render it impossible to say that the conflagration was a direct result of the oil spillage," however the court looks instead to the "circumstances as a whole rather than ... careful analysis of each link in the chain of events leading to the occurrence." In the end, the court insisted, an ordinary person would say that the cause of the fire was the spill of the oil. The Wagon Mound was thus found liable.

The matter then went on further appeal to the Lords sitting on the Privy Council. They examined the *Polemis* rule "that, if the defendant is guilty of negligence, he is responsible for all the consequences whether reasonably foreseeable or not"—at least in those cases in which the consequences are "direct." The Lords were uncomfortable with the emergence of this direct/indirect distinction and preferred instead to say that one is "responsible for the probable consequences of his act. To demand more of him is too harsh a rule, to demand less is to ignore that civilized order requires the observance of a minimum standard of behaviour." They preferred even more to say that liability for a consequence has and ought to be imposed only when it was reasonably foreseeable.[6] The lower courts were, therefore, overruled, and *Polemis* re-interpreted and swept away as "illogical and unjust." The Wagon Mound was held not to be responsible for the destruction of the wharf by the fire. Had Mort's Dock made a claim for the relatively small damage caused by the mucking oil on its property or because of the suspension of work while the oil's properties were investigated, it might have enjoyed success and thus some compensation. The fire, however, was unforeseeable.

Wagon Mound (No. 2)

If we stop here, then nothing terribly remarkable has transpired. *Polemis* is overruled, to be sure, but the case law still offers little in the way of guidelines for future courts. We might say that a defendant who allows oil to run freely into the harbor is negligent, but that for furnace oil, at least, the anticipated kind of injury is pollution but not fire. We might expect local law to develop a system of fines in order to discourage oil spilling or to require restitution for cleanup costs, but if it is so that this furnace oil is not a fire risk—as at least one expert declared to the manager of Mort's Dock—then the judges have simply tried to maintain

---

[6] The Privy Council cited *Palsgraf*, a case taken up below, toward this end, though it does not seem to have considered it closely; it refers to our famous and beloved American case as "Palsgref."

the notion of responsibility for all direct consequences. These judges might have found the Wagon Mound liable if the pollution had caused grave and immediate harm, as it might have if a sensitive victim had been in the water and was injured by contact with the oil, or if there had been a business on the bay that suffered great losses because the thick furnace oil mucked up its machines in the water or at water's edge. But given that the nature of the damage was destruction by fire, and fire is said not to be a foreseeable result when heavy oil spills, the Privy Council was simply advancing the idea that foreseeability is important not only in deciding whether a defendant is negligent but also in drawing the line as to which harms are then the negligent defendant's responsibility. *Polemis*, with its direct/indirect line-drawing inquiry, held to the contrary, of course, but the *Wagon Mound (No. 1)* alternative, if it is that, might well seem more sensible to most observers.[7]

But the skeptical reader might be on guard if only because even as the labels change, there remains the underlying problem of how to limit the chain of causation in some objective manner. Foreseeability is of little help in understanding *Wagon Mound (No. 1)* or this larger issue. The Privy Council would have us believe that a large amount of oil floating around an industrial wharf did not amount to a foreseeable fire risk, even though debris and welding operations were known to be present. Whether or not Mort's Dock should have relied on the opinion of one neighbor or should simply have realized that debris could help sustain a fire, it is hard to see how the Wagon Mound could get by without foreseeing the risk of fire from its spill.

All this, of course, is simply the story of the first Privy Council decision in *Wagon Mound (No. 1),* and there is more to our tale because of the separate case brought by the owners of the two ships damaged by the same fire. These ships, the Corrimal and the Audrey D were docked at the Sheerlegs Wharf for repairs when the fire broke out. And it this litigation, culminating in the Privy Council's decision in *Wagon Mound (No. 2)*, to which we now turn.

The Miller Steamship Company owned the Corrimal and claimed damages of £165,000.[8] R.W. Miller & Co., Ltd. owned the Audrey D, a smaller ship that was damaged in the amount of £1,000. The initial case

---

[7] Put differently, *Wagon Mound (No. 1)* may have survived as something of a fixture in American law casebooks simply because it stands in contrast to *Polemis*. The latter is cited for the idea of liability for surprising losses (albeit ones that happened very close, in time and space, to the negligent act) while *Wagon Mound (No. 1)* carries the banner for the notion of cutting off the chain of causation for things that are said to be unexpected or remote from a negligent act. Armed with the inexact language of foreseeability, courts can argue and draw lines as they please, choosing words and precedents from here and there.

[8] Australia would not convert to decimal currency until 1966, when the Australian dollar was born on "C–Day."

came out of the Supreme Court of New South Wales in 1963, almost two years after the Privy Council issued the final disposition in *Wagon Mound (No. 1)*. The case had been initiated many years earlier, prior to the final decision in *Wagon Mound (No. 1)*, but the owners of the damaged ships decided to await the completion of that matter before proceeding with their actions.

Undoubtedly aware that the cards were stacked against them because of the Privy Council's decision in the first case, plaintiffs now sought liability under two theories, negligence and nuisance. As to negligence, they attempted to establish that the fire at the wharf was in fact foreseeable. Plaintiffs seemed unconcerned that the earlier decision precluded this claim, or perhaps they were confident that their claim was about the scope of, rather than the revisited fact of, negligence. Judge Walsh, who heard this second case (and was not on the multi-judge panel in the first case), did indeed suggest that there was some greater evidence presented by the shipowners in their case that the fire was in fact foreseeable, but ultimately concluded that the fire was not foreseeable. On the other hand, Walsh accepted a second claim brought by these plaintiffs, that the oil spill was a common law nuisance and that, somehow, nuisance law does not require foreseeability; with *Wagon Mound (No. 1)* thus circumvented, the lower court then awarded the owners of the two ships £80,000, and £1,000, respectively.

The appeal went straight to the Privy Council this time, skipping the round of multi-judge review that took place in *Wagon Mound (No. 1)*. The five-member Council panel included two judges who participated in *Wagon Mound (No. 1)*, including Lord Reid who authored the decision in *No. 2*. Much of *Wagon Mound (No. 2)* is devoted to the rejection of the idea that there could be liability in nuisance law without foreseeability. And yet, *Wagon Mound (No. 2)* concluded that there was liability, and that the shipowners could collect, because the foreseeability test for negligence was met! Rather than overruling its prior opinion, the court simply insisted that the findings of facts supported the conclusion that the fire was in fact foreseeable. Judge Walsh, it will be recalled, found that the fire was not foreseeable—though he left some room for the Privy Council by suggesting that the latest presentation of facts tended to suggest more strongly than one would gather from *Wagon Mound (No. 1)* that the fire was foreseeable. The Privy Council simply inferred on its own that the fire was foreseeable, contrary to its own earlier ruling regarding the same event.

The *Wagon Mound* Paradox

The results in the two Wagon Mound cases are puzzling and even paradoxical. The Privy Council in *No. 2* rejected the idea that nuisance would support a claim for unforeseeable consequences, so we can not easily rationalize the two cases by saying that the second set of plaintiffs succeeded where the first failed because the later plaintiffs thought to bring a nuisance claim along with the argument that nuisance law provides for recovery even where consequences are unforeseeable.

Nor is the difference between the two cases easily traced to distinct lower court opinions. The lower court continued the pattern of *No. 1*, concluding that the fire was unforeseeable. An objective observer might have expected either the same result in the two cases or contrary rulings—but then with plaintiff succeeding in *No. 1* and failing in *No. 2*, contrary to the actual results. The fire in the *No. 2* was just as unforeseeable as in *No. 1*, for it was the same fire, but the loss was, if anything, less proximate, less direct, and more remote for the second plaintiffs because the ships caught fire after the wharf was aflame. If the passage of time is something that makes losses non-proximate, then the first thing to burn should be more proximate than the second and third.

The two Wagon Mound cases thus seem exceedingly strange. A thick oil spill spreads around and then catches on fire after welding restarts; a wharf and then two ships are damaged; the shipowners, but not the wharf-owner, recover. We might have been able to tolerate the reverse. Had Mort's Dock collected and the shipowners not collected, we could have understood the court as drawing a line in time between the first fire and then the second and third. Indeed, we might have said that the court was eager to find some liability, for without such liability and in the days before effective environmental protection statutes and agencies, and extensive clean-up requirements, spills of heavy oil that does not easily catch fire might otherwise go largely undeterred. A court might want to impose some liability, and yet still recognize that it needs to end the chain of causation somewhere. Recovery for the wharf but not for the vessels would have made this point dramatically apparent. But the Wagon Mound cases, as we have seen, do just the opposite. A single court, the Privy Council, reaches two results that defy logic, as the more proximate cause goes unrecompensed while the more remote ones generate liability even as all these losses come out of the same fire, foreseeable or unforeseeable as the case may be.

It is possible that this paradox is simply the product of change in the Privy Council's membership, or indeed of personality conflicts on the Council. *No. 1* was authored by Lord Simonds, an old school type even for a Lord. He had been knighted in 1937 and joined the Privy Council in 1944. *No. 2* was authored by Lord Reid, who was nine years younger, and certainly more liberal than, Simonds. Reid was an outspoken critic of the practice of suppressing minority viewpoints on the Privy Council, so it is possible that *No. 2* represents Reid's chance to overcome his defeat in *No. 1*, where he was likely overshadowed by Viscount Simonds.

Reid became senior Lord of Appeal in 1962, the year Simonds left the Council. It is often tempting to see important cases and statutes as the product of personalities and happenstance, but of course it is more instructive to see law as reflecting broader cultural and functional concerns. Given this larger goal, and the absence of any hard evidence about Reid's position in *Wagon Mound (No. 1)* or the relationship between Simonds and Reid, I set aside the idea that the two Wagon Mound cases simply reflect the influence or conflicting personalities of these two judges.

Multiple Tortfeasors

But imagine for a moment that the Privy Council knew precisely what it was doing and that law down under (and elsewhere) is not unfathomable but rather admirable and mysteriously elegant. The Privy Council's apparent inconsistency should, after all, be measured against the fact that when deciding against Mort's Dock in *No. 1* the Council must have known that claims regarding the Corrimal and the Audrey D were heading its way. The Privy Council could easily have issued consistent results, or even made the more remote loss be the one to go uncompensated, so that it is possible these judges meant to convey a message with their puzzling treatment of the two Wagon Mound cases. Let us try to set aside questions about foreseeability, and focus instead on the behavior and injuries at issue in these cases. The idea is to think of the proximate cause doctrine and the talk about foreseeability as tools rather than as central issues. Foreseeability may be the tail that wags a more important dog.

It may be useful to revisit the facts of these cases without any suggestion that they are about foreseeability and the questions with which we began, and with some skepticism about the language used by the New South Wales Court and the Privy Council. We begin with a major oil spill by the Wagon Mound followed by premature welding on Mort's Dock which causes a fire and leads to the destruction of the wharf owned by Mort's Dock and then also to the damage of ships owned by the Miller Steamship Company and the R.W. Miller Company. If the case arose today, Miller Steamship would surely sue both the Wagon Mound and Mort's Dock, which is to say the oilspiller and the firestarter, even as Mort's Dock would surely sue the Wagon Mound for the value of the former's wharf. In most jurisdictions, comparative negligence would govern the case, for this modern doctrine allows apportionment of blame, or damages, among several defendant-tortfeasors or between a plaintiff whose negligence contributed to the injury at issue and a defendant (or more than one) who also contributed to the problem. The doctrine facilitates partial recoveries, or the apportionment of losses across several responsible parties. Had the Miller Steamship brought such a suit, it might have expected to recover from both defendants in a manner to be allocated by the court. In turn, Mort's Dock, the defendant in one case and the plaintiff in the other—or simply a party in one large, modern comparative negligence lawsuit—might or might not collect from the Wagon Mound, depending on how the factfinder allocated fault between the Wagon Mound and Mort's Dock. For all the talk in the decision about Mort's Dock inquiring as to whether normal work could continue in the midst of the furnace oil, few readers will have thought that the resumption of welding was wise. It is difficult to correct for our hindsight bias, knowing as we do that fire broke out, but it does seem reckless to begin welding based on one opinion and with no extra precautions. It hardly seems likely that a careful enterprise would begin burning and welding in the midst of a harbor full of thick oil and with nothing more than the say-so of a neighbor as to the flammability of this kind of oil spread upon water. Mort's Dock would be more sympathetic if, for example, it had inquired into the dissipation properties of the heavy oil or the danger posed by the oil-soaked wharf. Nor is there any evidence that Mort's Dock brought in any firefighting equipment, experimented with flames on the oil slick in a confined space, or took other special precautions before normal welding resumed. Similarly, once its operations resumed, Mort's Dock might have continued to inquire about appropriate safety conditions, and it might at least have organized a work crew to clear away debris that floated under or near its welding sites. The modern reader will have observed that Caltex may also have been at fault because it gave poor advice, because some of the oil floating in the water came from its operation, or even because some of the debris that may have played a role in igniting the furnace oil could be traced to its property. A modern plaintiff might have sued three parties, the Wagon Mound for the spill, Mort's Dock for the welding, and Caltex for the reasons just sketched. Again, we would contemplate some allocation of liability to Mort's Dock. In the actual case, of course, the Wagon Mound was the lone defendant in the cases that made their way to the Privy Council.

Why did the shipowners not sue Mort's Dock? The central feature of every answer to this question is that comparative negligence, as between a plaintiff and defendant as well as among several defendants among whom contribution may be sought, was not available in this jurisdiction at this point in history.[9] A secondary answer is that the decline of Mort's

---

[9] Nor would joint, or joint and several, liability have been available. Joint liability can apply in situations where multiple defendants have acted in concert (as when two persons wrongfully shoot and injure a third) or where multiple wrongdoers have acted in a way such that any one of them alone would have caused the full damage even without the negligence of the other(s)—and where the wrongdoers seem about equally responsible for

Dock may have been apparent so that it was an unattractive defendant even when the cases were making their way through the lower courts. Today, the land that was once occupied by Mort's Dock is now Mort Bay Park, and the surrounding area has been transformed into an upscale destination with insufficient parking.[10] The thick oil and the debris are apparently, and finally, gone. The change in land use may reflect the fact that Mort's Dock was a declining, unattractive defendant.[11]

In a world without comparative negligence one normally chooses the most culpable party to sue, so that even if we think that the resumption of welding with no further precautions was careless, and even if we think that Mort's Dock was a thriving business, or land owner, capable of paying a tort judgment, it would still have been natural for suits to be filed against the Wagon Mound. It is also the case that Mort's Dock was a local business, while the Wagon Mound was British owned and took off for other waters as quickly as possible. These factors cut in opposite directions. Local courts might be thought more sympathetic to local businesses, though that sort of provincialism is usually associated with juries rather than judges. At the same time, it is easier to sue and collect when filing a claim against a fixed local establishment. We might, therefore, understand plaintiffs' focus on the Wagon Mound as the product of straightforward strategic thinking about bringing suit against the more culpable and less sympathetic wrongdoer. Moreover, the presence of some evidence that it was safe to weld in the midst of furnace oil actually made suit against the Wagon Mound yet more attractive, because this information would prevent Wagon Mound from simply saying that Mort's Dock had been an intervening wrongdoer that severed the chain of causation.[12]

---

the injury. There may be some relaxation of the first of these requirements, but joint and several liability is almost unimaginable in a case where two parties acting separately (not in concert) bring about a loss, and where judges and juries would not think of them as equally to blame.

[10] Scott Rochfort, *Mort Bay, Balmain,* Sydney Morning Herald, April 13, 2002, at Metro., 2.

[11] It is *not* the case that Mort's Dock chose not to rebuild in order to await real estate development and the profits it would bring. The property was purchased for public housing, and was not privately developed for some ten years.

[12] Similarly, a claim based on joint liability would have failed. Joint liability is *never* the rule where one tortfeasor is a much more serious or wrongful actor than the other. In modern times, plaintiff can bring a comparative negligence claim, and expect the factfinder to allocate responsibility among the defendants. In a case where the allocation is 85%–15%, for example, a plaintiff who brings a comparative negligence claim can expect recovery in that proportion, and in the event that one defendant is judgment proof, jurisdictions have diverse rules regarding the extent to which the remaining defendant can be called upon to make the plaintiff whole. In the era before comparative negligence developed, there would never have been joint and several liability—though there might have been had the

The central point is now before us. Among the many things that tort law aims to do, it seeks to deter wrongful actors by requiring such actors to pay when their negligent behavior causes harms. But what should tort law do when there is more than one negligent party? One possibility is of course to ask all the wrongful parties to pay some share of the losses they have together caused. We associate this strategy with the doctrine of comparative negligence, a doctrine that can apply to cases where a plaintiff and defendant have combined to cause injury but also to situations involving several negligent defendants. It is not a perfect rule, as for example when parties expect other parties to be judgment proof. But in most settings the prospect of some liability when one participates in a tort, along with the prospect of an increasing share of this liability the more other parties are well behaved, will encourage socially respectable and efficient behavior. In the absence of comparative negligence, foreseeability can be used to create a substitute means of deterring multiple parties, by allocating different losses to the several negligent parties. If Mort's Dock and the Wagon Mound were both at fault, comparative negligence would have us add up the losses to the ships and to the wharf, and then allocate this total between the two defendants. In turn, the foreseeability approach allocates not the total pool of losses but the individual plaintiffs, or assets, that are lost. One easy way to do this is to have the second negligent party, the wharf owner, simply absorb its own loss while the oil-spiller pays for the lost ships. Had the wharf suffered no damage at all, and had the two damaged ships sued separately, it is plausible that the courts would have found their way toward a solution in which Mort's Dock paid for one of the damaged ships while the oil-spilling Wagon Mound paid for the other (larger one, no doubt). Again, the court might have used the language of foreseeability and proximate cause to accomplish this allocation.[13]

A slightly simpler version of the story told here is that the first Wagon Mound case concerns a plaintiff that is contributorily negligent— but also a defendant that is poised to escape the scene with no liability at all. In such a situation, the moral might be, clever courts will nevertheless allow contributory negligence to apply so long as they see other cases on the horizon with which to deter the first wrongdoer. Mort's Dock fails to recover because it was likely careless, and the Wagon Mound is made to pay in *No. 2* in order to prevent it from going completely free. But the important thing is to see that the Wagon Mound

---

allocation been 50–50, but plaintiff would likely have collected 100% from the more responsible (85%) defendant.

[13] Other doctrines in tort law might do the same. Thus, assumption of risk and last clear chance may be applied in ways that spread liability across multiple wrongdoers, ensuring that every wrongdoer is deterred. But this larger claim takes us too far from our story.

Cases involve multiple parties, multiple losses and, very likely, an informed and sophisticated court that was able to make the entire story—spread out across multiple cases including one that might be filed later on—come out right. Taken one at a time, the cases seem inconsistent, but viewed as a whole and in the context of the overall goals of the tort system, the results are quite elegant.

Palsgraf Reconsidered

Consider now that most famous of all causation cases, *Palsgraf v. Long Island Rail Road*, decided seven years after *Polemis* but well before *Wagon Mound*. The Long Island Rail Road operated with crowded platforms and commuter trains, and their guards helped the pushing crowds on to train cars. As it turns out, the law had long helped plaintiffs recover for many kinds of injuries suffered on crowded train platforms and in the trains themselves. By the beginning of the Twentieth Century railroads were regularly paying (or settling cases) following injuries that could loosely be blamed on the railroads.[14] It appears that these payments did not cause the Long Island Rail Road to change things much; trains and platforms were extremely crowded during these peak years of mass transit, and the company appears to have decided that the gains from carrying extra passengers exceeded the losses associated with paying for those injuries which occurred.[15] Modern law and economics students will recognize this as an example of the idea that a party may behave the same when subject to a negligence rule as it will if subjected to strict liability. In any event, we can be sure that the *Palsgraf* court was aware of these frequent injuries and payments by the railroad, much as the first Privy Council was aware of the ships damaged by fire.

But Mrs. Palsgraf herself was not injured by simple jostling or pushing. In her case, the guards who pushed and pulled to help a passenger aboard caused this passenger to drop a parcel on the tracks, the parcel was an unmarked bag containing fireworks, the subsequent

---

[14] See James W. Ely, Jr., *Railroads and American Law* 221 (2001) ("On the whole, passengers received solicitous treatment from judges and legislators, a fact that seemingly contradicts the contention that the negligence standard was employed to hold down the operating costs of railroads.").

[15] I am unable to find evidence that the Long Island Rail Road employed guards for the purpose of pushing in more passengers at peak times during this period, though this was the practice for many years on the Interborough Rapid Transit (IRT) subway line in New York, and is to this day the case in Tokyo, where *shirioshi* do the job equipped only with white gloves. The role of these New York platform attendants is evidenced by the character Pusher Ross in the World War I movie, "Sergeant York." If there were such professional pushers at work in Mrs. Palsgraf's case, then it is even more apparent that the railroad internalized the costs and benefits by virtue of paying for injuries that the pushing practice generated.

explosion rocked and damaged the station's platform causing a stampede, and then either the rocking or the stampede caused some scales to
topple over and injure Mrs. Palsgraf.[16] Judge Benjamin Cardozo, writing
for the majority, famously found her injury too remote, but in (what we
will soon see to be) the most brilliant line of the opinion he says, "the
wrongdoer as to her [Mrs. Palsgraf] is the man who carries the bomb,
not the one who explodes it without suspicion of the danger."[17]

Hundreds and perhaps thousands of pages have been written about
Palsgraf, but I think we now see that a novel and attractive way to think
about it is as another substitute for, or precursor to, comparative
negligence. Arguably, there are two wrongdoers, the railroad and the
fellow who carries around fireworks in a bag in a crowded public place.
Cardozo might have liked to make both pay, perhaps by dividing the
damages between these tortfeasors. But in a system where only one is to
pay—and where it is plain that the railroad (if it continues to push and
pull passengers aboard) will pay another day because the usual portfolio
of bruised knees and broken limbs will come about—it is ingenious to let
the railroad go free and to encourage Mrs. Palsgraf, or future plaintiffs
like her, to sue the carrier of explosive fireworks. In this way, both
tortfeasors will be penalized and deterred when all is said and done.
Here we must look not to two cases decided by a single court, but rather
to the single case before a court along with another that it contemplates
(to be brought by a party yet unknown). The talk of the case may be
about foreseeability, but that factor is more of a tool than the main point
of the exercise.

Palsgraf is more elegant than *Wagon Mound* in this regard because
there is no contributory negligence by the injured plaintiff in *Palsgraf*.
Mrs. Palsgraf loses, at least in her suit against the railroad, despite the
fact that she (unlike Mort's Dock perhaps) is absolutely without fault. It
is therefore a cleaner example of the way in which unforeseeability can
do the work that comparative negligence might later take on. On the
other hand, *Wagon Mound* is a better vehicle for illuminating this role
for foreseeability because it is so striking that a single court imposed
liability in *Wagon Mound (No. 2)* after declining to do so in *No. 1*.
Palsgraf would be more like *Wagon Mound* if Cardozo had a second case
(that he could see coming his way) in which someone was injured yet
farther down the platform, perhaps because the scales fell and then
caused another parcel to fall and injure this second plaintiff. With two
plaintiffs' injuries to allocate in cases arising out of a single transaction,
Cardozo might well have allowed the second plaintiff to recover from the

---

[16] *Compare* John T. Noonan, Jr., *Persons and Masks of the Law* 119 (1976) *with*
Richard A. Posner, *Cardozo: A Study in Reputation* 38–39 (1990).

[17] Palsgraf v. Long Island R.R. Co., 162 N.E. 99, 100 (N.Y.1928).

railroad. One injury would be enough for the carrier of fireworks. Instead, Cardozo had to make do with the fact that the railroad had paid and could be expected to pay for injuries that occurred because of pushing alone.[18] Having come this far we can also see that *Polemis* is not necessarily at odds with either *Wagon Mound* or *Palsgraf*. A superficial reading puts these cases at opposite ends of a spectrum as to the role of foreseeability. In *Polemis* the plank-dropper pays for the unforeseeable explosion that occurs, while in *Wagon Mound (No. 1)* and in *Palsgraf* the unanticipated injuries are not charged to the original wrongdoers, the oilspiller and the pushy railroad. But seen through the lens of multiple wrongdoers, the cases are quite consistent. In *Wagon Mound (No. 1)* and in *Palsgraf* the defendants leave court unscathed because the courts see other defendants who need to be deterred with these very losses. Meanwhile, the defendants who are present in the first cases will be deterred elsewhere. In *Wagon Mound* that will happen in *No. 2*, the case brought by the fire-suffering shipowners, and in *Palsgraf* that will happen at the hands of past and (inevitable) future plaintiffs who are injured because of the crowds or guards. But in *Polemis* there is no multiple party issue, and perhaps we should take the *Polemis* approach, of all but ignoring foreseeability when it comes to damages and in this way limiting foreseeability inquiries to the negligence calculus, as following from the presence of but a single tortfeasor. With just one tortfeasor to deter, the argument goes, judges are more inclined to follow the thinskull rule and to avoid any artificial constructs that limit liability, including the degree/kind distinction.

It is interesting that on the Polemis the plank-dropper was very much a part of the shipping operation. A group of workers was hired to move containers of benzine from the hold of the Polemis to another location. It was while moving these containers, and with equipment brought on for that purpose, that a plank was dropped and the benzine ignited by a spark. The case is thus very much about a single tortfeasor and actually not a very good example of liability for unanticipated events because it is not particularly unforeseeable that leaking containers of a highly flammable substance might catch fire if heavy things are dropped

---

[18] Indeed, a simple view of *Palsgraf* is that where there are two tortfeasors involved in generating a loss, one subject to strict liability and the other to a negligence regime, then it is the negligent one that should be expected to pay. One leap here is the association of the railroad with strict liability, for in principle common carriers are strictly liable for damage to freight and not persons. Still, the cases and settlement practices of the pre-*Palsgraf* period suggest something akin to strict liability for mishaps in trains and on crowded platforms. *See supra* note 12. The idea itself, that as between the railroad and the carrier of fireworks, it is the more patently blameworthy carrier that should pay, can be said to anticipate cases like *Indiana Harbor Belt R.R. v. American Cyanamid Co.*, 916 F.2d 1174 (7th Cir.1990) (Posner, J.) (declining to find strict liability with respect to manufacturer and shipper of chemicals where other parties may have been negligent).

on or near them. Indeed, liability would have been found under the old manner/type approach. But even where the losses are quite unanticipated, the argument here is that with a single tortfeasor we should expect courts to be less inclined to use foreseeability as a tool for limiting damages. The unforeseeability limitation is seen as a means of saving damages for other wrongdoers, and where there are no other tortfeasors to deter there is less of a need to draw the foreseeable/unforeseeable line.

Foreseeability with Comparative Negligence and Other Regulatory Tools

This emphasis on unforeseeability as a tool with which to impose damages on additional tortfeasors, rather than as mechanism for limiting damages paid by the first and most obvious tortfeasor, raises the question of what becomes of unforeseeability when comparative negligence comes into play. If a modern court can use comparative negligence to deter multiple tortfeasors, perhaps because it becomes authorized to do so by the legislature, then what should be expected of (un)foreseeability? There is no need to answer this question in order to understand the four great cases discussed here because they predated the development of comparative negligence. But the question is surely an important one going forward inasmuch as contemporary legal systems have rather widely adopted comparative negligence. It is easy to imagine more liability for unforeseeable consequences, because there is no need to save consequences for other tortfeasors. But one can also imagine very little change in outcomes, with courts enjoying two tools, unforeseeability and comparative negligence, with which to deal with the challenges of multiple tortfeasors. In this regard, foreseeability may continue to be used as a means of systemic manipulation when some of the relevant wrongdoers are not before the court. I leave these questions for other classes and stories.

Somewhat similarly, the Wagon Mound might have been better deterred by environmental laws requiring the cleanup of oil spills, a requirement that oil-carrying ships post bonds to guarantee their clean and safe passage, and so forth. But these requirements, though familiar to the modern reader, had not yet developed when the great cases discussed here were decided. Modern regulatory systems take some of the burden off tort law by using such new tools to control the behavior of multiple parties in one environment. It may be that resourceful courts, following the lead of Cardozo and the Privy Council, would have made complicated new regulatory systems unnecessary. But again, the role of unforeseeability and the strategies that law has developed for regulating large numbers of parties whose activities can not always be easily traced to harmful consequences, are topics left for other books and courses.

6

Anita Bernstein

Hymowitz v. Eli Lilly and Co.:
Markets of Mothers

Back in the fifties, Shirley Hymowitz adored her doctor, a Park Avenue eminence named Ernest Gladstone. She remembered him later as "a man I had more faith in than God. He had delivered me, and he delivered my children." The young Brooklyn homemaker gave birth to her first daughter, Rita, in 1952, when she was 23, and her second daughter, Mindy, in 1954. Both pregnancies were fretful events. Shirley Hymowitz worried that they might not continue to term. "I was staining, and at the time it was considered a miracle drug," Mrs. Hymowitz said, recalling what the kind, father-like Dr. Gladstone prescribed for her. "I took more with Mindy because I bled more." Millions of pregnant American women—the estimates run as high as six million, and no lower than a million and a half—ingested DES during the decades following World War II, ostensibly to prevent miscarriages and make their babies healthier.[1] Not all of these consumers knew what they were ingesting— several believed their DES was a vitamin—and others never remembered the name of the substance. Shirley Hymowitz remembered. "When I took that drug, the name fascinated me. Stil*best*rol. I said, what a strange name."[2]

Growing up near the peak of the American baby boom, the Hymowitz sisters became "very different" people, as their mother saw them.

---

[1] The six million figure is from a *People* magazine feature, presumably verified in some way by fact-checking staff. *See Before His Cancer Ordeal, Lawyer Craig Diamond Defended DES Makers: Now He's Suing His Former Clients*, People, May 9, 1983, at 40. *See also* Shelly Squires, *DES Found to Pose Lifelong Risk*, The Record (Bergen County), Aug. 2, 1999, at H1 (quoting National Institutes of Health estimate of 4.8 million); Robert Meyers, *D.E.S.: The Bitter Pill* 13 (1983) ("At least 3 percent of the nation's current population was exposed . . .").

[2] Interview with Shirley Hymowitz (July 3, 2002).

"Rita's a very calm, gentle woman. She lives on a farm in Virginia. She has a daughter. She also had four or five miscarriages." Mindy Hymowitz grew up funny, tough, eager to reach for risks—"a pistol," recalled her friend Randy Deutsch.[3] When Mindy found out that she had been badly hurt—she had clear-cell adenocarcinoma of the vagina, a rare cancer almost never found in young women—and also that many well-informed observers blamed a negligent industry for that type of injury, she took a fighting stance. Lying in her hospital bed after her hysterectomy in 1979, weak and wracked with pain, the 24–year-old nurse stretched for the telephone and began calling lawyers, one after the next. "Somebody had to be held responsible," she later recalled, "and it certainly was not my mother."[4]

Biography of a Drug

Stilbestrol, also known as DES or diethylstilbestrol, is a synthetic version of estrogen. Though naturally present in both male and female bodies, estrogen is considered the principal female hormone. Scientists first isolated estrogen in the 1920s. From the start, physicians sought to prescribe it as a treatment for symptoms of menopause. But estrogen proved difficult to administer. Like many other hormones, natural estrogen is destroyed by saliva and gastric juices, and therefore cannot be taken orally. It can be injected, but to little profit for those who market it: Patients dislike injections.

Accordingly, researchers set out to find a way to redesign natural estrogen into a form that patients could take by mouth, in a pill. The first to succeed was an English team of scientists led by chemist-physician E.C. Dodds. His link to an overprescribed drug notwithstanding, Charles Dodds throughout a long, brilliant career opposed reckless medication. He spent time and effort in the 1930s pleading for more care in the dispensation of sex hormones, and also denounced "the general public's desire for the maintenance of youth and all that it implies, together with the successful exploitation of this trait by commercial firms." In the 1930s Dr. Dodds had the skills in biochemistry and endocrinology to understand, and perhaps even invent, a birth control pill and a "morning after pill," but he disapproved of these projects and would not touch them, believing that the female reproductive cycle was too delicate to be maneuvered in what would amount to an uncontrolled experiment.[5]

---

[3] Interview with Randy Deutsch (July 14, 2002).

[4] Quoted in Henry Gilgoff, *The DES Daughters Get Day in Court*, Newsday, May 1, 1989, Business, at 1.

[5] Meyers, *supra* note 1, at 42–43.

Dodds never patented his 1938 invention because his source of funding, a British Medical Research Council grant, required grant recipients to share their discoveries with the public rather than patent them for private gain.[6] By not patenting DES, Dodds made it easy for drug manufacturers to produce and sell it. Under the federal Food, Drug, and Cosmetic Act, newly enacted in 1938, anyone with Food and Drug Administration approval could manufacture or market an approved drug;[7] the lack of a patent saved DES manufacturers the expense of a license. Manufacturing this drug was like printing money: according to one judicial opinion, natural estrogen cost three hundred times as much as DES to manufacture.[8]

To get approval from the newly formed FDA, each would-be DES manufacturer was expected to file a new drug application. The 1930s version of a new drug application required the manufacturer to state the drug's chemical makeup, production methods, proposed labeling, and information about its safety and anticipated applications. Applicants did not have to say anything about efficacy then; the efficacy requirement arrived later in 1962. By the end of 1940, ten companies had submitted separate proposals to the FDA regarding stilbestrol.

In their applications, these drug manufacturers proposed selling DES to treat gynecological ailments. They made no reference to improving the outcomes of pregnancy. For reasons that are now not entirely clear, the FDA, after meeting with officials from the ten applicants, directed the companies to withdraw their separate applications and create one consolidated new-drug file. This file referred to no controlled human studies, said nothing about a known association between estrogen and cancer, and did not cite animal studies that might have suggested DES was dangerous. What the file did provide were numerous anecdotes about successful outcomes.[9]

---

[6] Roberta J. Apfel & Susan M. Fisher, *To Do No Harm: DES and the Dilemmas of Modern Medicine* 12–14 (1984); Meyers, *supra* note 1, at 11 (quoting Dodds).

[7] Martin v. Abbott Laboratories, 689 P.2d 368, 373 (Wash.1984); Ferrigno v. Eli Lilly & Co., 420 A.2d 1305, 1310 (N.J. Super. Ct. Law Div. 1980); Richard M. Russell, Note, *The Causation Requirement: Guardian of Fairness or Obstacle to Justice?—Making Sense of a Decade of DES Litigation*, 25 Suffolk U. L. Rev. 1071, 1072–73 (1991).

[8] *Ferrigno* at 1310.

[9] Lucinda M. Finley, *The Pharmaceutical Industry and Women's Reproductive Health: The Perils of Ignoring Risk and Blaming Women, in Corporate Victimization of Women* 59, 64–64 (Elizabeth Szockyj & James G. Fox eds., 1996). Today anecdotes about happy results are not considered good enough evidence to support the use of a particular drug. Clinicians expect data from randomized and controlled studies, showing that the drug yields better results than a placebo.

The FDA approved DES in 1941 to treat four conditions: menopausal disorders, gonorrheal vaginitis, senile vaginitis, and unwanted lactation. The approval did not extend to pregnancy, but physicians were free to dispense DES to pregnant women if they so chose. In approving the new drug, the FDA also directed the companies to work with the same formula in manufacturing DES, to develop uniform labeling for usage and recommended dosage, and to send their patient reports to the same consolidated file.

Soon manufacturers began to think about marketing DES to pregnant women. This marketing strategy—the companies' going beyond passive supply and expressly telling physicians that DES was good for pregnancy—required separate new approval from the FDA. Manufacturers were encouraged by early findings that natural estrogen could correct hormonal deficiencies that contributed to miscarriages, and by other studies that supported the hypothesis that stilbestrol functioned like natural estrogen for this purpose. In their supplemental new-drug applications, manufacturers relied on various medical school reports; they conducted very little research in-house.

The FDA approved the first plan to market DES as a miscarriage preventative in 1947. The new anti-miscarriage market caused DES sales to swell. Some manufacturers marketed stilbestrol generically; others promoted the product by a trade name. DES pills varied only by strength and external appearance, however, and so pharmacists frequently would fill prescriptions with whatever they had on hand in the right dosage, a practice of which manufacturers were aware.[10]

The drug filled a deep niche in American society after World War II, as citizens settled into their growing economy. With millions of servicemen just back from the war, couples had reason to view babies as anchoring their new, or newly reunited, marriages. In this climate a healthy child—or, in the later years of DES marketing, a child expected to be even *more* healthy than nature would have provided—warranted the most ardent pursuit.[11] The two decades right after the war also marked a high point of reverence for pharmaceutical innovation, in part because the arrival of penicillin was still a fresh memory. A genuine miracle drug, penicillin had only recently put dreaded conditions like syphilis and staph infection in their place. It made sense then to think that the next drug would be the next miracle. Pat Cody, founder of the patient advocacy group DES Action, said she shudders to think how much DES exposure would have occurred if manufacturers had been permitted to advertise prescription drugs directly to consumers in the

---

[10] See Russell, *supra* note 7, at 1073.

[11] See Meyers, *supra* note 1, at 16 (noting that "in postwar America, when pregnancy was so avidly sought by so many couples, a miscarriage could be enough to distort a woman's perspective, a family's peace, a couple's dreams").

1950s, as they do today: "Fifty million women, not five million," would have taken the drug, Cody estimated.[12]

Not everyone had access to DES, however. The exposed population was mostly white, upper-income, and reasonably well educated.[13] Sybil Shainwald, who went on to become a prominent lawyer noted for work in behalf of DES plaintiffs, remembered being too poor to get DES when she was pregnant in 1950. She couldn't afford to see an obstetrician, even though she, like Shirley Hymowitz, had worried about miscarriage because she had experienced bleeding. "I don't *think* I would have taken [DES]," she mused more than fifty years later. "I wanted a natural childbirth. I'd read *Childbirth Without Fear*," the bible of the alternative birth movement that went through six printings following its first publication in 1944.[14] But the point was moot: when she was a patient, Sybil Shainwald could afford only a general practitioner, a man who did not keep up with the latest pharmaceutical wonders. Women of her class received DES only under rare circumstances.[15]

Against the backdrop of enthusiasm for healthy babies and health-making pharmaceuticals, the manufacturers got a sales boost in 1952 when the FDA declared that stilbestrol was no longer a new drug. This FDA decision meant that any company could market DES for any purpose as long as it followed the standard formula and protocols of packaging. Hundreds of companies entered this lucrative market, promoting DES aggressively to physicians for prescription to pregnant women. Another significant event occurred in 1952: the first medical-journal paper questioning the effectiveness of DES as a miscarriage preventative was published.[16] The two 1952 events came together in an unfortunate way. As word got out that DES was perhaps useless to prevent miscarriage—indeed, later studies found that it seemed to make miscarriage *more* likely, not less likely[17]—manufacturers retreated some-what from the miscarriage promise and marketed DES more vaguely as a source of healthier, heartier, better babies,[18] a claim that the FDA did not ask them to support.

---

[12] Interview with Pat Cody (Aug. 1, 2002).

[13] Finley, *supra* note 9, at 67.

[14] Interview with Sybil Shainwald (Aug. 4, 2002).

[15] *See, e.g.*, Mink v. University of Chicago, 460 F.Supp. 713 (N.D.Ill.1978) (seeking damages for plaintiffs who were given DES without their knowledge or consent as part of a research study).

[16] David Robinson & Landrum B. Shettles, *The Use of Diethystilbestrol in Threatened Abortion*, 63 Am. J. Obstetrics & Gynecology 1330 (1952).

[17] Finley, *supra* note 9, at 66–67. *See also infra* notes 25–26 and accompanying text.

[18] Interview with Lucinda Finley (July 31, 2002). One 1957 advertisement in a medical journal touted DES in bold terms: "Recommended for routine prophylaxis in ALL pregnan-

Although DES never lost its FDA approval and is still occasionally prescribed today[19]—and can also be ingested via hormone-fed animals that are slaughtered to become meat[20]—the era of routine distribution to healthy women came to an end in 1971, when researchers published the first of a series of grim findings regarding DES children: Young women whose mothers had ingested DES were developing clear-cell adenocarcinoma of the vagina, a disease that strikes almost no woman absent DES exposure. The physician who won the most fame for the discovery was Arthur Herbst, whose report about teenage adenocarcinoma, published first in 1971, was reprinted in *Classic Pages in Obstetrics and Gynecology* in 1999.[21] A DES mother, unnamed in the literature, shares credit for discovering the connection. In 1969 gynecologist Howard Ulfelder, later a co-author with Herbst, was puzzling over having seen three young patients in three years with clear-cell adenocarcinoma, the disease that young women were never supposed to get. He remained puzzled when the third patient's mother remarked to him, "I don't think I ever told you that when I was pregnant with Shelley the doctor put me on stilbestrol because I had lost one pregnancy. Could that have anything to do with it?" Ulfelder doubted it, but checked with the mother of the second patient. Yes, said the second mother. She had taken DES. "I thought, My God ...," Ulfelder recalled.[22]

Soon came new reports of other conditions. Among them were adenosis, a growth of misplaced tissue, sometimes called "precancerous," that appears on the cervix or vagina and requires monitoring; infertility, miscarriages, and premature births; menstrual abnormalities; and an

---

cies ... 96 per cent live delivery with desPLEX [a trade name for DES] ...—bigger and stronger babies too. No gastric or other side effects with desPLEX—in either high or low dosage." *Reprinted at* http://www.aaronlevinelaw.com/des.htm (last visited Feb. 19, 2003).

[19] Charles B. Huggins won the Nobel prize in medicine for his use of DES in alleviating prostate cancer, a use that continues. Meyers, *supra* note 1, at 43–44.

[20] Unlike DES generally, DES as food for animals to make them bigger is a patented technology. The Iowa State College Research Foundation made millions on this patent, and built an auditorium with some of the income. Cynthia Laitman Orenberg, *DES: The Complete Story* 135 (1981). In 1979 the federal government banned feeding DES to food animals. The Department of Agriculture website now expresses doubt that anyone would violate this law, because other hormones, "such as trenbolone acetate and estradiol," are more effective than DES in promoting growth, and also easier to obtain. Nevertheless, in July 1999 the Swiss government complained that it had found DES in U.S. beef. *See* http://www.fsis.usda.gov/oa/background/des.htm. Robert Meyers believes that every American who ate meat before 1979 is a DES-exposed person. Meyers, *supra* note 1, at 202: "You didn't have to be pregnant to get DES in America: you just had to have a good meal."

[21] 181 Am. J. Obstetrics & Gynecology 1574 (1999). The original article is Arthur L. Herbst et al., *Adenocarcinoma of the Vagina: Association of Maternal Stilbestrol Therapy with Tumor Appearance in Young Women*, 284 New Eng. J. Med. 878 (1971).

[22] Quoted in Meyers, *supra* note 1, at 93–94.

array of psychological and emotional conditions that remain inadequately understood.[23] Researchers would later discover harmful effects in DES
mothers and sons. In November 1971, the FDA decreed DES contraindicated for use in pregnancy, and ordered manufacturers to warn physicians of its dangers.[24]

Negligence? Defectiveness?

Because DES won its fame in Torts on the question of "market
share," an observer can easily overlook the question of whether the
manufacturers could be held liable in tort. When they rule on the
question of whether to apply market-share liability, judges typically
begin by presuming that DES manufacturers could be found liable if the
identification problem were resolved. Were the manufacturers at fault?
Or, to speak in the jargon of products liability rather than torts, was
DES a defective product? Decades after ceasing to market DES to
pregnant women, the manufacturers of DES do not concede negligence
or defectiveness.

The Claim of Manufacturer Negligence and Product Defect

By 1939, before the FDA approved the marketing of DES for limited
clinical conditions, more than 40 articles "documenting carcinogenic
effects of natural and synthetic estrogens, including DES" had been
published in medical journals.[25] In 1939 and 1940, a Northwestern
University study found that "an alarming number" of the offspring of
pregnant rats that were fed DES had reproductive-organ anomalies:
misshapen uteruses, ovaries, and vaginas in many of the females, tiny
and malformed penises in a smaller number of the males.[26] DES manufacturers did not act in response to these findings.

DES had won a big publicity boost following research in the late
1940s by the husband-and-wife team of George Smith, a gynecologist,
and Olive Watkins Smith, an endocrinologist. The Smiths reported

---

[23] See Orenberg, *supra* note 20, at 54–75.

[24] Martin v. Abbott Laboratories, 689 P.2d 368, 374 (Wash.1984). The FDA was slow to
act. The 1971 findings were published in April, and the FDA did not declare DES
contraindicated for use in pregnancy until November. By contrast the New York state
health commissioner, Hollis Ingraham, immediately wrote to all practicing physicians in
New York with the news of the adverse findings. Ingraham urged the FDA to ban DES for
use in pregnancy, but the FDA did nothing for eight months, during which time an
estimated 60,000 more women received prescriptions for DES. Finley, *supra* note 9, at 68–
69.

[25] Finley, *supra* note 8, at 61.

[26] *Id.* at 62.

findings that suggested an association between DES ingestion and an unexpectedly large number of healthy full-term babies among women at high risk for pregnancy complications. But these findings were soon attacked as unsound. When researchers tried to replicate them with controlled studies (the Smiths' findings were mainly anecdotal), they found that DES was of no value in preventing miscarriage. Bed rest, not DES, probably deserved the credit when the Smiths' mix of bed rest and DES improved the outcomes of pregnancy.

In 1952, Columbia researchers announced that DES was "a dismal failure in the general treatment of threatened abortion." Later studies refuted the Smiths' claims that DES produced healthier babies, one going so far as to find it caused a statistically significant *increase* in miscarriages, premature births, and neonatal deaths.[27] Whereas many dangers of DES, such as the risk of clear-cell cancer and adenosis among daughters, did not reveal themselves for many years, lack of efficacy could have emerged quickly if the manufacturers had undertaken the kind of clinical trials that the FDA began to demand in 1962 before approving new drugs.[28] One might conclude that manufacturers marketed DES to improve pregnancy outcomes long after they knew, or should have known, that serious doubts had been cast on its effectiveness for this purpose.

In the early years of marketing, from 1941 to 1952, when DES was approved only to treat specific conditions in women, salesmen for the manufacturers encouraged physicians to dispense DES for a variety of other conditions.[29] Long after the Smiths' claims about pregnancy outcomes were debunked, these manufacturers repeated these dubious claims to physicians in their promotional materials.[30] Moreover, whereas the Smiths themselves had evaluated DES as a therapy for women at risk for losing their pregnancies, manufacturers touted the drug as a panacea, good for all pregnant women.[31] These marketing tactics appear in hindsight unbounded. "The drug manufacturers who jumped on the DES bandwagon either never made the computations or didn't care," says one website addressed to DES claimants, but the recommended

[27] *Id.* at 65–67.

[28] Apfel & Miller, *supra* note 6, at 24.

[29] *Id.* at 18.

[30] Finley, *supra* note 9, at 67.

[31] It is not clear how cautious the Smiths were in their endorsement of DES. *Compare* Apfel & Miller, *supra* note 6, at 24–25 (describing careful, narrow recommendations), *with* W.J. Dieckmann et al., *Does the Administration of Diethystilbestrol During Pregnancy Have Therapeutic Value?*, 66 Am. J. Obstetrics & Gynecology 1062 (1953) (claiming that the Smiths had "suggested that increasing amounts of diethystilbestrol should be administered to *all* women during pregnancy") (emphasis added).

dosage of DES given to pregnant women "was the equivalent of the estrogenic effect of 55,666 birth control pills."[32]

Defense attorneys contacted for this chapter refused to provide the manufacturers' side of the story, citing ongoing litigation, but over the years spokespersons for the DES industry have maintained that the manufacturers were not at fault. "Lilly relied on the universities to do all the testing," one Lilly lawyer told a reporter in 1979. "If I were Lilly, and you gave me $100 million, and you said, 'Okay, go test the drug in 1947,' " the most respected authorities to do the job would have been the Boston researcher Priscilla White, and George and Olive Smith. "They were state of the art," the lawyer, Edwin Heafey, continued. "They knew more about this subject than anybody alive."[33]

For her part, Olive Smith objected bitterly to the blight that DES reports had cast on the Smiths' long careers. The couple had been superstars: Olive was the first woman to get a Ph.D. from Harvard's medical school; George published his first ten papers when he was still a medical student. The two broke major ground in obstetrics and endocrinology, but are thought of today as wrongheaded researchers whose Harvard credentials helped to underwrite the spread of a toxic drug. In an interview published in 1983, the octogenarian Olive insisted that DES did not cause cancer, and that reproductive-organ anomalies in DES daughters could well relate to their mothers' having had similar problems.[34]

Collateral Estoppel on Negligence or Defectiveness?

The issues of negligence and defectiveness have remained disputed in DES litigation into the twenty-first century, even though the harmful properties of DES are today taken as fact in schools and departments of American universities and in the popular media. Yet this conclusion continues to be relitigated. Plaintiffs savor a 1979 precedent, *Bichler v. Eli Lilly & Co.*,[35] that deemed Lilly to have been negligent for not testing the drug on pregnant mice. Defendants retort that issue preclusion on the point is improper because different claimants report different injuries, and experience different medical histories. New York courts have held that a plaintiff's clear-cell cancer followed by a hysterectomy and vaginectomy is close enough to Joyce Bichler's injuries to warrant issue

---

[32] Aaron M. Levine & Assocs., *When the Cure Is Worse Than the Disease*, at http://www.aaronlevinelaw.com/des.htm (last visited Feb. 19, 2003).

[33] Quoted in Cynthia Gorney, *DES: Proving The Connection*, Wash. Post, Sept. 7, 1979, at C1.

[34] Meyers, *supra* note 1, at 57. The Smiths also maintained that they had found DES indicated only in a small number of pregnancies. *Id.* at 71.

[35] 436 N.E.2d 182 (N.Y.1982).

preclusion on the question of negligence; they have also held, however, that plaintiffs are not entitled to issue preclusion on proximate cause.[36] DES litigators have reported wins and losses for both sides in recent years; teratologists and epidemiologists continue to be employed as courtroom expert witnesses on negligence and defect.

What About FDA Negligence?

In Torts classrooms over the decades, law students have volunteered their disapproval of the Food and Drug Administration performance with respect to the regulation of DES and wonder why the agency has not been held liable for careless decisionmaking, given that careful decision-making (for example, like that of the distinguished FDA scientist Frances Kelsey, who reviewed an application to market another notorious drug, thalidomide, in the early 1960s) might have saved lives. Observers have objected to the FDA's passive acceptance of industry data on safety and efficacy, its unfounded expansion of manufacturer prerogatives in 1952, and its refusal to take a hint from the thalidomide disaster in 1962—admittedly, most of the DES damage was done by then—that drugs taken during pregnancy might harm offspring. Activist Pat Cody has some sympathy for the agency, especially regarding its decision to put so much faith in manufacturer data during the early years: the FDA "was new in 1938, part of the New Deal; they didn't really know what they were doing."[37] Later in the DES era, the latter half of the 1947–1971 marketing period, however, the agency does appear remiss.

The reason for nonliability is the continuing effect of sovereign immunity on tort litigation. Although many barriers to suing government have fallen, federal agencies remain mostly immune from liability for their discretionary functions—that is, for decisions based on considerations of social or economic policy.[38] Courts have interpreted discretionary-function immunity to be present whenever an official had discretion to adopt the policy that plaintiffs attack. Only if the official violated a binding rule or policy will the agency be liable.[39] Even though FDA officials were obligated to authorize only safe and effective drugs, and even though DES is in hindsight both unsafe and ineffective as both a miscarriage preventative and a promoter of fetal well-being, FDA staff

---

[36] Kaufman v. Eli Lilly & Co., 482 N.E.2d 63 (N.Y.1985); Schaeffer v. Eli Lilly & Co., 113 A.D.2d 827, 830 (N.Y.App.Div.1985).

[37] Interview with Pat Cody (Aug. 1, 2002).

[38] Federal Tort Claims Act, 28 U.S.C. § 2680(a) (2003); Berkovitz v. United States, 486 U.S. 531 (1988).

[39] United States v. Gaubert, 499 U.S. 315 (1991); Campbell v. United States, 167 F.Supp.2d 440 (D.Mass.2001) (noting presumption that government action is considered immunized).

did not violate a clear agency rule or policy when they allowed DES to be marketed.

As plaintiffs and their lawyers appear to have conceded, the FDA had discretion to make the choices it made. Few have even attempted to sue the FDA for DES injuries. Joseph Jamail, a legendarily successful personal-injury lawyer based in Texas, gave it a try in the 1970s on behalf of a client named Beverly Ann Gray. The complaint named the United States and Lilly as defendants. The court dismissed the United States from the case, holding that the FDA approval of DES fell under discretionary-function immunity.[40]

"DES Daughters" Emerge, and Seek Redress, in the 1970s

The 1971 withdrawal of DES as a miscarriage preventative marked a new era for both medical providers and the legal community. Arthur Herbst, the researcher who broke the news about a link between DES and cancer in the *New England Journal of Medicine*, continued his DES research after publishing his initial findings in 1971. He started keeping what became known as the Herbst Registry, a record of all known cases of clear-cell vaginal adenocarcinoma. DES daughters, including Mindy Hymowitz, had their names added to this registry when their physicians reported occurrences of this rare disease. Joyce Bichler, number 70 in the registry and author of the first DES memoir, wrote about the strong feelings her number provoked for her. *Only seventy?*, she thought. And also, *There are seventy others?*[41] Victim awareness, and a movement to the courts, grew in the 1970s.

Paul Rheingold filed the first multi-plaintiff DES lawsuit in 1974.[42] Motivated in part by the DES exposure of his daughter, Julia, Rheingold brought a class action against twenty drug manufacturers. The relief he sought included a national fund, research and treatment programs, and publicity to make DES daughters aware of their plight. What exactly this plight was, Rheingold could not say. The young class members had not

---

[40] Gray v. United States, 445 F.Supp. 337, 339–42 (S.D.Tex.1978). *Accord* In re Orthopedic Bone Screw Product Liability Litigation, 264 F.3d 344 (3d Cir.2001) (immunizing an FDA decision regarding a medical device); Stauber v. Shalala, 895 F.Supp. 1178, 1192 (W.D.Wis.1995) (rejecting consumers' claim against the FDA for approving the marketing of bovine growth hormone because plaintiffs could not prove that the decision to approve was arbitrary and capricious); Sharona Hoffman, *Continued Concern: Human Subject Protection, the Institutional Review Board, and Continuing Review*, 68 Tenn. L. Rev. 725, 743–44 (2001) (noting that a claim against the FDA based on injuries that occurred during a clinical trial is unlikely to succeed because of sovereign immunity).

[41] Joyce Bichler, *DES Daughter: The Joyce Bichler Story* 76–77 (1981).

[42] Rheingold v. E.R. Squibb & Sons, No. 74 Civ. 3420, 1975 U.S. Dist. LEXIS 14160 (S.D.N.Y. Jan. 27, 1975).

yet set out to have children, nor yet experienced adult life under conditions of uncertainty about reproductive health. In the past Rheingold had won notable victories in behalf of plaintiffs' groups. But here he lost, because of the inchoate nature of the harm. Rheingold could allege only exposure, and not a certain injury.[43] His action was dismissed. Undaunted by the class action defeat, Rheingold devoted time in the 1970s to individual claims.

Litigator Sybil Shainwald also spent the 1970s making her mark in New York DES litigation. As a junior lawyer Shainwald represented Joyce Bichler, who at age 17 had been through a hysterectomy and a vaginectomy.[44] Bichler was the first plaintiff to win damages from a jury—$500,000—in a DES cancer case.

As a litigant Bichler was lucky, despite her severe illness and wrenching surgeries: she escaped the Scylla of the statute of limitations (because she was young when she discovered her injury)[45] and the Charybdis of nonidentification. Bichler's mother remembered that her pharmacist had told her the drug came from Lilly, a contention that made Lilly a plausible defendant, even though the jury ultimately rejected Bichler's contention that Lilly had supplied Mrs. Bichler with the drug. And Joyce Bichler brought luck to her fellow plaintiffs too. While refusing to agree that Joyce Bichler had identified the right supplier, her jury found that "the defendant, Eli Lilly, and the other drug manufacturers [had acted] in concert with each other in the testing and marketing of DES for miscarriage purposes."[46] This finding rested in part on the coordination among manufacturers in seeking FDA approval decades earlier. Upheld by the Court of Appeals, the highest court in New York, the concert-of-action precedent permitted courts to hold any DES manufacturer liable in full for the amount of damages that a plaintiff suffered.[47]

New York Litigants Get Over Their Biggest Hurdle

The DES problem is familiar to any Torts student. Two hundred and sixty-seven manufacturers,[48] some of them with only brief experience marketing the drug ... nobody paying for patent licenses that might

---

[43] Stephen Fenicell & Lawrence S. Cherfoos, *Daughters at Risk* 168 (1981).

[44] Bichler, *supra* note 41, at 65–67.

[45] *See infra*, "New York Litigants Get Over Their Biggest Hurdle."

[46] Quoted in Bichler, *supra* note 41, at 180–81.

[47] Bichler v. Eli Lilly & Co., 436 N.E.2d 182 (N.Y.1982).

[48] Judicial opinions often avert to uncertainty about the number, but Robert Meyers says 267. Meyers, *supra* note 1, at 18–19.

have kept better track of sales ... most of the (pre-computer) pharmaceutical and medical records scattered ... some DES mothers deceased, or unable to recall what kind of pill they took ... But wait. Not so fast. From the New York plaintiffs' standpoint, these issues arose only secondarily.

Consider Mindy Hymowitz. In 1979, Hymowitz found out about her vaginal adenocarcinoma. She had been exposed to DES in 1954, before she was born. Thereafter, she had experienced no contact with the substance. Now, assuming the existence of a claim, tort law will ask: When did the tort happen? Surely Mindy's injury occurred before her birth in December 1954. Her claim would be negligence, and in New York, negligence claims are supposed to be brought within three years of the harmful contact. Plaintiffs get the clock turned off when they are minors, but that benefit runs out when they come of age: then the clock turns back on. Mindy Hymowitz hadn't let any time go by. She learned about the cancer in April 1979, at age 24; she underwent a hysterectomy a week later, and was calling for legal help from her hospital bed. Too late, the lawyers said. You're too old.

For DES claimants in New York, the statute of limitations was a far more pressing problem than identifying the defendant. If the statute could not be relaxed, or reinterpreted, or rewritten to permit them to sue, their claims would vanish. Defense litigators typically raise the statute of limitations as an affirmative defense long before they begin to dispute the merits of a claim. As Mindy Hymowitz learned in her hospital room, there was no point even thinking about liability unless the statute of limitations could be dealt with.

Veteran litigator Paul Rheingold recalled the grim work of explaining the statute of limitations, again and again, to his DES clients. They did not accept that the passage of time functions to cut off liability. In their view, what was wrong in the 1950s remained wrong in the 1980s; Mindy Hymowitz spoke for many DES claimants when she said that "[s]omebody had to be held responsible, and it certainly was not my mother."[49] Rheingold remembered one client in particular, Fran Fishbane, a painter and activist. In the mid–1980s Rheingold advised Fishbane that her cause was hopeless. "I told her she might as well just go home and cry," he said.[50] Fishbane duly went home, but instead of crying sketched him a pencil drawing of what she called a hue and cry. She drew angry women in a mob, holding up signs with slogans like "DES Sucks," a raging and protesting fury. Rheingold framed the drawing and hung it in his New York brownstone office, in a collection of law-themed art.

---

[49] See supra note 4 and accompanying text.

[50] Interview with Paul Rheingold (July 16, 2002).

The difficulty that Rheingold struggled to communicate came from a misfit between latent exposure and tort statutes of limitation. Statutes of limitations work well for claims based on traumatic injury—an intentional punch in the nose, or a collision that results from bad driving. With latent exposure, however, injuries take years to ripen, over a gap between what is called the time of exposure and the time of discovery. On this injustice, a bit of wit from Jerome Frank still gets quoted: "Except in topsy-turvy land, you can't die before you are conceived, or be divorced before you marry, or harvest a crop never planted, or burn down a house never built, or miss a train running on a nonexistent railroad."[51] It seems harsh to use the statute of limitations against a plaintiff who may have proceeded at lightning speed. Moreover, if the main purpose of statutes of limitation is to remind courts that memories get stale, and that factual evidence decays as it ages, such statutes offer less benefit for latent-exposure claims—where defendants typically are business enterprises with the capacity to keep records almost indefinitely—than they do for traumatic impacts.

The New York time-of-exposure rule for the statute of limitation was "a dinosaur," according to activist Jay Halfon, the director of the New York Public Interest Research Group (NYPIRG).[52] Other states had started to liberalize their statutes for latent exposure, but New York law held firm to the view that the DES clock had started to tick for Mindy Hymowitz in the mid–1950s, with only a brief, now-expired extension based on her infancy at the time of impact. Mindy and her mother Shirley knew they needed a new statute. The Hymowitzes began traveling to Albany to share their plight with lawmakers. A handful of other DES claimants would make the same trip. "I always saw the same people," Shirley recalled. NYPIRG coordinated the lobbying effort. The AFL–CIO, a leading voice for labor in Albany, joined the endeavor: it too wanted relief from the time-of-exposure cutoff, because many union members were in a similar position with respect to injuries they attributed to workplace exposure to chemicals like PVC in past decades. The governor of New York, Mario Cuomo, supported their cause. But the coalition met tough opposition from Republican leaders in the legislature, who viewed the time-of-exposure rule necessary to protect against unbounded litigation. "You could have driven companies out of the state," said Warren Anderson, the state senate majority leader, several years after the lobbying effort.[53] Eventually Anderson supported a com-

---

[51] Dincher v. Marlin Firearms Co., 198 F.2d 821, 823 (2d Cir.1952) (Frank, J., dissenting). Judge Frank may have won fame in *Dincher*, but he lost in the Second Circuit: his fellow judges did not agree with him, and Mr. Dincher's claim, for the loss of his eye, did indeed die before its conception.

[52] Quoted in Gilgoff, *supra* note 4.

[53] Quoted in *id.*

promise, the revival statute of 1986.[54]

Under this revival statute, some toxic exposure claims that would have been barred under the statute of limitations could be prosecuted in New York during a one-year window that ran from July 30, 1986 to July 30, 1987. In order to be revived, the claims had to allege injury from one of five substances: asbestos, tungsten-carbide, chlordane, polyvinyl chloride—or DES. Perhaps more important, the 1986 law also substituted a "time of discovery" trigger for the old time-of-exposure rule, opening the door for some future DES claims to reach the New York courts.[55]

Now the DES daughters of New York could sue. But sue whom? A minority of the plaintiffs knew which manufacturer had made the DES their mothers had taken, or could at least present evidence that one particular manufacturer was the source. Now and then pharmacy records were available; sometimes hospital records established at the plaintiff's birth noted whose drugs her mother had taken; some versions of DES pills were distinctive in dosage or appearance. Most plaintiffs, however, needed judicial help to get over the identification barrier.

Hymowitz Comes to the Court of Appeals

In the same decade that DES litigators like Rheingold and Shainwald were changing DES case law, a student built theory to accompany and shape this work. To pick up the summer credit hours that every evening student needed to switch into the day division, Fordham law student Naomi Sheiner chose professor Sheila Birnbaum's products liability class. In that class Birnbaum, who would leave Fordham a few years later to become a prominent defense lawyer, encouraged Sheiner to think about the DES cases just beginning to percolate through the courts. Sheiner set out to write a law review comment. Her market share argument developed in the summer of 1977, Sheiner recalled a couple of decades later, when she and a friend would drive to classes, kicking around ideas in the car. Back then, Sheiner thought of market share as a way to collect damages, not an approach to causation. "Of course, I had no idea how hard it would be to figure out market share," she said. Her paper, probably the most significant student-written publication in all of tort law, was almost strangled in its crib when a supervising editor at the law review dismissed it as "too theoretical."[56] Another editor rescued

---

[54] *See id.* Revival laws continue to be enacted occasionally, in New York and elsewhere. *See, e.g.,* N.Y. C.P.L.R. 214–e (Consol. 2002) (enacted 1997); N.J. Stat. Ann. § 2A:14–26 (West 2003) (enacted 1995) (reviving some claims against blood suppliers for HIV transmission).

[55] N.Y. C.P.L.R. 214–c(4) (Consol. 2002).

[56] Interview with Naomi Sheiner (Mar. 31, 1998).

the paper; it was published in 1978;[57] and the California Supreme Court relied on it when issuing the first market share liability decision in 1980, *Sindell v. Abbott Laboratories*.[58]

By 1989, the year *Hymowitz* was decided, Sheiner's market share idea had won some and lost some around the country, while Sybil Shainwald's preferred theory, concert of action, had won no judicial support outside New York. The *Sindell* decision on market share had been accepted in Michigan and Washington,[59] modified in a pro-plaintiff direction in Wisconsin,[60] and rejected in Missouri and Iowa.[61] *Bichler v. Eli Lilly and Co.* was still available as a Court of Appeals precedent on full concert-of-action joint liability—a much better theory for plaintiffs than market share, because so many defendants were unidentified and unavailable—but DES litigators had reason to doubt the solidity of this stance.[62] Hundreds of claims lay in wait in New York.

Hymowitz reached the Court of Appeals, the state's highest court, as a quasi-class action—that is, never certified as a class, but involving common injuries and the same allegations of tortious conduct against DES manufacturers. The court was presented with certified questions. Defendants contended that they should prevail where plaintiffs could not identify the manufacturer of her mother's DES, and also that the 1986 revival statute was unconstitutional. Ira Gammerman, the trial judge

---

[57] Naomi Sheiner, Comment, *DES and a Proposed Theory of Enterprise Liability*, 46 Fordham L. Rev. 963 (1978). On the success of this publication, see Howard Denemark, *How Valid is the Often–Repeated Accusation That There Are Too Many Legal Articles and Too Many Law Reviews?*, 30 Akron L. Rev. 215, 226 (1996) (counting 58 hits in the Westlaw JLR database, plus twelve federal court, and 17 state court, citations).

[58] 607 P.2d 924 (Cal.1980).

[59] Abel v. Eli Lilly & Co., 343 N.W.2d 164 (Mich.1984); Martin v. Abbott Laboratories, 689 P.2d 368 (Wash.1984).

[60] The Wisconsin Supreme Court held that a DES plaintiff could recover in full from just one manufacturer if she could prove that this defendant had marketed the type of DES that her mother took (that is, similar in color or shape or other identifiable appearance). The defendant would be free to implead third parties, and liability would be apportioned on many criteria, including market share. Collins v. Eli Lilly & Co., 342 N.W.2d 37 (Wis.1984).

[61] Zafft v. Eli Lilly & Co., 676 S.W.2d 241 (Mo.1984); Mulcahy v. Eli Lilly & Co., 386 N.W.2d 67 (Iowa 1986).

[62] In Bichler v. Eli Lilly & Co., 436 N.E.2d 182 (N.Y.1982), Lilly appealed the judgment entered on Joyce Bichler's $500,000 jury verdict. *See supra* notes 47–50 and accompanying text. Lilly objected to the application of concert-of-action liability. The Court of Appeals rejected this contention—but on procedural grounds, holding that Lilly had "abandoned or withdrawn" its efforts to gain contrary jury instructions at trial. *Bichler*, 436 N.E.2d at 187. The court seemed to frown on the plaintiff's strategy—concert of action against only one defendant—but declined to disrupt a finding against which Lilly had not fought vigorously at trial. *See id.* at 186.

handling DES cases in New York City, had ruled for the plaintiffs on these points.

DES litigation is famous today for its numerous defendants, but the New York plaintiffs were even more numerous. About 500 DES daughters had retained various lawyers, none of whom could be called a shrinking violet. Paul Rheingold popped his client Mindy Hymowitz at the top of the Court of Appeals caption. "It could have been Erin Murphy," Sybil Shainwald said with a little regret, more than twenty years later, remembering her own client. Also jockeying for influence were NYPIRG, which had led the fight for the revival statute, and the New York attorney general's office, which appeared as amicus. "Ego, power, and money," Paul Rheingold grinned, remembering conflicts among plaintiffs' lawyers over which of them would have to sit on the sidelines.[63]

Five Court of Appeals judges rather than the normal seven participated in *Hymowitz*: three judges—Joseph Bellacosa, Judith Kaye, and Richard Simons—recused themselves, and one, Milton Mollen, the presiding justice of the Second Department appellate court, sat as a replacement.[64] The court spent a full afternoon hearing arguments from several lawyers. Listening to the judges' questions, Rheingold had a distinct feeling that the Court of Appeals would endorse market share liability. The only suspense, he wrote soon after the decision, was over whether "defendants would be exculpated from responsibility and whether joint liability would be applied."[65]

The court issued its opinion on April 4, 1989. Chief Judge Sol Wachtler, whose career would crash into disgrace a few years later,[66] wrote for the 4–1 majority. *Hymowitz v. Eli Lilly and Co.*[67] upheld the revival statute against claims by the defendants that it violated their rights to equal protection and due process. Choosing among the theories that plaintiffs had invoked to hold all DES manufacturers liable, the court rejected both concert of action and "alternative liability," the

---

[63] Interview with Paul Rheingold (July 16, 2002).

[64] Paul D. Rheingold, *The* Hymowitz *Decision: Practical Aspects of New York DES Litigation*, 55 Brook. L. Rev. 883, 887 (1989). Rheingold dedicated this article to Mindy Hymowitz, his client, then enrolled in law school, noting "her courage to speak out against restrictive DES laws." *Id.* at 883.

[65] *Id.* at 887.

[66] Judge Wachtler was arrested in 1993 on charges of harassing and threatening a former lover; the New York tabloids enjoyed the detail that he had sent the woman's 14-year-old daughter a condom in the mail. He served more than a year in federal prison. Wachtler later attributed his behavior to manic-depressive illness. Sol Wachtler, *After the Madness: A Judge's Own Prison Memoir* (1997).

[67] 539 N.E.2d 1069 (N.Y.1989).

approach made famous in California's *Summers v. Tice*.[68] It accepted
market share liability, a variation on Sheiner's theme, where defendants
are liable to each plaintiff in proportion to their share of the DES market
at the time of exposure.

Of all the many questions that the market share concept raised—
among them, which years of sales, which dosages, and miscarriage DES
or all DES?[69]—the most fundamental related to geographic terrain.
Sindell had left the question unresolved. Florida, in a post-*Hymowitz*
decision, would later choose a much narrower market: it held that if the
mother had bought her DES from only one pharmacy, the market would
be the suppliers to that pharmacy.[70] Similarly, current case law in
Washington looks for a market "as narrow as possible."[71] *Hymowitz*,
however, issued an explicit judicial endorsement of a national market.

Hymowitz also held that defendants with a share of the market
could not escape liability based on what was known about the source of
DES in a particular instance of exposure. For instance, if a plaintiff's
mother testifies that her DES pill was a particular color and the
defendant can prove that it never made DES pills in that color, *Hymowitz* deems the defendant no less obliged to pay, still stuck with liability
in proportion to its share of the market at the time. It was only this last
piece of the majority opinion that did not win a unanimous court: Milton
Mollen, the replacement judge filling in from the Second Department,
wrote in a separate opinion that each defendant should be permitted to
exculpate itself.[72]

Mollen's opinion highlights an inconsistency worth noting. On the
one hand, when a plaintiff can identify one particular defendant, then
that defendant, if deemed negligent (or strictly liable), becomes liable for
all of her damages. No identification issue impedes the causation element of the plaintiff's case; she recovers in full.[73] On the other hand,
equally positive *non*-identification does not exonerate the defendant in

---

[68] 199 P.2d 1 (Cal.1948).

[69] *See infra* notes 80–83 and accompanying text.

[70] Conley v. Boyle Drug Co., 570 So.2d 275, 283 (Fla.1990).

[71] George v. Parke–Davis, 733 P.2d 507, 512 (Wash.1987); Martin v. Abbott Laboratories, 689 P.2d 368, 383 (Wash.1984) (establishing market share without settling geography
question).

[72] *Hymowitz*, 539 N.E.2d at 1081 (Mollen, J., concurring and dissenting).

[73] Sybil Shainwald, however, has reported that Lilly takes a contrary position in
settlement negotiations. "Even if I have an affidavit from the pharmacist" identifying
Lilly, she said, the company insists on proceeding on a market-share fractional basis.
Interview with Sybil Shainwald (Nov. 8, 2002). In principle, market share is supposed to be
used only when the plaintiff cannot identify the defendant supplier.

full. A manufacturer that can prove it was not the source of the mother's DES is nevertheless burdened with a market share of liability. Identified or unidentified, a defendant that sold DES can only lose, never win, on causation. As Mollen pointed out in his separate opinion, no other court had gone this far in a DES market-share ruling.[74] Others share his disapproval. "The *Hymowitz* decision is dangerous precedent," one student writer concluded promptly after the case was decided, "because it totally eliminates causation as an element of recovery, develops a theory which is plagued with internal inconsistencies, and establishes liability that far exceeds absolute liability."[75]

Among lawyers and litigants at the time of decision, *Hymowitz* provoked more moderate commentary. A Lilly spokeswoman seemed satisfied: *Hymowitz* struck "a reasonable balance between the interests of the plaintiffs and the interests of the defendants in the New York DES cases," she told a reporter.[76] For Sybil Shainwald, *Hymowitz* was a defeat. She, after all, had won *Bichler*, the concert-of-action precedent. Now her clients, and all DES claimants in New York, would have to chase numerous manufacturers whenever they could not identify the supplier in order to obtain judgments or settlements containing anything close to full damages: *Hymowitz* rejected joint liability, and treated market-share percentages as the maximum each unidentified defendant had to pay. Later Shainwald called the decade between *Bichler* and *Hymowitz* as a transition where the Court of Appeals grew "more conservative."[77] Her colleague and contemporary LeRoy Hersh, a Bay Area lawyer, agreed that the market share rule of *Hymowitz* was a disappointment, as had been the California market share holding nine years earlier.[78] Paul Rheingold, however, published a law review article soon after *Hymowitz* was decided, deeming market share superior to concert of action as a way to impose liability. Concert of action, Rheingold wrote:

---

[74] *Hymowitz*, 539 N.E.2d at 1082.

[75] Laura A. Abrams, Comment, *The DES Dilemma: A Study in How Hard Cases Make Bad Law*, 59 U. Cin. L. Rev. 489, 509 (1990).

[76] Quoted in Alvin E. Bessent, *Court Clears Path for DES Cases*, Newsday, Apr. 5, 1989, at 29.

[77] Interview with Sybil Shainwald (Aug. 4, 2002).

[78] Hersh remembers being at a social event one evening in 1980, aware that *Sindell* had just been decided that day but not yet told what the court had held. The news would be announced the next morning. At the gathering, Hersh encountered Justice Matthew Tobriner of the California Supreme Court. "Matt Tobriner said to me, 'The court's decision will make you very happy, LeRoy,' " Hersh recounted in 2002. "But as it turned out, it was a Pyrrhic victory." Interview with LeRoy Hersh (July 31, 2002).

had been rejected by every other state in the country which had the DES identification issue before it, although a number of them had adopted other theories. [Moreover], the briefs of virtually every defendant advocated, in one way or another, that, if the court was going to consider some legal theory shifting the traditional burden of identification away from the plaintiffs, market share was the most equitable of the devices.[79]

DES Litigation Practice in New York after *Hymowitz*

New York litigators now had to work with *Hymowitz*. As their architect-theoretician Naomi Sheiner could see only in hindsight, market share is extremely hard to do. For starters, not all manufacturers subject to jurisdiction could provide their sales figures for the relevant years. Even Lilly, an extraordinarily sophisticated defendant, a company that could provide the number of DES units it had made between 1942 to 1971—that would be 716 million—could not count the number of those units that went to pregnant women.[80] So much for the numerator of the fraction. The denominator remains even more elusive. Without the central recordkeeping that a patent license would have created, courts had trouble counting the total number of DES units sold.

The New York lawyers knew California had had a hard time following *Sindell*. The California Supreme Court had ordered a trial on the market share question; a rancorous and protracted hearing ensued. "We started by asking every company for their sales data, and then we started interpreting, massaging, mashing the data," recalled Roman Silberfeld, a plaintiffs' lawyer based in Los Angeles. "It was far from perfect, because the data were so bad."[81] Plaintiffs' attorneys described the San Francisco endeavor as too dependent on manufacturer self-reporting. Some of them thought that Lilly in particular got off easy, winning a market share apportionment that some said was perhaps half of the truth.[82] John McGoldrick, who once represented Lilly and went on

---

[79] Rheingold, *supra* note 64, at 886.

[80] Meyers, *supra* note 1, at 80. Cynthia Orenberg writes that Lilly claimed $2.5 million in total sales of DES to pregnant women, Orenberg, *supra* note 20, at 153—a figure that seems low.

[81] Interview with Roman Silberfeld (Aug. 16, 2002).

[82] Lilly drew less than a third overall in the San Francisco proceeding, with higher fractions in the early years and lower ones later. According to Robert Meyers, Lilly "made at least half, and possibly 75 percent of all DES sold in this country"—although not all of it was marketed under the Lilly name, and some of it was not used to prevent miscarriage. Meyers, supra note 1, at 79–80. It is hard to assess the charge that Lilly benefited from an unduly low market share assessment. If all the sales figures were too low, not just Lilly's,

to become general counsel of Bristol Myers Squibb, dismissed these speculations as a kind of backhanded compliment to a company that had a stellar reputation: "The pharmacist would say, 'I only carried Lilly,' the implication being, 'I only carried the best,' " he recalled.[83]

Soon after the *Hymowitz* decision came down, litigants took the New York market share fight to the grand Erie County courthouse in Buffalo. Judge James Kane, who presided, made no market share decision; the lawyers worked out their own deal regarding the national market that *Hymowitz* mandated they identify and measure. Under this settlement, finalized in 1992, the plaintiffs' side won a 10% increase per defendant over the California amounts, so that, for instance, a defendant assigned 20% in San Francisco would be assigned 22% in New York—an adjustment that still left their clients undercompensated, in their view. The lawyers for both sides crafted what they called "the grid" or "the matrix," a chart listing the years 1947 to 1971, when DES was marketed to pregnant women, and the market share of each corporation for that year.

With the grid in front of them, a plaintiff's lawyer like Paul Rheingold or Sybil Shainwald could sit down with a defense lawyer like John McGoldrick and look up the relevant year of exposure. Lilly, or any other defendant, would have an assigned market share for that year, and that fractional number would be multiplied by the value of the plaintiff's damages. In identifying damages, some lawyers preferred to work with broad classifications—cancer, infertility, miscarriage—whereas others preferred a more individualized assessment.

The grid facilitated settlement,[84] but some lawyers felt chafed by its static, bureaucratic approach to damages. In the early 1990s Shainwald, an early and energetic grid user, believed that plaintiffs' counsel in New

---

then the market share calculation would not have given Lilly any particular advantage among the defendants.

[83] Interview with John McGoldrick (Aug. 5, 2002). Roman Silberfeld agreed that the Lilly market share really did not exceed about thirty percent overall, mainly because the phenomenon of generic drugs did not develop until around 1953. From 1947 to 1953, Silberfeld believed Lilly did dominate the market. But generics quickly demoted Lilly to a much smaller share. Silberfeld added that Lilly had about three times the market share of the runner-up #2. Interview with Roman Silberfeld (Aug. 16, 2002).

[84] It was, however, only part of the process. Roman Silberfeld pointed out that the grid is particularly unenlightening in cases of partial identification—for instance, where the plaintiff's mother has a vague memory of taking a red pill (Lilly made DES in red, among other colors). Has the defendant been identified? Not clear. If this vague memory constitutes an identification of Lilly, then the market share grid is not supposed to be relevant. *See supra* note 73 and accompanying text. If Lilly has not been identified, then Lilly should not pay more in settlement than the grid suggests. In practice, however, the grid proved neither irrelevant nor outcome-determinative, just a part of the mix. Interview with Roman Silberfeld (Aug. 16, 2002).

York tended to settle too cheaply. Rankled by what she saw as the injustice of market share liability, so inferior to concert of action as a means to compensate plaintiffs, Shainwald sat down to think of a way to increase the DES settlement values—for cancer and infertility, the costlier injuries, in particular.

Shainwald decided to venture a reverse-bifurcated trial. In her plan, first the jury would consider damages; only afterwards would it consider liability. Shainwald had little precedent to cite in support of proceeding backwards. Although reverse bifurcation had been used in asbestos litigation, the tactic was, and remains, rare. But Judge Ira Gammerman, still handling DES trials in New York post-*Hymowitz* as he had done pre-*Hymowitz*, accepted the plan. He began presiding over a reverse-bifurcated, multi-plaintiff DES trial in early 1994.

Shainwald brought in California DES litigator LeRoy Hersh, and the two seasoned hands put together a notebook about each of the plaintiffs, containing undisputed facts—like the plaintiffs'age, education, experience, life activities—in which the jurors could write their own notes. Coming alive as individuals during the damages phase of the trial, these young women won significantly higher awards than their predecessors had achieved.[85] Shainwald remembered waiting nervously for the announcement of damages for her first plaintiff, Gina Cardinale. A hundred and fifty thousand, said the jury. Shainwald's heart sank. *Chicken feed*. Not remotely worth all the effort she and Hersh and the clients had put into the trial. *Oh no, if this is how the jury is pricing the cases ...*

"Two million," came the next award, for infertility, and Shainwald could resume breathing. Then came what she called "two tens and a twelve"—multimillion-dollar awards for vaginal adenocarcinoma, a landmark in damages litigation.[86] Swiftly the defendants settled; the negligence half of the bifurcated trial never took place.[87] The cost of doing DES business thirty years ago had just gone up.[88]

Epilogue

Observers expected DES claims to be filed through the 1990s and stop in 2001. The drug had been marketed to pregnant women until 1971, and reproductive-organ anomalies in DES daughters typically

---

[85] Lucinda Finley, *Female Trouble: The Implications of Tort Reform for Women*, 64 Tenn. L. Rev. 847, 863 n.60 (1997).

[86] Interview with Sybil Shainwald (Aug. 4, 2002).

[87] Interview with Sybil Shainwald (Nov. 8, 2002).

[88] Market share liability without concert of action liability or joint liability, however, meant that plaintiffs could collect only a fraction of the value of their injuries. *See DES Daughters Awarded $42 Million, But ...*, Nat'l L.J., Jan. 24, 1994, at 6 (quoting an estimate that 11 DES plaintiffs would recover no more than $400,000, despite the eight-figure sums that the jury awarded to them).

appear before age 21. The big cohort of baby boomers, which included Mindy Hymowitz, Joyce Bichler, and countless other DES daughters, did indeed conclude almost all its litigation before the end of the century. But DES claims have continued to be filed in the twenty-first century. One source of belated claims has been the availability of DES in the years after the FDA disapproved it as a miscarriage preventative; a few physicians, defying the ban, continued to prescribe it in the 1970s.[89] And so Sybil Shainwald, for instance, filed a claim in March 2002 in behalf of four DES daughters; the Washington, D.C. litigator Aaron Levine filed a claim in December 2001.[90] Enough time has passed since *Hymowitz*, however, to conclude the DES story with a retrospective on what this decision wrought.

Having arrived relatively late in the market-share case law *Hymowitz*, rather than *Sindell*, is the decision that best captures the social and legal phenomenon of DES exposure. Though not certified as a class, the hundreds of plaintiffs in New York stood in for millions exposed. The plaintiff named in the caption had the right condition: whereas Judith Sindell suffered from bladder cancer, a disease that usually develops without known DES exposure, Mindy Hymowitz's clear-cell vaginal adenocarcinoma marked a signature encounter.[91] The *Hymowitz* caption named lawyers who were already leaders of DES litigation, and the decision strengthened their leadership role. *Hymowitz's* declaration of a national market deemed DES an American public health problem rather than a questionable product distributed in isolated regional sales; this view of DES was congruent with DES consumer health-care activism at a national level. Encouraged by litigation like *Hymowitz*, feminist health networks, including Pat Cody's still-strong DES Action, have not only expanded awareness of this substance but also linked it to medical and pharmaceutical impacts on women's bodies generally.[92]

---

[89] Interview with Sybil Shainwald (Nov. 8, 2002).

[90] *DES:* Klein v. Abbott Labs, Pharmaceutical Litigation Rep., May 2002, at 4 (describing both cases).

[91] The adjective "signature" in toxic-torts scholarship connotes a very strong statistical association between an agent and an outcome of disease. More than 90% of mesothelioma cases, for instance, are attributable to asbestos exposure. Similarly, clear-cell vaginal adenocarcinoma bespeaks DES exposure. Margaret A. Berger, *Eliminating General Causation: Notes Towards a New Theory of Justice and Toxic Torts*, 97 Colum. L. Rev. 2117, 2121–22 (1997). *But see* Troyen A. Brennan, *Helping Courts with Toxic Torts: Some Proposals Regarding Alternative Methods for Presenting and Assessing Scientific Evidence in Common Law Courts*, 51 U. Pitt. L. Rev. 1, 21 (1989) (citing "[m]ore recent work" that finds "other causes of clear cell cancers").

[92] *See* Finley, *supra* note 85; Joan Steinman, *Women, Medical Care, and Mass Tort Litigation*, 68 Chi.-Kent L. Rev. 409 (1992), *reprinted in A Products Liability Anthology* 190 (Anita Bernstein ed., 1995).

What did *Hymowitz* achieve for plaintiffs? Many DES-exposed persons did not benefit from the decision. In contrast to powerful public awareness about—and courtroom victories by—DES daughters, DES grandchildren and sons are noteworthy for not emerging as a presence in the courts. Two years after *Hymowitz* the Court of Appeals, Wachtler again writing for the court, held that DES grandchildren had no claim against manufacturers for injuries sustained as a result of their mothers' reproductive-organ anomalies.[93] A malformed vagina or cervix that obstructs conception or full-term fetal development can be charged to DES manufacturers when the malformed plaintiff sues in her own behalf; but cerebral palsy in a neonate, the DES daughter's child, attributed to the same anatomical damages, cannot.

DES sons remain almost unseen on the litigation landscape. This obscurity is not for their lack of damages. Soon after the female-organ reports of the early 1970s, researchers found links between maternal ingestion of DES and epididymal cysts, sperm and semen abnormalities, microphallic penises (smaller than four centimeters when nonerect), difficulty in urination, and undescended testicles in DES sons[94]—an outcome consistent with findings from mice studies of the 1950s. Undoubtedly part of what obscures the injuries to DES sons is their relative lack of organ damage and the lack of a distinctive cancer. But these factual, objective conditions do not entirely explain the cultural invisibility of DES damage to men.[95]

The millions of offspring born to mothers who took DES during pregnancy, especially if they are in the majority that do not have cancer, might be seen as a privileged and powerful cohort—children of affluence and near-affluence, articulate, politically posed to claim rewards from the legislatures and the courts—and, as this book goes to press in 2003, at about the top of their earnings game. The shadow of DES in their lives does not obscure all the sunlight they enjoy. Most DES daughters will never develop clear-cell vaginal adenocarcinoma—even if the Herbst follow-up study, which found this cancer in only 1.4 per thousand

---

[93] Enright v. Eli Lilly & Co., 570 N.E.2d 198 (N.Y.1991).

[94] Orenberg, *supra* note 20, at 83–88; *see also supra* note 25 and accompanying text. Physicians and researchers also suspect a link between DES exposure and testicular cancer, although the evidence is ambiguous. Meyers, *supra* note 1, at 144–45, 150–52.

[95] Men do not readily identify themselves as DES victims. Two physician-writers, considering DES damage, speculate that whereas women know that their bodies will change whether they want change or not—all of them can expect at least menarche and menopause; most women will also experience pregnancy—men "are socialized from earliest childhood to idealize bodily integrity." Thus they feel less willing to admit that their bodies have been changed by forces they could not control. Apfel & Fisher, *supra* note 6, at 82–83. And because their genitals have more prestige than women's genitals, "there is also a greater tendency toward denial of this harm." *Id.* at 82.

daughters, undercounted the cancers.[96] Experts say that the majority of daughters born to mothers who took DES have some kind of reproductive-organ anomalies, but frequently the condition is benign: a small uterus, for instance, or adenosis that goes away. Although infertility has been a common problem for these women, 81 percent reached adulthood capable of having babies, compared to 95 percent of the unexposed population.[97] DES exposure did not stop Paul Rheingold's daughter from presenting him with grandchildren.[98]

"Our major cause of concern now," the chairman of obstetrics of a large research hospital said in 1989, "is the emotional problems."[99] Female reproductive anatomy had been problematic enough in American culture before DES exposure added its own measure of suspicion, shame, and blight. In the early 1980s activist Fran Fishbane expressed concern about the effects of identifying DES daughters as sexually pathological before they are old enough to make love: "Can a young woman who has associated pain and anxiety with her vagina from the age of 12 then feel pleasure in that same area when she becomes sexually active years later?" she asked.[100] Relations between DES mothers and their exposed daughters have been a key venue for the expression of distress. Roberta Apfel and Susan Fisher write that although often "the DES daughter will not experience anger at her mother for taking the drug," because she "will fully appreciate that her mother's intentions were absolutely the best," a "new stress situation" when it emerges can expose a suppressed rage.[101] Apfel and Fisher suggest that DES mothers may feel "uneasy about their mothering," apart from DES, and the toxic exposure their daughters suffered can become a focus of unrelated guilt and hostility.[102]

In more harmonious mother-daughter relationships affected by DES, guilt and blame are supposed to stay banished, but they linger. Joyce Bichler wrote in *DES Daughter* about watching her mother testify at her trial—a crucible of mutual pain, where each woman felt she had hurt the other.[103] Mindy Hymowitz used to say to Shirley, "Don't blame yourself,

---

[96] Gorney, *supra* note 33.

[97] Gina Kolata, *Fewer Problems: The Medical Record on DES Emerges After Years of Research and Anxiety*, N.Y. Times, Apr. 9, 1989, § 4, at 26.

[98] Interview with Paul Rheingold (July 16, 2002).

[99] Quoted in Kolata, *supra* note 97.

[100] Quoted in Orenberg, *supra* note 20, at 71.

[101] Apfel & Fisher, *supra* note 6, at 76–77.

[102] For one woman they describe, DES was proof that she was a bad and destructive mother and her daughter would do best not to heed her advice. *Id.* at 80.

[103] Bichler, *supra* note 41, at 147.

Mom." And Shirley was a trooper: "I told her, 'I never thought about it.' That wasn't true—I did—but it would have made her feel bad."[104]

Without Mindy there would have been no *Hymowitz*, and this story of *Hymowitz* concludes by remembering her. In 1987, while her claim was making its way to the Court of Appeals, Mindy enrolled in Brooklyn Law School as a night student, continuing to work as a nurse during the day. She graduated four years later. Cancer came back for Mindy while she was working as a medical malpractice litigator. Surgery for the cancer recurrence, which her doctors called successful, changed her bladder permanently: for the rest of her life, she would need catheters to empty it. Mindy carried the catheters in her purse and kept her spirits high.

In June 1996, grappling with her illness but active and outgoing, Mindy said yes to a blind date with John Cella, a trade-union paperhanger. They soon were married. "We were best friends right away," Cella remembered; he said he wished he could have met Mindy earlier to share more time with her before her death in October 1998. "I'll never get married again," Cella declared in 2002. "My friends tell me not to say that, but I know I never will, because I think about her all the time."[105] Shirley Hymowitz shared a similar feeling: "It never leaves you. I have pictures of her all over. I have a big 16 by 20 picture in my bedroom. I see her face every morning."[106]

Today Brooklyn Law School maintains a scholarship in memory of Mindy Hymowitz Cella. The school describes the scholarship as honoring "the named plaintiff in the landmark DES lawsuit *Hymowitz v. Eli Lilly*, [who] died at 43 years of age after a long and courageous battle with cancer. She had a nursing career before pursuing a legal education. As an associate of Aaronson Rappaport Feinstein & Deutsch, LLP, she focused on medical malpractice defense work. The firm established the scholarship to honor her loyalty, commitment and fortitude."[107]

She was buried in Pinelawn Memorial Park on Long Island, under a marker reading 1954–1998 for Mindy and 1947– for John. The stone is flat, by Pinelawn rules:[108] the cemetery wants to keep its grassy acres serene, never jarred by the force that a headstone would assert on the landscape. Mindy Hymowitz, a different sort altogether, preferred to stand up.

---

[104] Interview with Shirley Hymowitz (July 3, 2002).

[105] Interview with John Cella (Aug. 27, 2002).

[106] Interview with Shirley Hymowitz (July 3, 2002).

[107] www.brooklaw.edu/pages/index.php3?page=1234 (visited May 15, 2002).

[108] Interview with John Cella (Aug. 27, 2002).

* * *

As for market share liability, its story marks an oscillation between judicial activism and retreat from activism. Around the country, market share liability for other products has fared almost as poorly as DES-grandchild litigation.[109] Its biggest victory in New York has been a terse Appellate Division ruling about lead paint.[110] If this doctrine will remain confined to drugs that judges deem "fungible," as seems likely, then market share liability will recede as fungible drugs themselves recede. Charles Dodds' 1930s decision not to patent his invention stemmed from a disapproval of proprietary intellectual property as contrary to the public good. This stance has almost vanished among those who possess patentable innovations. To be sure, patents occasionally expire, and generic drugs keep the fungibility possibility alive. But short of a revolution in the practices of patenting and drug marketing, new defective drugs deemed fungible are unlikely to revive market share in the courts.[111]

In their rejections of market share liability, courts express their aversion to a judicial maneuver that looks like legislation. Both the real New York state legislature and the legislature-ish Court of Appeals chose to install prospective, policy-focused, aggregative legal change in the 1980s. New York's revival statute rescued DES claims from statute-of-limitations death. The same statute also replaced an old rule, time of exposure, with a new one, time of discovery, to aid plaintiffs against defendants. Three years later, the Court of Appeals used *Hymowitz* to legislate away the barrier of proving causation in fact. In further defiance of judicial tradition, *Hymowitz* held that a defendant that did

[109] Rejections of market-share liability include *Goldman v. Johns–Manville Sales Corp.*, 514 N.E.2d 691 (Ohio 1987) (asbestos); *Shackil v. Lederle Laboratories*, 561 A.2d 511 (N.J.1989) (DPT vaccine); and *Lee v. Baxter Healthcare Corp.*, 721 F.Supp. 89 (D.Md.1989) (breast implants). Hawaii accepted it for blood clotting protein, however, in *Smith v. Cutter Biological, Inc.*, 823 P.2d 717 (Haw.1991).

[110] New York City Hous. Auth. v. Lead Indus. Ass'n, 713 N.Y.S.2d 345 (N.Y.App.Div. 2000). Lead-paint litigation has had a rocky path. *See generally* Molly McDonough, *Poisoned by Paint*, A.B.A. J., July 2002, at 43, 44 (reporting that market-share claims against lead paint manufacturers have mostly failed).

[111] Although the intellectual property that Charles Dobbs abjured was a patent rather than a copyright, the Supreme Court's decision to uphold legislation extending the duration of copyrights, a subject with the same constitutional status as patents, is pertinent to the task of predicting whether fungible drugs will return to revive market share liability. *See* Eldred v. Ashcroft, 123 S.Ct. 769 (2003) (construing the "limited times" provision in the Copyright and Patent Clause of the United States Constitution not to invalidate a congressional extension). Heavy lobbying by copyright holders to gain the legislative extension, and the Court's acceptance of the protections that these sectors won from Congress, suggests a strengthening of the idea that those who hold intellectual property need not cede it into the public domain.

not cause injury to a plaintiff could be obliged to compensate her. It linked manufacturers together for furnishing the same product to a market, even when the manufacturers shared few if any other connections, and even though the Court of Appeals could no longer accept the concert-of-action conclusion that it had tolerated in *Bichler*. These legislature-like moves declared tort traditions inadequate to address the problem of DES injury, and jettisoned them in order to achieve better policy. To courts considering market share in later cases, such deviations from doctrine exceeded the bounds of what the judiciary could do. And so having disappointed plaintiffs in 1989 for not going far enough, *Hymowitz* stands judged for going too far.

This legacy of judicial discomfort and retreat should not surprise those who read the story about markets of mothers. Judges prefer a limited-powers role whose contours they can feel, even if they occasionally have trouble stating where judging ends and legislating from the bench begins. *Hymowitz* reached into the province of the legislature. But perhaps reaching is not so bad as neglecting to reach. American legislatures—from Congress on down—have shirked their obligation to promote public welfare through effective health-care policy. Dozens of millions of Americans without health insurance testify to this failure. As tort law likes to insist, actors who have a duty to act are just as responsible for their omissions as they would be for intentional, denominate, affirmative initiatives like *Hymowitz*.

7

Kenneth W. Simons

Murphy v. Steeplechase Amusement Co.: While the Timorous Stay at Home, the Adventurous Ride the Flopper

Introduction

"This young lad, with his sweetheart and some friends ... came down to this park that night to be amused, to that playground of the world, Coney Island, providing as it does, all kinds of entertainment, liquid, solid, things that make life more enjoyable, especially to those whose conditions of life were like this lad's was. He was a truck driver—he probably could not come to the Ritz–Carlton to a dance or anything of that kind, but he could go to Coney Island if he wanted to, and dance or do whatever else attracted him in the way of pleasure, and he could give the girl who was then his sweetheart, and now his wife, such delights as she could find in his companionship... So he went and bought a ticket, ... and having indulged himself in some of the pleasures that were there because of these devices, he finally landed upon this moving plane preceded by his friends, including his sweetheart, and when he got on there, he says a sudden jerk occurred and they were all thrown down, he striking his knee and getting this injury."

—Trial judge John M. Tierney, summarizing the testimony in the course of his instruction to the jury.

"The verdict is a moderate one, a very sensible one in my judgment."

—Trial judge John M. Tierney, in rejecting the motion of defendant to set aside the jury's verdict awarding $5000 to plaintiff Murphy

"The timorous may stay at home."[1]

—Justice Benjamin Cardozo, for the Court of Appeals, reversing the judgment of the trial court.

"[*Murphy*] makes one recall that time he/she fell head over heels for someone and felt like a jerk doing it."[2]

In Murphy v. Steeplechase Amusement Co., Judge Benjamin Cardozo of the New York Court of Appeals penned one of his most memorable opinions. A young man had stepped on "The Flopper," a ride at Coney Island featuring a fast-moving belt. He fell and suffered a fracture of his knee cap. In characteristically pithy and exalted prose, Cardozo explained that the plaintiff was not legally entitled to a recovery from the park for its alleged negligence:

> *Volenti non fit injuria* One who takes part in such a sport accepts the dangers that inhere in it so far as they are obvious and necessary, just as a fencer accepts the risk of a thrust by his antagonist or a spectator at a ball game the chance of contact with the ball... The antics of the clown are not the paces of the cloistered cleric. The rough and boisterous joke, the horseplay of the crowd, evokes its own guffaws, but they are not the pleasures of tranquility. The plaintiff was not seeking a retreat for meditation. Visitors were tumbling about the belt to the merriment of onlookers when he made his choice to join them. He took the chance of a like fate, with whatever damage to his body might ensue from such a fall. The timorous may stay at home.[3]

To this day, *Murphy* is regularly cited for the proposition that one who assumes the risk of a harm should not recover damages. We should be careful, however, not to be mesmerized by the eloquence of Cardozo's writing. A closer look at the case reveals that the plaintiff's claim was more plausible than Cardozo's dismissive opinion suggests. Cardozo is right to emphasize the significance in tort doctrine of a victim's consent to a risk. But his terse and epigrammatic opinion is stronger on rhetoric than analysis. Both the *Murphy* case and assumption of risk doctrine are more complex and more interesting than Cardozo's opinion implies.

---

[1] Murphy v. Steeplechase Amusement Co., 166 N.E. 173 (N.Y.1929).

[2] Paul Horowitz et al., *The Law of Prime Numbers*, 68 N.Y.U. L. Rev. 185, 198 n.49 (1993).

[3] 166 N.E. at 174.

The Opinion, at First Glance

On first reading, the opinion probably strikes most readers as utterly persuasive. In Cardozo's telling, the story is straightforward. James Murphy, "a vigorous young man," visits Coney Island with friends. (Notice the suggestive language: a "vigorous" and "young" rider would presumably relish a physical challenge.) Murphy and his friends observe other riders jump or tumble from the aptly named "Flopper." Murphy then chooses, for his amusement, to ride on a moving belt, realizing that there is a significant chance he will fall. That is precisely what happens. He says that the mechanism suddenly jerked and caused him to tumble, but, Cardozo believes, this claim is dubious at best: "One who steps upon a moving belt and finds his heels above his head is in no position to discriminate with nicety between the successive stages of the shock, between the jerk which is a cause and the jerk, accompanying the fall, as an instantaneous effect."[4] But in any event, even if a sudden jerk caused the fall, "the risk at greatest was a fall. This was the very hazard that was invited and foreseen."[5] Indeed, as Cardozo describes the case, Murphy does not merely decide to ride the Flopper notwithstanding the risk of a fall; he chooses to ride the device precisely *in order* to encounter that risk. "There would have been no point to the whole thing, no adventure about it, if the risk had not been there."[6] Justice Cardozo then concludes that there is insufficient evidence of negligence by the defendant and, in the paragraph quoted above, that plaintiff has assumed the risk. (The Latin phrase that Cardozo invokes—*volenti non fit injuria*—means "No injury or wrong is done to one who consents," expressing the idea that plaintiff has assumed the risk.[7])

On this view of the facts, it is easy to agree with the court's conclusion that, under any of the plaintiff's theories of negligence, he is not entitled to recover. Thus, the claim that the Flopper was operated at too fast and dangerous a speed, or that it improperly jerked suddenly, is negated by Murphy's appreciation that a fall was, in any event, an expected risk. And the claim that the park did not provide a proper railing or guard to prevent a fall is similarly unconvincing, if such a precaution would have defeated the "point to the whole thing," i.e., the excitement of confronting the risk.[8]

---

[4] *Id.*

[5] *Id.*

[6] *Id.*

[7] *See Black's Law Dictionary* 1569 (7th ed. 1999).

[8] The plaintiff also testified that he fell upon unpadded wood. However, the court correctly notes that the case did not go to the jury on this theory of defective padding, and that the evidence supporting the theory is relatively weak. 166 N.E. at 175.

Seductive as this account is, however, it both oversimplifies the facts and fails to elucidate the relevant legal principles.

A Closer Look at the Facts

An examination of the trial transcript and exhibits in *Murphy* reveals that the story told in Cardozo's opinion is inaccurate and misleading. Even as designed, the Flopper was more dangerous than the opinion implies. Moreover, Cardozo is too quick to assume that it did not malfunction with a jerk. At the same time, Coney Island also contained a number of rides more dangerous than the Flopper, a fact which may have subtly influenced Cardozo to conclude that Murphy assumed the risk.

First, how was the Flopper designed to operate? And how dangerous was it when it operated as intended? In answering these questions, we cannot rely on Cardozo's description of the Flopper, which is misleading in several respects. Consider the photograph and diagram (appearing at pp. 184–85) of the Flopper that were introduced at trial:

The belt was constantly moving at a rapid speed (as explained further below). Accordingly, great dexterity was required simply to step onto the device without falling, especially if you intended to stand rather than sit on the belt. (Indeed, it might have been safer, not to step on the belt, but to jump onto it with both feet.) And even if you intended to sit rather than stand on the moving belt, you would need to lower your body onto it very carefully. Thus, although the photograph of four children riding the Flopper depicts the device as a benign, pleasurable amusement, the accuracy of the photograph is highly questionable. The child at the very rear of the Flopper is sitting only inches from the end of the belt. How could she achieve this position, if the belt was always moving? And how could another child calmly rest her hand on the adjacent padding, while the belt was quickly moving? It seems very likely that when the photograph was taken, the belt was turned off.[9]

From Cardozo's account, the reader will likely assume that if the rider was standing on the moving belt of the Flopper, he was protected by padded walls immediately adjacent to the belt.[10] But in fact, on either side of the belt a padded floor extended more than six feet, so that the padded walls were actually located to the side of the rider but more than six feet away. The walls thus provided no protection against a fall occurring, and very little protection against the consequences of such a fall.[11] To be sure, the floor immediately adjacent to the belt was itself padded and thus provided some protection. However, Cardozo's description might create the incorrect impression that adjacent padded walls provided an added measure of protection.

Other features of the Flopper not described by Cardozo also suggest that it was less safe than Cardozo implies. In the first place, the belt on which the rider sits or stands is only 16 inches wide—much narrower than a standard escalator.[12] If a rider were standing on such a narrow

---

[9] Unfortunately, plaintiff's attorney makes no effort to explore these questions. Indeed, on cross-examination, Murphy testifies that the photograph is "way different" from what the actual Flopper looked like. Inexplicably, Murphy's lawyer does not pursue the point. It is also unclear why he did not take any photographs of the Flopper at the time of the accident. Such photographs might, among other things, have buttressed one of Murphy's strongest claims—that he was injured in part because his knee hit a portion of the device that was unpadded.

[10] "The belt runs in a groove, with padded walls on either side to a height of four feet, and with padded flooring *beyond the walls* at the same angle as the belt." 166 N.E. at 173–74 (emphasis added).

[11] To be sure, if padded walls *had* been located immediately adjacent to the belt, this might have been *more* dangerous in some case, insofar as riders would be more likely to fall directly onto the moving belt.

[12] For example, Hyundai's standard escalators have a minimum width of 594 mm, or about 24 inches.

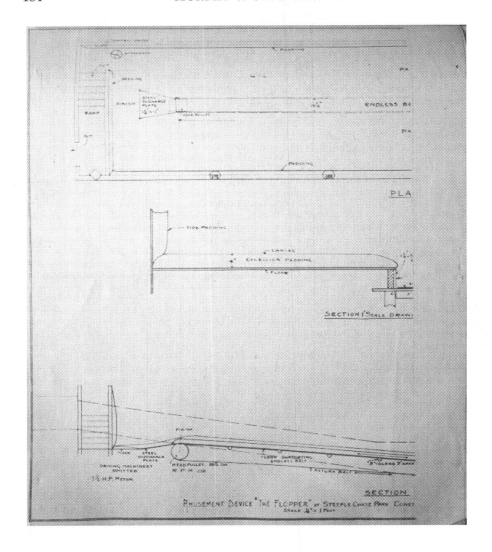

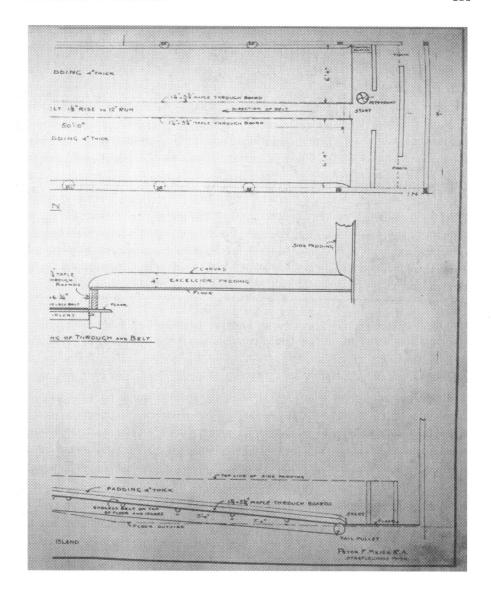

belt while it was moving quickly, he or she would have difficulty maintaining balance. And, although witnesses for the park indicated that adults could either stand or sit on the belt, few adults could comfortably fit on such a narrow belt in a sitting position.[13]

Moreover, if a rider was somehow able to maintain his balance on the Flopper for its full 50 feet until the end of the belt, he would fairly quickly run into a padded wall, which (according to the diagram) is located only six feet from the end of the belt. More likely, a rider able to get on the Flopper in the first place would either fall or deliberately jump off the belt before the end.

Cardozo's account also does not fully convey how quickly the belt was moving. The 100–foot belt traveled six revolutions per minute, which translates to just under 7 miles per hour (or 10 feet per second). By contrast, today's escalators typically travel 1–2 miles per hour,[14] and today's moving sidewalks (found, for example, in airports) typically travel 1–1.5 miles per hour.[15] Another instructive comparison is a tread-mill. Adults who run close to full speed on a treadmill achieve the same speed at which the Flopper operated. But on a treadmill, users typically increase their speed gradually, and indeed would be foolish to step on the treadmill when it was already moving at that speed. And, of course, a user of a treadmill runs in the direction *opposing* the movement of the belt; the opposition provides the user much greater stability than if he were to stand on a Flopper. (This author considered experimenting by stepping on a treadmill already moving at 7 miles per hour, but bowed to his family's contrary wishes. Readers are strongly advised to be timorous as well.)

On the other hand, it is worth noting that the incline of the belt was not as steep as the opinion might imply. It ascended only five feet over its fifty foot length; indeed, all of the witnesses who rode it testified that they believed it to be level.

So just how dangerous was the Flopper? From the above, clearly it would be a very tricky matter to step onto the fast-moving belt without falling, or to maintain one's balance once standing on the belt, or to depart the device without jumping or falling. How many actual injuries could be expected? The nurse at the emergency hospital connected to Steeplechase Park testified that she attended to others who fell from the

---

[13] However, a wider belt might be less safe for children. There was testimony that children usually sit down when they ride. And lowering a child to a sitting position might be more difficult and more dangerous if the belt were wider.

[14] Escalator speeds vary from about 90 ft/minute to 180 ft/minute; often, the maximum speed is 120 ft/minute.

[15] Various commercial web sites indicate this range of speeds. Moreover, by regulation, California limits speeds to 180 ft/minute. 8 Cal. Code Regs. § 3091(h) (2003).

Flopper, but she could not say how many, and none was very badly injured or had broken bones.

But of course Murphy did not merely claim that the Flopper was dangerous as originally designed: he also asserted that, after he placed one foot on the belt, it suddenly jerked, causing him and all of the other riders (six in total) to fall. His testimony to this effect is corroborated by two other riders—his girlfriend and his sister. On the other hand, the operator of the ride denied that the belt jerked.[16] Moreover, two witnesses for defendant testified that a smoothly operating belt of this design could not possibly jerk, causing Cardozo to observe: "If the movement was spasmodic, it was an unexplained and, it seems, an inexplicable departure from the normal workings of the mechanism."[17]

Cardozo is quick to conclude that the evidence of a sudden jerk is

---

[16] This testimony by the operator, James Erllo, could have been crucial. Unfortunately, his fuller explanation of how the accident occurred is opaque at best, perhaps because of language difficulties. The testimony does provide some comic relief:

[Direct examination by attorney for defendant:]

Q: At the time of the happening of the accident could you see the belt?

A: Yes, sir.

Q: Did the belt jerk at the time of the accident?

A: It never jerked the belt.

Q: What?

A: Don't jerk the belt, the belt was all right.

Q: What are you saying, say it again?

A: I say the belt was never jerked, it was all right.

Q: Did the belt jerk at the time of the happening of the accident?

A: No.

. . .

Q: Did you see the plaintiff fall down?

A: I seen him, yes.

Q: Did you see the plaintiff fall down, just say yes or no?

A: Yes.

Q: Did he fall down?

A: Just flopped down, that is all.

[By the court:]

Q: Flopped?

A: Just laid down.

Q. He was on the Flopper?

A. On the Flopper.

The attorney for Murphy did not even bother cross-examining Erllo about the circumstances of the fall.

[17] Murphy v. Steeplechase Amusement Co., 166 N.E. 173, 174 (N.Y.1929).

too weak to support the verdict[18]—too quick, in my view. In so concluding, he departs from the deferential role that appellate judges ordinarily
demonstrate towards a trier of fact. Two other witnesses did testify in
support of Murphy's claim that a sudden jerk caused the accident.
Although they are interested witnesses, and although the operator
testified to the contrary, this credibility determination should have been
left to the jury. To be sure, Cardozo is understandably doubtful that
Murphy could really tell whether he was thrown off the fast-moving belt
when he first stepped on it because it suddenly jerked, or merely because
he couldn't keep his balance. After all, assuming no jerk, a person is
most likely to lose his balance on the fast-moving ride at the moment he
steps on it. But the jury might also have believed the testimony of
Murphy and the two other witnesses that all six riders of the Flopper
were thrown off the belt at the same instant, and this testimony
certainly supports the claim of a sudden jerk.

Perhaps Cardozo was displeased by the trial court's instruction to
the jury, which strongly suggested that the evidence in the case did
demonstrate a sudden jerk:

> Now, you see in the plaintiff an unusually big, strong, husky lad. Is
> it probable that he would have fallen down upon that ground and
> broken his knee unless there was some impelling cause producing
> that result? Would all of his companions be thrown down to the floor
> without some sudden jerk?
>
> You men, in your own experience, perhaps, have put your foot upon
> moving platforms or escalators... Did you fall if the thing ran
> smoothly?
>
> . . .
>
> Now, this device was called a Flopper. ...[I]n determining the
> probabilities of this situation, your inquiry is, why was it called a
> flopper if it ran smoothly?

These comments are indeed surprisingly obtuse, and perhaps one-sided.[19]
Nevertheless, it would have been much more appropriate for the Court

---

[18] "[Murphy] cannot help himself to a verdict in such circumstances by the addition of
the facile comment that it threw him with a jerk, for he cannot readily differentiate
between a jerk that causes a fall and a jerk that is the immediate effect of a fall." 166 N.E.
at 174.

[19] Obviously, if a belt is very fast-moving, a rider can easily fall, even if the belt
operates smoothly. The trial judge's comparison to a slow-moving escalator is therefore
very misleading.

Other aspects of the instruction are also problematic. For example, the court's original
instruction does not mention assumption of risk at all. When defendant requests such an
instruction, the court provides one, but the resulting instruction does not clarify that
assumption of risk is a full defense to liability:

of Appeals to reverse because this instruction was erroneous or misleading, rather than because the evidence was insufficient.

Before we turn from the facts to the legal doctrine, it is worth placing *Murphy* within a broader factual context, one that might have affected Cardozo's view of the case. The accident occurred at Coney Island. In 1925, Coney Island was not just any amusement site. It was, in the trial court's apt phrase, the "playground of the world."

Consider first what we know about other amusement rides that Murphy himself sampled. To enter Steeplechase Park, Murphy first passed through the Barrel of Love, which has been described as follows:

> a slowly revolving, giant cylinder of polished wood, about fifteen feet long, through which a person by careful diagonal movement could pass in dignified erectness or by losing footing could end up in an intimate arm-and-leg tangle with complete strangers. Many a boy met girl that way.[20]

Murphy also rode the Whirlpool, or Human Roulette Wheel, a large revolving platform 30 feet in diameter, with room for 20 people, which flung passengers sitting on it to the perimeter.[21] Finally, Murphy answered "yes" when defense counsel asked him, of the other amusements in the park, "You saw a great many people tumbling around and enjoying themselves?" and "[Y]ou had a lot of fun watching other fellows receive falls and bumps of various kinds, didn't you?"

Another amusement at the park at this time was the Human Pool Table, a large surface containing 24 large rotating discs. Adjacent discs revolved in opposite directions. The people became "players" as they attempted to cross its flat surface, but lost their footing as they were spun in every direction and became entangled with others players. Steeplechase also contained: the Cakewalk (the floor shook when a person attempted to walk on it); the Panama Slide (which dropped people into a bowl); and the Grinder (a large "sausage machine"; people entered one end, squeezed through soft rollers, and were dumped out at the other end).[22]

[Defendant's lawyer]: I ask the Court to charge the jury that the plaintiff assumed the natural open and obvious risks of the normal and natural operation of this amusement device.

[The court]: So charged, if you find they were open and obvious, then he did assume them.

[20] Oliver Pilat & Jo Ranson, *Sodom by the Sea: An Affectionate History of Coney Island* 135 (1943).

[21] Murphy answers "yes" when asked, "You went in some kind of a slide and then you were propelled down on a movable table and you skidded around that and went off?"

[22] Steeplechase's attorney mentions the Cakewalk and Panama Slide.

In the words of one contemporary account:

> A chief pleasure of battered souls, one notices at once, is battered bodies. Here is a device where half a dozen of us sit in a flat-bottomed bowl and fall downhill, around curves, against posts, whirling at dizzying speed, jolted, sick and happy. Further on we do the same thing without the intervention of the bowl, sliding in a polished chute. Probably the pleasure of the latter comes from wondering about slivers. ... After you have done any of these things, you stand and watch other people repeating your agonies, and seeing them ridiculous you have all the contemptuous superiority of a new fledged sophomore hazing a freshman.[23]

Justice Cardozo was undoubtedly aware of Coney Island's general reputation as a locus of thrill-seekers. His view of the Flopper, and of Murphy's likely attitude towards its possible dangers, might have been colored by the plain fact that the Flopper was only one of many rides at Coney Island designed or expected to cause frequent falls.

A Closer Look at the Doctrinal Analysis

The brief analysis in *Murphy* of relevant legal doctrine is opaque and incomplete. That is a shame, because the vivid fact pattern in the case presents a wonderful opportunity for exploring the doctrinal issues posed by a victim's supposed consent to a risk. Let's put some flesh on the bare bones of Cardozo's analysis.

Lack of Negligence versus Assumption of Risk

Murphy is usually understood as a classic illustration of assumption of risk doctrine: one who voluntarily encounters a known risk is barred from recovery if the risk comes to fruition and he suffers harm. But is that actually the basis of the Court of Appeals' decision? Or does the court believe that Steeplechase Amusement Company was not negligent in the first place? Or, finally, is there really any difference between these questions? In other words, is there any difference (other than formal legal labels) between concluding that Steeplechase was not negligent, and concluding that Steeplechase was negligent but Murphy is barred by his assumption of risk?

Cardozo's opinion, alas, does not directly answer these questions. On the one hand, the opinion intimates that negligence (or breach of duty) and assumption of risk are separate inquiries. Thus, after describing the different types of negligence that plaintiff asserts, the court finds insuffi-

---

[23] Bruce Bliven, *Coney Island for Battered Souls*, The New Republic, Nov. 23, 1921. For historical accounts of Coney Island, see John F. Kasson, *Amusing the Million: Coney Island at the Turn of the Century* (1978); Pilat & Ranson, *supra* note 20.

cient basis for finding that the belt was out of order; then, after assuming arguendo that the jerk was established, the court employs an explicit analysis of assumption of risk, in the next paragraph that begins *"Volenti non fit injuria."* And yet, on the other hand, the court never clearly distinguishes the "no negligence" and assumption of risk arguments analytically: Cardozo moves back and forth between them abruptly and without explanation.[24]

All of this is rather curious, since New York law at the time clearly did differentiate the two inquiries: plaintiff must prove defendant's negligence as part of his prima facie case; but even if he succeeds in establishing that case, defendant escapes liability if he establishes as a defense that plaintiff assumed the risk. Indeed, only two years earlier, Cardozo himself authored an opinion that not only identified the distinction but relied upon it in denying recovery. In *Yaconi v. Brady & Gioe, Inc.*,[25] a longshoreman noticed a large spot of grease or oil, about a yard square, in the hold of the ship that he and the rest of his crew were unloading. He asked that the boss be notified to have it covered with sawdust or a piece of wood. An hour later, no such precaution had been taken. Plaintiff fell and broke his leg. Justice Cardozo, writing for the Court of Appeals, first found sufficient evidence of negligence. But he continued:

> The question remains whether there was an assumption of the risk. The danger was obvious. Not only was it obvious, but the plaintiff marked and understood it. ... The plaintiff..., knowing all the chances, was willing to go on in danger. The delay of a few minutes would have been enough, for if another did not bring the sawdust, he could have gone for it himself. The alternative was his, either to stop for this brief time, or to go on at his own risk. To his undoing he chose the risk.[26]

---

[24] Thus, in the third paragraph, Cardozo emphasizes the assumption of risk argument, noting the name "the Flopper," the participants' awareness of the risk, and the idea that the adventure would have been pointless absent the risk of a fall. In the fourth, he emphasizes that plaintiff took a chance, but then explains the plaintiff's alternative theories of negligence. In the fifth, he mainly discusses the inadequate proof of negligence, but at the end emphasizes that in any case, the risk of a fall is what was invited and foreseen (implying that such a risk is assumed by plaintiff). In the sixth and most famous paragraph, he underscores plaintiff's choice to encounter the risk. In the seventh, he states that "[a] different case would be here" if the risks were unknown or unknowable, or were much more serious in magnitude or frequency. But he does not clarify whether the case would be different because there would then be negligence, or because there would then be no assumption of risk. In the eighth paragraph, he observes that negligence could indeed be proven by inadequate padding, though the case did not go to the jury on this theory.

[25] 158 N.E. 876 (N.Y.1927).

[26] *Id.* at 877–78. *See also* Heck v. Lehigh Valley R.R. Co., 149 N.E. 835, 836 (N.Y.1925) (Cardozo, J.) (distinguishing breach of duty from assumption of risk).

Accordingly, the court reversed the judgment for the plaintiff and ordered the complaint dismissed.

Precluding recovery in *Yaconi* seems extremely harsh, and we will consider below the wisdom of the traditional doctrine of assumption of risk that bars recovery in such circumstances. But notice how readily Cardozo distinguishes in *Yaconi* between the question of negligence and the question of assumption of risk. The key to negligence is whether the defendant has created an unreasonably great risk. The key to assumption of risk is whether the individual victim was aware of that risk, and yet voluntarily chose to confront it. (If another longshoremen slipped on the oil without having observed it, assumption of risk would not bar his recovery.)

Why aren't the two issues distinguished more clearly in *Murphy*? Because, in some circumstances, the issues are indeed substantively identical, or nearly so.[27] To understand this point, consider the four different theories of negligence asserted in *Murphy* in more detail.

With respect to two of Murphy's theories of negligence, it is pretty easy to distinguish the questions. First, suppose Murphy was able to show that the padding on the surfaces of the Flopper was badly worn or inadequate, so that he hit exposed wood when he fell. Permitting such a dangerous condition to develop is clearly negligent. But it is a separate question whether a rider is aware of this risk. If he is, yet chooses to ride, he assumes the risk; if he is not, he does not.

Second, suppose Murphy could show that the Flopper was not operating smoothly, but with a series of violent jerks that caused much more severe falls than would normally be expected. It would be negligent to continue operating the device; such a "Superjerking Flopper" would, in Cardozo's language, be "too perilous to be endured." But suppose that a particular plaintiff observed the higher level of risk from the Super-jerking Flopper, yet decided to ride it. He would likely be barred from recovery, under the traditional doctrine of assumption of risk. A customer unaware of the risk, by contrast, would not be barred. (Below, I will explore more carefully whether the "negligent jerk" theory is persuasive on the actual *Murphy* facts.)

However, with respect to the claim that the Flopper traveled at an excessive speed, and the claim that it should have had a guard rail, it is difficult, if not impossible, to separate the question of negligence from

---

[27] In other opinions, Cardozo treats no negligence and assumption of risk as alternative or perhaps equivalent grounds for the decision. In *Dougherty v. Pratt Institute*, for example, a window washer died after falling from a window not equipped with a hook to which he could have attached his safety belt. Cardozo treats this obvious danger as both refuting plaintiff's claim of breach of duty and as establishing the plaintiff's assumption of risk when he continued to work. 155 N.E. 67, 68 (N.Y.1926).

the question of assumption of risk. Both speed and omission of a guard were inherent characteristics of the Flopper, providing part of its appeal. A very slow-moving Flopper wouldn't "flop" anyone, nor would it create the pleasurable sensation of speed; it would essentially be a moving sidewalk. A Flopper with a sturdy railing would essentially be a gently sloping escalator. And in either case, in the immortal words of bluesman B.B. King, "The thrill is gone."[28]

The crucial and surprising analytic point is this: the legal relevance of the device's speed or lack of a guard can be described in *either* of two ways. First, we might say that it is not negligent to offer these sorts of risky amusement rides to a willing public. Second, we might say that, whether or not the offering of such a ride (given its speed and lack of a sturdy railing) is negligent, any rider who is aware of the relevant risks but nevertheless chooses to take the ride legally assumes those risks. In this context, the two descriptions are virtually the same, for both rely on the idea that the defendant should not be liable if he offers a risky but socially acceptable activity in which participants elect to participate.[29]

The Negligence Claim in Murphy

Let's take a closer look at Murphy's theories of negligence. As we've seen, a critical question at trial was whether the belt suddenly jerked, thus causing Murphy's fall and injury. Would a positive answer demonstrate that Steeplechase was negligent? Not necessarily. For example, suppose it could be shown that one of the riders deliberately pulled hard on the belt, causing the sudden jerk. Unless such an act was foreseeable and could reasonably be prevented, Steeplechase would not be responsible. On the other hand, if a sudden jerk occurred but no explanation was offered, many courts would treat this as strong circumstantial evidence of negligence, sufficient to permit the jury to find that Steeplechase must have been negligent (for example, in failing properly to maintain the mechanism or to inspect the belt for hidden objects that could cause a jerk).[30]

---

[28] B.B. King, *The Thrill is Gone*, on *Completely Well* (MCA 1969).

Compare another New York case involving a victim of a Coney Island ride. In *Reinzi v. Tilyou*, Michael and Frances Reinzi took the Steeplechase ride (which gave Steeplechase Park its name), sitting on a wooden horse in a track that curved and dipped, simulating a horse race. The stirrup broke, and both fell off. The court (with Cardozo concurring) found sufficient evidence of negligence, and, perhaps with *Murphy* in mind, further noted: "This is not a case where the fun came from being thrown off the horses. That was not a part of the sport." 169 N.E. 101, 103 (N.Y.1929).

[29] In the terminology of many modern courts, the first characterization describes the category of "primary" assumption of risk, while the second describes the category of "secondary" assumption of risk.

[30] The circumstantial evidence doctrine, which goes by the name of res ipsa loquitur, permits a jury to find negligence despite the absence of specific proof of negligence, if the

In *Murphy*, however, the parties disputed whether a sudden jerk had occurred, not whether, if it did occur, Steeplechase was negligent. And, as I've suggested, Cardozo was too skeptical of Murphy's proof (offered by three witnesses) that the belt did jerk. On the other hand, Steeplechase's witnesses did testify, without contradiction, that it was not physically possible for the belt to jerk. At the very least, one would expect Murphy's attorney to have produced expert testimony to the contrary—for example, testimony explaining that if a shoe or foot were lodged underneath the belt, or if the belt was turned off while several riders were standing on it, it could suddenly jerk.[31] Cardozo's impatience with the "jerk" allegation is thus understandable.

If the belt did not actually jerk, is there a plausible argument that Steeplechase was negligent in some other respect? The excessive speed and inadequate railing arguments appear to be weak, for reasons noted above. Still, if Murphy's lawyer had been more diligent, he might have made the arguments plausible. What if he had interrogated the attending nurse more closely on the question of frequency of injuries? Suppose she revealed that every week, she treated a dozen people for injuries from falls? It would then have been a much closer question whether the intrinsic nature of the Flopper was simply too dangerous—"too perilous to be endured."[32] After all, the Flopper had only been in operation for less than one year when Murphy was injured. Perhaps Steeplechase

accident is of a type that ordinarily does not occur if due care is used. Res ipsa has sometimes been invoked in cases of amusement rides and escalators. *See, e.g.*, Brown v. Winnwood Amusement Co., 34 S.W.2d 149, 153 (Mo.Ct.App.1931) (upholding use of res ipsa to demonstrate negligence when a roller coaster suddenly jerked, and distinguishing *Murphy* on the ground that the Flopper "was intended to make one fall"); O'Callaghan v. Dellwood Park Co., 89 N.E. 1005 (Ill.1909) (cited in *Murphy*) (upholding use of res ipsa to demonstrate negligence when scenic railway suddenly stopped, apparently because of something on the track).

[31] In its brief on appeal, Steeplechase asserts: "Any start or stop of the belt would necessarily be gradual because of the natural tendency of all driving belts to slip when power is applied or shut off." However, this assertion is not supported by trial testimony or any reference to a secondary source. Steeplechase also states that "any change of speed of the belt could have resulted only from a fluctuation in the electric current supplied by the Brooklyn Edison Company, of which there is no proof and which is so unusual that we may with reason believe that it did not occur." Finally, Steeplechase notes the possibility that "some sudden break in the device might jam the belt and stop its movement," but, Steeplechase correctly observes, no evidence of any such break or defect was introduced.

[32] Indeed, that might have been the view of Justice O'Brien, who dissented in *Murphy*, without opinion, merely citing the recent case of *Tantillo v. Goldstein Brothers Amusement Co.*, 162 N.E. 82 (N.Y.1928). In that case, the plaintiff was offered free admission to a vaudeville show if he participated in an act. As requested, he ran on a treadmill to the amusement of the audience. But he was then catapulted off, and the person who was supposed to catch him fell on plaintiff and broke his arm. The court upheld a judgment of negligence, finding that the act was inherently dangerous. Presumably O'Brien believed that in *Murphy*, too, the activity was inherently too dangerous.

should have anticipated that a serious accident of the sort Murphy suffered was bound to occur, and sooner rather than later.

To underscore the point, imagine that Steeplechase decided to triple the speed of the Flopper, from approximately 7 miles per hour to 21 miles per hour. At that rate, one would expect anyone trying to stand on this "Superfast Flopper" to fall, and a substantial number to receive injuries, some of them serious. In dictum, Cardozo makes it clear that some activities are simply too risky, in light of the seriousness or frequency of expected injuries.[33] And he appears to endorse this judgment even if the participants are fully aware of the risks and choose to encounter them. In other words, with especially dangerous activities, liability will ensue notwithstanding both the argument that it is not negligent to offer such an activity to willing participants, and the argument that such participants are legally barred by assumption of those risks. Once again, application of either doctrine, negligence or assumption of risk, results in the same legal conclusion (though here, each permits liability instead of precluding it).

The Assumption of Risk Claim in Murphy

Three aspects of Murphy's assumption of risk argument deserve a closer look: first, Cardozo's supposition that it is irrelevant whether the jerk occurred; second, the question of how subjective and specific his appreciation of the risk must have been; and third, the question whether his choice to confront the risk was sufficiently voluntary.

Reconsider one of Cardozo's most important and striking arguments in *Murphy*. In his view, it is legally irrelevant whether a jerk occurred, even though the dispute over this factual issue was absolutely central at the trial. "Whether the movement of the belt was uniform or irregular, the risk at greatest was a fall. This was the very hazard that was invited and foreseen."[34] And Cardozo would presumably argue that even if the Flopper malfunctioned as badly as suggested in the "Superjerking Flopper" hypothetical above, Murphy should not be able to recover, if the only risk at issue was a fall.

---

[33] *See* 166 N.E. at 174–75:

A different case would be here if the dangers inherent in the sport were . . . so serious as to justify the belief that precautions of some kind must have been taken to avert them. . . . A different case there would also be if the accidents had been so many as to show that the game in its inherent nature was too dangerous to be continued without change. . . . [The nurse's testimony that she had treated some injuries at the Flopper] is not enough to show that the game was a trap for the unwary, too perilous to be endured. According to the defendant's estimate, two hundred and fifty thousand visitors were at the Flopper in a year. Some quota of accidents was to be looked for in so great a mass.

[34] *Id.* at 174.

This argument is much too facile. Not all falls are alike. A fall due to a sudden, unanticipated jerk might well differ from a fall due to jumping off a smoothly moving belt, and even from a fall due to losing one's balance on such a belt. In the first place, the fall due to the jerk might be more severe: it might throw the rider farther or much more rapidly, especially if the jerk was extremely sudden and sharp. In the second place, while riders probably have at least a modest ability to anticipate and thus guard against the consequences of a fall off a smoothly operating belt, a rider is much less able to protect himself when he has no reason to anticipate a jerk. (This might, indeed, explain why Murphy, a "vigorous young man," suffered such serious injuries, even though he probably anticipated the possibility of a fall from a fast but smoothly operating belt.) Many riders might have considered the speedy but continuously operating belt an enjoyable challenge: could they keep their balance without falling? But if they had known that the belt would suddenly jerk, making a fall virtually inevitable, they might have found the challenge too risky. Or, at the very least, they might have proceeded with much more caution, maintaining a greater distance from other riders and otherwise preparing themselves for any sudden lurch.

If we reject as simplistic Cardozo's argument that "the risk at greatest was a fall," then his conclusion that Murphy assumed the risk of a fall due to a jerk no longer follows. For the risks one legally assumes are defined narrowly, in light of the individual plaintiff's actual appreciation of the risk. And the nature, as well as the level, of the risk is relevant.[35] Since Murphy might have viewed the risk from a jerk-induced fall as greater, or more difficult to guard against, than the risk from more foreseeable types of falls, he would only have legally assumed the latter risks

Consider another assumption of risk opinion written by Cardozo, in which he clearly views assumption of risk as requiring subjective appreciation of the precise risk that leads to plaintiff's harm. In *Schmitt v. City of Syracuse*,[36] a seventeen year old boy who heard explosions of dynamite rode his bicycle to the scene and was badly injured by a further explosion.

The plaintiff may have known that dynamite was being exploded and that dynamite was dangerous, but it cannot be said as a matter

---

[35] Indeed, recall Cardozo's concession that if Murphy had been injured because the padding was inadequate, Murphy could obtain recovery. But this would be true even if an injury so suffered was no more severe than an injury suffered because of a legally assumed risk. Compare Murphy fracturing his knee because of a mild fall on an unpadded surface, with his fracturing his knee because of a more serious fall on a padded surface after falling off a smoothly moving belt. The injuries are the same, but a court might conclude that the risk of the second is legally assumed, while the risk of the first is not.

[36] 128 N.E. 119 (N.Y.1920).

of law that he knew or should have known that the work done at the Ford car, which was that of preparing the charges and not that of exploding dynamite, was necessarily dangerous or that he fully appreciated the extent of the risk. At most, he was a loiterer or casual observer upon the street and was not a spectator voluntarily consenting to or assuming the risk of injury.[37]

To be sure, it is *possible* for a rider to assume the risks even from a *jerking* moving belt. Imagine that Steeplechase offered two Floppers side by side. One was the actual Flopper, designed to operate smoothly; the other was the "HerkyJerky Flopper," running a little slower, but periodically and unpredictably jerking. Murphy, after observing riders falling off each Flopper, decides to ride the HerkyJerky. Under traditional doctrine, he would have assumed the risk of injury from such a fall— either because offering the HerkyJerky is not considered to be negligent, or because a participant will be viewed as voluntarily encountering a known risk. Of course, in the *Murphy* case itself, we would need proof that Murphy appreciated the actual risks of a jerk-induced fall, not just the risks of a fall caused by the smoothly operating belt that he had witnessed. And that proof is lacking.

This feature of traditional assumption of risk doctrine—its focus on subjective appreciation of risk—raises another doubt about Cardozo's analysis. How does he conclude that Murphy subjectively appreciated the risk of a fall at all, much less a fall induced by a jerk? Cardozo emphasizes the objective facts, that many of the riders did indeed fall, and also the subjective choice of Murphy's girlfriend: " 'I took a chance,' she said when asked whether she thought that a fall might be expected." Cardozo continues: "Plaintiff took the chance with her..."[38] But *her* testimony that she expected a significant risk of a fall does not demonstrate that *he* believed the risk of a fall was significant. Perhaps he believed there was only a small risk that he himself would fall, and only an insignificant risk of a fall serious enough to cause injury.[39] And perhaps his reason for taking the ride was not to enjoy the thrill of a fall

---

[37] *Id.* at 120–21.

Consider also *Larson v. Nassau Electric R.R. Co.*, 119 N.E. 92 (N.Y.1918). A motorman was crushed when an air brake of a railroad car failed to work properly. Defendant argued that plaintiff was aware of the defect and assumed the risk of injury from it. But, writing for the court, Cardozo noted that plaintiff had noticed a similar defect in the past, yet it had not led to harm. Thus, '[w]e cannot say as a matter of law that he appreciated the danger' and should have taken steps to avoid it. "A jury must say whether the risk was so obvious or so imminent as to cast that duty upon him. He may have known that there was a defect, but it does not follow that he knew the danger." *Id.* at 93.

[38] 166 N.E. at 174.

[39] Murphy did testify to some appreciation of the risk, but he did not go as far as his girlfriend in conceding that he "took the chance." Here is his testimony on cross-examination:

or a near-fall, but to enjoy the sensation of speed. In this light, Cardozo's claim that there would be no point to the ride absent a substantial risk of a fall is unpersuasive; although many participants may have wanted to fall, or may have wanted to see others fall, other participants (including Murphy) could have had different but equally intelligible motives. To be sure, there is indeed sufficient evidence in the record to support a finding that Murphy subjectively appreciated the risks of injury from a fall. But such a finding hardly follows from the fact that his girlfriend appreciated those risks.

A final issue relevant to the legal analysis in *Murphy* is whether Murphy's choice to encounter the risk was sufficiently *voluntary* to count as assumption of risk. At trial, Murphy testified that he believed he was required to ride the Flopper in order to get to other amusements in the park. This, he said, was part of his reason for riding the Flopper. Others in his group shared this belief. On the other hand, two witnesses for Steeplechase testified, without contradiction, that there was no actual necessity; the park was so constructed that one could indeed reach the other amusements without riding the Flopper. This dispute was a key issue at the trial.[40]

Yet Cardozo's opinion does not even mention the issue of necessity. Perhaps he concluded that the proof, showing no actual necessity to ride the Flopper in order to get to other rides, moots the issue. But that conclusion would be incorrect. If Murphy honestly and reasonably believed that he had no alternative way of getting to other amusements, then that belief, even if mistaken, might be enough. For in other necessity cases, courts routinely examine the issue from the perspective of reasonable foresight, not hindsight. Consider cases where the plaintiff attempts to rescue someone endangered by defendant's negligence.[41] If,

---

Q: Did not you expect to fall off when you got on this thing?

A: Well, I don't know.

Q: Well, did not you expect to?

A: I expected some but not what I got.

Q: Were not the other people who were getting on this device falling off?

A: Some did and some did not.

[40] Indeed, Murphy's claim of necessity was part of the basis for the trial court's decision denying Steeplechase's motion to dismiss.

Arguably, even if Murphy needed to travel through the Flopper amusement area to access other portions of the park, he could have walked alongside the Flopper, rather than riding it. However, it is not clear from the diagram that this was a feasible option. Given the location of the attendant at the start of the belt, and given the presence of other riders, a patron might have been required to step on the Flopper initially in order to reach the ride exit.

[41] Under assumption of risk doctrine, such cases are usually treated as rendering the plaintiff's choice to confront the risk not "voluntary." *See Restatement (Second) of Torts* § 496E(2)(a), illus. 2 & 3 (1965).

from the perspective of foresight, the rescue seems to have some reasonable chance of success, then the plaintiff will be entitled to recover, and will not be barred by contributory negligence or assumption of risk, even if, after the fact, it turns out that the rescue effort was futile.[42]

Cardozo might have been unimpressed with Murphy's necessity argument for another reason. An amusement park customer who is required to participate in a particular amusement in order to get to other rides arguably still has a sufficient choice that his decision counts as a voluntary assumption of risk: he still can choose whether to attend or remain in the park at all. Nevertheless, if rides are indeed linked in this way, the customer should not be deemed to accept the risk unless he is aware of it; and Murphy's claim is that he was *not* so notified when he entered the park. (Notice after entry is also problematic; in the actual case, it is unclear whether Murphy could have obtained his money back if he had chosen to leave.) In any event, the court should have offered a fuller analysis of this issue.[43]

Murphy and Contemporary Tort Doctrine[44]

The doctrinal analysis in *Murphy* is disappointingly opaque, if not unpersuasive. But the case was decided in 1929. As we progress into the

[42] *See* Eckert v. Long Island R.R. Co., 43 N.Y. 502 (N.Y.1871); *see also* Wagner v. Int'l Ry., 133 N.E. 437 (N.Y.1921) (a Cardozo opinion that mainly establishes that the original tortfeasor remains a proximate cause of the rescuer's injury, but also seems to provide that the rescuer is entitled to recover (notwithstanding possible claims that the rescuer was contributorily negligent or assumed the risk) so long as his rescue effort was not reckless). As the court concludes: "Whether Herbert Wagner's fall was due to the defendant's negligence, and whether plaintiff in going to the rescue, as he did, was foolhardy or reasonable in the light of the emergency confronting him, were questions for the jury." *Id.* at 438.

[43] There is some reason to believe that Cardozo would have taken a dim view of the necessity argument if he had addressed it. In *Yaconi v. Brady & Gioe, Inc.*, discussed above, Cardozo observes that the employee "knew there was no pathway to his work except across the spot of danger. . . . In going on with the work, he made the risk his own." 158 N.E. at 877–78 (N.Y. 1927). Many courts, at least today, would reason otherwise. If, in order to continue working, one must confront a risk negligently created by defendant, many jurisdictions would treat the risk as not voluntarily assumed. *See Restatement (Second) of Torts* § 496E (1965).

In the workplace, most accidents are now covered by worker's compensation, a statutory no fault liability scheme that eliminates the defense of assumption of risk entirely.

[44] For some accounts of the development of assumption of risk doctrine, and arguments about its current vitality, see John L. Diamond, *Assumption of Risk After Comparative Negligence: Integrating Contract Theory into Tort Doctrine*, 52 Ohio St. L.J. 717 (1991); Kenneth W. Simons, *Assumption of Risk and Consent in the Law of Torts: A Theory of Full Preference*, 67 B.U. L. Rev. 213 (1987); Kenneth W. Simons, *Reflections on Assumption of*

21st century, does tort doctrine offer greater clarity? Is there now a consensus about how to analyze jerking (or nonjerking) Floppers? I'm afraid not.

Modernists have indeed tried to reform assumption of risk doctrine, and to some extent they have succeeded. In a nutshell, the developments since 1929 are as follows. First, comparative fault, permitting negligent plaintiffs to obtain at least partial recovery, has largely replaced the rule that such plaintiffs are completely barred from recovery. But assumption of risk, insofar as it is still recognized as a defense, is normally a complete defense. Thus, although in 1929 a plaintiff would be denied any recovery if his behavior was classified as assumption of risk *or* as contributory negligence, today it makes a big difference how that behavior is classified. Second, the traditional assumption of risk defense has been rejected in an increasing number of states. And the modern conventional wisdom is that that defense should be abolished and replaced by (or merged into) a comparative fault framework. On this view, any case that would in the past have been classified as "victim assumption of the risk of the injurer's negligence" should now be reclassified, and must fall into one of two categories:

(1) If the victim who chose to encounter the risk acted *unreasonably*, she might obtain partial recovery (depending on the applicable comparative fault rules);

(2) Alternatively, if the victim who chose to encounter the risk acted *reasonably* or without fault, she obtains full recovery.

(This reclassification occurs, of course, only in those cases where the defendant was found to have been negligent in the first place.)

The new approach has been officially endorsed by the Restatement (Third) of Torts,[45] and it works well in many cases. Reconsider *Yaconi*, for example. Today, most courts would conclude that a worker who tried without success to have a dangerous workplace condition remedied and who continued to work in the face of the danger should not be denied all recovery based on assumption of risk. At worst, he might be partially at fault if he could have performed his work without endangering himself, but unreasonably failed to do so. At best, he is not at fault at all and is entitled to a full recovery.

But does this approach always work? Specifically, are there cases in which a defendant was negligent, the plaintiff was not negligent, and yet the plaintiff should be precluded from recovery because of her consent

---

Risk, 50 UCLA L. Rev. 481 (2002); Stephen D. Sugarman, *The Monsanto Lecture: Assumption of Risk*, 31 Val.U. L. Rev. 833 (1997). For a more philosophical account, see 3 Joel Feinberg, *The Moral Limits of the Criminal Law, Harm to Self*, chs. 20, 22 (1986).

[45] *Restatement (Third) of Torts: Apportionment* § 2 cmt. i; § 3 cmt. c (1998).

to, or her voluntary choice to confront, a known risk? If such cases do exist, then the modern conventional wisdom is wrong, and assumption of risk has a continuing role to play.

Return to the "Superjerking Flopper" hypothetical. Suppose the Flopper is badly malfunctioning on a given day, operating with a series of unpredictable, violent jerks that produce much more severe falls than it normally causes. And further suppose that Patrick, a Coney Island regular who is quite familiar with the Flopper, is fully aware of these facts, but is delighted to see that the ride has become more challenging. He chooses to ride, falls, and suffers an injury. Should he be entitled to recover? On the modern approach, it appears, he should. For it seems that Steeplechase is negligent for operating the Superjerker, while it is not at all clear that Patrick is even partially at fault simply because he chooses, for his own purposes, to take this risk. After all, the timorous will stay at home; the mildly adventurous will choose to ride only a properly operating Flopper; but the true thrill-seekers might reasonably, and without fault, choose to ride a Superjerker. And yet is it not clear that these faultless adventurers should not be entitled to recover?

The modernists who advocate abolishing assumption of risk do have an answer. In cases such as Patrick electing to ride the Superjerker, they might agree that recovery should not be permitted. But they would explain this conclusion by re-characterizing the case: they would assert that Steeplechase is *not negligent*, after all, in offering even this very risky ride to those who obtain distinctive benefits from encountering its risks. More generally, they will treat many cases formerly characterized as assumption of risk as, instead, cases where the defendant either owed "no duty" to the plaintiff or did not breach that duty. Thus, to invoke two of Cardozo's own examples in *Murphy*, the owner of a baseball stadium has no duty to screen all of the seats, since spectators in less dangerous locations generally prefer the better view to the slight increase in safety. And fencers do not owe an absolute duty not to injure each other; rather, a "fencer accepts the risk of a thrust by his antagonist" and (the modernist would say) is owed only a limited duty because, again, "[o]ne who takes part in such a sport accepts the dangers that inhere in it in so far as they are obvious and necessary."[46]

Well, which approach is better—the approach that says participants in a game (and operators of amusement rides) do not breach a duty if they fail to eliminate the inherent risks of the activity, or the approach that says that participants "assume" such risks? There are some differences, apart from labeling, between the two approaches. The assumption of risk approach tends to be more individualized and subjective, focusing on the actual appreciation of risk of the plaintiff who was injured. The

---

[46] Murphy v. Steeplechase Amusement Co., 166 N.E. 173, 174 (N.Y.1929).

no duty approach tends to be wholesale, rather than retail, focusing on the risks that most participants would appreciate, but not examining the actual understanding of the individual plaintiff. The no duty approach is therefore more categorical, and typically more protective of defendants.[47]

As further examples of the individualistic approach, recall some of the *Murphy* scenarios we explored above. Suppose many riders of the Flopper would care whether the belt jerked suddenly, because they wanted the challenge of keeping their balance, not the almost certain effect of a fall. But suppose Murphy himself wouldn't care; he loves to fall, and the harder and more sudden, the better. Then, on the individualistic assumption of risk approach, his claim would be barred. And conversely, perhaps Murphy's girlfriend took the chance, while his state of mind was different; he was confident he could keep his balance, and would not have taken the risk if he thought the chance of injury was more than trivial. Then he would not have assumed the risk of injury from a Flopper that he did not realize might suddenly jerk.

The consensual rationale that underlies both assumption of risk and the no duty approach would seem to support the more subjective approach, at least in principle. However, under this approach, the legal resolution potentially turns on difficult matters of proof. Advocates of the "no duty" approach would say that it is not worth preserving a legal defense that depends on such fine distinctions. The debate is an ongoing one. Still, whichever is the better doctrinal approach, notice that a similar policy underlies each—namely, the idea that often, consent to a risk is sufficient to preclude negligence liability. And notice that this policy is quite different from the comparative fault idea, under which it is only justifiable to reduce (much less preclude) a plaintiff's recovery if the plaintiff acted in an unreasonable or faulty way. For, under either doctrinal variation of the consensual approach, the adventurous as well as the timorous can be acting reasonably or without fault.

The view that assumption of risk has largely been "abolished" is therefore somewhat misleading. It is true that the traditional assumption of risk doctrine, barring a plaintiff from recovery whenever he makes any minimal choice to confront a known risk, is overbroad. (Recall *Yaconi*). This broad version of assumption of risk is rarely followed today. However, a number of states continue to employ a narrower assumption of risk defense. And even where assumption of risk is formally abolished as a distinct doctrine, its consensual rationale underlies a variety of no duty (or limited duty) rules. Moreover, in factual contexts such as the Flopper, when a participant chooses an

---

[47] Also, the plaintiff bears the burden of proving duty, while the defendant has the burden of proving assumption of risk. In borderline cases, plaintiff would prefer the assumption of risk approach, because of the shifted burden.

activity at least in part because of, and not merely in spite of, the risks that it poses, this consensual rationale seems especially persuasive, whatever label is attached to it.

Finally, even in *Murphy*, Cardozo acknowledged that if the injuries were "too serious" or "too frequent," recovery would be allowed. Perhaps he assumes that no participant would voluntarily consent to a risk of serious or frequent injuries on an amusement device. Or perhaps he endorses a straightforwardly paternalistic approach, believing that, although such consent occasionally occurs, the law should ignore it in order to protect victims from their own extremely ill-advised decisions. Contemporary tort law clearly does recognize limits to consent doctrines: in products liability, for example, consumers can sometimes recover for a design defect even if it is open and obvious.[48] If such limits are accepted, however, then, once again, they can be expressed doctrinally in two different ways—either in the form of an expanded duty rule (a duty to protect victims from foolish decisions) or in the form of a special limitation on assumption of risk.

Why is *Murphy* Considered an Important Case?

Murphy continues to be cited frequently and is prominently featured in many torts casebooks as a primary illustration of assumption of risk. What explains its continuing reputation as a classic torts case? Three main reasons, I believe: *Murphy*'s recognition of the principle that liability for the inherent risks of an activity is often unwarranted; the vivid fact pattern; and the striking vitality of Cardozo's writing.

First, *Murphy* memorably exemplifies the point that some activities have inherent risks that are also part of their attraction. And Cardozo's opinion cogently argues that victims who suffer harms arising from such risks normally should not be able to obtain compensation. This lesson remains relevant today for injuries occurring, not just in amusement parks, but also in a wide range of recreational sports and activities.

Unfortunately, in other respects, the legal analysis in *Murphy* is not especially strong, nor is it path-breaking. *Murphy* did little to clarify existing legal rules, nor did it move the law in a new direction. Cardozo's other opinions on assumption of risk are similar: although they sometimes offer more in the way of clarification,[49] they apply but do not remake existing doctrine.

---

[48] *See Restatement (Third) of Torts: Products Liability* § 2 cmts. d, l (1998).

[49] *See, e.g.*, Maloney v. Cunard Steamship Co., 111 N.E. 835, 837 (N.Y.1916) (explaining that it would be perverse "if the law required us to hold that a servant who heedlessly incurs a risk is in a worse plight than a servant who voluntarily accepts the same risk";

Still, Cardozo's contribution here is distinctive in one way: his opinions vividly bring out the factual context of assumption of risk doctrine, reminding the reader of the social practices and customs underlying a plaintiff's decision to confront a risk. His opinions typically begin with a cinematic narration of the injury. Doctrinal standards often first appear more as background props than as primary actors. But the technique is a sly one: when he tells a compelling story, he also insinuates that the legal standard is as compelling as the tale. In the end, the reader (or viewer) comprehends the facts and the law as one.

Murphy undoubtedly has colorful, memorable facts. You cannot read the case without developing a mental picture of the Flopper and of Murphy's fall. (Unfortunately, there is reason to doubt that the picture painted in the opinion accurately depicts the real Flopper and the real accident, as we've seen.[50]) Moreover, the fact pattern is both simple and suggestive. Virtually any significant issue in the law of assumption of risk (or limited duty due to participants' consent) can easily be teased out through slight variations of the facts.

The story, then, is compelling and vivid. But another reason for *Murphy*'s iconic status is Cardozo's marvelous writing style. His exalted rhetoric is distinctive, arresting and irresistible. These qualities are exhibited in most of Cardozo's opinions, though *Murphy* is one of the best exemplars.[51] Judge Richard Posner observes: "The power of Cardozo

---

thus, one cannot infer contributory negligence from the mere use by a servant of an appliance furnished for his use).

[50] The opinion paints a picture of the Flopper that is possibly misleading and incomplete, for Cardozo suggests that the padded walls were adjacent to the belt, and he does not address whether the riders reasonably believed that it was necessary to ride the Flopper in order to get to other amusements. The opinion also paints a picture of the accident (the belt did not jerk) that the jury might reasonably have rejected.

[51] Here is a small selection of pithy aphorisms and nimble turns of phrase drawn from a range of Cardozo's tort opinions, many of which are staples of the first year torts class:

Danger invites rescue.

Wagner v. International Ry., 133 N.E. 437, 437 (N.Y.1921).

[T]he orbit of the danger as disclosed to the eye of reasonable vigilance [is] the orbit of the duty.... Life will have to be made over, and human nature transformed, before prevision so extravagant can be accepted as the norm of conduct....

Palsgraf v. Long Island R.R., 162 N.E. 99, 100 (N.Y.1928).

A statute designed for the protection of human life is not to be brushed aside as a form of words, its commands reduced to the level of cautions, and the duty to obey attenuated into an option to conform.

Martin v. Herzog, 126 N.E. 814, 816 (N.Y.1920).

In *Pokora v. Wabash Ry.*, one of the few memorable tort opinions that he had occasion to write once he had joined the United States Supreme Court, Cardozo suggested a "need for caution in framing standards of behavior that amount to rules of law. The need is the

... is to a great extent that of a rhetorician—a poet—rather than that of an analyst, or of an advocate or practitioner of pragmatic jurisprudence."[52] Whether or not this assessment is valid as a general matter, it accurately characterizes Cardozo's opinion in *Murphy*.

Conclusion

Alas, most of the grand amusements of Coney Island are no more.[53] Steeplechase Park closed in 1964; the two other major parks operating in Coney Island in the first decades of the 20th century had already closed by then. The Flopper itself was in operation for no more than two years, and I have found no record of a similar ride in recent times.

But imagine that a lawyer-turned-entrepreneur with fond memories of her first year Torts class were to recreate the Flopper. Would it be a success? I doubt it. The significant risk of physical injury from the frequent falls would, I suspect, scare away too many potential riders. And it is hard to compete with modern roller-coasters and similar high-speed rides, which offer much greater excitement, and over a much longer period of time, without the obvious risk of immediate physical injury.

Nevertheless, if a contemporary amusement park did offer the Flopper, and another James Murphy fell off, suffering injury, what result? Some courts would agree with Cardozo and find such an amusement device similar to the risky activities of skiing or riding a horse:

---

more urgent when there is no background of experience out of which the standards have emerged. They are then, not the natural flowerings of behavior in its customary forms, but rules artificially developed, and imposed from without." 292 U.S. 98, 105 (1934).

Finally, in a case involving a seaman who fell off a tugboat as it turned, Cardozo explained that proof of negligence was lacking. The concluding language prefigures the great epithet from *Murphy*, "the timorous may stay at home":

> A boat is not unseaworthy because there are spaces here and there where a seaman, if awkward or inattentive, may find it possible to fall. . . . The mariner on the dizzy mast has this at least in common with his sheltered brother in the harbor, that the work of each is on the waves. One who would shun their perils wholly, should stay upon the land.

Brick v. Long Island R.R. Co., 157 N.E. 93, 94 (N.Y.1927).

[52] Richard A. Posner, *Cardozo: A Study in Reputation* 56–57 (1990). Another illuminating biography of Cardozo is Andrew L. Kaufman, *Cardozo* (1998). Also instructive is Warren Seavey, *Mr. Justice Cardozo and the Law of Torts*, 39 Colum. L. Rev. 20 (1939).

[53] A major exception is the Cyclone, one of the most famous roller-coasters in history, opened in Coney Island in 1927 and still running today. "With its clattering 85–foot drop reaching speeds of 60 miles an hour, the Cyclone prompted as brave a soul as Charles Lindbergh to remark that it was 'scarier than flying.' " See *The Riegelmann Boardwalk Is Built*, at http://www.pbs.org/wgbh/amex/coney/peopleevents/pande10.html (last visited Feb. 18, 2002).

they would conclude that the risks, if adequately disclosed, are of a type and degree that the organizer can legitimately create without liability, and that the participant can acceptably assume. But other courts would differ. Even if the fall was not due to a jerk, but only to the speed of the mechanism, they might find the device "too perilous to be endured," in Cardozo's words.

The timorous can indeed stay at home. But it does not follow that the adventurous must always take their lumps with no hope of compensation.

8

Kenneth S. Abraham

Rylands v. Fletcher: Tort Law's Conscience

Rylands v. Fletcher[1] will not go away. Though the rule the case now stands for has turned out to be very limited, considerably more than a century after the case was decided the idea behind it still threatens to escape and do mischief throughout the law of torts. That idea, of course, is strict liability: the notion that injurers should be liable for the harm they cause, regardless of whether they are negligent. Let loose completely, this idea would swallow up much of the rest of accident law. There would be little remaining negligence law, because there would be no need for it. Yet, although the idea of strict liability has never gained anything even close to dominance, neither has it stayed respectfully in its place. *Rylands* is tort law's conscience, an always-available alternative to the negligence system that persistently causes us to examine the justifications for the limitations on liability that are inherent in a body of accident law based primarily on negligence.

The power behind the idea of strict liability is all the more remarkable once we understand how little strict liability there actually is in contemporary tort law. *Rylands* was at first squarely rejected by many courts in the United States. But the small pockets of strict liability that remained subsequently evolved into something broader, and by the mid-twentieth century *Rylands* was the seminal case in a body of strict liability law on ultrahazardous activities that had the potential for significant expansion. In certain respects the American law of strict liability definitely was broader than the law of Great Britain, which after all had given birth to *Rylands*.

---

[1] Fletcher v. Rylands, 3 H. & C. 774 (Exch. 1865), *rev'd,* L.R. 1 Exch. 265 (Exch.Ch. 1866), *rev'd,* L. R. 3 H. L. 330 (1868).

But as it turned out, there was never any further expansion in the scope of strict liability. And with the perspective of another half-century, the overall picture suggests that *Rylands* and the rule that has evolved from it have a very minor place in American tort law. Today the vast majority of modern tort cases involve auto accidents—quintessentially a domain of negligence liability. A second major category of tort litigation—products liability—is now recognized to be largely a regime of negligence rather than strict liability. What have come to be called "toxic torts" involving environmental exposures sometimes involve strict liability, but more often turn on negligence or breach of statutory duty. The domain of employer's strict liability, *respondeat superior*, depends for its application on the negligence of the employee. And even in the classic situation for which *Rylands v. Fletcher* is the model—harm resulting from a dangerous use of land—some jurisdictions apply strict liability to only one activity: blasting. Other states apply strict liability to a few additional activities, but everywhere the approach is limited in scope.

The story of *Rylands v. Fletcher*, therefore, is not so much a story of legal change or of the evolution of the law, though it is that in part. Rather, the story of *Rylands* lies in the idea of strict liability, and the power of that idea to influence our way of thinking about tort law, far out of proportion to the contemporary influence of this idea on the particulars of legal doctrine.

The Parties and The Litigation

Rylands was a suit by the operator of a coal mine against a mill owner who had built a reservoir to create power for his mill. The reservoir burst and flooded the mine. To understand the decision, and the doctrine for which the decision has come to stand, in a sense that is all we need to know. But as so often happens when we descend below the rarified air of an appellate opinion, the facts surrounding *Rylands* are messy. Appreciating the historical context in which the case arose can add richness and texture to our understanding of the litigation that gave rise to the rule for which *Rylands* now stands.

Thomas Fletcher operated a number of collieries, or coal mines, in Lancashire County, England, around the middle of the nineteenth century.[2] He began mining coal at several sites on the lands of Lord Wilton in this area in 1850. The land was about two miles outside of the small industrial town of Radcliffe. An aerial photograph today shows it to partly suburban subdivisions and partly farms. During Fletcher's time,

---

[2] Fletcher is identified as the owner of seven different active mines in North and East Lancashire alone as of 1869. *See Collieries of the United Kingdom at Work in 1869*, at http://freepages.genealogy.rootsweb.com/?cmhrc/lom69.nel.htm.

land uses in the area probably were more diverse. Among other things, however, this was unmistakably coal mining country. As of 1869, shortly after the decision in *Rylands*, there were over two hundred collieries in this part of Lancashire alone.[3]

The coal deposits at one site that Fletcher was working, the Red House Colliery (what we can call "parcel one"), led beyond the boundary of the lands of Lord Wilton and under the land of two other parties ("parcel two" and "parcel three"), who granted Fletcher the right to mine under their lands as well. Apparently the shafts that Fletcher worked became physically linked with, or at least were directly next to some other, long-abandoned shafts of another mine, or mines, eventually terminating either directly under or right at the border of yet another piece of land which also was owned by Lord Wilton ("parcel four"). At some point after 1855 Fletcher stopped working the Red House Colliery, though his right to work it seems to have continued.

John Rylands, who was to become the defendant, leased parcel four from Lord Wilton. Rylands was a very wealthy man. The "Wellington of Commerce," he was sole owner of a firm that manufactured linen, huckaback, diaper, calico, check, and gingham. It was the largest company of its kind in the cotton industry, and the largest employer in England, having 12,000 employees in seventeen separate mills.[4]

In 1860 Rylands constructed a reservoir on the land he was leasing from Lord Wilton in the same vicinity as Fletcher's mine, in order to assist in providing power to a cotton mill that Rylands already had in operation. The mill contained 600 looms and was powered by steam generated by the burning of coal. The reservoir was to be a source of additional water for generating the steam, and would be fed by drainage from nearby fields as well as by another reservoir at slightly greater distance and higher elevation. In fact the mill was not on the same land as the reservoir, but on what seems to have been Rylands' own adjoining land ("parcel five"). Since the water would have to pass over the intervening two parcels of land (under which the abandoned coal shafts also passed), Rylands may have needed the permission of these two landowners. Whether he had this permission is beside the point, but the very fact that five different parcels of land (and what lay beneath some of them) figured in the case in one way or another suggests just how bound up with ideas about the right to use land the issues raised in *Rylands* actually were.

---

[3] *Id.*

[4] *See* A. W. B. Simpson, *Legal Liability for Bursting Reservoirs: The Historical Context of* Rylands v. Fletcher, 13 J. Legal Stud. 209, 239 n.117 (1984).

Rylands hired a contractor to dig the reservoir. The fact that the reservoir was "dug" rather than constructed by building up an embankment in order to dam a stream was of some significance in the England of that decade, as we will see later. Large dams and the reservoirs that resulted typically were constructed by embanking, or "impoundment," whereas small reservoirs such as the one Rylands dug were more like artificial ponds that were created by excavating a depression in the land. In the course of construction, Rylands' contractor discovered five old shafts lined with timber walls. The shafts were filled with marl or soil of the same kind that immediately surrounded them. The contractor did not know or suspect that these shafts communicated with old mines, although it was later found that the contractor (but not Rylands) was negligent in not taking their existence into account in designing the reservoir to withstand the pressure of the water it would contain.

The reservoir was finished early in December, 1860. It had been partially filled with water when, on December 11, one of the shafts underneath it burst downward. It seems apparent that the way the shafts were filled made them unable to withstand the increasing water pressure that developed as the depth of the reservoir increased. The water found its way through the burst shaft into the abandoned shafts underneath the reservoir, then made its way into the various shafts that Fletcher had previously worked, and eventually ended up flooding the Red House Colliery.

In an area where coal mining was as prevalent as it was in Lancashire at the time, this kind of occurrence was not uncommon, although typically flooding was from mine to mine. Abandoned or disused mines filled with water, and because records of the location of old mines were poor, the diggings of new mines sometimes unexpectedly encountered old shafts and released water that had collected in them.[5] Exactly what Rylands' engineer and contractors had seen or understood about the old shafts is not clear. But it seems likely that the finding that they were negligent rested at least in part on what they should have known about the prevalence, appearance, and permeability of abandoned mine shafts—especially in an area as full of coal mines as northeast Lancashire during that period.

Fletcher at first successfully pumped the water out of the mine, but then the boiler for the pump's engine burst, throwing parts several hundred yards, injuring half a dozen people, and demolishing buildings on the site. A mine inspector then warned Fletcher of his potential responsibility for injury and damage if he continued the effort, and he gave up trying.[6] Eleven months after the reservoir failed, Fletcher

---

[5] *Id.* at 241.

[6] *Id.* at 242.

brought an action against Rylands (and the manager of his mill, Jehu Horrocks, whose name the case bears but who otherwise disappears from the story), alleging negligence in the design and construction of the reservoir. Neither the contractor nor the engineer they employed were named as defendants, perhaps (as Professor Simpson speculates) because they were bankrupt.[7]

The path the case then took is especially interesting. It came on for trial in August, 1862. But apparently there was some question whether the defendants could be held liable in negligence under these circumstances. Although the contractors hired by the defendants to dig the reservoir were negligent, it was not clear whether Rylands himself had been. And although it had long been established that an employer was strictly liable "vicariously" for the negligence of his employees under the doctrine of *respondeat superior*, the contractors were not employees of the defendant, but independent contractors. Whether and under what circumstances (if any) one who employed an independent contractor could be held vicariously liable for the negligence of that contractor had not yet been definitively decided.

Probably for this reason, the case was referred to an "arbitrator"—something like a special master today, who is entitled to find facts and identify legal issues for decision by the court that appoints him. It is not clear whether the arbitrator was at that point given the authority to state a "special case"—that is, to formulate a question of law for the court. Some time later, however, on December 31, 1864, the arbitrator was given the authority to state a special case for a court called the Exchequer of Pleas. There was a stipulation by the parties that the proper verdict if there was liability would be for £5000.[8] This sum was fictional, however, and was merely used to round out the arbitrator's decision, for eventually the parties agreed (privately) on the proper amount of damages to be awarded if the plaintiff succeeded. We never learn this sum. The arbitrator found that although the contractors were negligent, the defendants were not. But the legal question the arbitrator's findings posed for the Exchequer of Pleas—the first court whose opinions are usually set out in the casebooks—had changed. That question was now whether Rylands could be held liable without fault, even if he was not vicariously liable for the negligence of the contractor. Resolution of the vicarious liability issue was left for the future.

---

[7] *Id.* at 243.

[8] This included "£348 for equipment lost in the mine, £331 for pumping expenses, £202 for loss of interest if the plaintiff was a tenant from year to year (alternatively £670 if he was entitled to a lease for sixteen years from 1855) and £56 loss of profit up to the point of abandonment." *Id.* at 242, n.128.

How had the question in the case been so radically transformed? The answer seems to lie in an event that had intervened between the time Fletcher filed suit and the time (December 31, 1864) the arbitrator was empowered to state a special case. On March 12, 1863, a very large dam at Sheffield, in Yorkshire, known as the Dale Dyke embankment, which had been built to create a reservoir, had failed. The resulting flood killed at least 238 people and flooded some villages in the valley below it to a depth of nine feet. Over 20,000 people suffered loss and needed public relief as a result.[9] They consulted a prominent attorney, Sir Hugh Cairns, who advised them that the statute authorizing construction of this dam to create a public reservoir also provided that the company that had built it was strictly liable for the personal injury and property damage resulting from its failure.[10] The Dale Dyke disaster garnered enormous publicity and was a matter of considerable public controversy. Legislation regulating large dams was introduced in Parliament (though never enacted) and a commission was formed to deal with the problem of how to provide compensation to the thousands of victims in need of it.[11]

Large dams built by water companies were almost always the product of special legislation, and any liability arising from their malfunction would correspondingly have been handled by legislation. Nevertheless, as a result of the Dale Dyke disaster, the general question of how the common law would handle liability for damage caused when they burst was probably on lawyers' and judges' minds at the time. Thus, although the reservoir at issue in *Rylands* was small (probably only 1.5 acres), private, and was built by excavating a hole in the ground rather than building up a major embankment, clearly the case was moved from the back burner to center stage in order to address the issue of common law strict liability. The judges at every level in *Rylands* were almost certainly well aware of the Dale Dyke disaster and concerned about the application of their decision to the general problem of dangerous dams and reservoirs. Thus, an obscure and very local case that began with straightforward allegations of negligence was transformed into a claim of strict liability with obvious significance for a potentially national problem.

As is well known, when the case was revived before the Exchequer of Pleas, that court denied Fletcher's claim by a vote of 2 to 1. For the most part the opinions at this first court to address the strict liability issue in *Rylands* are rooted in the doctrinal technicalities of the time. The judges disagreed about whether the suit sounded in trespass, case, or nuisance, and their votes turned on that issue. But as Professor

---

[9] *Id.* at 228.

[10] *Id.* at 233.

[11] *Id.* at 213–15.

Simpson has pointed out, the recognition that the law governing potentially large-scale dam disasters might also be at stake shows through in the opinions.[12] For example, explaining why in his view Rylands was not strictly liable, Baron Martin noted that "It does not appear that there was any embankment or that the water in the reservoir was ever above the level of the natural surface of the land,"[13] thus preserving a possible distinction between the failure of large, above-ground dams and the kind of underground leakage that occurred in *Rylands*.

In two successive appeals, however, Fletcher's strict liability claim succeeded. At the first level above the Exchequer of Pleas, in the Exchequer Chamber, Justice Blackburn set out a broad rule:

> We think that the true rule of law is, that the person who for his own purposes brings on his lands and collects and keeps there anything likely to do mischief if it escapes, must keep it in at his peril, and, if he does not do so, is prima facie answerable for all the damage which is the natural consequence of its escape. He can excuse himself by shewing that the escape was owing to the plaintiff's default; or perhaps that the escape was the consequence of vis major, or the act of God; but as nothing of this sort exists here, it is unnecessary to inquire what excuse would be sufficient.[14]

Blackburn's opinion is well known for its reference to "anything likely to do mischief if it escapes."

On appeal to the House of Lords, the Exchequer Chamber's decision was affirmed. One of the two opinions was by the Lord Chancellor, Hugh Cairns, who as a practising attorney had been consulted by the plaintiffs in the Dale Dyke disaster a few years before.[15] Setting out the "principles" on which the case was to be determined, Cairns distinguished between "natural" and "non-natural" uses of land:

> [I]if in what I may term the natural user of that land, there had been any accumulation of water, either on the surface or underground, and if, by the operation of the laws of nature, that accumulation of water had passed off into the close occupied by the Plaintiff, the Plaintiff could not have complained that that result had taken place . . .

---

[12] *Id.* at 246.

[13] 159 Eng. Rep. 737, 745 (1865).

[14] L. R. I Exch. 265, 279–80 (Exch. Ch. 1866). Like Martin's opinion below, Blackburn's opinion also reveals his awareness of the Dale Dyke disaster, in its reference to the tendency of escaping water to do damage by "drowning," though of course there was drowning at Dale Dyke but none in *Rylands*. *Id.* at 286. *See* Simpson, *supra* note 4, at 251 for this insight.

[15] *Id.* at 233.

On the other hand, if the Defendants, not stopping at the natural use of their close, had desired to use it for any purpose which I may term a non-natural use, for the purpose of introducing into that close that which in its natural condition was not in or upon it ... then for the consequence of that, in my opinion, the Defendants would be liable.[16]

It is interesting that not only these courts, but also many subsequent commentators, have been of two minds about the character of the case at the time. On the one hand, it is said that neither Blackburn nor Cairns thought that they were saying anything exceptional. Precedents imposing strict liability under various circumstances abounded. There had long been strict liability for trespassing animals, and although the matter was now in doubt, the strict liability-like tort of trespass *vi et armis* had until recently been clearly available to redress direct, violent harm regardless of negligence.[17] On the other hand, some of the arguments of counsel that are set out in great detail in the original reports assert that Fletcher's claim amounted to a case of first impression. And when the time came to decide the case and justify their decisions, Cairns made almost no reference to precedent, and the precedents to which Blackburn referred seem far removed and only distantly relevant to the problem at hand. Something important definitely was going on here, although its precise nature may have been a matter of disagreement at the time. Clearly, however, the overall flavor one gets from reading the full opinions in the original reports is that we are witnessing the beginning of something new, not the middle of something routine.

To appreciate what was new, it helps to understand that *Rylands* was decided at a moment (or at least during a period) of transition between the old, procedure-dominated writ system, and our modern, substance-driven approach to law. Before, cases had to fit into procedural pigeon holes. The mere fact that there was strict liability for trespassing animals would have had no necessary relevance to whether there was strict liability for bursting reservoirs. This was true not only in Great Britain, but in the United States as well. Writing several decades later, when the substantive approach to law had gained complete dominance, Professor Bohlen described the old procedure-based regime. The common law, he said,

> ... was regarded as perfect, and as such, almost sacred from even inquiry or criticism, not only as a system but as habitually classified into groups or categories, each separate and distinct. Each category was self-sustaining, its existence was its justification. However closely allied any two or more groups of these might be,

---

[16] L. R. 3 H. L. 330, 338–39 (1868).

[17] *See, e.g.*, Scott v. Shepherd, 96 Eng. Rep. 525 (K. B. 1773).

however superficial the differences in the situations with which they dealt, there appeared to the legal mind of the era no need but rather something approaching impiety in seeking to find some general principle as their common basis. There was no effort toward generalization . . .[18]

But by the time *Rylands* came on for decision the old conception of law, and the old reluctance of the courts to generalize, was dissolving. It was therefore possible for the first time for judges to think more generally—that is, substantively—about the proper scope of liability for accidental harm. Thus, the sense that something new was being decided in *Rylands* stems, I think, from the generality of the principle on which the opinions by Cairns and Blackburn are based. The courts spoke broadly of natural and non-natural uses of land and about things likely to do mischief if they escaped. The substance of the rule they propounded was emphatically not limited to reservoirs, or understandable only in a particular procedural context, as it might well have been under the old writ system. Rather, the courts in *Rylands* were attempting to state a rule about the circumstances under which defendants would be held to a higher standard than merely avoiding negligence in the use of their land. They were stating a general rule about property use, property rights, and strict liability. The scope of that rule may have been uncertain after *Rylands*, but the fact that the decision stood for a generally applicable substantive principle, whether broad or narrow, should not have been. Today that may seem only natural, and to be what judicial decisions always do. But to English judges at the time of *Rylands* the idea that there were general rules applicable to broad categories of activity would have at the least seemed to be something of a departure from the past.

The Reception and Evolution of the Rylands Doctrine: A Tale of Two Systems

For a good fifty years after *Rylands* was decided it was controversial, especially in the United States. This was for a number of reasons. First, the scope of the holding was uncertain and potentially very broad. Read literally, Lord Cairns' test for strict liability—the "non-natural" use of land—could apply to virtually anything other than the escape of dead leaves or tumbleweed from one property to another. Second, in the United States the establishment of negligence as the principal basis of liability for physical damage had only recently been fully accomplished.

To many courts *Rylands* seemed like a return to the ancient regime that had finally been rejected. As Chief Justice Doe of New Hampshire put it in an often-quoted opinion,

---

[18] *See* Francis H. Bohlen, *The Rule in* Rylands v. Fletcher, 59 U. Pa. L. Rev. 298, 316 (1911).

Everything that a man can bring on his land is capable of escaping,—against his will, and without his fault, with or without assistance, in some form, solid, liquid, or gaseous, changed or unchanged by the transforming processes of nature or art,—and of doing damage after its escape.... Even if the arbitrary test were applied only to things which a man brings on his land, it would ... ignore the rights growing out of a civilized state of society, and make a distinction not warranted by the enlightened spirit of the common law; it would impose a penalty upon efforts, made in a reasonable, skillful, and careful manner, to rise above a condition of barbarism.[19]

Until recently the received view was that, like New Hampshire, most nineteenth-century courts rejected the *Rylands* doctrine in name, but began nonetheless to apply strict liability in fact to harm caused by particular activities. For example, many courts in the nineteenth century, both before and after *Rylands*, held that there was strict liability for damage caused by explosives. The result of the decisions on blasting and other activities, it was said, was a body of slowly accumulating precedents that ultimately amounted to adoption of the rule in *Rylands*.[20]

Recent scholarship, however, has revealed that this story oversimplifies how these cases actually developed.[21] Although there were a few immediate rejections of *Rylands* in the 1870's, in short order there developed a split of authority, with at least as many courts citing *Rylands* favorably or expressly accepting it as rejecting it. It is especially interesting that the event that may well have solidified the evolution in favor of *Rylands* was the 1889 Johnstown Flood, in which a reservoir in Western Pennsylvania burst, destroying an entire town and killing 2000 people.[22] Just as in England, where the notorious collapse of the Dale Dyke dam during the pendency of Fletcher's suit against Rylands seems

---

[19] Brown v. Collins, 53 N.H. 442, 448 (N.H.1873).

[20] *See, e.g.*, William L. Prosser, *The Rule in* Rylands v. Fletcher, *in Selected Topics on the Law of Torts*, 135, 149 (1953); *see also* David Rosenberg, *The Hidden Holmes: His Theory of Torts in History* (1995), in which Professor Rosenberg argues that the almost universal view that Holmes and others such as Chief Justice Doe believed in limiting liability to negligence is inaccurate. Rosenberg contends that Holmes actually supported broad foresight-based strict liability, rejecting only cause-based strict liability.

[21] *See* Jed Handelsman Shugerman, *The Floodgates of Strict Liability: Bursting Reservoirs and the Adoption of* Fletcher v. Rylands *in the Gilded Age*, 110 Yale L.J. 333 (2000); Jed Handelsman Shugerman, *The Rhetoric of Morality and Economics in American Tort Law, 1870–1940* (unpublished manuscript, on file with the author). Much of my account in this and the following several paragraphs draws heavily and directly from Shugerman's valuable work. It would be going only slightly too far to place quotation marks around these entire paragraphs.

[22] For the full history of the flood and its aftermath, see David G. McCullough, *The Johnstown Flood* (1968).

to have influenced the ultimate decision in that case, the Johnstown Flood probably affected some American courts in its aftermath.

The disaster at Johnstown achieved enormous notoriety, not only because of the death and destruction it caused, but because of the people involved. The reservoir and the South Fork dam creating it had been purchased by a group calling itself the South Fork Fishing and Hunting Club in 1879. After the Club renovated it, the reservoir covered 450 acres and was one of the largest artificial collections of water in the country. Despite many warnings to the Club and considerable anxiety expressed by the townspeople living below, the dam was allowed to deteriorate. When the dam finally burst, the disaster drew all the more public attention because the members of the Club that owned it included Andrew Carnegie, Andrew Mellon, and Henry Clay Frick, all three among the wealthiest people in America. Newspapers filed daily, sensational reports from the scene. Yet when the Club denied responsibility and contributed little to compensate the Johnstown victims, the public's anger grew and publicity escalated. David McCullough calls the Flood the country's "biggest news story since the murder of Abraham Lincoln."[23] Perhaps in part because there was never a recovery in negligence against the Club or its members, in the years following the Flood the trend in the case law seemed to turn more noticeably—though never unanimously—in the direction of *Rylands*.[24]

However, although reservoir accidents gave rise to the decision in *Rylands* and perhaps to its gradual acceptance in the United States, in neither England nor the United States was the bursting of a dam a common enough occurrence to make a real dent in the history of tort law. Indeed, Professor Simpson notes that in the seventy years after *Rylands* there were only two serious dam failures in England, neither resulting in a lawsuit.[25] Moreover, after 1930, there have been "no serious dam failures in Britain, though there exist many ancient dams, some very ill maintained, and in the whole long curious story the only individual in Britain who ever seems actually to have employed the rule in *Rylands v. Fletcher* to recover damages for a burst reservoir is Thomas Fletcher himself."[26] For this reason, *Rylands* obviously has contemporary significance because of the general rule that grew out of it, not because of its application to reservoirs.

---

[23] *Id.* at 203.

[24] For discussion of this evolution in the case law, *see* Jed Handelsman Shugerman, *The Floodgates of Strict Liability: Bursting Reservoirs and the Adoption of* Fletcher v. Rylands *in the Gilded Age*, 110 Yale L.J. 333 (2000)

[25] Simpson, *supra* note 4, at 261.

[26] *Id.* at 262–63.

Just as *Palsgraf*[27] is not really about scales, *Rylands* is not really about reservoirs. Over time, what has mattered is not whether *Rylands* was applied to reservoirs, but whether and when there has been strict liability for injury and damage caused by dangerous activities more generally. On this issue, developments on the two sides of the Atlantic took somewhat different paths to what have turned out to be reasonably similar ends.

British Developments

In Great Britain and the Commonwealth, over nearly a century and a half, the *Rylands* doctrine has stayed reasonably close to its origins. The potentially broad test for liability about which the American courts had been so concerned—the "unnatural" use of land—was defined and thereby confined to what amounted to "unusual" uses. For example, in *Rickards v. Lothian*,[28] in an appeal from Australia, the House of Lords held that the principle underlying *Rylands* did not support the imposition of liability for damage caused by the overflow of water from a sink on the top floor of a building. One ground of the decision was that the tap had been turned on and the waste pipe plugged by vandals; but another was that

> It is not every use to which land is put that brings into play that principle. It must be some special use bringing with it increased danger to others, and must not merely be the ordinary use of the land or such a use as is proper for the general benefit of the community ... The provision of a proper supply of water to the various parts of a house is not only reasonable, but has become, in accordance with modern sanitary views, an almost necessary feature of town life.[29]

In short, a "natural" use was an "ordinary" one; to be non-natural a use must be extraordinary.

Eventually two other significant limitations on the scope of the *Rylands* doctrine became clear. Both emerged in *Read v. J. Lyons & Co., Ltd.*,[30] in which an inspector for the British Ministry of Supply during World War II was injured when a shell exploded in the course of her inspection of a munitions plant. The House of Lords denied recovery, ruling both that *Rylands* could apply only to substances that "escape" from the defendant's land and that, in any event, *Rylands* does not apply

---

[27] *See* Palsgraf v. Long Island R.R., 162 N.E. 99 (N.Y.1928).

[28] [1913] AC 263, HL.

[29] *Id*. at 280–81.

[30] [1947] AC 156, HL.

strict liability to actions to recover damages for personal injury, but only to property damage. Since the inspector in *Read v. J. Lyons* was injured within the factory, and since the only damages claimed were for personal injury, she could not recover without proof of negligence.

The final move in the confinement of *Rylands* came a decade ago, in *Cambridge Water Co., Ltd. v. Eastern Counties Leather, PLC.*[31] This was a case in which the chemicals used by a leather manufacturer in the tanning process had been spilled over time and eventually migrated into a community water supply several miles away. There was a finding of fact that, at the time the contamination occurred, it was not foreseeable to the defendants that small quantities of contaminants would find their way into the water supply and migrate such a distance.

In a decision that seems to have drained virtually all significance from the *Rylands* rule as a separate doctrine, the House of Lords held that, in effect, this rule was merely a version of the law of nuisance, applied to isolated escapes of substances from land rather than continuing interferences by one land use with other uses. Further, the court confirmed what probably had always been the case in view of Blackburn's reference to things "likely" to do mischief if they escape—that a foreseeability requirement also applied to any claim based on the *Rylands* rule. As a consequence of *Cambridge Water Co.*, far from being a broad-based ground for imposing strict liability, in Great Britain and the Commonwealth *Rylands* has become an extremely limited, nuisance-based exception to the general rule that there is no liability for property damage in the absence of negligence.

The American Story

As I noted earlier, in the nineteenth century there was a split of authority among the states as to whether and when the rule in *Rylands* applied. As time went on more states seemed to accept the doctrine, but of course the question is what they were accepting. Even before *Rylands* a number of states had imposed strict liability for damage caused by explosives used for blasting, and this became the paradigm strict liability activity. Other activities also sometimes became subject to strict liability, including not only the use of explosives but also their storage, and the transmission of electric power. But in many states the number of activities that were subject to strict liability was very limited; and quite a number still refused to apply *Rylands* to the collection of large amounts of water.

The scope of the *Rylands* doctrine, even where it was accepted, was therefore not entirely clear. Writing in 1911, long before the limited

---

[31] [1994], 1 ER 53, [1994] 2 AC 264.

character of the *Rylands* doctrine was recognized in England, Professor Bohlen argued that differences between the attitudes of the two countries and the backgrounds of English judges explained why the *Rylands* doctrine had at that point received limited acceptance in the United States and, even when it was accepted, narrow application.[32] In England, Bohlen contended, the passive enjoyment of land was valued far more than in the United States, where active use took priority. *Rylands,* he said, privileged the former over the latter. The aristocratic background and aspirations of the English judges who had decided *Rylands*, Bohlen thought, reinforced this preference for land-owning over land-using. Bohlen's materialist theory of what lay behind the decision was eventually disproved, at least in part, when in 1940 a lawyer from New York then serving in the Coast Guard (and apparently with time on his hands) looked into the actual backgrounds of the judges who had decided *Rylands*, and found that Bohlen's class-based explanation did not hold water, as it were.

Most of the judges involved in the case turned out to be from mercantile or otherwise non-aristocratic families.[33] For example, Baron Bramwell, who in dissent in the Exchequer of Pleas had argued for strict liability, was the son of a banker, and was believed by counsel practicing before him "to be firmly convinced that railroads needed judicial protection from juries."[34] This was hardly an attitude favoring the passive use of land over activity. Justice Blackburn had merely been a poor barrister before his elevation to the bench—"Mr. Justice Blackburn does not appear at any time to have commanded a large practice,"[35] and he "possessed none of the advantages of person and address which make for success in advocacy."[36] And Lord Cairns was a self-made man, born in County Down, Ireland, the son of a former Captain of the Forty-seventh Foot.[37]

Thus, the backgrounds of the judges in *Rylands* did not reveal a prejudice favoring passive over active land use. Nor did the results in the case law by the turn of the century reflect that distinction as the basis for decision. So what exactly was going on? By the 1930's there had been enough cases for the newly-founded American Law Institute to state in

---

[32] *See* Francis H. Bohlen, *The Rule in* Rylands v. Fletcher, 59 U. Pa. L. Rev. 298, 373, 411 (1911).

[33] *See* Robert Thomas Molloy, Fletcher v. Rylands: *A Reexamination of Juristic Origins*, 9 U. Chi. L. Rev. 266 (1940).

[34] *Id.* at 276–77.

[35] *Id.* at 279 (quoting London Times, Jan. 10, 1896, at 6).

[36] *Id.* (quoting 1 *Dictionary of National Biography* 203 (Supp. 1901)).

[37] *Id.* at 285.

its Restatement of Torts that there was strict liability for harm caused by what it called "ultrahazardous" activities.[38] Ironically, the Reporter for the Restatement was the same Professor Bohlen who two decades earlier had called into question the motives of the judges who decided *Rylands*. Although the Restatement recognized the American strict liability decisions, it nonetheless reflected Bohlen's ambivalence about *Rylands* itself, and took no position on whether the case law dictated liability on the particular facts of *Rylands*, stating, "*Caveat*: The Institute expresses no opinion as to whether the construction and use of a large tank or artificial reservoir in which a large body of water or other fluid is collected is or is not an ultrahazardous activity."[39]

Surveying the cases in order to discern a rule for which they did stand, Bohlen and his colleagues found that two principal factors determined whether an activity was ultrahazardous. The first was the dangerousness of the activity. The second was how common the activity was for the area in which it was conducted. The more dangerous and uncommon the activity, the more appropriate the label "ultrahazardous" and the more it warranted strict liability for the harms it caused.

The dangerousness criterion reflected the reluctance of some nineteenth and early twentieth-century courts to accept *Rylands* by name but their inclination nonetheless to impose strict liability selectively, in such paradigm cases as the use of explosives. As time went on, the activities the courts ruled were subject to strict liability had expanded to include other dangerous (though perhaps not quite so dangerous) activities, including the storage of substances that could explode if mishandled, such as oil or gasoline. The adjective used in the title of the newly recognized form of liability, "ultrahazardous," suggested that the degree of danger posed by an activity was the principal criterion on which the strict liability decision would be made. The more dangerous the activity, the less likely that a negligence regime could reduce its risks to an acceptable level and therefore the stronger the argument for strict liability. In *Rylands* terms, the more dangerous an activity, the more "non-natural" it was.

The commonness strand, however, added something that also had been influencing strict liability decisions. This strand was the legacy of the idea behind the rule in *Rylands* itself—that whether an activity was "non-natural" was not an absolute but a relational question. A reservoir might be common in mill-dam country, but uncommon elsewhere. An oil drilling rig might be common in certain counties in Texas, but not in northern California.[40] The more common an activity in a particular area,

---

[38] *See Restatement of Torts* § 519 (1934).

[39] *Id.* at § 520 cmt. c.

[40] *See, e.g.,* Turner v. Big Lake Oil Co., 96 S.W.2d 221 (Tex.1936).

the less reason there was to suppose that the defendant was more familiar with the risks posed by an activity and better situated to control these risks than potential victims. In this setting, it seemed, the threat of liability for harm caused by negligence would be sufficient to promote optimal levels of safety. Nearby property owners—who might well be engaging in the activity themselves—would also be aware of these risks and with the available means of controlling them, by virtue of their own familiarity with activity that was common in the area. But other things being equal, when an activity was uncommon in an area, the party engaging in it would be in the best position to determine whether engaging in it was worthwhile, in light of his special knowledge of the inevitable risks that the activity would impose on its neighbors, even if carefully conducted.

Moreover, the Restatement contained none of the restrictions on the scope of liability that later found their way into the modern British version of the *Rylands* rule. The basis of liability was that an activity was ultrahazardous, whether there was an escape of anything from land or not. And the liability in question was not limited to damage to real property; on the contrary, it encompassed liability for personal injury as well.[41]

Whatever disagreement there may now be among legal historians about the receptiveness of late nineteenth and early twentieth-century courts to *Rylands*, clearly the Restatement went beyond the facts of *Rylands* itself and provided the ingredients of a full-blown regime of activity-based strict liability. Liability could be imposed even without an "escape" of a "substance" from the defendant's land; recovery was permitted not only for property damage, but also for personal injury; and the conditions triggering strict liability were both generally-stated and, potentially, broadly applicable.

It may seem surprising that, although the rule for which *Rylands* seemed to stand started out quite broadly in Great Britain and quite narrowly in the United States, by the 1930's the attitudes of the two systems appeared to be in the process of reversing. By the time of the first Restatement, in the United States *Rylands* stood for a general principle that at least had the potential to expand, but on the other side of the Atlantic what the case stood for was being contained. Far from being surprising, however, this seeming reversal tells us something important about the differences between the two systems, certainly then and probably still.

By the 1930's in the United States both the courts and the academics who wrote the Restatement were much more willing to use the common law as a deliberate instrument of public policy than their

---

[41] *Restatement of Torts, supra* note 38, at § 519.

counterparts in Great Britain. As the limitations of an exclusively
negligence-based system of liability became evident, American jurisprudence reacted and began to flirt with the idea of enterprise-based strict
liability.[42] Liability for damage caused by ultrahazardous activities was
an important feature of this idea. But in Great Britain the courts were
more reluctant to use the common law in instrumental fashion. The idea
of enterprise-based responsibility therefore emerged more openly in the
realm of politics, culminating in the election of a Labor Party government and the consequent ouster of Winston Churchill as Prime Minister
shortly after the end of World War II in Europe. What was an incipient,
implicit socialism in the American law of torts and tort theory was more
explicit in British politics but less evident in the common law of Great
Britain.

It is easy to see how the incipient American movement toward a
more general regime of enterprise-based strict liability might well have
produced a significant alternative to the negligence system. The dangerousness criterion might have evolved so as to encompass far more
activities, and the uncommonness requirement might have withered
away. Injuries caused by dangerous products might eventually have been
brought under the enterprise liability umbrella. Automobile-related injuries might even have become subject to some form of strict liability as
well.[43]

The proof of the pudding, however, is in the eating. Over the
ensuing decades the case law accumulated and filled in the interstices of
the Restatement doctrine, but strict liability for dangerous activities
never seriously competed with negligence as a basis of liability. Rather,
state by state, activity by activity, particular context by particular
context, the courts imposed or declined to impose strict liability. By the
mid–1960's there were enough additional decisions to warrant reconfig-
uring a renamed "abnormally dangerous" activity rule in the Restatement of Torts (Second) to take account of six factors.[44] Three of these
were aspects of dangerousness, two were aspects of commonness, and
one was based on the value of the activity to the community.[45] Looking
back at all this after the six decades of litigation that followed the first

---

[42] See G. Edward White, *Tort Law in America: An Intellectual History* 106–10 (1980).

[43] See, e.g., Hammontree v. Jenner, 97 Cal.Rptr. 739 (Cal.Ct.App.1971) (rejecting the application of strict liability to auto accidents).

[44] *Restatement (Second) of Torts* §§ 519–20 (1977).

[45] The third restatement now in draft returns to a more concise test based on the two main factors, rejecting the social value of the activity as a factor, on the ground that the courts have largely disregarded this in their decisions. *See Restatement (Third) of Torts: Liability for Physical Harm (Basic Principles)* § 20 & cmt. k. (Tentative Draft No. 1, 2001).

Restatement, Professor Jones summarized the patchwork quilt of liability and no-liability that had emerged:

> The paradigm case is use of high explosives such as dynamite and nitroglycerin.... Yet there is surprising reluctance to invoke the rule of strict liability in cases involving other explosive substances such as propane gas. When construction and other activities cause damage through vibrations (in a manner similar to blasting with high explosives) the courts again invoke strict liability; but other claims premised on construction activities, indistinguishable in principle, typically require negligence. Negligence is also the general rule for escape of water and escape of fire. For radioactive emissions, strict liability is the rule; but claims based on toxic fumes unjustifiably require a showing of negligence.... [I]njuries caused by electric power lines are governed by negligence ...[46]

Even this division suggests greater uniformity than actually exists. Not only do different states have different rules for different activities; in addition, because context—commonness in the area—may have a bearing on the outcome, strict liability decisions tend to be made at a comparatively low level of generality. One cannot always simply make a list of activities that automatically do or do not result in strict liability for the harm they cause. In this sense the principle that what constitutes a nuisance depends on time and place, under which the *Rylands* rule has been completely subsumed in Great Britain, also exercises influence in strict liability actions on this side of the Atlantic. Thus, the context-dependent, or relational character of strict liability helps to explain what might otherwise seem to be the surprisingly small number of activities that trigger strict liability.

A second explanation, I think, turns on changing social perceptions of risk. The dangerousness requirement that is so central to strict liability doctrine depends for its content on both ordinary attitudes toward risky activities and on the technological state of the art. Given the direction in which both these phenomena have evolved over time, it is no surprise that there has been no growth in the number of activities considered abnormally dangerous. On the whole, life has been getting safer, both in the eyes of the public and in fact. Hurtling along a highway in a metal container at over 60 miles per hour is not considered dangerous, though it once would have been. Flying in an airplane thousands of feet above the ground was once a daredevil activity; now it is routine. As we become used to activities that were once perceived to involve high risk—as activities become common—we come to think of them as normally rather than "abnormally" dangerous.

---

[46] William K. Jones, *Strict Liability for Hazardous Enterprise*, 92 Colum. L. Rev. 1705, 1715–16 (1992).

But these attitudes are not merely the product of our greater familiarity with dangerous activities. Dangerous activities have in fact tended to become safer over time, at least in part because of technological advances that make them less likely to cause harm if they are carefully conducted. Very steadily and over a long period of time, life has been getting safer, not more dangerous.[47] In the 1940's the introduction of radar made flying much safer; now global satellite positions systems add another measure of safety. The introduction of seat belts in motor vehicles in the 1960's was followed by shoulder belts, which were followed by front-seat air bags, which have now been followed by side-door air bags. Ground damage caused by aviation was once subject to strict liability; now it is not. Driving never was, largely because it so quickly became "common" everywhere, but it followed the same path of technological evolution. If activities such as these can be made largely safe through the exercise of reasonable care, then imposing strict liability for harm the activities cause is not necessary. And it is technological contributions that have made it possible for activity after activity to be conducted safely. One lesson we can draw from these and similar advances is that, where strict liability could have gone, technology may have made it unnecessary to go.[48]

Ultimately, however, the explanation for the narrow domain that strict liability occupies in American tort law is that broad-based enterprise strict liability would be inconsistent with our values and politics. Although nuances within tort law may reflect purely internal legal considerations, the overall outlines of tort liability must and do reflect our social and political values. In general we are comfortable imposing strict liability for physical harm caused by unusually dangerous activities and by a product's departure from its intended design (so-called "manufacturing" as distinguished from "design" defects). But in the absence of either situation, imposing liability is likely to seem unfair unless the defendant was at fault in some identifiable way or has special cost-bearing capacity. Strict liability is therefore reserved for those few cases in which, despite the absence of real fault, we are comfortable imposing liability because of the risk-allocation and risk-spreading advantages of doing so.

[47] For example, between 1950 and 1980 the rate of accidental death in the United States declined from 60.6 to 46.7 per 100,000 persons. *See* George L. Priest, *Understanding the Liability Crisis, in New Directions in Liability Law* 199 (Walter Olsen ed., 1988). By 1990 the rate was 32.5 per 100,000, and by 1998 it had further declined to 28.5 per 100,000. *See Statistical Abstract of the United States* 91 (2000).

[48] It is true that these examples omit reference to such "modern" risks as exposure to dangerous chemicals in the environment. But in general we have tried to address these risks—and probably have been successful in reducing them—through the enactment of regulatory statutes rather than through tort law.

Keeping Tort Law Honest

If the rule in *Rylands* has come to be merely a branch of nuisance law in Great Britain, and if strict liability has such spotty and limited application throughout the United States, then why does *Rylands* belong in the handful of highly-celebrated tort cases whose stories are worth telling? What makes it one of tort law's greatest hits?

The answer, I think, is that because most tort law is accident law, and most accident law is negligence law, almost all the other celebrated cases are negligence cases.[49] This includes even *Escola* (discussed in Chapter 9), whose significance, after all, lies not in the decision itself but in Justice Traynor's concurring argument that the majority should not have rested its decision on a negligence theory, but should have adopted strict products liability. And what was once Traynor's vindication, the adoption of strict products liability by Restatement (Second) of Torts § 402A in 1965, has now become the story of the decades-long dawning recognition that virtually all of products liability (with the very limited exception of liability for "manufacturing defects") is in fact based on negligence, not strict liability.[50]

Consequently, *Rylands* is the first and foremost exemplar of the strict liability alternative to negligence liability for accidental personal injury and property damage. As such an exemplar, *Rylands* has both conceptual and normative significance. Even from an entirely conceptual standpoint, understanding strict liability helps us to understand negligence. We can better understand what it means to engage in "unreasonably" dangerous conduct if we appreciate the baseline against which this concept is defined. For example, deeply understanding the "objective test" for negligence requires recognizing the sense in which that test contemplates the possibility that certain defendants actually may be held strictly liable for their "negligence." A sub-normal defendant who is not capable of complying with the objective standard of reasonableness is held liable nonetheless. That is a version of liability without "fault." Similarly, it is not possible to evaluate the operation of *res ipsa loquitur* without appreciating the range of cases in which that doctrine may result in some defendants being held strictly liable. Under *res ipsa*, although a particular kind of accident may not ordinarily happen in the absence of negligence, such an accident still may have happened without negligence in this particular case. Yet the defendant may be held liable

---

[49] The one exception in this volume is *Vincent v. Lake Erie Transportation*, and even that case is usually taught and discussed under the rubric of privilege, not as a step in the evolution of strict liability.

[50] *See Restatement (Third) of Torts: Products Liability* § 2 cmt. a (1998).

anyway. This too is a version of strict liability. In short, to understand negligence, sometimes we must first understand strict liability.

But of course we study strict liability not only for conceptual clarity, but for normative reasons as well. We study *Rylands* not only because of what it was and is, but also because of what it might have been and might still become. If history had been different, a broad version of the principle underlying *Rylands* could have been the basis for development of a modern regime of strict liability for personal injury. Although history did not work out that way, the idea that the full costs of the injuries that are characteristic of certain activities should be shouldered by enterprises engaged in those activities, regardless of fault, still has considerable normative appeal. In every negligence case in which a defendant is held to have acted reasonably, a defendant avoids liability and an injured party goes uncompensated. An alternative to negligence liability that would hold enterprises responsible for the risks they take, and afford compensation to individuals who are injured when these risks materialize, continually forces us to ask, why not adopt strict liability? In this sense strict liability is tort law's conscience.

There are good, some would say compelling, answers to the question that this conscience keeps posing: socially desirable levels of activity may be depressed if actors are held liable for the results of reasonable conduct; other methods of compensating for misfortune, such as private or socially-provided health and disability insurance can be used to protect personal injury victims whose injuries were not caused by negligence; and the monetary costs of passing out compensation through litigation exceed the sums that actually find their way into the pockets of victims—we can spend our compensation dollars more effectively outside of tort law than within it. But these answers do not always satisfy us; again and again we are drawn back to *Rylands* and the idea of strict liability.

Sometimes the idea even leads us beyond the bounds of tort law itself. It is the idea behind *Rylands* that supplies the theory underlying such far-reaching alternatives to tort liability for accidental injury as workers compensation, and proposals for no-fault medical and products liability compensation systems.[51] Without the theory that risky activities should pay their own way, even if carefully conducted, these alternatives to tort law could not have been imagined; instead there would be negligence and negligence alone as the basis for liability, across the board. The *Rylands* rule and its potentially greater scope open up ways to think about the variety of settings in which it might make sense to dispense with the negligence principle altogether and develop very differ-

---

[51] For analysis, see Kenneth S. Abraham, *The Forms and Functions of Tort Law* 250–51 (2d ed. 2002).

ent approaches to liability and compensation that do not rely on tort liability, the courts, or litigation.

All this may seem to place excessive emphasis on a nineteenth-century case about a small reservoir in the English countryside. *Rylands* is after all merely an emblem for an idea that draws its strength from many other sources. But as an emblem, *Rylands* makes strict liability always at least theoretically available as an alternative to negligence, and as the basis for alternatives to tort law altogether. For this reason, the viability of the negligence requirement, and the meaning of negligence, are always potentially open to question. In this sense strict liability is tort law's conscience—always present, if only in the background, to ensure that proof of negligence is what justice and sound public policy require in the case at hand. And it was in *Rylands v. Fletcher* that the modern idea of strict liability was born.

9

Mark Geistfeld

Escola v. Coca Cola Bottling Co.: **Strict Products Liability Unbound**

On August 21, 1941, during the dinner shift at Tiny's Waffle Shop in Merced, California, a waitress Gladys Escola began restocking a refrigerator with bottles of Coca Cola. After placing three bottles in the refrigerator, she picked up the fourth from a case that had been delivered two days earlier by the Coca Cola distributor. Suddenly the bottle exploded, lacerating her finger for over five inches along the web between the first finger and thumb. The injury and ensuing operation involved the cutting of muscles, blood vessels and nerves. The resultant permanent tenderness and pain in the scar left Gladys partially incapacitated in her work as a waitress.

A claim for workers' compensation resulted in a payment of $42.60 to Mrs. Escola, an amount that did not cover her medical expenses and lost wages.[1] Alleging two counts of negligence, she commenced a tort action against the Coca Cola Bottling Company of Fresno, the company that had filled and distributed the exploding bottle.[2] Based on the doctrine of res ipsa loquitur, the jury awarded Mrs. Escola compensatory damages of $2,900. Defendant appealed, and the case ultimately worked its way up to the California Supreme Court.

---

[1] Opening Statement by Melvin Belli, Reporter's Transcript on Appeal, Escola v. Coca Cola Bottling Co., 150 P.2d 436 (Cal.1944) (No. S.F. 16951). Unless otherwise noted, descriptions of the case are derived from the published court opinions or the parties' appellate briefs.

The fact that Mrs. Escola was not fully compensated for her lost wages is typical in proceedings for workers' compensation. See infra note 59 and accompanying text.

[2] Two other Coca Cola corporate defendants were named in the complaint, but the case against them was dismissed prior to trial.

At each stage, the merits of the case were decided by application of res ipsa loquitur. The import of the case, however, has little to do with that important evidentiary doctrine. In an opinion concurring with the Supreme Court's affirmance of the jury award, Justice Roger Traynor argued that the award should be affirmed on grounds of strict liability rather than negligence. According to Traynor, strict liability followed from the defendant's breach of the implied warranty of merchantability, an action grounded in tort law rather than contract law as courts had previously assumed. By freeing the implied warranty from contractual restrictions, Traynor helped set in motion the forces that would lead to the widespread adoption of strict products liability. Traynor invoked other reasons for the rule of strict liability that provided important judicial support for enterprise liability, a theory of tort liability developed by the Legal Realists that has had enduring impact on tort doctrine and scholarship.

The Litigation

In the two counts of her complaint, Mrs. Escola alleged that defendant negligently sold to her employer a bottle with a dangerous latent defect, and that defendant negligently bottled or manufactured the injury-causing bottle.

The trial attorney for Mrs. Escola was the famous "King of Torts" Melvin Belli.[3] In his opening statement, Belli declared "We are going to rest our case completely on the doctrine we call res ipsa loquitur: The thing speaks for itself. Our theory of the case is that we have no way of showing any specific act of negligence."

Mrs. Escola testified that around noon on August 19, 1941, one of defendant's employees delivered several cases of Coca Cola to Tiny's Waffle Shop. He placed them on the floor next to an ice cream cabinet behind the customer counter. Mrs. Escola said that two days later, around 6:00 p.m., she placed the top case of Coca Cola on top of the ice

---

[3] At the time Belli was not known as the "King of Torts." He was so crowned in a Life Magazine article published in 1954. His attention-grabbing activities ranged from a role in a Star Trek episode to his representation of Jack Ruby, the man who killed John F. Kennedy's assassin, Lee Harvey Oswald. Consequently, "it's easy to forget Belli's place in the annals of American law. In his heyday, he was a brash maverick who turned accepted notions of corporate responsibility on their head. His genius was not so much as an innovator but as a popularizer of new trial techniques, most notably the use of demonstrative evidence in civil disputes. A prolific writer and speaker, Belli trained scores of plaintiff's lawyers, judges, and civilians about the evolution of tort law. And along the way, he helped the Association of Trial Lawyers of America, as it's known today, unite plaintiffs' lawyers in a way that the American Bar Association had never done."

Krysten Crawford, *Melvin Belli (1907–1995): Tortious Maximus*, Am. Law., Dec. 1999, at 36.

cream cabinet, opened the door of the refrigerator and started to move each bottle individually from the case to the refrigerator. The fourth bottle exploded shortly after she lifted it from the case. A customer testified that she was directly observing Mrs. Escola and did not see the bottle strike any object from the time it was removed from the case until it broke. It sounded "just like a fruit jar would blow up." The manager of Tiny's said the noise was like a "pop."

D. Walter Mullins, the defendant's employee who had delivered the Coca Cola from the defendant's warehouse in Fresno to Tiny's Waffle shop, testified that on prior occasions he had found broken bottles of Coca Cola when he took cases out of the warehouse. He never made inquiries concerning the reason for the breakage.

In its defense, defendant called three witnesses. The first, the manager of the Coca Cola Bottling Works of Fresno, testified about the bottling procedures. The bottles are used "over and over again," so they are visually inspected four different times for defects. "The work is not strenuous. We want the men to be more efficient so we give them a rest. If a bottle is cracked or if it is chipped it is what we consider a defect and we throw the bottle out."

Defendant's next witness testified about the different characteristics of breaks that occur in Coca Cola bottles when caused by different forces. Based on the characteristics of the breakage that caused Mrs. Escola's injury, he concluded that "internal pressure alone" could not have caused that break. Instead, the type of diagonal break described by Mrs. Escola "does result from holding the cap and striking a blow within two or three inches of the top."

The defendant's final witness, another expert, also concluded that the type of break described by Mrs. Escola "would definitely not be caused either by thermal shock or by internal pressure alone. In my opinion, such a break most likely would be caused by external force."

This witness also testified about the manufacturing procedures for the bottles. One out of 600 bottles are randomly tested for quality control. These machine tests are "pretty near" infallible. Inspectors also would check for defects. "Every now and then we do get bottles that have a defect and such bottles are thrown out."

Apparently, then, defendant sought to show that the break was caused by an external force that could have occurred only during delivery or after defendant had given up possession of the bottle. On the basis of this evidence, defendant moved for a directed verdict. Plaintiff's counsel argued that even the defendant's evidence permitted an inference that a defective bottle might have "sneaked through." The court denied the motion and then instructed the jury, which returned a verdict for the plaintiff. Defendant appealed.

In its appellate brief, defendant argued that the case was directly controlled by a recent decision involving an exploding bottle, *Gerber v. Farber*.[4] The *Gerber* court rejected a finding of negligence based on res ipsa loquitur, concluding that the defendant bottler did not have exclusive control of the instrumentality. This factual setting was "basically identical with the instant case" according to defendant Coca Cola, thereby mandating reversal of the judgment for Mrs. Escola.

In a split opinion, the appellate court agreed, holding that the factual discrepancies between the two cases are "inconsequential."[5] Because Mrs. Escola had not offered proof of careful handling by the retailer following delivery, she had failed to establish that the defect existed while the defendant possessed the bottle. The court also stated that plaintiff had failed to present "any evidence of negligence on defendant's part," and expressed concern that if a manufacturer were to be held liable in these circumstances, "he then becomes an insurer."

The dissent rejected the majority's reliance on *Gerber*. In *Gerber*, the defendant bottler had given possession of the bottle to an independent distributor, who carried the bottle on his truck for a week. Once the bottle was delivered to the restaurant, it was accessible to customers who might have mishandled it. On these facts, the defect in the bottle was no more attributable to the bottler than to the independent distributor or customers, thereby negating the element of exclusive control with respect to the defendant bottler. The dissent distinguished *Escola* on the ground that the defendant was both the bottler and distributor, giving it "exclusive control until the case of Coca Cola was placed under the counter. From the evidence, it is a reasonable inference that no one touched the case until plaintiff started to place the bottles in the refrigerator." Having shown that the element of exclusive control was sufficiently established, the dissent concluded that Mrs. Escola had proven that the defendant was negligent, since a bottle would not explode "unless someone was negligent."

The dissent clearly has the better argument regarding exclusive control, particularly as a customer had testified that Mrs. Escola did not mishandle the bottle while lifting it. Yet the dissent's argument is undermined by the assertion that an exploding bottle necessarily implies negligence on someone's part. An exploding bottle could be the inevitable result of reasonable, though imperfect quality-control measures. The fact of an exploding bottle does not necessarily mean someone was negligent, contrary to the reasoning of the dissent.

---

[4] 129 P.2d 485 (Cal.Ct.App.1942).

[5] 140 P.2d 107 (Cal.Ct.App.1943).

On what basis, then, did Mrs. Escola show that the exploding bottle more likely than not was the result of negligence? Defects surely result from negligence, but res ipsa loquitur requires a showing that the defect more likely than not resulted from negligence rather than reasonable, though imperfect quality-control procedures. This was the fundamental issue for the California Supreme Court on appeal, as it had no difficulty in finding that the element of exclusive control was established.[6] The Court's reasoning about the sufficiency of the evidence illustrates one of the central points made by Justice Traynor in his famous concurrence.

In evaluating the issue whether the defect was attributable to the defendant's negligence, the Court begins with an ambiguous statement of the relevant inquiry:

> An explosion such as took place here might have been caused by an excessive internal pressure in a sound bottle, by a defect in the glass of a bottle containing safe pressure, or by a combination of these two possible causes. The question is whether under the evidence there was a probability that defendant was negligent in any of these respects. If so, the doctrine of res ipsa loquitur applies.

Properly framed, the question is whether the evidence would enable a reasonable juror to conclude that the defect more likely than not was attributable to negligence. There will always be "a probability" of defect and "a probability" that the defendant was negligent. Res ipsa loquitur requires more exacting evidence. The plaintiff must have evidence showing that defects ordinarily do not occur without negligence on someone's part (with the requirement of exclusive control connecting that negligence to the defendant).

The Court found there was such evidence of negligence. If the defect involved an overcharge, "an inference" of negligence arises "[a]s it is a matter of common knowledge that an overcharge would not ordinarily result without negligence." If the defect pertained to the bottle itself and "were visible, an inference of negligence would arise from the failure of defendant to discover it. Where defects are discoverable, it may be assumed that they will not ordinarily escape detection if a reasonable inspection is made."

The only remaining issue concerned the possibility that the defect was latent. Such a defect was highly likely. The bottles were used "over and over" as one witness testified. Repeated use can create latent defects like hairline fractures in the glass. The bottle exploded due to a fracture of some type according to the testimony of defendant's expert witnesses. The evidence that latent defects ordinarily do not occur without negligence therefore was the crucial issue in the case.

---

[6] 150 P.2d 436 (Cal.1944).

The Court found the evidence of negligence to be sufficient in that regard as well:

> [According to the testimony of one of defendant's expert witnesses] there is available to the industry a commonly-used method of testing bottles for defects not apparent to the eye, which is almost infallible. Since Coca Cola bottles are subjected to these tests by the manufacturer, it is not likely that they contain defects when delivered to the bottler which are not discoverable by visual inspection. Both new and used bottles are filled and distributed by defendant. The used bottles are not again subjected to the tests referred above, and it may be inferred that defects not discoverable by visual inspection do not develop in bottles after they are manufactured. Obviously, if such defects do occur in used bottles there is a duty upon the bottler to make appropriate tests before they are refilled, and if such tests are not commercially practicable the bottles should not be re-used. This would seem particularly true where a charged liquid is placed in the bottle. It follows that a defect which would make the bottle unsound could be discovered by reasonable and practicable tests.

This reasoning does not withstand scrutiny. The Court assumes that latent defects would be detected by appropriate testing; otherwise the bottles should not be reused. Why should the bottles not be reused if they cannot be perfectly screened for latent defects? The test referred to by the Court involved the machine testing of one in every 600 newly manufactured bottles. To be "almost infallible" with respect to used bottles, virtually every one would have to be tested. What if the cost of such testing is disproportionately high to the benefit? If so, the test is not required as a matter of reasonable care. And if used bottles necessarily have some probability of containing a latent defect, it does not follow that the bottles should not be reused. The total elimination of risk is not a necessary requirement of reasonable care. Latent defects therefore can occur without negligence, so each instance of a latent defect could be the inevitable result of a less than perfect, though reasonable mode of testing. Due to this possibility, for the Court to conclude that latent defects do not *ordinarily* occur without negligence, it would need evidence showing that most defects are attributable to negligence rather than imperfect, reasonable quality-control measures. There was no such evidence. Mrs. Escola had not established that the defect more likely than not was attributable to negligence, one of the required elements for establishing negligence liability on the basis of res ipsa loquitur.

As it stands, *Escola* merely illustrates how courts improperly applied the doctrine of res ipsa loquitur in cases involving defective products. *Escola* nevertheless has become one of the most important tort cases in the United States because of the concurrence by Justice Roger Traynor, which adopted a position that had not been argued by any of the parties.

"In my opinion it should now be recognized that a manufacturer incurs an absolute liability when an article that he has placed on the market, knowing that it is to be used without inspection, proves to have a defect that causes injury to human beings."

Traynor observed that if the mere existence of a defect is sufficient to establish negligence on someone's part as it appears to have been in *Escola*,

> the negligence rule approaches the rule of strict liability. It is needlessly circuitous to make negligence the basis of recovery and impose what is really liability without negligence. If public policy demands that a manufacturer of goods be responsible for their quality regardless of negligence there is no reason not to fix that responsibility openly.

Traynor then provided the reasons of public policy that justify strict liability for defective products. These reasons were based both on precedent and concerns of injury prevention and compensation. The reasons were subsequently invoked some twenty years later to justify section 402A of the *Restatement (Second) of Torts*, the basis of the modern tort regime of strict products liability.

Escola and the Emergence of Strict Products Liability

Today it may seem surprising that an exploding-bottle case would play such an important role in the emergence of strict products liability. In the 1940s such cases were common. "Every state developed case law on exploding bottle cases. In Los Angeles County, the largest, busiest trial court district in California, juries reached verdicts in an average of one to two exploding bottle cases a year during the 1950s."[7]

Even though product cases like those involving exploding bottles were common, products liability had not been identified as a field of torts.[8] "Indeed, the subject of manufacturer or retailer liability for defective products was of minor scholarly significance during the 1930s and 1940s."[9]

Not only did Traynor's concurrence help to create the field of products liability, it significantly bolstered the reputation of the Califor-

---

[7] Benjamin T. Field, *Justice Roger Traynor and His Case for Judicial Activism* 157 (2000) (unpublished Ph.D. dissertation, University of California Berkeley) (citations omitted). The citation in the first footnote above comes from this source.

[8] George L. Priest, *The Invention of Enterprise Liability: A Critical History of the Intellectual Foundations of Modern Tort Law*, 14 J. Legal Stud. 461, 497 n.238 (1985) ("The Index to Legal Periodicals introduced the category 'Products Liability' for the first time in 1965, recording entries from 1961–64.").

[9] *Id.* at 462.

nia Supreme Court. Traynor was appointed to the California Supreme Court in 1940, and during his 30–year tenure on the Court it gained the reputation as the leading state court in the nation.[10] A significant source of the Court's reputation came from its products liability decisions, beginning with Traynor's concurrence in *Escola*.

Traynor's concurrence reflected his more general approach to judging.[11] "A law professor [and highly regarded tax scholar] at Berkeley before becoming a judge, Traynor was particularly conversant with academic literature and notably adept at its use.... More than anything else, Traynor brought academic sources within the range of cognizable authorities for a court—they were for him the equivalent of past decisions."[12] Traynor wrote 75 law review articles in addition to authoring 892 opinions for the Court.[13] Not surprisingly, Traynor was deemed to be "a law professor's judge" by highly regarded scholars.[14]

Traynor's reliance on academic sources is evident in the *Escola* concurrence. Equally evident is another hallmark of his judging: "a patient craftsmanlike working out of things within the frame of reference he has been given by existing law."[15]

The influence of *Escola* stems from Traynor's masterful reliance on existing law coupled with a persuasive conceptual justification for the position. The result is an opinion that was both traditional and revolutionary. Its reliance on precedent and common-law reasoning explains its ultimate widespread, noncontroversial acceptance. The conceptual justification for the result, in turn, helped to dramatically alter the prevailing

---

[10] *Cf.* Lawrence Friedman et al., *State Supreme Courts: A Century of Style and Citation*, 33 Stan. L. Rev. 773, 805 (1981) (study finding that during Traynor's tenure, the California Supreme Court became the most frequently cited court by courts in other jurisdictions). For discussion of the range of issues addressed by the Court's numerous landmark opinions, see Robert L. Rabin, *Rowland v. Christian: Hallmark of an Expansionary Era*, in this volume.

[11] For studies of Traynor's approach to judging, see Field, *supra* note 7; G. Edward White, *Tort Law in America: An Intellectual History* 180–210 (softcover ed. 1985) [hereinafter *Tort Law*]; G. Edward White, *The American Judicial Tradition: Profiles of Leading American Jurists* 292–316 (1976) [hereinafter *Profiles*].

[12] White, *Tort Law*, *supra* note 11, at 183.

[13] Field, *supra* note 7, at vii.

[14] Harry Kalven, Jr., *Torts: The Quest for Appropriate Standards*, 53 Cal. L. Rev. 189, 189 (1965). *See also* Louis Jaffe, *Res Ipsa Loquitur Vindicated*, 1 Buffalo L. Rev. 1, 13 (1951) ("We professors prefer Judge Traynor's clear, analytic approach.").

[15] Kalven, *supra* note 14, at 191. *See also* White, *Tort Law*, *supra* note 11, at 189–90 ("[Traynor's] effort, like that of Cardozo in his innovative decisions, was to create an impression that flows naturally from a canvass of available sources and arguments; that one had only to think the problem through and one would arrive at the solution.").

conception of tort law. "[A] conceptual revolution that is among the most dramatic ever witnessed in the Anglo–American legal system."[16]

Traynor's critical doctrinal argument sought to unbind the implied warranty of merchantability from contract law. After the landmark case of *MacPherson v. Buick Motor Co.*,[17] a seller's duty for defective products no longer depended upon a contractual relationship ("privity") with the injured party. The scope of the tort duty was not defined in contractual terms, but what about the content of duty? The answer, Traynor argued, could be derived from *MacPherson*. After pointing out that the retailer is under an "absolute liability to his customer" for implied warranties that include a "warranty of safety," a warranty that is "not necessarily a contractual one," Traynor then invoked the logic of *MacPherson*:

> The liability of the manufacturer to an immediate buyer injured by a defective product follows from the implied warranty of safety attending the sale. Ordinarily, however, the immediate buyer is a dealer who does not intend to use the product himself, and if the warranty of safety is to serve the purpose of protecting health and safety it must give rights to others than the dealer. In the words of Judge Cardozo in the *MacPherson* case: "The dealer was indeed the one person of whom it might be said with some approach to certainty that by him the car would not be used. Yet the defendant would have us say that he was the one person whom it was under a legal duty to protect. The law does not lead us to so inconsequential a conclusion." While the defendant's negligence in the *MacPherson* case made it unnecessary for the court to base liability on warranty, Judge Cardozo's reasoning recognized the injured person as the real party in interest and effectively disposed of the theory that the liability of the manufacturer incurred by his warranty should apply only to the immediate purchaser. It thus paves the way for a standard of liability that would make the manufacturer guarantee the safety of his product even when there is no negligence.

Having shown that *MacPherson* supported strict liability based on the implied warranty, Traynor needed to connect that principle to the case at hand. California had already extended warranty protection to an injured party without contractual privity in cases of contaminated foods, and Traynor found "no reason to differentiate" those hazards from others inherent in defective products. By analogy, then, California law supported warranty liability—and therefore strict liability—in cases lacking privity. And lest there be any concern about the inappropriate-

---

[16] Priest, *supra* note 8, at 461.

[17] 111 N.E. 1050 (N.Y.1916). For a detailed examination of this case, see James A. Henderson, Jr., *MacPherson v. Buick Motor Company: Simplifying the Facts While Reshaping the Law*, in this volume.

ness of relying on the warranty to define the content of a tort duty, Traynor pointed out that an "action on a warranty 'was, in its origin, a pure action of tort,' and it was only late in the historical development of warranties was an action in assumpsit [or contract] allowed." The quotation was attributed to separate works by Ames and Williston, illustrative of Traynor's reliance on impressive scholarly sources, including works by Bohlen, Prosser, and Llewelyn, throughout the concurrence.

Traynor's strongest doctrinal support for strict liability came from the contaminated food cases. In these cases, some courts had relied on the warranty theory to award tort damages on the basis of strict liability, even though the parties were not in privity.[18] Consequently, Traynor's doctrinal argument importantly depends on his claim that there is no distinction between the hazards posed by contaminated foods and those posed by defective products. The distinction was critical to the various courts that had limited strict liability to contaminated foods, yet Traynor had good reasons for rejecting the distinction. Prior to *MacPherson*, the existence of a tort duty depended on whether the product was imminently or inherently dangerous. The distinction between an imminently or inherently dangerous product and a defective product was rejected by *MacPherson*: "If the nature of a thing is such that it is reasonably certain to place life and limb in peril when negligently made, it is then a thing of danger [and subject to a tort duty.]"[19] By this same reasoning, the distinction between contaminated foods and other defective products should be rejected, since defective products are "reasonably certain to place life and limb in peril," making them "a thing of danger" subject to a tort duty.[20] By eliminating the distinction between the contaminated food cases and others involving defective products, the logic of *MacPherson* implies that the duty imposed on sellers in the contaminated food cases extends to other defective products. Traynor could defensibly conclude that *MacPherson* "paved the way" for strict liability.

The logic of *MacPherson*, the contaminated food cases, and the historical tort pedigree of warranties enabled Traynor to show how strict liability for defective products could be derived from established legal principles and precedent. A warranty implied by law is not based on consent and therefore is not necessarily contractual in nature. As revealed by the contaminated food cases, a warranty is implied by law for

---

[18] *See* William L. Prosser, *The Assault Upon the Citadel (Strict Liability to the Consumer)*, 69 Yale L.J. 1099, 1103–10 (1960).

[19] MacPherson v. Buick Motor Co., 111 N.E. 1050, 1053 (N.Y.1916).

[20] Not surprisingly, the collapse of the distinction between the contaminated food cases and others involving defective products provided the doctrinal impetus for strict products liability. *Cf.* Prosser, *supra* note 18, at 1110–14.

the purpose of protecting the health and safety of those who might be harmed by defective products, a purpose of tort law. To serve that tort purpose, the implied warranty must extend from the manufacturer to foreseeable users of the product, an extension justified by *MacPherson*. The warranty is breached by a defective product. The fact of defect thus triggers tort liability, regardless of the care exercised by the seller. Hence manufacturers should be strictly liable in tort for defective products.

The evident fairness of this result explains why sellers of defective products were routinely found to be liable under the doctrine of res ipsa loquitur, no matter how much care was exercised by the seller.[21] If defect alone establishes negligence, a seller is always liable for defective products. Negligence becomes equivalent to strict liability. Rather than base liability on the "needlessly circuitous" use of negligence, Traynor showed why there was no doctrinal reason not to "openly" impose strict liability on those who sell defective products.

Despite the force of Traynor's logic, it did not immediately move the courts or scholars. Not a single member of the *Escola* Court joined his concurrence, and it would be some time until the California Supreme Court adopted Traynor's position.

The next exploding-bottle case reached the Court five years later, and the Court again based liability on res ipsa loquitur.[22] As in *Escola*, Traynor thought the liability was based on "spurious application of the rules developed to determine the sufficiency of circumstantial evidence in negligence cases." Traynor again advocated that liability be based on strict liability for the reasons he gave in *Escola*. No member of the Court accepted Traynor's argument for strict liability.

In 1958, the Court considered another exploding-bottle case, this time finding that res ipsa loquitur was inapplicable because the plaintiff had failed to establish that the defect existed while the bottle was possessed by the defendants.[23] Traynor concurred with respect to the defendant manufacturer and dissented with respect to the defendant bottler, arguing that the defect probably existed while the bottler had possession. Traynor concluded that the bottler should be strictly liable for reasons given in the *Escola* concurrence. Once again, he was the lone advocate for strict liability.

---

[21] *See id.* at 1115 (observing that cases in which the application of res ipsa loquitur has been denied "are so extremely rare as to be almost negligible . . . . once the cause of the injury is proved to lie with the defendant, once it is brought home to his plant, the jury finds for the plaintiff").

[22] Gordon v. Aztec Brewing Co., 203 P.2d 522 (Cal.1949).

[23] Trust v. Arden Farms Co., 324 P.2d 583 (Cal.1958).

Traynor was influencing the Court, however. In a 1960 case, the Court held that warranty liability could be imposed on the manufacturer of a defective grinding wheel that blew up in the plaintiff's face.[24] Although the plaintiff was a worker who was not in contractual privity with the manufacturer, the whole Court (except Traynor) nevertheless supported warranty liability because employees are "members of the industrial 'family' of the employer." This reasoning, of course, is consistent with Traynor's argument in *Escola* that the implied warranty does not depend on privity. Gladys Escola, after all, was also in the "industrial family" of her employer, and so the warranty between Coca Cola and her employer should also have extended to her by this reasoning. Traynor agreed with the majority that the plaintiff worker should recover for his injuries, but for the reasons he had given in *Escola* and subsequent decisions.

Finally, in 1963 Traynor persuaded the entire Court to impose strict liability on the manufacturer of a defective power tool in the landmark case *Greenman v. Yuba Power Products.*[25] As in *Escola*, none of the parties had made an argument concerning strict liability.[26] Three new justices had been appointed to the Court, but three others adopted Traynor's position despite their earlier refusal to do so. Writing for the Court, Traynor stated: "We need not recanvass the reasons for imposing strict liability on the manufacturer. They have been fully articulated." In support, Traynor cited his *Escola* concurrence, cases in other jurisdictions, an influential law review article by William Prosser, and the torts treatise by Harper and James.

These academic citations reflected the emerging scholarly consensus on the issue. But like Traynor's colleagues on the California Supreme Court, legal academics did not immediately appreciate the *Escola* concurrence. In an article published in 1949, Prosser limited the *Escola* concurrence to food cases.[27] A highly regarded law review article published in 1951 documenting the rise of absolute liability does not cite *Escola*.[28] And even Fleming James, one of the staunchest advocates of

---

[24] Peterson v. Lamb Rubber Co., 353 P.2d 575 (Cal.1960).

[25] 377 P.2d 897 (Cal.1963).

[26] Field, *supra* note 7, at 172–73.

[27] William L. Prosser, *Res Ipsa Loquitur in California*, 37 Cal. L. Rev. 183, 224–25 (1949). Traynor's *Escola* concurrence had also justified strict liability because the defect violated a criminal statute involving foods and their containers. That aspect of Traynor's analysis, however, was tangential to his overall approach, as revealed by his invocation of *Escola* in later cases not involving food products.

[28] Charles O. Gregory, *Trespass to Negligence to Absolute Liability*, 37 Va. L. Rev. 359 (1951).

strict liability during this period, was slow to appreciate the import of *Escola*.[29]

In the mid–1950s, the problem of product defects started to gain the attention of scholars, and by the end of the decade products liability had become a prominent tort issue. At this time, it was evident that Traynor's arguments for strict liability were influencing the California Supreme Court as reflected in its "industrial family" decision. In 1961, the American Law Institute adopted a draft rule imposing strict liability on sellers of food products, leaving open the question whether the rule should apply to other products.[30] In 1962, the draft extended strict liability to both food and products for "intimate bodily use," and again the draft was approved by the Institute. *Greenman* was decided in 1963. In 1964, the American Law Institute approved yet another draft, section 402A of the *Restatement (Second) of Torts*, that applies strict liability to defective products.[31]

By 1971, 28 states had adopted the rule of strict liability for product defects; by 1976, 41 states had adopted it. In adopting the rule, state courts frequently cited *Greenman* as a "seminal" or "landmark" case, often noting the widespread influence of Traynor's analysis in *Escola* and its "genesis of the movement toward strict liability."[32] Legal scholars also jumped on the bandwagon, arguing that sellers should be strictly liable for product defects.[33]

The rapid adoption of strict products liability was attributable to broader social forces:

> One feature of public thinking in the 1960s was that major American corporations—and in particular, the Big Three automakers—were economic colossi that could easily bear whatever burdens might be imposed on them by way of regulation or liability. A second feature of public opinion was that these corporations should not be held in high respect; indeed, they should be frequently distrusted.... During the 1960s, the consumer movement was gaining force; this movement portrayed innocent consumers as needing strong protection from manufacturers, which frequently treat consumers in shabby ways.... The willingness of courts in the late 1960s to impose strong liabilities on major corporations (especially product

---

[29] Priest, *supra* note 8, at 499.

[30] For a description of the history of the American Law Institute's legislative history regarding section 402A, see *id.* at 512–14.

[31] *Restatement (Second) of Torts* § 402A (1965).

[32] Field, *supra* note 7, at 185.

[33] *See id.* at 186; Priest, *supra* note 8, at 511.

manufacturers) was certainly facilitated by this discrediting of corporations that was occurring in the public outlook.[34]

The judicial acceptance of strict products liability was also greatly facilitated by the way in which Traynor grounded the rule in established legal doctrines pertaining to warranties and the rejection of privity following *MacPherson*. For example, in discussing the history of the rule of strict liability, the *Restatement (Second)* states that courts had applied strict liability to food products for a long time, and that over time

> the courts have become more or less agreed upon the theory of a "warranty" from the seller to consumer, either "running with the goods" by analogy to a covenant running with the land, or made directly to the consumer. Other decisions have indicated that the basis of recovery is merely one of strict liability in tort....
>
> Recent decisions, since 1950, have extended this rule of strict liability beyond the seller of food for consumption....[35]

The correspondence with Traynor's concurrence is striking. The *Restatement (Second)* then explains why courts had taken so long to adopt Traynor's position:

> A number of courts, seeking a theoretical basis for the liability, have resorted to a "warranty" .... In instances this theory has proved to be an unfortunate one. Although warranty was in its origin a matter of tort liability, and it is generally agreed that a tort action will still lie for its breach, it has become so identified in practice with a contract of sale between the plaintiff and defendant that the warranty theory has been something of an obstacle to the recognition of the strict liability where there is no such contract. There is no thing in this Section which would prevent any court from treating the rule stated as a matter of "warranty" to the user or consumer.[36]

Apparently, then, the influence of *Escola* was delayed due to conceptual barriers. Courts had been conceptualizing warranties in contract terms.[37] Scholars had not yet conceptualized products liability as a field of torts. With the passage of time, these barriers were overcome by the force of Traynor's argument. The *Escola* concurrence had an evident and substantial influence on the emergence of strict products liability, pro-

---

[34] Gary T. Schwartz, *The Beginning and the Possible End of the Rise of Modern American Tort Law*, 26 Ga. L. Rev. 601, 615 (1992).

[35] *Restatement (Second) of Torts* § 402A cmt. b (1965).

[36] *Id.* cmt. m.

[37] For a particularly well-known and influential example, see *Henningsen v. Bloomfield Motors*, 161 A.2d 69 (N.J.1960).

viding a particularly good example of the more broadly based "legalist reformation" that was occurring in this period.[38]

Escola and the Expansion of Products Liability

Strict liability applies to product "defects." The definition of defect based on a warranty concept could have been largely limited to construction or manufacturing flaws.[39] Nevertheless, the concept of a product defect quickly expanded beyond construction or manufacturing defects. By the late 1960s courts were finding defects in the design of the product itself.[40] "During the 1970s the defective warning field erupted, and the liability of manufacturers expanded dramatically."[41]

The expansion of tort liability to encompass design and warning defects can also be traced to the *Escola* concurrence, because Traynor did not rely exclusively on the warranty argument to justify strict liability. No court or judge had previously justified strict liability by combining *MacPherson*, the contaminated food cases, and the tort pedigree of the implied warranty. To persuade others that his legal analysis yielded the correct conclusion, Traynor provided public policy rationales for the rule that imply manufacturer liability for design and warning defects. The most important contribution to tort law made by the *Escola* concurrence may well reside in this aspect of Traynor's analysis.

Traynor's reliance on public policy rationales was consistent with the jurisprudence of the time. When *Escola* was decided, Legal Realism was the dominant jurisprudential approach at the leading American law schools.[42] Prior to joining the California Supreme Court in 1940, Traynor had been a law professor for over ten years at a leading law school. Not surprisingly, Traynor's concurrence in *Escola* reflects the influence of Realism tempered by the constraints of judging.[43]

---

[38] The "legalist reformation" movement sought the goal of "social change and the expansion of existing hierarchies to include people who had previously been made subordinate" within a framework that "did not repudiate the commitment to the rule of law...." William P. Nelson, *The Legalist Reformation: Law, Politics, and Ideology in New York 1920–1980*, at 7 (2001).

[39] Typically the design and warning of a product function exactly as the seller had intended, so a warranty concept based on the seller's intentions ordinarily would apply only to construction or manufacturing defects.

[40] *See* Heaton v. Ford Motor Co., 435 P.2d 806 (Or.1967).

[41] Priest, *supra* note 8, at 523.

[42] *See* White, *Tort Law, supra* note 11, at 63.

[43] Like the Realists, Traynor rejected the notion that the law consists of fixed principles. Consequently, Traynor accepted the Realist position that judges often made law by relying on extra-legal factors. "He did not, however, share the anxiety of many of the

The Legal Realist movement rejected the form of legal reasoning in which conclusions are derived solely from the legal principles immanent in doctrine (the jurisprudence of "legal science").[44] For the Realists, a legal rule should be analyzed in terms of its impact rather than derivation. "Alongside an expanded definition of 'law' and lawmaking went an expanded awareness of the role of the legal system as an instrument of public policy.... With the advent of Realism arguments based on public policy considerations revived."[45]

To be persuasive to other judges, Traynor had to marshal doctrinal support for the rule of strict liability. To be persuasive to the Realist legal scholars, Traynor needed to show why his doctrinal arguments made good public policy. Thus, for Traynor the legal issue presented by *Escola* reduced to the following inquiry: "If public policy demands that a manufacturer of goods be responsible for their quality regardless of negligence there is no reason not to fix that responsibility openly."

Part of the public policy argument addressed the doctrinal issues discussed earlier. The other aspect of Traynor's public policy argument provided the conceptual basis for expanding tort liability to include design and warning defects:

> Even if there is no negligence, ... public policy demands that responsibility be fixed wherever it will most effectively reduce the hazards to life and health inherent in defective products that reach the market. It is evident that the manufacturer can anticipate some hazards and guard against the recurrence of others, as the public cannot. Those who suffer injury from defective products are unprepared to meet its consequences. The cost of an injury and the loss of time and health may be an overwhelming misfortune to the person injured, and a needless one, for the risk of injury can be insured by the manufacturer and distributed among the public as a cost of doing business. It is to the public interest to discourage the marketing of products having defects that are a menace to the public. If such products nevertheless find their way into the market it is to the public interest to place the responsibility for whatever injury they may cause upon the manufacturer, who, even if he is not negligent in the manufacture of the product, is responsible for its reaching the market. However intermittently such injuries may occur and however haphazardly they may strike, the risk of their

---

Legal Realists over the absence of fixed legal principles or their cynicism about the legitimacy of judge-made law." Field, *supra* note 7, at 19–20. Rather, Traynor thought that process constraints and rationality legitimated judge-made law. *See* White, *Profiles, supra* note 11, at 292–316.

[44] *See* White, *Tort Law, supra* note 11, at 20–62.

[45] *Id.* at 72.

occurrence is a constant risk and a general one. Against such a risk there should be general and constant protection and the manufacturer is best situated to afford such protection.

These considerations of public policy identified by Traynor involve deterrence—the ability of a legal rule to reduce risk—and risk distribution—the ability of a legal rule to spread risk by functioning as a form of insurance.

The deterrence argument made by Traynor is quite sound and prescient for its time. Traynor assumes that manufacturers have knowledge of product risks (they can "anticipate" risks) whereas consumers do not. As he elaborated later in the concurrence, the methods of mass production mean that the

> consumer no longer has means or skill enough to investigate for himself the soundness of a product, even when it is not contained in a sealed package, and his erstwhile vigilance has been lulled by the steady efforts of manufacturers to build up confidence by advertising and marketing devices such as trade-marks.

As Traynor subsequently phrased the problem in *Greenman*, consumers in the modern economy are "powerless" to protect themselves.

Traynor's deterrence argument for strict liability accordingly claims that when manufacturers have knowledge of product risk and consumers do not, then tort liability is required to ensure that manufacturers supply the appropriate amount of safety. This conclusion is fully supported by modern economic analysis.[46] The conclusion is prescient because "information economics," which today is a well-studied field examining how informational disparities affect market transactions, had not been developed in Traynor's time.

But the informational disparity identified by Traynor merely justifies tort liability. In principle, negligence liability could largely solve the safety problem.[47] Traynor addressed this issue with an analysis that again is quite sound.

As discussed earlier, Traynor pointed out that the negligence regime for defective products effectively functioned like strict liability, because

---

[46] *See* Mark Geistfeld, *Products Liability, in* 3 *Encyclopedia of Law and Economics* 347 (Boudewijn Bouckaert & Gerrit De Geest eds., 2000), *available at* http://encyclo.findlaw.com.

[47] The standard of care can be set so that it attains the same amount of per product risk that would occur in a regime of strict liability. The two liability regimes can create different levels of total risk, however, because total product consumption is likely to be higher under negligence than strict liability due to differing effects of these liability rules on consumer perceptions of the product's full price (purchase price plus expected injury costs borne by the consumer). *See id.*

the doctrine of res ipsa loquitur was not being applied properly. Standing alone, this argument would not justify strict liability, as the problem could be solved by more stringent jury instructions or appellate review. Traynor, though, had not completed this line of argument.

Traynor also observed that a negligence rule, if properly applied, would involve insurmountable problems of proof. "An injured person . . . is not ordinarily in a position to refute [the manufacturer's evidence of reasonable care] or identify the cause of the defect, for he can hardly be familiar with the manufacturing process as the manufacturer himself is."

This evidentiary problem creates a risk-reducing role for strict liability. The amount of product safety effectively induced by a negligence standard depends upon the available evidence concerning the range of safety investments that could be made by the manufacturer. If a particular safety investment is required by the standard of reasonable care but the plaintiff is unable to prove as much, a manufacturer that fails to make the investment will avoid negligence liability.[48] The threat of negligence liability therefore does not give the manufacturer an incentive to make such investments. Strict liability, by contrast, would create such an incentive. A strictly liable manufacturer is concerned about minimizing the sum of its safety expenditures and liability costs, so it makes any safety investment that reduces liability in a cost-effective manner. Consequently, a strictly liable manufacturer may make safety investments that it would forego in a negligence regime. If so, strict liability would reduce risk compared to a negligence standard.[49] A deterrence rationale for strict liability therefore can be derived from the evidentiary problem with negligence liability that Traynor had identified.

---

[48] *See, e.g.,* Cooley v. Public Serv. Co., 10 A.2d 673 (N.H.1940).

It is not doubted that due care might require the defendant to adopt some device that would afford [reasonable protection against the injury suffered by plaintiff.] Such a device, if it exists, is not disclosed by the record. The burden was on the plaintiff to show its practicality. Since the burden was not sustained, a verdict should be entered for the defendant.

Id. at 677.

Shifting the burden of proof to the defendant would address the problem, but that rule requires the defendant to prove a negative. To avoid liability, the defendant would have to show that no untaken precaution exists that would satisfy the requirements of reasonable care and would have prevented the injury. The difficulty of satisfying such an evidentiary burden could effectively convert the negligence rule into one of strict liability. In that event, the burden-shifting negligence rule would be less desirable than strict liability due to the higher litigation costs associated with the reasonable-care inquiry.

[49] *See* Steven Shavell, *Strict Liability Versus Negligence,* 9 J. Legal Stud. 1 (1980) (showing how strict liability can reduce risk by reducing "activity" levels, where "activity" is any aspect of risky behavior that is outside the ambit of negligence liability due to evidentiary limitations).

Traynor also claimed that strict liability further serves the public policy of insuring consumers against injuries caused by product defects. (And Mrs. Escola could properly be analyzed as a consumer for this purpose.[50]) This insurance argument can be illustrated by an advertisement (appearing on the next page) discussed by plaintiff in her brief to the intermediate appellate court:

> [In the advertisement] we find the picture of a startled yet happy individual taking a bottle of beverage from an ice chest. He is startled because the bottle is exploding, but he is at the same time happy (at least the advertisement would have us believe) because he knows that a certain insurance company ... will pay him $10,000 for the loss of an eye from an exploding bottle! The caption of the both disastrous and yet happy event is *"Injured by exploding bottle."*

Plaintiff discussed the advertisement to show that "it is *common knowledge* that these bottles of carbonated beverage do explode." The advertisement also highlights the desirability of insurance (the source of "happiness" for the accident victim) and the corresponding fact that individuals are willing to pay for it. In effect, Traynor showed that these characteristics of the insurance transaction would be retained if manufacturers were strictly liable.

As Traynor observed, "the risk of injury can be insured by the manufacturer and distributed among the public as a cost of doing business." Like other costs, the cost of tort compensation is included in the price of the product paid by the consumer. Hence consumers pay for the compensation provided by the manufacturer and are happy to have such insurance, because it protects them from the "overwhelming misfortune" of an uncompensated physical injury. That outcome is not unfair to the manufacturer: it is "responsible for [the product] reaching the market" and receives premium payments (via higher product prices) for the insurance.

---

[50] The employer of Mrs. Escola was the direct purchaser of the product, and so it would pay for the insurance provided by strict liability. But in a well-functioning labor market, the employer must compensate the employee for any job-related risks. Mrs. Escola clearly faced a risk of uncompensated loss despite the availability of workers' compensation. *See supra* text accompanying note 1. Rather than paying Mrs. Escola a higher wage for facing the risk associated with uncompensated injuries caused by product defects, her employer could provide compensation by purchasing tort insurance. To determine whether the tort insurance is desirable, the employer would compare the insurance premium to the cost of the uncompensated risk—the same type of decision faced by a consumer.

This argument effectively undermined a reason frequently given by courts for rejecting liability without fault. As the intermediate appellate court in *Escola* concluded, Mrs. Escola must lose without proof of fault, because if the manufacturer were liable in these circumstances, "he then becomes an insurer." At the time "it was customary for courts to oppose any legal development that would, in their judgment, render the defendant an 'insurer' of the plaintiff's safety."[51]

The courts had been taking this position because tort cases during this period typically involved automobile accidents and other accidental injuries between strangers who had no pre-existing relationship. When the parties to an accident have no pre-existing relationship, tort law provides the primary means of allocating the benefits and burdens of the risky behavior. A potential injurer (like a driver) benefits from the risky activity (driving), whereas a potential victim (pedestrian) faces the risk of injury. Each incurs her own precautionary costs. How tort law should distribute these benefits and burdens between the two parties is an issue of fairness not present in the products liability context. As Traynor recognized and as products liability law now acknowledges, any tort burdens incurred by the manufacturer are passed onto the consumer in the form of higher prices, eliminating any consideration of how tort liability affects the manufacturer (the potential injurer).[52] The fairness question in products liability cases thus fundamentally differs from other tort cases that require consideration of how tort liability would affect the potential injurer. Due to this difference, there is nothing inherently unfair about turning the manufacturer into an insurer. Traynor's analysis in this respect is both sound and consistent with other tort doctrines.[53]

Having shown that the tort insurance would not be unfair, Traynor needed to establish its desirability. Insurance, of course, is desirable, but who should provide it? The answer seemed obvious to Traynor. "Those

---

[51] Mark C. Rahdert, *Covering Accident Costs: Insurance, Liability, and Tort Reform* 67 (1995).

[52] *See Restatement (Third) of Torts: Products Liability* § 2 cmt. f at 23 (1998) (stating that "it is not a factor . . . that the imposition of liability would have a negative effect on corporate earnings or would reduce employment in a given industry").

[53] Tort law traditionally has been analyzed in terms of how the liberty interests of potential injurers conflict with the security interests of potential victims. *See, e.g.*, Oliver Wendell Holmes, *The Common Law* 144 (1881) (stating that tort law "is intended to reconcile the policy of letting accidents lie where they fall, and the reasonable freedom of others with the protection of the individual from injury"). If the fairness of a tort rule depends on how it mediates these conflicting interests, and if the nature of the conflict changes with context as Traynor in effect observed, then it follows that the substantive content of tort rules should reflect these contextual changes. For an argument that the important tort doctrines can be interpreted in this manner, see Mark Geistfeld, *Negligence, Compensation, and the Coherence of Tort Law*, 91 Geo. L.J. (forthcoming 2003).

who suffer injury from defective products are unprepared to meet its consequences." By contrast, "the risk of injury can be insured by the manufacturer." Consequently, "the manufacturer is best situated to afford such protection."

Given the assumption that the manufacturer is the entity best able to provide insurance (an important issue to be discussed later), Traynor's public policy argument provides a compelling justification for strict liability. Not only would strict liability reduce risk relative to a regime of negligence, it would create a desirable form of insurance.

Much like Traynor's warranty argument influenced section 402A of the *Restatement (Second) of Torts*, so did these policy arguments. According to Traynor, strict liability is required for deterrence purposes due to the lack of consumer information about product risk. Correspondingly, strict liability under the *Restatement (Second)* "applies only where the product is, at the time it leaves the seller's hands, in a condition not contemplated by the ultimate consumer, which will be unreasonably dangerous to him."[54] "The article sold must be dangerous to an extent beyond that which would be contemplated by the ordinary consumer who purchases it, with the ordinary knowledge common to the community as to its characteristics."[55] Strict products liability under the *Restatement (Second)* therefore applies only when consumers are not well informed of risk, the situation in which tort liability serves the deterrence purpose identified by Traynor.

Indeed, the *Restatement (Second)* provides the virtual entirety of Traynor's public policy argument:

> On whatever theory, the justification for the strict liability has been said to be that the seller, by marketing his product for use and consumption, has undertaken and assumed a special responsibility toward any member of the consuming public who may be injured by it; that the public has the right to and does expect, in the case of products which it needs and for which it is forced to rely upon the seller, that reputable sellers will stand behind their goods; that public policy demands that the burden of accidental injuries caused by products intended for consumption be placed upon those who market them, and be treated as a cost of production against which liability insurance can be obtained; and that the consumer of such products is entitled to the maximum of protection at the hands of someone, and the proper persons to afford it are those who market the products.[56]

---

[54] *Restatement (Second) of Torts* § 402A cmt. g (1965).

[55] *Id.* at cmt. i.

[56] *Id.* at cmt. c.

By adopting Traynor's public policy arguments for strict liability, the *Restatement (Second)*, whether intentionally or not, provided the policy rationale for extending tort liability beyond exploding bottles and other construction defects.[57] Product designs frequently involve risks not adequately understood by the ordinary consumer, and a defective design poses unreasonable risks. Tort liability for design defects therefore is needed to ensure reasonably safe product designs, and the resultant tort insurance is properly provided by the manufacturer for the benefit of consumers and users. So too, if the product warning does not apprise product users of risks that would not otherwise be known to them, the product is dangerous beyond the extent contemplated by the ordinary consumer and is defective. Again, tort liability is needed to give manufacturers an incentive to remedy the defect, and the insurance entailed by such liability is desirable. The expansion of strict products liability to include design and warning defects therefore can be traced to the *Escola* concurrence.

Strict liability for design and warning defects, however, has turned out to be indistinguishable from negligence. The reason involves the definition of "defect." A construction or manufacturing defect is easily defined as a departure from the product's design or intended function. A soda bottle, for example, is not designed to have hairline fractures, so the existence of such fractures renders the bottle defective. A design or warning defect, by contrast, has no obvious definition other than as a departure from what the design or warning *should* have been. A design or warning should be reasonable, making the defect inquiry for designs and warnings no different than the reasonableness inquiry characteristic of negligence liability. Consequently, a rule of strict liability for design and warning defects is merely another name for negligence liability.[58]

Design and warning cases are governed by negligence principles because the rule of strict liability is limited to product defects. Absent the defect requirement, product sellers would be liable for all product-caused injuries, eliminating any role for negligence principles. The defect requirement therefore raises interesting questions about *Escola*. Is that requirement consistent with the *Escola* concurrence, even though it reintroduces negligence principles in design and warning cases? Or does the concurrence support a rule of strict liability for all product-caused injuries, regardless of defect? Quite likely, these issues were not considered by Traynor when he wrote the concurrence. The significance of an

---

[57] *Cf.* George L. Priest, *Strict Products Liability: The Original Intent*, 10 Cardozo L. Rev. 2301 (1989) (arguing that strict liability under section 402A was intended to cover only construction or manufacturing defects).

[58] *See Restatement (Third) of Torts: Products Liability* § 2 (1998).

opinion, though, can be determined by the force of its logic rather than its author's intentions.

These issues can be considered in terms of the relationship between *Escola* and enterprise liability, a theory of tort law seeking to justify strict liability for all injuries caused by business enterprise, not just those caused by product defects. Many scholars believe that the *Escola* concurrence effectively adopts enterprise liability. If so, the concurrence would be inconsistent with the limitation of strict liability to defective products. Alternatively, if the concurrence does not fully embrace the tenets of enterprise liability, then those reasons may help to explain why modern products liability law has limited strict liability to product defects, despite the reintroduction of negligence liability in design and warning cases. The story of *Escola* thus concludes with the theory of enterprise liability.

Escola and Enterprise Liability

The theory of enterprise liability grew out of the workers' compensation statutes that were adopted by state after state between 1910 and 1920. These statutes removed workplace injuries from the tort system, giving workers a right to compensation for injuries arising out of the workplace. The right to compensation is strict; no fault of the employer is required. The employee typically receives full compensation for the medical and rehabilitation costs of the injury and limited compensation for lost wages.[59] The compensation is determined on a scheduled basis by an administrative tribunal.

During the decades that followed the widespread adoption of workers' compensation, tort scholars sought to identify the justifications for workers' compensation in an effort to determine whether other areas of tort law required similar reforms.

> It was widely accepted that losses from injuries to workers represented a "cost" of enterprise and that the compensation statutes served to internalize those costs to the responsible corporate decision makers. It was also accepted that businesses could bear those costs more adequately than injured workers could because businesses could pass them along to consumers in the price of their products.[60]

The concepts of cost internalization and risk-spreading form the

---

[59] For an overview of workers' compensation systems, see 1 American Law Institute, Reporters' Study, *Enterprise Responsibility for Personal Injury* 105–27 (1991).

[60] Priest, *supra* note 8, at 466 (citations omitted).

theory of enterprise liability developed by the Legal Realist scholars.[61] According to that theory, strict liability should apply to business-caused injuries, because such liability internalizes the cost of injury to the business and optimally spreads risk.[62] The concept of cost internalization is related to risk reduction. The incentive that businesses have to reduce costs would lead them to reduce their liability costs by adopting safety measures and reducing injuries (and liability payments). The concept of risk distribution or insurance is based on the premise that the business can bear injury costs better than injured individuals.

Thus, at the time *Escola* was decided, scholars had already been analyzing tort law with the public policy rationales that Traynor so effectively employed. Indeed, cost internalization and risk spreading were among the list of reasons providing "a considerable impetus" for the rule of strict liability according to William Prosser in his 1941 treatise.[63] In *Escola*, Traynor heavily relied on Prosser's work. Traynor's arguments regarding cost internalization, the difficulties of proving negligence, the tort origins of warranty actions, and the ability of manufacturers to spread risk via price increases were all drawn from his friend William Prosser.[64]

Traynor's reliance on Prosser, however, does not diminish the significance of *Escola*, which converted Prosser's list of reasons into a cohesive conception of strict liability.

It was one thing for Prosser to collect authorities, marshal reasons, and argue for strict liability in the abstract; another for Traynor to show, through an impressive synthesis of case law and academic writing, the apparently obvious advantages of strict liability for defective products. Traynor's *Escola* opinion came at a time when strict liability theory was in an embryonic state; he gave it a model for practical application.[65]

Traynor's application of enterprise liability was so farsighted that tort scholars, including Prosser, did not see for some time how the

---

[61] For extensive discussions of the development of enterprise liability, see Virginia E. Nolan & Edmund Ursin, *Understanding Enterprise Liability: Rethinking Tort Reform for the Twenty-first Century* (1995); Priest, supra note 8; Rahdert, *supra* note 51.

[62] *See* Priest, *supra* note 8, at 463.

[63] William L. Prosser, *The Law of Torts* 688–93 (1941).

[64] For a detailed comparison, see White, *Tort Law*, *supra* note 11, at 198–201. "Prosser and Roger Traynor were friends and often intellectual allies: their partnership was a significant event in the intellectual history of torts in America." *Id.* at 179. Traynor, for example, recommended three candidates for a new dean at Boalt Hall, and Prosser was selected from that group. Field, *supra* note 7, at 167. "Traynor later sat on Prosser's committee on the Restatement (Second) of Torts." *Id.*

[65] White, *Tort Law*, *supra* note 11, at 200.

theory of enterprise liability applied to product-caused injuries.[66] Instead, tort scholars at the time were discussing compensation plans for other injuries, such as those caused by automobile accidents.[67] Traynor did not develop the theory of enterprise liability, but he was the first to see clearly how it would apply to the problem of product-caused injuries. Consequently, Traynor has been called the "judicial architect" of enterprise liability.[68]

Despite the association between Traynor and enterprise liability, he never judicially accepted the full implications of the theory. If strict liability would reduce risk and provide optimal insurance when the defendant is a business organization, then these rationales imply that strict liability should not be limited to injuries caused by product defects. Consumers who suffer injuries from nondefective products, after all, would benefit from the insurance afforded by strict liability, and such liability could reduce risk as well.[69] The tenets of enterprise liability accordingly imply that strict liability should not be limited to defective products. Nevertheless, Traynor "repeatedly refused to apply strict liability in cases that did not involve a defective product, even where the defendant was a business."[70]

The most obvious reason why Traynor limited strict liability to defective products is that he justified the rule with the implied warranty. The implied warranty is breached by an exploding soda bottle; it is not breached by nondefective products, which by definition are appropriately safe or fit. The implied warranty does not support a rule of strict liability for nondefective products, so Traynor limited the rule to product defects.[71] He conceptualized strict products liability as the unbinding of

---

[66] *See supra* notes 27–29 and accompanying text. Although Prosser had listed deterrence and risk-spreading among the various rationales for strict liability in his 1941 treatise, he was relying on the work of other scholars who had not yet made the connection between enterprise liability and product injuries. Prosser also was not persuaded by these two rationales. Years later, he said the deterrence rationale had "a specious and unconvincing sound, and would appear to have been concocted in the heads of professors rather than based on any realities of the situation," whereas the manufacturer's ability to spread risk by procuring "[l]iability insurance is obviously not to be ignored; but it is a makeweight." Prosser, *supra* note 18, at 1120–22.

[67] *See especially* Committee to Study Compensation for Automobile Accidents, *Report to the Columbia University Council for Research in the Social Science* (1932).

[68] Nolan & Ursin, *supra* note 61, at 114.

[69] The potential risk reduction stems from the different impact that negligence and strict liability have on consumer perceptions of product price. See supra note 47.

[70] Field, *supra* note 7, at 180.

[71] Traynor's insistence on doctrinal support for strict liability was consistent with the evolutionary change in jurisprudential thinking that took place following *Escola*. At the

warranty liability from contractual restrictions, and that conception depends on the warranty and the associated requirement of defect.[72]

Traynor's unwillingness to expand strict liability beyond product defects may also have stemmed from his awareness of a major problem posed by enterprise liability. As he later observed, the defect requirement means "the manufacturer is not an insurer for all injuries caused by his product."[73] The limit on manufacturer-provided insurance did not trouble Traynor, suggesting that he recognized the limitation of the insurance rationale for strict liability.

Indeed, this limitation is implied by the *Escola* concurrence. In arguing that strict liability would provide desirable insurance, Traynor assumed that manufacturers could purchase insurance whereas the public could not. The insurance rationale therefore was contingent in this regard. If facts pertaining to the availability of insurance changed, then the insurance rationale might also change. More precisely, if changed circumstances placed consumers in the better position for procuring insurance, the insurance rationale as articulated in *Escola* would counsel against tort insurance in favor of these other insurance mechanisms. In that event, tort liability would be justified only on grounds of risk reduction or deterrence, resulting in the limitation of strict liability to product defects. Such liability utilizes manufacturer-provided insurance (tort damages) only as a means of giving product sellers an incentive to supply nondefective products.

This contingency in Traynor's insurance argument may also explain why he adhered to the requirement of defect. At the time *Escola* was decided, health insurance was not widely available.[74] As compared to no insurance, the insurance supplied by manufacturer liability would be desired by consumers. To be sure, consumers also would want insurance for injuries caused by nondefective products, but Traynor first needed to

---

time *Escola* was decided, Realism was the dominant jurisprudence. The Realist position, however, did not necessarily require doctrinal support for a given legal position. The jurisprudence that followed Realism, by contrast, emphasized rationality in the law, consisting both of continuity (via reliance on precedent) and desirability in light of changed social conditions. *See* White, *Tort Law*, *supra* note 11, at 139–79.

[72] *Cf.* Roger J. Traynor, *The Ways and Meanings of Defective Products and Strict Liability*, 32 Tenn. L. Rev. 363, 366 (1965)("The reasons justifying strict liability emphasize that there is something wrong, if not in the manner of the manufacturer's production, at least in his product.").

[73] *Id.* at 366–67.

[74] Health insurance in the United States was a product of the depression in the 1930s and World War II; it was not until the mid–1950s that a sizable portion of the population had such insurance. *See* Rashi Fein, *Medical Care, Medical Costs: The Search for a Health Insurance Policy* 21–24 (1986); Paul Starr, *The Social Transformation of American Medicine* 240, 327–28 (1982).

persuade others that strict liability was appropriate for defective products. By the time Traynor's argument was accepted in the 1960s, circumstances had changed. A sizable portion of the population had health insurance, such insurance was widely available, and government-funded social insurance programs had expanded substantially.[75] Today the vast majority of accident victims receive some compensation from their own insurance policies and government programs.[76] This change in social facts has altered the relevant insurance considerations in a manner that undercuts the extension of strict liability to nondefective products.

Consider again the insurance advertisement discussed earlier. Consumers need not purchase insurance (via higher product prices) from strictly liable manufacturers. Instead, consumers can purchase their own insurance, commonly called "first-party insurance," just like the individual in the advertisement. Alternatively, the insurance can be provided by the government. These types of insurance have many cost advantages over the tort insurance provided by product sellers, commonly called "third-party insurance." The primary reasons for the cost differential between the two insurance mechanisms are the event that triggers coverage and the scope of coverage.[77]

The coverage supplied by first-party insurance policies is triggered by the fact of loss (like medical expenses for health insurance), whereas the cause of loss ordinarily is not relevant. The fact of injury or loss usually is easy to prove (submitting bills), so policyholders typically do not need a lawyer to receive insurance proceeds. By contrast, accident victims must hire a lawyer to receive the tort insurance provided by strict liability. In part, a lawyer is needed to help establish that the plaintiff's injury was proximately caused by a product sold by the defendant. Often, many products are causally implicated in an accident, and a potentially contentious and costly factual inquiry may be required to resolve the liability question.[78] Many items of tort damages are also

[75] *See* Fein, *supra* note 74; Starr, *supra* note 74; 3 Fowler V. Harper et al., *The Law of Torts* § 13.1 at 127 (2d ed. 1986) (describing growth in social-insurance programs).

[76] *See* Deborah R. Hensler et al., *Compensation for Accidental Injuries in the United States* 108 (1991) (summarizing study which found that 85% of all accident victims received some compensation from their own insurance and public programs)

[77] First-party insurance may also be cheaper due to its comparative advantage in minimizing the costs of moral hazard and adverse selection. *See* Richard A. Epstein, *Products Liability as an Insurance Market*, 15 J. Legal Stud. 645 (1985); George L. Priest, *The Current Insurance Crisis and Modern Tort Law*, 96 Yale L.J. 1521 (1987). *But see* Jon D. Hanson & Kyle D. Logue, *The First–Party Insurance Externality: An Economic Justification for Enterprise Liability*, 76 Cornell L. Rev. 129 (1990) (arguing that first-party insurance creates a moral hazard problem that would be eliminated by enterprise liability).

[78] *See* Mark Geistfeld, *Implementing Enterprise Liability: A Comment on Henderson and Twerski*, 67 N.Y.U. L. Rev. 1157 (1992). Rather than merely raising the transaction

difficult and costly to prove. The resultant litigation expenses increase the cost of tort insurance, which largely explains why even in a tort regime of strict liability, the administrative costs of third-party insurance per dollar of coverage significantly exceed the administrative costs of first-party insurance.[79]

Tort insurance imposes other additional costs on consumers. The scope of coverage provided by tort insurance is not extensive enough for consumers, as it does not cover losses unrelated to product use. To cover these contingencies (like medical expenses due to illness), individuals must purchase other insurance. But since first-party insurance coverage typically is triggered by the fact of loss rather than its cause, individuals who have such insurance might receive double compensation when injured by products. The health insurer, for example, is obligated to pay whenever the policyholder suffered an insured-against loss (medical expenses), and the manufacturer is obligated to pay tort damages for such loss (due to the collateral-source rule) even though the consumer received the health insurance proceeds. Double recovery can be avoided if the health insurer exercises a contractual or statutory right to indemnification out of the tort recovery received by the policyholder (known as "subrogation"). The separate legal proceeding, however, often is complicated and costly due to the need to determine which part of the tort award or settlement is covered by the insurance policy. Consequently, insurers do not always exercise this right. Insurance provided by product sellers therefore may be an inefficient form of double insurance or otherwise increase the administrative cost of first-party insurance policies, providing another reason why consumers might have lower total insurance costs if sellers were not strictly liable for all product-caused injuries.

In acknowledgement of the problems posed by tort insurance, the theory of enterprise liability includes various proposals for reducing insurance costs, such as limitations on damages for pain and suffering.[80] In Traynor's view, these reforms required legislative action.[81] Unable to judicially implement the required reforms, Traynor properly limited the

---

costs of enterprise liability, some argue that the problem of multiple causes would render enterprise liability unworkable. *See* James A. Henderson, Jr. & Aaron D. Twerski, *Closing the American Products Liability Frontier: The Rejection of Liability Without Defect*, 66 N.Y.U. L. Rev. 1263 (1991).

[79] For more extensive discussion with a heuristic assessment of the cost differential, see Mark Geistfeld, *Should Enterprise Liability Replace the Rule of Strict Liability for Abnormally Dangerous Activities?*, 45 UCLA L. Rev. 611, 625–33, 639–46 (1998).

[80] *See generally* Nolan & Ursin, *supra* note 61.

[81] *See* Seffert v. Los Angeles Transit Lines, 364 P.2d 337 (Cal.1961) (Traynor, J., dissenting).

insurance rationale to injuries caused by defective products. So limited, tort liability minimizes consumer insurance costs while giving product sellers an incentive to supply nondefective products.

This limitation of the insurance rationale for tort liability has been widely recognized. "Where courts (and sometimes legislatures) have embraced the insurance rationale, they usually have done so in a cautious, qualified manner."[82] The contingency inherent in the *Escola* insurance rationale therefore explains why strict liability has been limited to product defects, even though that limitation has reintroduced negligence liability for design and warning defects.

For this same reason, the *Escola* concurrence does not effectively adopt the theory of enterprise liability. But by accepting some tenets of enterprise liability, the *Escola* concurrence facilitated the expansion of tort liability to cover other injuries caused by businesses. Injuries caused by professional negligence, for example, were no longer immune from tort liability, illustrating the pervasive impact that *Escola* and enterprise liability have had on modern tort law.[83]

---

[82] Rahdert, *supra* note 51, at 59.

[83] For discussion of the influence of enterprise liability on professional negligence, *see* Robert L. Rabin, *Some Thoughts on the Ideology of Enterprise Liability*, 55 Md. L. Rev. 1190 (1996). The influence of *Escola* becomes readily apparent once malpractice is analogized to the defective provision of a service. Like design and warning defects, the issue of defectiveness in the provision of services ordinarily must be determined by negligence principles. Given the analogy with defects, the appropriateness of negligence liability for malpractice follows from the same analysis Traynor employed in *Escola*. For other examples of how enterprise liability has influenced modern tort law, see James A. Henderson, Jr., *Echoes of Enterprise Liability in Product Design and Marketing Litigation*, 87 Cornell L. Rev. 958 (2002); Gregory C. Keating, *The Theory of Enterprise Liability and Common Law Strict Liability*, 54 Vand. L. Rev. 1285 (2001); Nolan & Ursin, *supra* note 61, at 125–37; Schwartz, *supra* note 34.

10

Stephen D. Sugarman

Vincent v. Lake Erie Transportation Co.: Liability for Harm Caused by Necessity

The Storm and the Escape of the Reynolds

In the evening of November 27, 1905, a ferocious storm struck Duluth, Minnesota. Although Duluth's port in the early 20th century was one of the busiest in the world, by 10:30 p.m. that night shipping traffic had been suspended. A combination of fierce winds that eventually reached about 70 miles an hour and heavy snow brought visibility down to nearly zero. The storm caused rough and high waves that pounded against and over Duluth harbor's many docks. With gale winds that did not abate until mid-day on the 28th, the tempest left great destruction in its wake.

Eighteen ships were damaged or destroyed by the storm, including the Mataafa, a 430 foot long iron ore carrier, whose name the storm has since carried. Thirty-six lives were lost, as well as considerable cargo. Afterward, many old-time Duluth seamen swore that the Mataafa Blow was the worst they had ever known, and Duluth weather records show that it would be another 70 years before the area experienced as severe a storm.

The steamship S. C. Reynolds, subsequently known to generations of law students, was one of many vessels to enter Duluth harbor earlier in the day of the big storm. Built in 1890 for the Lake Erie Transportation Company, a subsidiary of the Wabash Railway, the Reynolds had always plied the Great Lakes as a cargo ship. That season she was under charter to Anchor Lines out of Toledo, Ohio, and on this voyage she was set to discharge most of her cargo at the City Dock in the port of Duluth. More than 250 feet long, 40 feet wide, and made of steel, the Reynolds was under the command of Captain T. C. Herrick. Herrick had been a captain of steamships for more than thirty years and had been sailing freighters into Duluth for more than ten.

Like many other captains that day, Herrick was no doubt initially pleased with the fairly calm weather he found at Duluth upon the Reynolds' arrival late in the afternoon of the 27th. Another big storm had passed through Duluth on November 23–24, and the end of the fall season was fast approaching, as Duluth's port was traditionally closed to shipping from the start of December until April, owing to the rugged winters along the western shores of Lake Superior.

As the Reynolds came abreast the City Dock between 4 and 5 p.m. that afternoon, those in charge of the dock positioned her, not along side the dock where she would be closest to the shore, but rather along the exposed end of the dock that stuck out into the harbor. There was nothing uncommon about docking at this location, however, and a crew of stevedores was on hand to unload the cargo, which commenced around 5 p.m. Following a break of about an hour for dinner, the work continued until it was completed at around 10:30 p.m.

Although the storm was then raging, Captain Herrick nonetheless sought to push off, and signaled to the Union Towing and Wrecking Company to send tugs for assistance, which was the routine practice in heavy weather. No tugs were provided, however, because those in charge of Union Towing had concluded by then that it was too dangerous, even with tugs, for any ship to attempt to leave the port.

At that point, Captain Herrick concluded that it would be foolhardy to try to leave on his own. So, rather than pushing off, he ordered his men to do what they could to secure the Reynolds to the dock. Herrick was by then clearly aware that were his ship to come free, it would likely crash into another ship or some other pier or perhaps simply sink because of the rough seas in the harbor. His crew's effort, which involved the ongoing replacement of ropes as they chaffed, was a success, and the Reynolds was saved the fate of the many other vessels that were lost during the night and the next morning. Eventually, in the afternoon of the 28th when the storm subsided sufficiently, the Reynolds safely pulled away from the City Dock.

The Lawsuit–Participants, Pleadings, and Trial

Although the Reynolds escaped the Mataafa blow unscathed, the owners of City Dock claimed their property was seriously damaged by the Reynolds' relentless pounding into the dock during the storm. As a result, plaintiffs R. C. Vincent and Lillian M. Kelly filed a lawsuit in state court against the Lake Erie Transportation Company, owner of the Reynolds. Plaintiffs sought damages in the amount of $1200 (roughly the equivalent of $25,000 today).

Vincent v. Lake Erie Transportation Co.[1] is famous now as the seminal case in which a party, acting out of necessity, intentionally enters (or uses) another's property for his benefit, and, even though that necessity privileges the entry (or use), the actor is nonetheless held liable for harm done to the property regardless of whether the actor was at fault or not. Although not typically characterized in this way, this is a form of strict liability imposed on permissible self-help efforts, and it stands in contrast to most of contemporary tort law that conditions recovery on proof of fault.

Vincent now appears in all of the leading casebooks and in the Restatement of Torts as part of the law of intentional torts. But, as will be explained, before the case reached the Minnesota Supreme Court it was formally cast as one involving the defendant's negligence, although the plaintiffs' lawyer appeared to oscillate between two very different notions of what it means to be negligent. The majority of the Minnesota Supreme Court viewed the case very differently, handing down a memorable opinion filled with intriguing analogies that are perhaps far less persuasive than the justices imagined. But that is getting ahead of our story.

Vincent pitted two experienced Duluth attorneys against each other. Plaintiffs engaged E. F. Alford from the Duluth firm of Alford & Hunt. Alford had been admitted to the Minnesota bar in 1893 and had served in the Minnesota legislature from 1900–02. Duluth admiralty lawyer Henry Ransom Spencer represented the defendant. Spencer too had served in the Minnesota legislature, and in 1895 he had published a Treatise on the Law of Marine Collisions. Although Alford and Spencer surely knew each other, this did not prevent both from vigorously making objection after objection to questions put to witnesses by the opposing lawyer during the trial.[2]

---

[1] 124 N.W. 221 (Minn.1910).

[2] Alford had originally filed Vincent and Kelly's claim in federal court in admiralty. The appropriate scope of admiralty jurisdiction was contested in that era, however, and at that very time defendant's lawyer Spencer was involved in a case that was decided by the U.S. Supreme Court on February 24, 1908. In that case, *Duluth and Superior Bridge Company v. Steamer "Troy,"* 208 U.S. 321 (1908), owners of a draw bridge brought an action *in rem* against the steamer Troy that struck and damaged the bridge. On the same day, the Court first decided a case concerning a ship that damaged a dock, a pier, and a bridge, and concluded that those properties pertained to commerce on land and were not aids to navigation in the maritime sense. Cleveland Terminal & Valley R.R. Co. v.

Vincent was tried before Judge Josiah D. Ensign and a jury of twelve, with the trial commencing on September 14, 1908. This was less than four months after the state court complaint was filed, an incredibly rapid pace for litigation as compared with common experience today.[3]

At the pleading stage, Alford squarely cast the plaintiffs' lawsuit in terms of fault, claiming that the defendant had negligently kept the Reynolds tied to the plaintiffs' dock. In presenting the plaintiffs' side of the case at trial, however, Alford did not even to try to prove that Captain Herrick had been negligent in the way we now understand the term. Alford first called two witnesses who basically testified that they saw the ship tied to the dock and they saw the damage it did to the dock. These two witnesses were F. H. Bidwell, who was the manager of the City Dock at the time of the famous storm, and W. H. Brewer, who had then been an assistant to Bidwell and who had become the dock manager by the time of trial. Alford also called R. C.Vincent, one of the plaintiffs, and offered depositions and interrogatories of two additional witnesses, O. S. Olson and George Vincent. Alford's purpose was to use the testimony of these three men to prove the amount of damages that the Reynolds did to the dock.

Nowadays, we clearly understand that negligence requires a showing by the plaintiff that a reasonable defendant would have acted differently. Therefore, based on the evidence discussed so far, if Alford's claim is to be viewed as truly based on our current understanding of negligence, his was a very aggressive position, because it essentially asserted that the reasonable thing to have done was to sacrifice the Reynolds. Although it is not known from the historical record how much the Reynolds was worth at the time, it seems clear that its value was a great deal more than the amount of the damage it plausibly could have done to the dock. Hence, if Captain Herrick were to be judged at fault, it seemingly would be for causing a small harm by failing to incur a much larger one. In the 21st century at least, it is hard to view someone as negligent on that basis.

It is not surprising therefore, that, when the plaintiffs completed their part of the case, Spencer, the defendant's lawyer, moved to have the case dismissed on the ground that no proof of fault had been offered.

Cleveland Steamship Co., 208 U.S. 316 (1908). On that basis, the Court concluded that there was no U.S. admiralty jurisdiction over the matter merely because a ship was involved (contrary to what then appeared to be the law in England). That decision doomed the plaintiff's case in the *Troy* decision as well, and, in light of these outcomes, Alford refiled his claim a few months later in state court.

[3] Yet, it is to be noted that the depositions used at trial had been taken earlier while the case was pending in federal court, *see supra* note 2.

Although there seemed to be considerable merit to the defendant's legal position, Judge Ensign denied the motion.

Notwithstanding the way we would today interpret his pleadings, it appears that, in presenting his case, Alford was actually relying upon the legal theory that, if plaintiffs could prove that the defendant's ship damaged their dock, they were entitled to recovery, unless the defendant could prove that the harm was the result of an inevitable accident. Moreover, Alford viewed the idea of an inevitable accident narrowly. In effect, his position was that if there was any way that the defendants could have avoided the harm to the dock but they chose not to take that step, the accident was not inevitable. Clearly, Alford believed he would win were this legal theory accepted because harm to the dock presumably could have been avoided had the Reynolds merely been cut loose, albeit with the probable loss of the ship (and possible damage to other ships or docks in the harbor). Put differently, because the defendants chose to keep the vessel securely tied to the dock, this made the harm to the dock no longer an inevitable accident, but rather something of a deliberate outcome.

This way of thinking might imply that one should be deemed "negligent" for knowingly taking a substantial risk to another, regardless of the reasonableness of that risk—a very different view of negligence than we have today, but one which was supported as late as 1951 in a well known concurring opinion by Lord Reid in a famous English case involving a passerby who was struck by a cricket ball that was hit beyond the cricket field.[4]

Later, in his brief on appeal, Alford traced his legal theory to a maxim from Blackstone: *Sic utere tuo ut alienum non laedas*—use your own property in such a manner as not to injure that of another.[5] A narrower way of putting this claim might be to restrict it to instances in which the defendant intentionally used and then harmed the plaintiff's property in order to obtain a benefit from that property. Either way, although it seems odd today to consider it necessarily *blameworthy* merely for one to put her interests ahead of those of another, possibly Alford sensed that what people would find blameworthy was the failure to offer to pay for the harm done in such instances.

Oddly, Alford appears to have had something of a change of heart later in the trial, because, after the defendants put forward their side the case, he belatedly introduced evidence seemingly intended to prove specific acts of negligence by the defendants after all—the failure initially to tie up the Reynolds elsewhere than at the exposed edge of the dock,

---

[4] Bolton v. Stone, [1951] A.C. 850.

[5] 3 William Blackstone, *Commentaries* 217.

the failure to move the Reynolds earlier in the evening during the unloading as the weather turned worse, and the failure to move the Reynolds to a position of greater safety along the side of the dock after the unloading was completed. If proved, any of these would certainly have been a proper ground for finding the defendants at fault in today's sense, thereby clearly vindicating Alford's initial pleading.

However, from the written record of the testimony, the evidence Alford presented concerning the defendant's fault seems weak. Moreover, by that point in the trial, the defendant had already introduced considerable testimony by other experienced local ship captains, sailors from the Reynolds, and seamen who had staffed tugboats in Duluth harbor on the day of the storm to the effect that Captain Herrick had, in all respects, acted reasonably.

Because the Reynolds had been in the Duluth harbor several times earlier that season, Herrick was surely well aware of where he might tie up. But he testified that on November 27, 1905 the Reynolds was put where she docked at the direction of those operating the dock, and there is no evidence that anyone thought that a foolish thing to do at the time. Indeed, Herrick stated that at around 5 p.m., when he tied up to the dock, the weather conditions were not unusual and that he had actually steamed into the dock without the assistance of tugboats. Alford challenged no aspect of this part of Herrick's story on cross-examination.

Apparently in hopes of helping to prove the great danger she faced if the Reynolds were set loose late in the evening without the assistance of tugs, Spencer sought to have several of his witnesses testify as to the many other ships that went down in the Mataafa storm. But Alford objected to such questions at every opportunity, and Judge Ensign sustained those objections. The effectiveness of those objections must be doubted, however, first because a few witnesses off-handedly blurted out references to the storm and its general consequences before objections could be made, and, second, because surely every juror in the case must have been well informed about the Mataafa storm anyway.

In rebuttal to Spencer's side of the case, Alford introduced the pretrial deposition he had taken of Herbert W. Richardson, who had been in charge of the United States Weather Bureau at Duluth on the days of the storm, as well as two exhibits, which were the official weather records made by Richardson on those two days. The first of these exhibits shows that the wind, which was less than 20 miles an hour before noon, had picked up to 34 miles an hour by 4:52 p.m. the approximate time when the Reynolds docked. The exhibit also shows that snow began at 6:30 p.m. and that the wind continued to increase reaching 54 miles an hour at about the time the Reynolds had finished unloading and 62 miles an hour by 11:58 p.m. According to the second exhibit, the wind continued at more than 60 miles an hour during the night, reaching a maximum of 68 miles an hour between 8 and 9 a.m. on the 28th. At noon, however, it suddenly calmed down considerably, and by 1 p.m. on the 28th was back to below 40 miles an hour for the rest of the day. The first exhibit also shows, and Richardson confirmed this in his deposition, that a storm warning had been given at 10:00 a.m. on the 27th (which warning was also published in the evening paper) with all ships told to remain in port because of the very dangerous storm that was expected (although notes on the exhibit show that in fact several large craft actually departed late in the afternoon, presumably around the time the Reynolds docked).

The problem with this evidence from the perspective of proving fault on the part of Captain Herrick is that the dock manager Bidwell and his assistants surely were also aware of the storm warning and yet did nothing to direct Herrick to tie up the Reynolds at what might possibly have been a safer spot along side the City Dock instead of out at the end where she was placed. Indeed, to the extent that the failure to act on Richardson's storm warning made Captain Herrick negligent, that failure to act implied contributory negligence on the part of those in charge of the dock (which would have been a complete defense in the early 1900s). So, too, as for moving the ship either before or after the unloading was complete, again there was no suggestion from the dock operators that, in view of the storm warning and the increasing wind, they believed that the Reynolds should be shifted.

To bolster the assertion that the Reynolds should have been moved to a safer place, Alford called Captain Alexander McDougal. McDougal claimed that the proper, and rather easy, thing to do was to shift the Reynolds away from the end of the City Dock to the side, where she would be more sheltered by lying between the City Dock and the next dock to the west. McDougal asserted that this is what Herrick should have done earlier in the evening as the storm grew, and that this is as well what Herrick should have done once the unloading was complete and the tugboats were unavailable. Moreover, Captain McDougal testified that had the Reynolds been moved as he proposed, then not only would the dock not have been battered, but the Reynolds itself would not have been harmed. If believed, this is rather powerful expert testimony for the plaintiffs.

Yet, in his cross-examination, Spencer made considerable headway in undermining McDougal's credibility on the issue of what Captain Herrick should have done. Most importantly, McDougal, who was age 62 at the time of the trial, conceded that he had not been active as a captain for a quarter of a century, had not been present in Duluth during this storm, and had last commanded a wood, not a steel, ship. Although there is no way to know, it would be surprising if McDougal's testimony was ultimately convincing to the jury. As Spencer later wrote in his brief on appeal: "By reading the testimony of Captain McDougall [sic] it is apparent that he has reached that complacent period in life when old men look back upon what they did, when young, when everything is measured by the magnified prowess of their own youth."

At the end of the trial, Judge Ensign rejected Spencer's motion for a directed verdict for the defense, and then both sides submitted jury instructions. Alford's proposed instructions make no mention of negligence or any of the alternative actions that Captain McDougal argued Captain Herrick should reasonably have taken. Instead, Alford stuck with the approach underlying his initial presentation of the plaintiffs' case—that if the Reynolds damaged the dock, the defendants were liable unless the damage was the result of an inevitable accident.

Spencer's proposed instructions first include the proposition that if the defendant had acted lawfully and with the proper precautions, any harm to the dock was the result of an inevitable accident. They also include the conventional fault-based proposition that no recovery is to be allowed if the master and crew of the Reynolds "endeavored by every means consistent with due care and caution and a proper display of nautical skill to move said steamer from plaintiffs' dock after delivery of the goods consigned to the City dock..."

Judge Ensign generally accepted Alford's proffered jury instructions, rejected most of Spencer's and went on to give a rambling, repetitive, somewhat incoherent and, to today's way of thinking, internally conflicting set of instructions to the jury.

On the one hand, Judge Ensign repeated several times that the jury had to find that the defendant was negligent before it could find for the plaintiffs, and this was the one important place in which he actually gave Spencer's requested instruction about fault just quoted above. But the judge also gave the plaintiffs' requested jury instructions about the defendant being liable if its ship caused harm and this was not the result of an inevitable accident narrowly defined (having refused Spencer's requested instruction to include within the definition of an inevitable accident harm that occurs notwithstanding due care having been taken by the defendant). Ensign also put forward Blackstone's maxim noted earlier about using your property in a way that it does not injure another. He then further stated, "The defendant had no right to save its ship at the expense of the plaintiffs and if it was to save—that is, in saving its ship—if it was so saved and damage was done to the defendant [here Ensign must mean either "by" the defendant, or to the "plaintiff"] by reason of its laying at the dock and being saved, *and the defendant was negligent*, then the defendant should be liable for that damage." (emphasis supplied)

If the jurors followed Ensign's instructions, they probably would have been puzzled by exactly what they were supposed to decide if they concluded that the harm to the dock was not an inevitable accident in the narrow sense, but that the defendant had exercised due care under the circumstances by choosing to keep the Reynolds tied up.[6]

On September 17, 1908, the jury in the *Vincent* case returned a verdict in favor of the plaintiffs in the amount of $500. As noted above, Alford had claimed damages of $1200. There are two very different explanations for the size of the award.

One explanation is that the jury believed that the dock was damaged in the amount of approximately $1000 but that, despite the judge's instructions, the jurors thought it fairest for the loss to be shared by the two essentially innocent and reasonable parties. On this theory, the jury deemed the Reynolds' operators to be at fault even though they were not, but then asked them to pay for only half of the harm done. While completely at odds with tort law's all-or-nothing outlook (especially in an era when contributory negligence was a complete defense), what might be termed a "compromise" verdict would be viewed by some as a highly just result.

A different explanation rests on the difficulties that Alford had in proving what might have been thought a simple point—the amount of damage to the dock. As already noted, his strategy was to have plaintiff R. C. Vincent testify as to how much he paid to fix the dock and then to use a deposition from O. S. Olson, the foreman for Whitney Brothers who repaired the dock, to confirm that they indeed did the work and that is what they charged for it. But Spencer sniped at this effort relentlessly. One attack was that Whitney Brothers might have overcharged. Another was that they might have billed for repairs that had nothing to do with damage done during the Mataafa storm. Along these lines Spencer insinuated that since Olson had not been there at the time of the storm and did not make the repairs until June 1906, Olson could have no idea whether he was actually repairing damage done later on by other ships, well after the Reynolds was long gone. During all of this, despite a slew of Spencer objections, Alford somehow managed to get Vincent to estimate, based on his expertise in the business, that the damage done to the dock was about $1000 and to disclose that Whitney Brothers' repair bill was $932.09. Alford also disclosed that the dock, in good repair, was worth about $23,000.

---

[6] This was a disappointing performance from a prominent judge who, having gone on the St. Louis County (Duluth) bench in 1889, had many years of judicial service by the time the *Vincent* case came before him. Having originally moved to and opened his law practice in Minnesota in 1868, Ensign was one of a group of men granted a franchise for a street railway in Duluth and he became a director of the First National Bank of Duluth. A Republican, Ensign was elected Mayor of Duluth in 1880 and again in 1884.

Spencer did not give up, however. One defense witness, Peter Grignon, who had been repairing docks in Duluth for 10 years, claimed that the cost of repairs should only have been $400. Spencer called several other witnesses who testified that the storm itself battered the dock and caused it harm. Surely this damage was not chargeable to the defendant, even if Captain Herrick had been at fault in not moving the Reynolds. Indeed, some defense witnesses asserted that the Reynolds never actually touched the dock. Rather, although it was tossed about by the waves and the wind, and although it was carefully tied to the dock by ropes, the ship somehow miraculously avoided striking the dock itself. On this theory, presumably, all of the harm was done by the storm on its own. However, evidence from plaintiffs' witnesses that repairs were needed only at the place on the dock where the Reynolds was tied up seemed to counter this argument rather persuasively. Nonetheless, it is possible that after all of this question-raising, the jury concluded that the amount of harm actually done to the dock by the ship was just the $500 it awarded.

The Appeal

Six months later, on March 20, 1909, Spencer filed motions for a judgment notwithstanding the verdict and in the alternative for a new trial. These were denied, and on May 24, 1909, Spencer served on Alford a notice of appeal to the Minnesota Supreme Court. This section critically examines the arguments made in the briefs for both sides, and provides a background against which the court's opinion, discussed later, can be viewed.

Spencer's brief on behalf of the defendant was a very substantial piece of work. Nearly 80 pages in length, it alleged 33 errors in the trial of the case—14 concerning rulings on matters of evidence, and 15 concerning charges to the jury, plus the failure of the judge to grant Spencer's four motions—to dismiss, for a directed verdict, for a judgment notwithstanding the verdict, and for a new trial.

As might be expected, Spencer argued that, apart from the testimony of Captain McDougal, which he dismissed as unpersuasive, there was no evidence upon which the jury could find that Captain Herrick was negligent. And Spencer cited several cases in which ship and railway owners had escaped liability for damage done by their property because the defendants had not been at fault. These cases appear to be ones in which storms of various sorts overwhelmed the defendants' efforts, such as blowing the defendant's ship into the plaintiff's barge. Just as he claimed at the trial, Spencer asserted that the harm to the plaintiffs' dock in the *Vincent* case was also the product of an inevitable accident.

When he came to discuss jury instructions that Spencer argued should not have been given, he gave special focus to the instruction quoted earlier in which Judge Ensign talks about the defendant having no right to save its ship at the expense of the plaintiff. To this Spencer argued "As between two equally innocent parties, how can the Court saddle such a damage on to one rather than the other?"

In support of the view that in such circumstances the loss should fall on the plaintiffs, Spencer cited the case of *The Chickasaw*,[7] a case decided by what was then a federal court of appeals for Western Tennessee. There a steamship, the Chickasaw, was in the process of taking on coal from a barge that was tied up along side the steamship when a large piece of timber suddenly floated down the river and struck the barge. When it seemed clear to the Chickasaw operators that the barge was about to sink and smash into their boat, those in charge ordered the lines to the barge cut so as to avoid the injury. Alas, rather than harmlessly sinking, the barge floated down the river and struck another steamship. The owners of that ship sued the owners of the Chickasaw, but the defendants won the case. Although a case in admiralty and hence perhaps not technically applicable to common law decisions, the *Chickasaw* decision might seem at first blush quite parallel to the *Vincent* case. After all, the Chickasaw operators acted to save their own property at what turned out to be the expense of the plaintiff, and yet the defendant was held not liable.

But in deciding the *Chickasaw* case, the court stated that it was "not foreseen" that the coal barge would keep afloat and therefore be in a position to harm the plaintiff's ship. To try to fit within this phrasing, Spencer then stated about the Reynolds, "There was no design to shift the danger to the plaintiffs by remaining at the dock. In fact it was not anticipated that any damage would be done." The problem with this argument, of course, is that when Captain Herrick decided not to depart and instead ordered the Reynolds secured to the City Dock, damage to the dock was hardly unforeseeable.

Alford's brief for the dock owners began with a statement that might seem surprising in view of what seemed to be Alford's legal position earlier. In that statement Alford simply argued that the defendant was evidently negligent—negligent in initially tying up at the exposed end of the dock when a storm was plainly brewing, negligent in continuing to unload rather than moving the ship as Captain McDougal testified should have occurred as the storm grew, and negligent again in not sliding the ship into a safer location after the unloading was finished. According to Alford, by keeping the Reynolds at the exposed end of the dock, the defendant unreasonably endangered the plaintiff's dock and

---

[7] 41 F. 627 (C.C.W.D.Tenn.1890).

was properly found liable by the jury for the harm done. One explanation for Alford taking this approach, of course, is that his clients won below and the trial judge, arguably, charged the jury in terms of negligence; therefore, to protect his verdict, Alford might have felt no need to argue for the Blackstone maxim or any other legal theory that sounded more like strict liability.

However, as soon as he began the "argument" section of his brief, Alford immediately returned to the Blackstone maxim. Moreover, he deftly turned the defendant's reliance on the *Chickasaw* case around by emphasizing what was noted above—namely that *if* the foreseeable consequences of cutting the coal barge loose would have been to harm the plaintiff's steamship, *then* the implication (albeit not the holding) of the *Chickasaw* decision was that the defendant would have been liable. And here in the *Vincent* case, Alford must have felt on reasonably safe grounds in asserting that the natural and probable consequence of tying the Reynolds to the City Dock during the ferocious storm was damage to the dock.

Notice that Alford might also have distinguished the *Chickasaw* case in a different way. There, the Chickasaw operators in no way used the plaintiff's steamship in order to obtain a benefit from it; but in *Vincent*, those in charge of the Reynolds clearly did use the plaintiffs' property in order to obtain a benefit. Alford, however, did not pursue this line of argument.

The Decision in Vincent v. Lake Erie Transportation Co.

The five-member Minnesota Supreme Court heard the case and on January 14, 1910 issued a divided (3–2) opinion upholding the plaintiffs' victory in the court below.[8] This section provides a detailed description and critique of the reasoning offered by the majority, as well as a few words about the disappointing quality of the dissent.

Associate Justice Thomas Dillon O'Brien, who had been appointed to the Court only a few months earlier, wrote the opinion for the majority.[9] Justice O'Brien quickly dispatched the claim that Captain

---

[8] 124 N.W. 221 (Minn.1910).

[9] Voting with O'Brien were Chief Justice Charles Start and Associate Justice Calvin Brown. Associate Justice Charles Lewis wrote the dissent, in which Associate Justice Edwin Jaggard joined. All but O'Brien were Republicans. Start had been first elected Chief Justice in 1894. Brown was elected as an Associate Justice in 1898. Lewis went on to the Court in 1900 and Jaggard in 1904. Before coming on to the Court, Jaggard was a member of the law faculty at the University of Minnesota and authored a *Handbook of the Law of Torts*, first published in 1893. Hence, all but O'Brien had at least a reasonable amount of judicial experience when the *Vincent* case came before them.

Herrick had been negligent, notwithstanding the apparent jury finding that he was. As O'Brien saw it, even if it might have been possible to move the Reynolds in the way imagined by plaintiffs' witness Captain McDougal, it was not negligent to fail to try. Rather, according to O'Brien, the record clearly supported the defendant's position that it was "prudent seamanship" to keep the Reynolds where she was once the cargo was unloaded. As for any possible fault in not moving the ship earlier, O'Brien simply concluded that the storm turned out to be far more violent than could have reasonably been anticipated and therefore it was plainly reasonable both to dock where the Reynolds first tied up and to keep her there during the early evening of November 27 as she was being unloaded. In short, by the time it was appreciated just how ferocious the Mataafa blow was becoming, it was too late to expect Captain Herrick to do more than he did, which was to tie down as snugly as possible.

O'Brien also made clear that had the Reynolds damaged property in the Duluth harbor as a result of what Alford had termed an inevitable accident narrowly defined, then the defendant would not be liable. O'Brien gave two such examples: 1) a ship entered the harbor and was blown against the dock, or 2) a ship was tied to a dock but was blown loose by the storm and struck another ship or dock.

This case, however, was different. Here, rather, "the defendant prudently and advisedly availed itself of the plaintiff's property for the purpose of preserving its own more valuable property..." and for the consequences of those "deliberate... and direct efforts" the defendants were liable. No mention was made either of Blackstone's maxim or the holding and dicta of the *Chickasaw* case.

One explanation for O'Brien's approach in crafting the *Vincent* opinion is suggested in a memorial published in the Minnesota Reports following O'Brien's death in 1935. Among the tributes to O'Brien from various judges is this observation by then Justice Royal A. Stone, who had been O'Brien's law partner during much of the period 1907 to 1923: "He was frank in expressing his dislike for the mounting volume of law books and for the increasing vogue of the case lawyer. Against their technique, he wanted liberty to invoke and apply, to the ever changing situations presented by human evolution, those principles that would work out what to him seemed justice."[10]

Simply put, O'Brien must have believed it was only fair that the owners of the Reynolds pay for the damage done to the dock, even if damaging the dock was a reasonable thing to do. So, rather than offering a close analysis of legal doctrine, O'Brien put forward, with a certain rhetorical flourish, five plausible analogies. This was not reasoning by

---

[10] 198 Minn. xli (Minn. 1935).

analogy in the traditional sense, in which the outcomes of actual cases are analogized to the case at bar as a way to justify the decision in the current case. Rather, this was an attempt to pile up several examples in which it seemed intuitively fair to O'Brien that the party in the position of the defendant in *Vincent* should have a legal obligation to pay for the injury in question.

Two of these analogies are variations on actual cases, neither of which was cited by either of the lawyers in *Vincent*. One is the now famous case of *Ploof v. Putnam*.[11] There, under stress of unexpectedly bad weather, a sloop tied up at a private dock at an island on Lake Champlain, Vermont, but was unmoored by the agent of the dock owner, with the result that the boat, its cargo and the boat owner and his family suffered injuries. *Ploof* itself held that it was not a trespass to tie up to the dock in such circumstances of "necessity," with the consequence that the dock owner's agent had no right to remove the boat from the island. Rather, to unmoor the boat was a wrongful act entitling the boat owner to damages. To this O'Brien added in his *Vincent* opinion: "If, in that case, the vessel has been permitted to remain, and the dock had suffered an injury, we believe the ship owner would have been held liable for the injury done."

Although the Vermont Supreme Court might have awarded damages to the dock owner under the circumstances supposed, it might not have, as this issue was clearly not addressed in *Ploof*. But, again, O'Brien was not relying on *Ploof* as legal precedent. Rather, O'Brien is best seen as asserting that it is only fair that, in return for the privilege of using the dock in circumstances of necessity, the ship owner in *Ploof* would have a legal duty to pay for any harm he did to the dock.[12]

O'Brien next offered a variation on the then recent Minnesota

---

[11] 71 A. 188 (Vt.1908).

[12] In a recent article about the *Ploof* case, Professor Joan Vogel discloses that the dock owner was a wealthy absentee yachtsman from New York, someone who might well not have had the sympathy of the Vermont courts. Joan Vogel, *Cases in Context: Lake Champlain Wars, Gentrification and* Ploof v. Putnam, 45 St. Louis U. L.J. 791 (2001). Superficially, this information might not only help to explain the result in *Ploof*, but also it might cast doubt on O'Brien's prediction about what the Vermont courts would have done had the ship damaged the dock. On the other hand, Vogel further explains that the people in the boat were known in the area as thieving pirates and that the agent for the dock owner, like probably most such agents in the area, was undoubtedly on notice to keep this particular family off the premises in light of all sorts of objects having gone missing in recent years. Moreover, Vogel further shows that the French–Canadian background of the boat-owing family may have caused it to be more disliked in the Lake Champlain area than was the absentee New York dock owner. This additional information about the real story behind *Ploof* makes it even more uncertain exactly how O'Brien's hypothetical case would actually have been decided.

Supreme Court decision in *Depue v. Flatau*.[13] In the actual case a traveler, who had come to the defendants' premises to consider buying their cattle, claimed that he became so ill after dining in the defendant's home as to be unable to travel safely on his own. Nonetheless, the plaintiff asserted, the homeowners compelled him to leave, and when the traveler suffered harm from being stranded out in the cold night, he sued his allegedly ungenerous hosts. Although the trial court had dismissed the case, the Minnesota Supreme Court (before O'Brien went on the bench) concluded that the hosts owed their visitor a duty of due care, and sent the case back for trial to determine whether the defendants were aware of the plaintiff's condition and if so whether sending him home on his own was an unreasonable thing to do. This is, essentially, the same case as *Ploof*. O'Brien again rhetorically asked, "If, however, the owner of the premises had furnished the traveler with proper accommodation and medical attendance, would he have been able to defeat an action brought against him for their reasonable worth?" As with the *Ploof* hypothetical, O'Brien's strategy is to get the reader to agree with him as to what would be fair in this hypothetical case and then by analogy to agree with the Court's outcome in *Vincent*. Of course, the answer to O'Brien's hypothetical question was in no way decided in *Depue* and, in any event, a legal action by the providers of care might well have been brought in contract for the value of the services provided, and that difference might make any decision in the hypothetical *Depue* case weak legal precedent for *Vincent*. But, again, it would be a mistake to view O'Brien as resting his argument on any particular legal doctrine.

O'Brien sought further to persuade the reader by imagining that, for the purpose of tying the Reynolds tight against the City Dock, the ship's employees had simply helped themselves to someone else's ropes that they found lying on the dock. Even if this use of the ropes were fully justified, O'Brien asserted that surely the ship owner would be liable to the ropes owner. This is more of the same type of argument already discussed. O'Brien cited no authority for the legal outcome he imagined and he provided no real argument for why the ship owner would indeed be liable to the ropes owner. Presumably, he found self-evident the fairness of his assumed outcome.

On closer examination, the rhetorical power of this hypothetical case is somewhat compromised. First, had the ropes merely been used and then returned after the storm died down and the ship could sail away safely, it is by no means obvious that the ship owner would owe the ropes owner something like the rental value of the ropes for the night. Moreover, even had the ropes broken and been made useless by the force of the storm, would everyone really agree that the ship owner had to pay

---

[13] 111 N.W. 1 (Minn.1907).

for the loss? Suppose the ship had been tied to the dock by the ropes and then had been blown loose by the storm, thereby destroying the ropes? Elsewhere in O'Brien's opinion he stated that in such event the ship owner would not be liable if the loose ship then bashed into something causing harm. On that assumption, liability to the ropes owner is surely not self-evident.

O'Brien next argued that in times of "public necessity" the government may take private property for public purposes, but when it does so, it is obligated to provide compensation to the property owner. Here he was of course invoking the "just compensation" principle of the Fifth Amendment. By analogy, he was suggesting that surely when someone takes property for private purposes, there is all the more reason to insist on compensation.

There are at least three problems with this comparison, however. First, government is a very good loss spreader and that alone might be a reason for imposing liability on the state that might not so readily apply to private persons. Second, because those with political power could be invidiously selective in terms of whose property they take for public purposes, Fifth Amendment rights might be seen as vital in helping to assure that when government takes private property there is a good economic reason for doing so. These fears of invidious selection might well not apply to rare private necessity situations illustrated by *Vincent*. Third, and perhaps far more damning, in truly analogous settings of government takings *in emergency situations of necessity*, it turns out that the law, both at the time and today, is actually the opposite of what O'Brien suggests. That is, where, for example, public officials reasonably destroy private property for a greater public good in the face of forces comparable to the storm in *Vincent* (e.g., a huge fire), the victims must bear their losses themselves—notwithstanding that the rest of the citizenry broadly benefited from the action by public officials on their behalf.[14] In short, on closer examination, this analogy offered by O'Brien perhaps better supports the dissent.

Finally, O'Brien offered a religious-based analogy. He noted that theologians believe that a starving man may morally take food from another to save his life. But then, O'Brien asserted, surely such a man would have an obligation to pay for the food taken when he is able to do so. O'Brien was not asserting that theologians have taken a position on what the law is on this question. Presumably their concern, in any event, would have been with whether there is a moral obligation to repay. O'Brien's idea must have been that once the reader agrees there is a

---

[14] *See, e.g.*, Surocco v. Geary, 3 Cal. 69 (Cal.1853); Harrison v. Wisdom, 54 Tenn. (7 Heisk.) 99 (Tenn.1872); *Restatement (Second) of Torts* § 196 (1965).

moral obligation to repay, then it follows that there should also be a legal obligation—an obligation that applies by analogy to *Vincent*.

O'Brien was of Irish ancestry and a devout Catholic.[15] Yet, despite his religious background, in preparing his opinion in the Vincent case O'Brien apparently did not consult the writings of the great 13th century Catholic theologian Saint Thomas Aquinas, who actually deals with this matter in his famous *Summa Theologica*.[16] After asking whether it is lawful to steal through stress of need, Aquinas concludes that one may "take secretly and use another's property in a case of extreme need: because that which he takes for the support of his life becomes his own property by reason of that need." He also states that in such cases "all things are common property" and that taking another's property when in "imminent danger" is not theft or robbery. Although Aquinas does not squarely address the obligation to repay, the implication of his notion that in times of necessity what human law normally terms private property becomes common property as a matter of natural law is that there is no obligation to repay.

Moreover, even if there were a moral obligation to offer to pay for the food, it does not necessarily follow that the person from whom the food was taken should be given a legal right against the formerly starving man. Surely most decent people, if asked, would happily provide the food for free in order to save the other's life—at least if they are not asked too often. Of course in the O'Brien–Aquinas example, the person was not asked to provide the food, and instead it was simply taken. This setting might suggest to some that, later on, the starving man should at least offer to pay for the food as an expression of gratitude. But then surely many people would refuse that offer if made and would find it ungracious to accept the money that was tendered. In short, whether it is appropriate to grant a legal right to a possibly ungracious host against an arguably ungrateful food-taker is a difficult question.

Given O'Brien's seemingly dismissive attitude towards the growing proliferation of reported cases, it is probably not surprising that his

---

[15] At the start of the 20th century, Minnesota was predominantly Republican, Protestant and Scandinavian. Quite exceptionally John Johnson, a Democrat, was elected governor, and in 1905 he appointed O'Brien, a fellow Democrat, to be insurance commissioner, a post he held for two years. But, although O'Brien was possibly the second most prominent Democrat in the state at that time, he was not viewed as a viable candidate to succeed Johnson because of his Irish Catholic background. Nonetheless, O'Brien was appointed by Johnson on September 1, 1909 to the Minnesota Supreme Court for a term ending January 1, 1911. In that era, there were contested partisan elections to serve on the Minnesota Supreme Court, and when O'Brien ran for a full term in November, 1910 he was defeated by David Simpson, as the Republican slate was victorious for all state offices. Hence, his service on the Court lasted but 16 months.

[16] Thomas Aquinas, *Summa Theologica* Part II–II, Question 66, Article 7.

opinion pays no attention to the English law on this subject. Nevertheless, the classic early 17th century decision in *Mouse's Case*[17] seems inconsistent with O'Brien's analysis in *Vincent*. Although not cited in the briefs, *Mouse's Case* was cited in *Ploof*. When an unexpected storm on the Thames threatened to sink the Gravesend ferry, a passenger deliberately threw some of the cargo overboard, thereby saving himself, the ship, the crew, the other passengers, and the other cargo. The owners of a casket that was sacrificed for the common good sued the passenger-hero for their loss. But the court held for the defendant, saying that it was lawful, under circumstances of necessity, to have tossed the casket overboard and that no compensation was owed. To be sure, one could distinguish *Mouse's Case* from *Vincent* on the ground that different rules should apply to cases such as the former where property is sacrificed to save lives and those like *Vincent* where merely other property is saved (although had Captain Herrick actually set out in the Reynolds in the teeth of the storm, surely life as well as property would have been at risk). But, given several of the analogies O'Brien put forward, this is a distinction that his analysis rejects. Others might seek to distinguish *Mouse's Case* from *Vincent* on the ground that the passenger defendant in the former case acted on behalf of a much wider public and not merely for his own benefit. But, once more, given the analogy O'Brien offered based on his view of public necessity cases, it would be difficult for him to have suggested such a distinction.[18]

Mouse's Case was re-affirmed in the case of *Cope v. Sharpe (No. 2)*,[19] a case that was wending its way through the English courts at the very moment of *Vincent,* and hence perhaps the decision was not readily available to the Minnesota Supreme Court when it was preparing the *Vincent* opinion. In *Cope,* the plaintiff leased his land to the defendant for pheasant hunting. A fire broke out on the plaintiff's land that threatened some pheasants nesting nearby. The defendant came onto the land and set fire to some heather, in effect to create a firebreak to protect the pheasants. This act was judged to be reasonably required by

---

[17] 12 Co. 63, 66 Eng.Rep. 1341 (K.B.1609).

[18] Some have suggested that in the circumstances of *Mouse's Case* the damages incurred by those who owned the property that was thrown overboard would have been paid for as a group by those whose property was not sacrificed under the principle of "general average" that applies to admiralty cases. Because of ambiguities in the reporting of *Mouse's Case*, however, this is not clearly the outcome of that case. It is also arguable that had the plaintiff's casket not been tossed over, it and the entire ship would have been lost, so that there was no loss "caused" by the tossing for which the plaintiff there should recover. And *Vincent* is clearly different on that ground. Yet, this "no cause in fact" argument is perhaps too clever because surely some other property could have been sacrificed instead, thereby saving the casket and the ship.

[19] 26 T.L. R. 172 (Eng. K.B.D. Dec 15, 1909), [1912] 1 K.B. 496.

necessity at the time, even though, in the end, it turned out to be unnecessary in fact. The plaintiff sued for trespass and the court held for the defendant, making it clear that the defendant not only had the right to enter the land to create the firebreak, but also that he was not liable for any damage done thereby. Because property was damaged out of necessity in order to save even more valuable property, this case seems highly analogous to *Vincent*—but opposite in result.

In sum, the analysis put forward in the opinion by O'Brien is not likely to convince those who start out far more uncertain about the proper outcome of the case than O'Brien must have been.

Justice Lewis' dissent is also disappointing. It basically asserts that liability in American tort law should be based on fault and the defendant here was not at fault, as the majority itself recognized. The dissenters did not believe that so much should turn on whether additional cables were used to secure the ship to the dock. Lewis asked, suppose Captain Herrick happened to use cables at 5 p.m. that were strong enough to hold the ship throughout the night. Since the eventual strength of the storm was not to be anticipated at that time, how could securing the ship at 5 p.m. be seen as a foreseeable sacrificing of the plaintiffs' property for the benefit of the defendant? And if not, Lewis asserted, the majority would seemingly have found against the plaintiffs. But for Lewis, having the outcome of the case turn on when the cables were tied had no moral force.

Yet, it is actually not at all clear that the majority would have sided with the defendant in the example given by Lewis. While it is true that the late-night tying of extra cable was a fact emphasized in O'Brien's opinion, surely the majority, if pressed, could as easily have adopted Alford's position for the plaintiffs that it was the deliberate choice not to cut the Reynolds free that was crucial and which distinguished this case from those other examples that O'Brien gave in which he said the victim would have to bear the loss brought about by a storm (e.g., where the ship was blown loose from the dock). In short, the dissent failed to provide a thoughtful analysis of why there should not be liability without fault in circumstances like those at issue in *Vincent*.[20]

It is unlikely that either the majority or the dissent in *Vincent* had even the slightest expectation as to how famous a case this was to become. Indeed, at the outset it drew little attention. Although the

---

[20] That the former torts professor Justice Jaggard joined Lewis in dissent is not surprising. In his 1895 treatise on torts, *supra* note 9, Jaggard offered two sections (numbers 50 and 51) that deal with issues of "necessity" and the use of self-help to protect one's property. Although he did not discuss cases that are precisely the same as *Vincent*, the general thrust of his analysis of many earlier cases was that no liability attaches to reasonable behavior carried out by "necessity."

Duluth newspapers covered the Mataafa storm for days in great detail, they barely noted the lawsuit against the owners of the Reynolds. The day the trial started, two local papers carried small stories to that effect, and during the trial brief mention of the case generally appeared in slight stories about the local court's calendar that day or the prior day. When the verdict was given, a short mention of that appeared, but there does not appear to be even the slightest mention of the Minnesota Supreme Court's decision in either the Duluth or Minneapolis papers.

Insurance

In thinking about the *Vincent* facts today, scholars are likely to ask about the role of insurance in this situation. In 1910, unsurprisingly, no mention was made of insurance in the briefs or in the opinions in *Vincent*. After all, the conventional view of tort law has long been that insurance should be irrelevant to the outcome of a case.

On the defense side, liability insurance has traditionally been understood simply as the vehicle by which the defendant has arranged in advance to satisfy its obligation after a decision to award damages has been made. Imposing liability *because* of the availability of liability insurance has conventionally seemed altogether unfair.

In more recent times, of course, there is a very different perspective on this matter. While insurance in the particular case is generally seen as irrelevant, the role that liability insurance generally can play in spreading losses for a category of injuries in question is viewed by many commentators and some courts as highly relevant to the decision to impose liability on the relevant defendants, and especially the decision to impose liability without fault. After all, strict liability, in effect, makes the defendant the insurer of the plaintiff, and it is through the purchase of liability insurance that the defendant typically fulfills that role.

So, too, the common law position on "collateral sources"—that they are to be ignored—has traditionally meant that the existence of first party casualty insurance on the plaintiff's side is also not to count in deciding the outcome of a plaintiff's tort case or the amount the victorious plaintiff should recover. Yet, here too, changes have been made and proposed. Now, many states require the jury to be told of collateral sources, presumably with the intention that juries will ordinarily reduce the tort awards they make accordingly. This view envisions tort's role as one of filling in the compensation gaps.

Even more radically, many have argued that, because the transactions costs of operating the tort system are so huge, liability insurance is a very expensive way to provide victims with insurance. From this outlook, some have proposed that attention should be given to whether there isn't a better way of making sure that victims have their own insurance.[21]

Hence, the availability of insurance in a situation like that which happened in *Vincent* might be viewed as far more pertinent today than it was then. Nonetheless, it is at least worth noting that by the time of *Vincent* the then fairly new market in liability insurance was reasonably well in place. So, too, of course, was the older market in first party casualty insurance, which was available to the owners of the Reynolds to provide coverage in case their ship was damaged or lost, and which was also available to the owners of the City Dock to provide coverage in case their dock was damaged for example by a fire or by a storm or, indeed, by the Reynolds in the way it was.

One caveat to these points is that many marine insurance policies in force in Duluth at the time had end dates, such as October 31. The idea seems to have been that, although the Duluth harbor wasn't generally closed until December, conditions in November were dangerous enough that insurers didn't want to cover the risk. It is not altogether clear whether this end date generally applied only to casualty insurance for ship owners, to all casualty insurance, or even, in some instances, to both casualty and liability insurance policies.

Another ambiguity as to liability insurance coverage is that these policies have long been written to cover liability arising from "accidental" harm so as not to provide insurance for those who engage in intentional wrongdoing. It is not entirely clear how this language would be read in circumstances such as *Vincent* where tort liability is seemingly based upon intentional conduct that is not wrongful.

Whatever the general practice, based upon the testimony of Mr. Vincent, it appears that the defendants indeed were insured in this instance and that there was no problem of coverage because of the deliberate conduct of Captain Herrick. On direct examination Alford asked Vincent, "what is your business now?," and Vincent replied, "Well, I have no particular business, particularly. I am plaintiff in this case, I might say, against the Liability Insurance Company. That is my business now at the present time."

Whether or not the plaintiffs had casualty insurance is uncertain. In any event, it is important to appreciate that this case, which for some is a matter of such moral moment, might well have been, at base, a fight between two insurance carriers. And surely today we would expect that both ship owners and dock owners ought to be able to obtain insurance to cover harm to the dock of the sort that occurred in *Vincent* (a point further elaborated below).

---

[21] *See generally* Stephen D. Sugarman, *Doing Away With Personal Injury Law* (1989).

Scholarly Understandings of the Law Prior to *Vincent*

The Harvard Law Review noted and favorably commented on the *Ploof* decision right after it was decided in 1908, stating further that there was as yet no authority on the question of whether the dock owner might successfully sue for damages done to his property had he allowed the ship to remain there during the storm (i.e., the issue raised by *Vincent*).[22]

For its proposition about the lack of precedent, the Harvard Law Review cited Professor Henry Terry's 1884 treatise, where Terry thoughtfully pointed to what he saw as two clashing principles.[23] On the one hand "small violations of rights ... must in exceptional circumstances be allowed in order to prevent vastly greater evils, and people must be left free to do such acts when the occasion calls for them without being checked by fear of legal liability." On the other "a person who does such acts for his own sole benefit ought to make a compensation for any substantial damage done by him in so acting ... [in contrast to] ... the general policy of the law ... to let accidental damage lie where it falls." As to his preference, Terry came down in favor of the latter, by way of analogy to the principle governing "takings" of private property for public use. (As noted already, however, it turns out that destruction of private property by public officials in circumstances of public necessity has not been deemed a "taking" and has not attracted strict liability in tort in the way that what might be termed the private "taking" did in *Vincent*.)

Terry's treatise made an oblique reference to Oliver Wendell Holmes, and in fact Holmes broadly addressed the issue raised by *Vincent* in his famous lectures on The Common Law, published in 1881, to which Terry was referring.[24] Holmes pointed out that in the 1648 English case of Gilbert v. Stone,[25] a man, who was in fear of his life because of threats by twelve armed men, entered another's property and

---

[22] *Necessity as an Excuse for a Trespass Upon Land*, 22 Harv. L. Rev. 298 (1908–09). The view that the law on the question raised in *Vincent* was unresolved at the time of the case was also embraced by a note in the Lawyers Reports Annotated (a forerunner of ALR) that accompanied its printing of the *Vincent* decision, *Liability for Injury to Wharf by Vessel Attached Thereto during a Storm*, 27 L.R.A. (N.S.) 312 (1910).

[23] Henry Terry, *Some Leading Principles on Anglo–American Law* 423 (1884).

[24] O.W. Holmes, *The Common Law* 147–49 (1881).

[25] *Id.* at 148. Henry Weeks published *The Doctrine of* Damnum Absque Injuria *Considered in its Relation to the Law of Torts* in 1879. That Latin phrase refers to instances in which a person suffering a loss does not have an action for damages against the person causing it. Weeks restated the rule, later clearly embraced in *Ploof*, that one may enter another's land because of necessity and not be liable for trespass. As for liability

took a horse. As Holmes put it, "In such a case, he actually contemplates and chooses harm to another as a consequence of his act. Yet the act is neither blameworthy nor punishable." (Here Holmes must mean "punishable" to refer to criminal law.) In the very next sentence, however, Holmes stated, "But it might be actionable, and Rolle, C.J. ruled that it was." Yet, a few paragraphs later, Holmes further stated, "It is doubtful, however, whether the ruling of Chief Justice Rolle would now be followed. .... [because more recent statements of the law suggest that] ... an act must in general not only be dangerous, but one which would be blameworthy on the part of the average man, in order to make the actor liable."

None of this scholarly authority was cited by either the lawyers or the two opinions in *Vincent*.

How the *Vincent* Decision was Received

Very soon after *Vincent* was decided, both the Harvard and Columbia Law Reviews came down in favor of the result in the case. The brief Harvard note first disparaged the contemporaneous English decision in *Cope v. Sharpe* as unfairly "allowing one man for his own benefit deliberately to thrust a burden upon another."[26] This time the Harvard editors endorsed Terry's preferred resolution to the effect, as they put it, "the owner should be compensated for the loss occasioned by his being forced by law to become the means of saving another from a greater loss." The Harvard editors further opined "The law should look on the matter as a judicial sale of the use of land and give the owner a remedy upon a theory analogous to quasi-contract"—by which they apparently meant to invoke Terry's analogy to public takings of land. The Columbia editors discussed and appeared to approve of *Mouse's Case* but somehow do not recognize its seeming conflict with *Vincent*, whose outcome they favored because of the "equities" in the case.[27]

By contrast, writing on *Cope v. Sharpe* in Canadian journals supported that decision but failed to note its apparent inconsistency with *Vincent*.[28]

---

for damage done while on the land of another, Weeks did not take a position, but instead referred, at p. 118, to dictum in a Pennsylvania Supreme Court case from 1841, *Chambers v. Bedell*, 2 Watts & Serg. 225 (Pa.1841), suggesting somewhat equivocally that while a person may be able to go onto another's property to retrieve his own chattel, he may be required to "repair" any damage done in the process.

[26] *Trespass to Realty*, 23 Harv. L. Rev. 490 (1909–10).

[27] *Trespass–Necessity*, 10 Colum. L. Rev. 372 (1910). Professor John Henry Wigmore included *Vincent* in his 1912 casebook *Selected Cases on the Law of Torts*, without comment but with reference to the Harvard and Columbia notes.

[28] *See, e.g., Emergency as a Justification for Trespass*, 52 Canadian L.J. 101 (1915).

Moreover, a small volume providing practical advice for captains whose ships are in collisions was published by The American Steamship Owners' Mutual Protection and Indemnity Association, Inc. in 1919. Seemingly oblivious to *Vincent*, the author stated "Damage done to docks or wharves should also be promptly reported. If the damage is caused by fault in the handling or managing of the vessel, she is liable therefor. No liability, however, exists against the vessel unless the damage was caused by her fault."[29] The author went on to tell the captain to file a Note of Protest in situations when bad weather occasions a loss.

In short, in the decade after it was decided, *Vincent* had gained attention at least in some quarters, but had been subjected to no serious analysis. This was soon to change because of the work of Professor Francis Bohlen.

Bohlen had only referred to *Vincent* in a footnote to *Ploof* in the 1915 edition of his torts casebook[30] but by the second edition, published in 1925, *Vincent* and *Ploof* were both fully included.[31] More importantly, Bohlen's prominent article *Incomplete Privilege to Inflict Intentional Invasions of Interests of Property and Personality* appeared in the 1925–26 volume of the Harvard Law Review.[32] In addition, Bohlen, who had been named as the Reporter for the first Restatement of Torts in 1923, went on to give both *Ploof* and *Vincent* a prominent place in the Restatement.[33] Whereas the Restatement and its comments make no real attempt to justify the *Vincent* outcome, Bohlen's article does—about which more will be said below.

After Bohlen's article appeared, the correctness of *Vincent* seems to have been taken for granted. It was favorably cited, for example, in several articles concerning airplane ground damage, and Professor Fowler Harper embraced Bohlen's "incomplete privilege" analytical structure in the first edition of his treatise published in 1933,[34] the forerunner of the current multi-volume torts treatise carrying the names of Harper, James and Gray.[35]

---

[29] W.H. LaBoyteaux, *Handbook for Masters* 33 (1919).

[30] 2 Francis H. Bohlen, *Cases on the Law of Torts* 920 (1915)

[31] Francis H. Bohlen, *Cases on the Law of Torts* 104–110 (2d ed. 1925).

[32] Francis H. Bohlen, *Incomplete Privilege to Inflict Intentional Invasions of Interests of Property and Personality*, 39 Harv. L. Rev. 307 (1925–26).

[33] The principles of *Ploof* and *Vincent* as Bohlen interpreted them now appear in section 197 in the Restatement (Second).

[34] Fowler Vincent Harper, *Treatise on the Law of Torts* 138–39 (1933).

[35] Fowler V. Harper et al., *The Law of Torts* (2d ed. 1986).

In short, Bohlen's analysis was the first of what, in more recent years, has become a torrent of serious academic writing about *Vincent* and analogous problems by both legal scholars and moral philosophers. Like Bohlen, nearly all of these authors have defended *Vincent* as correctly decided, but for a remarkable variety of quite different reasons.

The Importance of *Vincent* Today

For nearly a century now, *Vincent* has been a mainstay among the cases included in leading torts casebooks. Its great importance, however, hardly stems from its role in anchoring one small corner of the law of intentional torts, and surely not as a special piece of the law of trespass to land. Reported cases that are factually very similar to *Vincent* are few in number, although it has been cited from time to time over the years, and surely American scholars would say it decidedly remains "good law."

For the torts instructor and torts student, *Vincent* presents a vivid example of liability imposed in the absence of fault—to be compared with other islands of non-fault liability in what otherwise is a sea of liability based on negligence. The other major islands are strict liability for abnormally dangerous activities, strict liability for products containing manufacturing defects, and, some would argue, vicarious liability for the torts of one's employees.

The breadth of the moral principle that seems to underlie the majority's opinion is quite uncertain. The Blackstone maxim, for example, could easily be re-cast more sweepingly like this: If, for your own benefit, you expose another to a risk of harm, it is only fair that you should compensate the other if the foreseeable harm actually occurs, even if it was reasonable to act as you did. But, if this broad principle about risking another's interest to further your own were accepted, it would require overturning a great deal of established tort law. Many examples could be given, in which, under today's law, the defendant escapes liability because of the absence of negligence and because the danger from the risk taken is not sufficiently large or uncommon to invoke the law of abnormally dangerous activities.

Notice that the position of the Restatement of Torts (Second) that there should be strict liability for ground damage done by airplanes that crash without fault[36] well fits this more sweeping phrasing of the Blackstone maxim. Yet, many states today have rejected the Restatement position on airplane ground damage.[37] Reconciling that trend with *Vincent* may seem quite difficult.

---

[36] *Restatement (Second) of Torts* § 520A (1965).

[37] *See generally Restatement (Third) of Torts: Liability for Physical Harm (Basic Principles)* 350–54 (Tentative Draft No. 1, 2001), where then Reporter Professor Gary

On the other hand, as suggested earlier in passing when discussing the plaintiffs' reliance on the Blackstone maxim in their appellate brief, the *Vincent* principle could be cast far more narrowly: one is liable without fault if one intentionally uses another's property for one's own benefit and in the process damages that property (or even more narrowly, if one permissibly trespasses on another's land out of necessity and in the process damages the other's land or property on the land). But, of course, to justify only the narrower rule would require explaining why, for example, only intentional harm is covered and not merely knowingly exposing the other to a risk of harm. And, so too, one would have to explain why it is not sufficient that the victim's property was foreseeably harmed by the defendant's selfish act, but that the injurer must also actually benefit from the use of the victim's property.

For scholars, *Vincent* has become especially important because it, or another now-famous hypothetical in the same vein, has been featured by so many writers in recent years. That other example imagines a careful solo hiker whose life is threatened by an unexpectedly fierce storm and who happens onto an unoccupied cabin.[38] The hiker then forces her way in and eats sufficient food and burns sufficient wood to keep herself alive until the storm passes. It is assumed that breaking into the cabin and consuming the food and wood are altogether reasonable under the circumstances of necessity. Indeed, most would probably assume that had the owner of the cabin been there, she surely would have had a moral duty to welcome in the hiker and warm and feed her, and that any decent person would certainly have done that and never given a thought to charging for her charity. However, in the hypothetical the cabin owner was not there, and the hiker has not yet offered to pay for the cost of the food and wood. And so, as in *Vincent*, we are presented first with the question of whether there is a moral duty of the hiker to repay and second whether the hiker should be legally liable to pay if the cabin owner sues for that loss. Simply put, this is a replay of *Vincent*, but in an entirely non-commercial setting in which life is clearly at stake.

In this now vast literature, nearly all of the writers on this topic either take *Vincent* as obviously reflecting the proper result or else argue strenuously for why it is the proper result.[39] Liability of the hiker is

---

Schwartz suggests that it is difficult to reconcile the position of the *Restatement (Second)* with either the law on the books or the principles underlying strict liability for abnormally dangerous activities. Professor Schwartz recommended withdrawing the special section 520A and leaving the *Restatement (Third)* silent on this specific issue.

[38] *See* Joel Feinberg, *Voluntary Euthanasia and the Inalienable Right to Life*, 7 Phil. & Pub. Aff. 93, 102 (1978); *see also* Jules L. Coleman, *Risks and Wrongs* 282 (1992).

[39] *But see* Guido Calabresi, *Cost of Accidents*, 169 n.28 (1970); Phillip Montague, *Rights, Permission, and Compensation*, 13 Phil. & Pub. Aff. 79 (1984); Howard Latin,

similarly treated. Yet, the supporters of the *Vincent* result offer so many different justifications that one is entitled to be suspicious of this united front.

Bohlen provided a structural home for the problem by locating it in the world of intentional torts and specifically within the topic of trespass to land. Normally, when someone trespasses on your land, you have a self-help right to gently expel them; you need not tolerate them and sue them later in court. This is what the defendant in *Ploof* claimed as his right. But *Ploof* concluded that what would normally be an intentional trespass by the sloop owner was not a trespass after all because of the exigency of the storm. Necessity gave the sloop owner the privilege to enter the land so that he was not a trespasser. In that event, the land owner had no right to expel him. By doing so, the defendant improperly "trespassed" on the interests of the sloop owner.

Deeming this right of the sloop owner to use the land of another as a "privilege" is consistent with intentional tort doctrine generally. For example, you may harm someone in a way that would otherwise be a battery if you are exercising the "privilege" of self-defense. "Consent" is also frequently said to give one the privilege to impose harm that otherwise would be tortious.

But if the sloop owner in *Ploof* had the privilege to trespass, what is the analytical move that imposes liability on him for harm he causes to the dock? Bohlen's solution is to term his entry only an "incomplete privilege"—a privilege to dock but not a privilege to escape liability for the harm to the dock.

There is nothing wrong with this language. But it is worth noting that most of the law of intentional torts does not come in this form. If one looks beneath the labels, most of the time one is liable for an intentional tort because one has acted wrongfully, and where one has not acted in a socially unacceptable way, that is where one typically has a complete privilege and is not held liable. In short, the liability without fault that is created by the conditional or incomplete privilege approach embraced by Bohlen for the necessity setting is atypical.

In any event, Bohlen's offered justification for granting only an "incomplete privilege" is largely the same sense of fairness that Justice O'Brien felt—because the party acting out of necessity benefited from his action, it is only fair that he pay for the harm he caused.[40]

Problem-Solving Behavior and Theories of Tort Liability, 73 Cal. L. Rev. 677, 705–10 (1985).

[40] For an early critique of the Bohlen argument, see Robert Keeton, *Conditional Fault in the Law of Torts*, 72 Harv. L. Rev. 401 (1959).

Notice that *Vincent* wasn't actually the ideal case factually for embracing this "incomplete privilege" notion because, unlike the sloop owner in *Ploof*, the ship owner in *Vincent* clearly had a right to tie up in the dock quite apart from necessity. Simply put, the ship owner and dock owners in *Vincent* had a pre-existing contractual relationship with each other, and one wonders whether the case should somehow have been analyzed as a matter of contractual interpretation. While intriguing, this is not altogether promising, however.

Presumably, it is generally understood that once you unload your ship, you normally are to push off. Indeed, normally the ship operator is eager to push off to carry on with business. Recall that the Reynolds carried some remaining cargo to unload elsewhere. On the other hand, it is hard to imagine that it was understood that a ship was required by contract to set off in the face of a storm like the Mataffa Blow. But if we understand the Reynolds as remaining at the City Dock under implied terms of the contract instead of by the legal right of necessity, that hardly seems determinative as to who should pay for the damage to the dock. While the dock owner could have provided expressly by contract that the ship had to pay for damages to the dock, so too the ship owner could have sought a provision exempting it from liability in such circumstances. It seems clear, however, that no one thought to deal explicitly with this issue. While, for some, the failure of the parties in *Vincent* to provide for this contingency should be held against the plaintiff (who should be entitled to his regular "dock fees" and nothing more), others would not be convinced by an argument that hopes to stimulate better advance planning as to risks when neither of the two commercial actors had done so. Hence, a contracts approach probably leaves one pretty much in the same place as a torts approach—that is, trying to decide what would be the appropriate "implied term."

Some scholars with an economics orientation have noted that it probably doesn't really matter who in *Vincent* is held liable.[41] This is because, in the end, regardless of the rule, the harm to the dock will eventually be paid for by buyers of the cargo. That is, under the *Vincent* result, ship owners will directly pass on this cost of doing business in what they charge to carry cargo. And under the opposite result, dock owners would increase their dock fees, which would then also be passed on in one way or another to those whose cargo is handled at the docks.

Under this view, it is helpful that everyone understands what the tort rule is so that insurance companies get their pricing right. If the damage to the dock is to be a cost of dock owning, then casualty insurers need to factor this risk into the premiums they charge. But if the

---

[41] *See, e.g.*, Dale Broeder, *Torts and Just Compensation: Some Personal Reflections*, 17 Hastings L.J. 229 (1965).

damage to the dock is to be a cost of ship owning, then liability insurers need to factor this risk into the premiums they charge. For the benefit of both shipping companies and dock operators, it would be better not to overpay for insurance coverage. Of course, the parties could possibly contract around any uncertainty in the law, but a clear rule makes that unnecessary and probably cheaper.

Which way this cuts in terms of deciding how *Vincent* should be decided is not self-evident, however. If first party insurance is cheaper to administer than liability insurance, that cuts against the *Vincent* result. Yet, the *Vincent* result makes is unnecessary to determine whether the ship owner was actually at fault, as would be required if the rule were one of negligence liability instead of strict liability. If fault must be determined, then considerations of access to evidence might also be relevant. But in the end this might only justify shifting the burden of proof to the defendant rather than, in effect, conclusively presuming against the defendant via a rule of strict liability.

Economics oriented writers have offered other insights into the *Vincent* problem as well. A central concern of theirs is the incentive effects of law, and an early argument was that if *Vincent* had been decided the other way, then the dock owner would have an incentive to cut the ship loose. By being assured of compensation, the argument goes, the dock owner won't engage in this self-protection effort.[42]

This argument is very delicate for "law and economics" devotees, however, because the *Ploof* rule itself is supposed to deter dock owners from cutting loose ships that are privileged to dock out of necessity. To argue that a further incentive is required to channel the dock owner's conduct in the proper way threatens to undermine the fundamental "law and economics" understanding of tort law. That is, the stick of liability is supposed to be enough, with a "carrot" of compensation not needed.

Others, less concerned with the niceties of economic models, might retort that absent the *Vincent* rule the dock owner might just take a chance, cutting the ship loose, in the hopes that it will not sink or damage other property. But such a dock owner might well also fear that the compensation legally promised by *Vincent* might never be forthcoming, given insolvency and other concerns, and might well cut the ship loose even after *Vincent*. The actual circumstances of the *Ploof* case are probably a good example of this. In sum, this sort of speculating isn't altogether satisfying.

Those who think about economic incentives have another arrow in their quiver. Absent *Vincent*, they might argue, property owners may take steps to make it more difficult for others to exercise the privilege to

---

[42] For an early formulation of this idea, see Clarence Morris, *Torts* 42–46 (1953).

trespass by necessity. They might invite us to imagine a cabin owner putting on locks and installing windows that the stranded hiker cannot break and an absent dock owner putting out spikes or other dangers that prevent someone else's ship from docking. Abstractly, there may be something to this concern. But it seems quite far-fetched in the setting of both *Vincent* and the cabin owner hypothetical. That is, the City Dock owners could hardly expect to carry on their business at all if they made it difficult for ships like the Reynolds to dock, even ships that suddenly appear at the dock in a storm. And cabin owners who would try to prevent break-ins surely are most worried about vandals who have no necessity to enter the cabin. To imagine a cabin owner who would make it more difficult for stranded innocent hikers to break in, having already protected the cabin to discourage vandals, is to imagine a person who is unlikely to exist in the real world. The same point goes for the *Ploof* setting. It is quite imaginable that absent dock owners at that time would have portable docks dismantled in the off-season in order to try to prevent "pirates" and other evil doers from gaining access to their property. But after whatever sort of prevention measures have been taken against that risk, it is hard to imagine the owners making it yet additionally more difficult for possible entrants out of necessity. This is not to argue that no property owners would ever respond in this way had *Vincent* been decided otherwise, but only that such perverse behavioral responses seem fanciful in the cases that have been given the main scholarly attention.

Rather than raising economics concerns, some scholars have asserted considerations of fairness. One way to put their point is that the ship owner in *Vincent* and the hiker in the cabin case are "unjustly enriched" if they are able to benefit from the use of the victim's property without paying for the harm done.[43] This is not the place to provide a substantial analysis of the law of "unjust enrichment." However, one point can be made.

To be sure, those who exercised self-help to rescue themselves in these examples were enriched by their efforts (or at least avoided a loss), and this came at the expense of someone else. Yet, whether that enrichment was "unjust" is exactly the issue that these problems raise. Put differently, should these harms be understood to have been caused by unexpectedly large storms, in a world in which dock and cabin owners well understand that they are financially at risk in many ways when dangerous storms pass by? Or should these harms be seen as costs of hiking or ship owning for which those engaged in those activities should

---

[43] *See, e.g.,* Daniel Friedman, *Restitution of Benefits Obtained Through the Appropriation of Property or the Commission of a Wrong,* 80 Colum. L. Rev. 504, 541 (1980); Howard Klepper, *Torts of Necessity: A Moral theory of Compensation,* 9 Law & Phil. 223 (1990); Ernest Weinrib, *The Idea of Private Law* 196 (1995).

be responsible? If there is good reason to adopt the latter understanding of these events, then it would be "unjust" not to hold the hiker and ship owner liable. But absent a convincing reason, their enrichment does not yet seem "unjust." In short, "unjust enrichment" might be the label one would want to put on the case if, for some other reason, it was concluded that the ship owner and/or hiker should bear the loss occasioned by the storm.

As just noted, these "necessity" cases involve self-rescue efforts. Some scholars, therefore, have thought about the problem in the wider context of the way that tort law treats rescues.[44] This line of inquiry is also stimulating, but not ultimately satisfying. The cabin owner and the dock owner, had they been at their property at the moment of the storm, would generally have no duty to rescue those in need. That is, the common law imposes no duty to rescue strangers even when such an effort is virtually costless (a rule, it should be noted, that is much criticized by many scholars). At least in the *Ploof* and hiker examples, then, the property owners could sit by and do nothing. (Notice again how the *Vincent* facts raise extra complications here.) But, of course, most people would view such property owners as despicable. In any event, the necessity doctrine provides that the parties at risk can at least help themselves.

What, then, does the lack of a duty to rescue imply when someone out of necessity reasonably damages the property? One view might be that since the property owner had no legal duty to come to the aid of another—no obligation to be a rescuer—then if that owner is involuntarily made a rescuer, that owner ought to be compensated. That is the result of the *Vincent* rule. But there is a different view. The morally right thing is to rescue, even if for certain historic, procedural, and/or other reasons tort law does not actually create a legal duty to do so. In that case, being forced to rescue, as it were, is being forced to do what you morally should have done. Hence, one could argue, there is no reason to provide a cause of action to vindicate someone's callous selfishness. This would lead to a rejection of the *Vincent* rule and would mean that, on both sides of the rescue question, the law would keep out.

In the end, resolving this argument may come down to determining what sort of society we live in, or want to live in. Is ours a society in which property rights should be selfishly held and given strong legal protection, or do we want a society—as suggested in the writings of Aquinas—in which what is personally owned for most circumstances becomes common property to be taken and used by others in occasional and special circumstances of necessity? Without resolving that broader

---

[44] *See generally* George Fletcher, *Corrective Justice for Moderns*, 106 Harv. L. Rev. 1658, 1670–71 (1993).

question, it may not be possible to come to a satisfying determination of whether *Vincent* was rightly decided.[45] Moreover, in digging deeper into how property rights should be defined in our society, it might turn out that we would want different answers depending upon such matters as the commercial status of the parties, whether life or merely property is at stake, and/or whether a relatively modest or a large amount of damage was suffered by the plaintiff.

For now it perhaps suffices to insist that the *Vincent* result is not the only imaginable outcome of the case. Not only were there two dissenters, but also the Anglo–Canadian law appears to remain to the contrary. *Cope v. Sharpe* has not been overruled,[46] and the opinion in a much more recent Canadian case, with facts very much like those in *Vincent*, points to a result quite the opposite of *Vincent*.[47]

The End of the Story

Although the Reynolds escaped harm in the Mataafa storm, her luck eventually ran out. She was sold by the Lake Erie Transportation Company in 1911 and then resold in 1912. In 1915 she was rebuilt for ocean service and sold once more. In 1917 ownership finally passed to the U.S. Steamship Company of New York, under whose proprietorship she was torpedoed and sunk by a German submarine off the coast of France on May 18, 1918.

---

[45] *See, e.g.*, George C. Christie, *The Defense of Necessity Considered from the Legal and Moral Points of View*, 48 Duke L.J. 975 (1999).

[46] *See, e.g.*, R.W.M. Dias and B.S. Markesinis, *Tort Law* 507–12 (2d ed. 1989) where *Cope v. Sharpe* is shown to be the law, although the authors criticize the thinking behind the case. For a similar analysis, see John G. Fleming, *The Law of Torts* 104–07 (9th ed. 1998).

[47] Munn v. "Sir J Crosbie" [1967] 1 Ex. C.R. 94. *See generally* Allen M. Linden, *Canadian Tort Law* 79–81 (5th ed. 1993).

Contributors to *Torts Stories*

Kenneth S. Abraham is Robert E. Scott Distinguished Professor of Law and Class of 1966 Research Professor, University of Virginia School of Law.

Anita Bernstein is Sam Nunn Professor of Law, Emory University School of Law.

Mark Geistfeld is Professor of Law, New York University School of Law.

Stephen G. Gilles is Professor of Law, Quinnipiac University School of Law.

Daniel J. Givelber is Professor of Law, Northeastern University School of Law.

James A. Henderson, Jr. is Frank B. Ingersoll Professor of Law, Cornell Law School.

Saul Levmore is Dean & William B. Graham Professor of Law, University of Chicago Law School.

Robert L. Rabin is A. Calder Mackay Professor of Law, Stanford Law School.

Peter H. Schuck is Simeon E. Baldwin Professor of Law, Yale Law School.

Kenneth W. Simons is M. L. Sykes Scholar and Professor of Law, Boston University School of Law.

Stephen D. Sugarman is Agnes Roddy Robb Professor of Law, University of California at Berkeley School of Law.

*

Acknowledgments

Kenneth S. Abraham would like to thank Vincent Blasi, G. Edward White, Jennifer Mnookin, and Jed Handelsman Shugerman for helpful comments.

Anita Bernstein thanks Lucinda Finley for sharing her expertise in the DES litigation, and David Garrow and Leslie Griffin for helpful comments on the manuscript.

Mark Geistfeld expresses his thanks for helpful comments from Eleanor Fox and William E. Nelson.

Stephen G. Gilles would like to thank Neal Feigenson and Michael Green for helpful comments.

James A. Henderson, Jr. acknowledges the research assistance of Josh Chandler.

Saul Levmore acknowledges the research assistance of Dean Bachus.

Robert L. Rabin thanks Marc Franklin and Lawrence Friedman for helpful comments, and Barrett Hester for research assistance, as well as footnote formatting on the entire manuscript.

Peter H. Schuck and Daniel J. Givelber acknowledge the research assistance of Evan Young.

Kenneth W. Simons would like to thank David Albeck and Chris Marx for helpful comments, and Jason Hall for research assistance.

Stephen D. Sugarman would like to thank Debby Kearney for reference assistance.

†